Contents

Part One

Burdens, Sorrows and Sins

I

Once more the swan had spread its wings across the roof. This morning it was distinctly yellow with a feathery brown border which indicated that there had been heavy rain during the night. A shower, and the patch of damp was hardly visible; a downpour, however, sought out the cracks between tiles and joists and soon insinuated water down the attic walls to paint that full-blown fowl on the plaster of the back room ceiling.

In the corner bed, Mirrin Stalker snuggled down under the patchwork quilt. Only the tip of her nose protruded as her dark sleepy eyes ruefully contemplated the swan, an uncharitable talisman all too familiar during the wet Scottish winter. The swan meant rain, and rain meant mud: mud meant boots, and boots meant skinned heels and chapped ankles. Mirrin sighed at the prospect of discomfort, and tilted her head an inch from the pillow to learn what the hour might be.

Punctual Kate, Mirrin's elder sister, and the family's most reliable clock, was half through dressing. Mirrin watched as she looped her hair into a trim coronet, then completed the process of buttoning her bodice. Never any rush with Kate; no infuriating fumbling with mismatched buttons, bent hooks, or strings which had slithered out of chemises and shifts. She envied Kate's innate tidiness, but knew better than to try to emulate it.

Luxuriating in the big warm bed, she wriggled deeper under the clothes. Thank God, she could lie snug for another few minutes. Mirrin loved the soft feather-filled mattress. She and Kate had inherited it a year ago when their father had strained his back and had moved his sleeping quarters to the hard palliasse in the kitchen alcove. It had been a poor exchange for her mother, who had never suffered a muscular twinge in her life; though she had known pain of other kinds, and much of it. All Flora Stalker's children had been born in this very bed, except the poor unnamed wee mite who had made his entry into the world unexpectedly early when Flora had been alone in the house, and had fluttered out his few brief moments of existence on the flagstones of the kitchen floor. Neighbours and relatives had said it was God's Will; the way things were for common folk, that there was no help for it. Mirrin did not subscribe to popular opinion. There was neither dignity nor decency in what had happened to Mam and – though she had been only eleven years old at the time – the incident had stirred Mirrin's rebellious instincts.

'Not for me,' she murmured. 'By God, it'll not be like that for me.'

'What are you mutterin' about, Mirrin?' Kate tapped the hummock of her sister's knees. 'Come on: high time you were up.'

'Och, not just yet.'

'Mam'll be shoutin' in a minute.'

Struggling stoically from under the quilt, Mirrin stretched her arms above her head, pulled herself into a sitting position, feet flat on the mattress, and combed her fingers through her hair. In the shrunken faded pink flannelette nightgown she looked younger than her eighteen years.

Yawning, she said, 'Not ... much ... of a mornin'?'

'No, but at least it's dry,' Kate said.

'Dry? Then how did the bird get there?'

Kate too was acquainted with the swan's significance.

'Must have rained itself out early,' she said. 'Now come on, Mirrin. Things have been bad enough this mornin'. Mother had a right bit of bother in gettin' Dougie up. Him an' Da were late leavin' for work. Don't you make it worse.'

With sudden vigour, Mirrin said, 'Right!'

She rolled from the bed, stamped her feet, and peeled the nightgown over her head. Naked as the day she was born, she padded to the dresser by the curtained window, poured water from an iron jug into a tin basin and sponged her face and body thoroughly. Cold robbed her of breath, made her whistle through her teeth. Groping, she found the towel on the bed-end and dried herself briskly.

From the narrow single cot against the wall, Betsy Stalker complained, 'You're not at that again, Mirrin?'

'Toughens you up,' said Mirrin, shivering.

'Aye, you're tough enough already,' Betsy put in, before cowling the blankets over her ears and turning her face to the wall again. Nothing could now be seen of her except the fine sausage-shaped ringlets of hair which she tended with such careful vanity that, even in sleep, they obediently retained their bounce and curl.

At fourteen, Betsy was the youngest of the three Stalker girls. Like her twin brother, Drew, she still attended the parish school and was thus entitled to enjoy an extra half hour in bed. Nobody grudged her the privilege: it would end all too soon, with the summer term, in fact, then Betsy too would be committed to early rising like the rest of them.

By now Alex Stalker and his middle son, Dougie, would be crawling along the ramp of the bottom level of the pit, heading, with the day shift troupe, for the coal-face and another ten hours of toil on their knees. In a half hour or so, Mirrin would also be up at Blacklaw colliery, and another work day would be in full swing for them all.

Kate was still policing her sister, making sure that Mirrin did not cause further disruption to the daily ritual which had already been delayed by Dougie's reluctance to get his back off the bed.

Making shrill chirruping noises against the cold, Mirrin hauled on her clean shift and heavy drawers and, hopping, furled her black stockings over her shapely legs.

'I don't see why you can't just have a warm wash at night like everybody else, Mirrin.' Kate was uncommonly waspish today.

'I don't mind cold water.'

'Must you be so ... so shameless about it?'

'I'm not ashamed of what I've got ...'

'Mirrin: really!' Kate exclaimed; and, from the cot, Betsy giggled drowsily.

A loud rap on the door put an end to the debate.

'Kate,' Mam Stalker called, imperiously. 'Are y'ready t'serve the porridge?'

'Make sure it's not lumpy,' Mirrin said.

'Just for that,' said Kate, without a trace of malice, 'I'll make sure your share's like a turnip field.'

As Kate went into the kitchen, Mirrin propped a square of mirror on the pillow and, kneeling, spent another minute combing her thick, dark hair. Not vain like young Betsy, she enjoyed the sensual satisfactions of the daily toilet for their own sake, as bracers against the harsh, comfortless environment in which she lived and worked.

By the flicker of the tallow stump which Kate had left on the stool, Mirrin casually studied her features. She had the straight Stalker nose and determined chin, but the wide, frank mouth was all her own. Not even her oldest brother, James, whom everybody in Blacklaw thought handsome, had quite such a generous gob. Impudently, she stuck out her tongue at her own image, stuffed straggles of hair under the pins, snuffed out the candle and went quickly through the low doorway into the kitchen.

While the bedroom had been gloomy and cold, the kitchen was already bright and warm. A fire burned cleanly in the grate under the stove, sparking light from the brass tea-caddy on the mantelpiece, shining on the willow-pattern plates which were racked on the top shelf of the dresser and seldom brought down for use. A scrubbed deal-topped table in the middle of the room had seven chairs round it; a fairly sorry collection, save for the one used by the head of the household which, larger than the others, had arms, and a cushion in a crochet wool cover.

Bowls and mugs were on the table, though the plates from which Alex and Dougie had hastily supped breakfast had already been rinsed, dried and put back in the cupboard. Porridge slurped in the black iron pan on the hob, and the fat-bellied teapot cocked a snoot at it for its rough-hewn manners. The sodden smells of sweat and steam coaxed out of the damp pit-clothing which had been draped over chair-backs round the fire mingled with the acrid aroma of stewing tea and the mealy savour of porridge. They were the smells of all colliers' houses, common to every cottage and row in Blacklaw, and went quite unnoticed.

Kate had already ladled porridge into two bowls and, standing, was spooning her portion into her mouth. Kate was never quite her placid self until she had eaten and, even then, had no time for conversation in the morning.

Drew, too, had come down for breakfast. Unlike Betsy, he did not care to lie long in the morning, and was praised by Alex for his diligent habits. The boy had taken his bowl to the window, and was seated by it, holding his spoon in one hand and a newspaper in the other, peering at the print as he ate. It was a typical pose, absorbed, almost secretive. Mirrin knew she would get no change out of Drew. Not that she wanted it. They were held only by the bond of kinship, Drew and she; neither much liked the other, though for no apparent reason.

Ignoring him, Mirrin moved towards the stove.

'About time,' said Flora Stalker. 'I'm wearin' myself thin tryin' t'rout this family from their beds every day.'

Mirrin lifted the porridge bowl from the table and, toasting her back at the fire, ate the coagulating oatmeal without real hunger.

There had been many days in the past when Alex's meagre wage had been pared away to meet 'economies' within the pit; then a simple cup of porridge had seemed like a feast and had been savoured with great relish by hungry mouths. But things were not so bad for the Stalkers now, with three wages coming in and the prospect of Betsy and, maybe, Drew bringing home a little more money for the purse before the summer was out. James was away on his own, married and a father in his own right, quite fit enough to see that his wife and bairn did not starve.

Still, Mam complained. She was no whiner, not like some of the tartars in the village, but she had grown into the habit of making bitter jokes about her girth and her children's sloth, factors which contained little enough truth. As it was, Flora Stalker was content with her lot, and chivvied the family from a position of strength, secure in her husband's love and her children's unwavering loyalty.

One thing Flora was not, and that was thin. In the past year or two she had thickened, putting on the kind of weight which

13

was considered a sign of good health. Her features were not fat, however, merely strong and big-boned. She had the same dark eyes as her daughters. Lately, her brown hair had become flecked with grey and she spent much time sorting the bun at the nape of her neck to disguise the pallid, tell-tale strands. Though she would never admit to favouritism, her affinities were with Kate, who was so much like her in some ways; and with Dougie, the cheerful, grinning, sixteen-year-old who, though not as broad or handsome as James, was never moody or depressed by the lot he had drawn in life, by the prospect of forty years or more spent in the dark of the seams, grinding himself up small to earn his quota of bread and tea.

'I don't know what's wrong wi' Dougie these days,' Flora said.

'He's learnin' not t'like the early rise,' said Mirrin.

'He never complains,' Flora said, defensively.

'He'll learn that, too, soon enough. Wait 'til he starts t'think just what he's got t'get up for.' Mirrin would argue at any hour of the day or night, could turn an innocent remark into a challenge for debate with natural ease; a trait inherited from her father. 'A coal-face shifter at sixteen, my God! He should still be at school.'

'He didn't like school,' put in Drew, mildly, without looking up from the back issue of the *Glasgow Herald*. 'He told me himself that he thought school was for cissies, an' that learnin' was a waste o'time.'

'Don't you listen t'him, then,' Kate advised.

Flora Stalker did not add comment: secretly she was inclined to share Dougie's suspicion of book learning. She had been brought up in a household where nobody could read or write. It was only after her marriage to Alex that she had made the effort to master letters, mainly at her husband's insistence. There was, perhaps, a faint priggishness in Drew's remark about his brother.

Putting the empty porridge pot in the sink, Flora said, 'Dougie's doin' a man's job now an' it's a mercy for you, lad, that things are not what they were, or you'd be underground too, howkin' coal t'fill baskets, or workin' a vent-rope for four-teen hours . . .'

Drew sighed, not audibly: he had heard the chant a dozen times before. Though he did not appear to brush his mother's reminiscence aside, he discreetly lowered his eyes to the news-paper again.

'Aye, things are just wonderful, now,' said Mirrin, with a trace of sarcasm.

'Don't start,' Kate warned, in a murmur.

'Haven't time, anyway,' Mirrin replied.

She put the bowl on the table, swallowed tea from her mug, then seated herself on the edge of her father's chair and reached for her boots. They had almost dried out after Satur-day's soaking. She extracted the balls of newspaper from inside and, taking a fresh strip from an old *Advertiser*, tore it in half and quickly fashioned two paper tapes to protect her stocking heels.

'Dougie's started shavin',' she announced.

'How d'you know that?' Flora asked, disappointed that she had not been the first to learn her son's secret.

'Saw him,' said Mirrin. 'Late last night; Da was instructin' him, only the old man kept burstin' out with laughter. Dougie finally got a bit annoyed an' sliced a piece off his delicate hide.'

'Is that what the blood was?' Flora said.

'Aye, you'd think they'd butchered an ox between them,' said Mirrin. 'Still, whatever the rest o' us might think about Dougie bein' a man, it seems nature's catchin' up with him whether we like it or not. Next thing, it'll be girls.'

'That's enough, Mirrin!' Flora Stalker said.

It was well known that she resented the need to give her strapping sons into another woman's charge; she had only really thawed towards James's wife, Lily, after the girl had proved her worth by presenting her with her first grandchild, a boy at that. There would be weeping and wailing the day Dougie got himself snared by a rose-cheeked lass, and a full-scale investigation made into her merits before Flora would let her lovely wee son follow his instincts unchecked.

Finishing her lacing, Mirrin stood up and experimentally drummed her boots on the floor; then, indefatigably high-spirited, accelerated the rhythm into an impromptu dance, kicking her heels and shaking up her skirts until even Drew glanced up from his reading and grinned.

'Aye,' Flora declared. 'We'll see if you're as bright at the day's end, miss.'

'Hard work,' said Mirrin, 'never killed Kelly's donkey.'

'Huh!' said Flora Stalker, then, relenting, gave Mirrin a curt hug and a pat on the rump to send her on her way to work.

The door closed behind the girl. For a few minutes the echo of her footsteps lingered on the pavement outside, then died away.

Flora Stalker wiped her hands on her apron, and glanced at the wagging clock on the wall.

'Three awa' an' two t'go,' she said, firmly. 'Kate, away an' waken Betsy; there's a good girl.'

'Yes, Mam,' Kate said, and for the first time that morning, smiled. Within the house the day, at last, had steadied to an even keel.

*

The rain which had swept intermittently from the west for days on end had dwindled and died out. The blustery wind was more persistent, though, and continued to rattle slates, slap ropes and cables and clatter the rusty scraps which had blown down into the village from the pit-head workings. A milky light bathed the low hills of the neighbouring country; but that was cattle land, and the colliers claimed that farmers always had the best of the Scottish weather. Closer, at Northrigg and the home pits on the edge of Blacklaw village, slag heaps maintained their watch on the sky, grey, bald-crowned and dismal as ever. Rain or shine, thought Mirrin, there was little enough glint in Blacklaw.

The village comprised two rows of brick-built cottages, a brace of shops, a thriving public house and, in a lane stem-ming from the thoroughfare, a red sandstone kirk and its graveyard. The Stalkers' house was the last in the row. The street lifted ahead of Mirrin, climbing gradually to the colliery gates. Though hardly a garden suburb, Blacklaw was not the meanest village in the area. Once the cottage roofs had been of turf, but Houston Lamont had refurbished them. Some eight or nine years ago, in a mood of progressiveness and generosity, about the time his son had been born, Lamont had contracted to have all his tied properties limewashed and slated. Uncharitable elements in the community attributed his action to cunning, but, for the most part, Lamont's stock with his miners suffered no harm at all by the improvement scheme. Mirrin did not know the reasons for the coalmaster's action; all she could now remember was the excitement of those summer months, with slaters' drays lined along the street and strange workmen from Hamilton and Crosstrees flirting with the village lassies and getting themselves drunk at the dinner break. One slater had even wooed Kate. But Kate had been far too sensible to be fooled by his blandishments; which was just as well since the rogue later proved to have a wife and bairns in Lanark. Since then Kate, like Blacklaw, had grown older and plainer. Nobody courted her now with serious intentions.

There were many women in the street, young and old. The first haul of the day would be up soon, grinding out of the bowels of the earth on the end of its slender cables to the whining of the high wheel. The women worked at the sorting tables and the long troughs down which the coal was poured and shaken. It was a damned sight better, Mirrin supposed, than being stopped over like a mule all day, with a hun'weight of the heaviest in a creel on your back and a series of dangerously flimsy ladders to ascend from level to level. That sort of murderous slavery had ended only a few decades ago, and several folk in Blacklaw could still recall firsthand the deaths, disasters and diseases of those days and made them sound worse than the collective Plagues of Egypt. The troughs were bad enough; out in the open yard, with only leaky tin roofs to umbrella the rain in the wet months, and a filthy river of coal endlessly flowing from the wagon tips, shovelled along by a combination of steam engine's belts and the spades of boys and crippled miners not fit for underground work.

Coal, coated in dust, hard, gritty and clinging, was the source of fulfilment for all their needs and comforts. It was everywhere; in every pore, in the nostrils, the lungs, the hair roots, and the corners of the eyes, under the fingernails deep as the cuticles, infiltrating even the most secret parts of a woman's body. It was the main chemical element in the air they breathed, and tinted the water which sluggishly flowed from taps and pumps. The burns were coal-black, the river Shennan coke-grey, and the buds on the trees uncurled from their winter's sleep with coal grit embedded in their tender folds.

All day long Mirrin, and forty like her, pored over the tables and troughs and sorted the valuable stuff, cleaning out stones and clay dods and bits of rusty metal which somehow got churned up with the pure, black mineral on which all their lives depended. *That*, in the opinion of men, was fit work for women.

By now the day-shift would be at the face, the changed shift tucked up in their beds, sleeping the sleep of sheer exhaustion. Hennigan's shop was open for business, and women crowded its narrow doorway, buying a pie or a quarter loaf for the midday meal. As always, Kate had packed a bannock and cheese into a newspaper and put it safe in her sister's coat pocket.

Mirrin skirted a puddle in the road and let the shawl fall back off her shoulders. She joined the stream of women and girls making for the gates, for the shed where they could leave their coats and shawls and wrap themselves in heavy canvas aprons, garments which made bending difficult and slowed their walk to a senile sort of shuffle. For the most part, spirits were high, and greetings and jocular remarks were shouted from one group to another. Mirrin was too bold an individual to be popular with many of her co-workers, but her quick wit and her flair for humour could not be ignored.

She came up behind a cluster of five girls, all of her age and former schoolmates. They were bunched round in a secretive conclave, whispering furtively over a postcard which one of them had produced.

'Showin' off your smutty pictures again, Mary?' said Mirrin, in passing. 'Havin' a brother workin' on the bum-boats has done your education a power o'good.'

Flushing slightly, Mary Nichol glanced up. In her hand Mirrin glimpsed a sepia-coloured card, printed with what looked like four rolls of uncooked dough engaged in a wrestling bout. Mary quickly palmed the card and tucked it away in her pocket.

'Our Jackie's no' a bum-boat man: he's an ensign.'

'Aye,' said Mirrin. 'An ensign on the Clyde ferry.'

'He'll take his ticket,' Mary Nichol shouted. 'You'll see.'

Mirrin had a stinging retort on the tip of her tongue, but her reply was cut short by the appearance of two other girls from a doorway just ahead of her: Deirdre Collins and her aunt, Essa, both in their twenties and as alike as podded peas.

'Hullo, Mirrin,' they said in unison.

'Hullo.'

Together, the three girls walked the last hundred yards to the gates.

Essa said, 'Here, did you hear about Janet?'

'Which Janet?' said Mirrin.

Deirdre said, 'Janet Mackenzie: big Tam's daughter.'

'Her that worked at Lamont's house,' Essa added.

'What about her?'

'Walked out on him,' said Essa.

'I thought she needed the work?'

'Couldn't stand it,' said Deirdre.

'An' she'd only been there since Christmas,' said Essa.

Confidentially, Deirdre gripped Mirrin's shoulder. 'Expected too much of her, if y'ask me.'

'Who? Lamont?'

'Aye, the master himself, if y'ask me,' said Deirdre.

'Have y'spoken t'Janet?' said Mirrin.

'She's left the village,' said Essa, knowingly. 'Packed her bags on Saturday afternoon and was gone out of Blacklaw on the Sunday mornin' train.'

Mirrin stared quizzically at the Collins girls for a moment: she did not doubt their word, only their interpretation of the facts of the matter. It was quite likely that Janet Mackenzie *had* walked out on her employer. She wouldn't be the first girl to have quit domestic service in the coalmaster's house. But

Mirrin gave little credence to the rumours which circulated among some of the local girls, rumours which hinted that Houston Lamont was a lecherous old devil. For one thing, Lamont was hardly old; for another he was married to the kind of wife who would keep a sharp eye on her servants' behaviour and put hems on her husband; lastly, the coalmaster did not strike her as the sort of man who would demean himself by chasing maids – especially maids like Janet Mackenzie, who had a face like a sow, and a figure to match. Mirrin would believe most things about Lamont, but not that. If Janet had left, the chances were she had been caught pilfering, or had taken the huff at something trivial.

Mirrin hesitated and glanced back. The colliery fence did not quite cut off the view down the long scoop of the main street. Away in the distance, a full mile from the end of the village, a high dyke and a wealth of handsome oaks marked Houston Lamont's estate. Many of the older generation considered it fitting that Mr Lamont's dwelling should have more than its share of greenery. After all, he *was* the mine owner, and, being rich, educated and powerful, attracted such favours naturally. Mirrin did not fall in with the theory that Lamont was one of God's elect. The traditional awe of servants for master had been partially rinsed out of her by the conversations of her father and his friends. She was only a girl, of course, and a good-looking lass at that: consequently, her opinions were not taken seriously by the district's militants. Even her father and brothers treated her political fervour as something of a joke. By the Stalker women, her outspokenness was regarded as brazen and brash and a continual source of embarrassment. For all her loathing of Lamont and his class, Mirrin could not set much store by the latest piece of gossip. However, she was sensible enough to hold her tongue and let the Collins girls prattle on about the habits of the country gentry and the Lamonts in particular, as they hurried over the cobbles, through the gates, and came along the crowded lane under the towers of the winding gear.

All around her now were Lamont's men, Lamont's hirelings, Lamont's machines, and the black dross which lay at the root of Lamont's wealth. For all that, at the beginning of another week, Mirrin could not help but feel a certain security within the ugly confines of the pit-head. None of the colliers were ever long enough away to view the place in correct perspective. It was their homesteading, their estate, and they had as much subtle pride in it as if their names had been stamped across the deeds of ownership and scribbled on the contracts.

Beneath her feet the seams of coal radiated outwards across Lanarkshire, deep, rich, and inexhaustible as the earth itself. Even the raddled landscape was not without a certain weird beauty of its own.

Still listening to the girls' catalogue of scandal, which was now expanded to include other village notables, Mirrin looked at the polished shine of the pewter-coloured bogies, at the rufus-red of the corrugated iron sheds, and the iridescent sheen of the coal itself which, pulled up from the belly of the earth, was beginning to ripple down the chutes, just like a stream. Overall, Blacklaw surely had to be one of the ugliest spots in all Scotland; but even here, sometimes, there was a pitiless kind of beauty.

As they hung up their coats in the shed, and wrapped the stiff canvas aprons round their waists, Deirdre Collins said, 'She'd have done better t'stay here, if y'ask me.'

'Janet was no worker,' Mirrin said. 'She was always as lazy as sin.'

Essa gave Mirrin a sly glance. 'Y'don't have t'be a worker t'get on in this world, not if you're a lassie.'

'What's that supposed t'mean, Essa?'

'If Janet had had your looks, Mirrin Stalker, she . . .'

'My looks!' Mirrin answered. 'What does a girl need looks for? All y'need in this job is a strong pair of arms.'

Before either of the girls could say more, Mirrin turned and strode off towards the troughs.

It wasn't the first time that her looks had been used against her by women who called themselves her friends; nor would it be the last, she supposed. But their hints meant nothing. This was the place for her. She was strong and healthy and young, and had her family, her politics and her job, and even a beau of sorts, if you could call Rob Ewing that. No, there was nothing much wrong with being eighteen and a sorter in Blacklaw Colliery.

Mirrin Stalker started work at ten minutes past seven o'clock. By noon of that day, Monday, 19th March, 1875, she would wish herself a thousand miles from Lamont's colliery, and everything it stood for in the history of Blacklaw.

*

The schoolhouse was out to the west, nearer the village than Lamont's oaks, a tight, hunchbacked building with a spit of sparse grass which served as a playground, and an iron bell in a tower perched over the dominie's parlour. At eleven on the dot, the bell clapper dinged a half dozen times and from doorways front and rear one hundred and twenty boys and girls rushed, brawling and yelling, to seize the pleasure of ten minutes' break from the rigours of free education.

Through the midst of this swarming and disorganized bedlam, three boys walked soberly across the playground and stopped by the comparative privacy of the gate.

The tallest, Henderson by name, had the startled expression of a snared rabbit. McLaren, the stoutest, was moon-cheeked and sly-eyed and had hair the colour of a wheatstook. Drew Stalker, smallest of the trio, was sallow, solemn, dark-haired and neat; his face betrayed no emotion at all, a fact which considerably riled his captors.

The boys halted by the gatepost. Drew hesitated, his view of the yard blotted out by the bullies and his back already against the stone pillar.

'You're a right rotten tyke, Stalker,' McLaren snarled. 'Told old Guthrie on us, did you?'

'I never told him anythin'.'

'Aye, but you did,' McLaren insisted. 'How else was he to know we had them test answers wrote out on a bit of paper?'

'He saw you squintin' at them.'

'Naw, he never,' said Henderson.

'We should've hammered you this mornin' when we made you copy them out for us,' McLaren said.

'Well, we'll hammer him now,' said Henderson.

'You were lucky the dominie only took the paper away,' said Drew mildly.

'Only took the paper away,' mimicked Henderson. 'Listen Stalker, I dropped in the last three tests, an' if I drop in this one m'father'll murder me. He's for me stayin' at the school 'til I'm fifteen. But the board'll not select me if I fail.'

Drew said nothing.

'Bash the wee pig,' McLaren advised.

A group of older girls and boys hovered some twenty feet away. Fine they knew what was afoot, but none had the gumption to stick up for Drew Stalker. He had no close pal in all the school. Even his twin sister Betsy had hidden herself away.

The point was, he *hadn't* piped to old Guthrie. Secretly, however, he was delighted that Henderson's and McLaren's cribbing had been spotted by the eagle-eyed dominie. There was justice in it, the kind of justice which appealed to his Stalker blood.

Where had Henderson and McLaren been all those evenings when he was shivering in the backyard shed? He was dispatched there by his father because the house held no corner quiet enough for serious study-work. Most of the other village boys were up by the shale bings chasing rats or laying snaps for hares, or dunting a clooty ball about the forecourt of the *Lantern* pub.

Aye, Drew knew what they said about him, chanting the dirty rhyme about Stalker the Swat.

If they could have seen him in the shed, huddled on top of the wash tub because the floor was swimming with mud, peering at his books by the glimmer of a penny dip, shaking crawlies from his hair, and shuddering with cold; if they could have seen him then ... No, they wouldn't have respected him. On the contrary, they'd just have laughed louder and added more verses to the song.

A fist jabbed at him.

He tried to side-step, but McLaren had him pinned by the shoulder.

'Give'm the pincer,' Henderson advised.

McLaren's finger and thumb reached for Drew's nose.

Drew jerked his head. He was lighter and faster than his assailants. He ducked suddenly, wrenched at the arm, and darted past the fat boy.

Off balance, McLaren tottered and fell. For an instant he sprawled on his back, mouth wide with astonishment, then he struggled to his feet and tore after Drew to seek recompense for the insult to his pride.

Many children were watching now. The spectators made a loose ring round the three lads, Drew in the centre.

Stalker was always fair game and put up a sly fight. The real excitement came when Henderson had him on the ground, battering him red. It was always the same: the bouts had the inevitability of ritual.

Drew crouched, arms out to parry any sudden rush. Provided he kept alert, he might be able to evade them long enough for the bell to save him from too much punishment. He faced across the playground towards the school dyke and the slope above Poulter's burn. The landscape seemed no more than a flat screen against which Henderson and McLaren were glued like paper scraps.

Something twitched on the border of his vision.

He glanced up, away across the wall, and stared.

Henderson's knuckles cracked into his mouth. He felt skin split and blood ooze over his lip. Henderson struck him again, on the cheek. Still Drew did not move, standing stooped, face tilted, blood dripping from his chin. His eyes were round and glassy as marbles.

On the slope above the burn, the chestnut tree quivered once more.

Incredulously, Drew shook his head.

The barren and stunted tree had developed life. It swayed sluggishly, first to one side and then to the other.

'Look!'

He pointed, arm, wrist and finger rigid.

All the spectators, including the bullies, turned. As if to please him, the tree swayed violently, showering twigs and withered leaves to the grass.

'Da!' Henderson murmured. 'Daddy!'

24

A low moan rose from the children.

A great rumbling roar disturbed the atmosphere. A series of vibrations shook through the earth. In the dominie's tower, the bell clanged quizzically, then was mute.

The tree rose abruptly into the air, trunk, roots, fibres all shot clear of the ground, as if some petulant giant had punched it from below. For a second it hung suspended, then arched away and crashed down into the burn fifty yards to the south.

In the school yard no child moved, heads all turned, bodies frozen in attitudes of play; then the main door was flung open and Dominie Guthrie ran out, followed by Mr Spence, and two young, scared student teachers.

'Children! Children! Attention!'

Guthrie's reedy command was swallowed up in the bedlam. His appearance had broken the awful spell.

Girls screamed and clapped their hands to their ears. Infant school pupils fled in confusion, tumbled, picked themselves up, scurried hither and thither, wailing, sobbing, lost. Older boys simply stood stock still, white-faced, unaware of what was required of them.

Guthrie came out into the playground, arms raised, brows drawn as if in temper.

'Please, children! Attention!'

The more intelligent settled and had just begun to draw towards the man, when the ground directly beneath the school jarred and trembled, and a report like cannon-shot cracked overhead. It was followed immediately by another, then another, a whole fusillade of echoing explosions.

In a frenzy of terror, the children scattered.

Blood dripping from his mouth, Drew found himself running too, caught in the crowd which streamed through the gate and along the footpath into the kirk lane.

The colliery hooter blared stridently.

Drew rounded the gable of the kirk hall and saw smoke peppered with sparks coil darkly over the pit-head. Even as he came within sight, the pall burgeoned into a roaring column which shot from the top of the winding shaft two hundred feet into the air.

He shied and clung to the dyke.

Rabbity chin wobbling with tears, Henderson overtook him. 'Aw, Drew!' he cried. 'It's the pit. An' it's m'Daddy's shift.'

But Drew had guessed that already. It was his father's shift too: his father and brothers were deep that morning, deep down at the bottom level.

Without a word, Drew ran on again.

*

In the last house in Main Street, Kate Stalker felt the first tremor of the explosion as she replaced the teapot on the hob. Swinging, she clutched at the table, gawping stupidly at the brown rivers of tea spilled from the overturned mugs. In the chair in the corner, the big woman raised her head. Every bit of expression had drained from her face, so that it resembled one of the potato heads which Betsy used to draw, primitive shapes for eyes and mouth, and nothing more.

'Mother . . .'

Kate stepped round the table towards the woman. Three blasts battered the narrow room. Pictures on the wall tilted wildly, and the dresser dishes chattered against their restraining rods. A bowl hopped from the flat-topped board and broke into fragments on the floor.

Understanding swarmed through the defences which shock had flung around her brain: Flora Stalker hauled herself out of the chair and reeled towards the door.

'Alex?' she cried peevishly. 'Alex?'

Snatching up a plaid wool shawl, Kate ran out into the street after her mother and draped the comforter round the woman's shoulders as best she could.

The woman still sounded oddly vexed.

'Not *my* laddies,' she declared. 'Oh, God, not *my* boys.'

Blacklaw Main Street was as Kate could never have imagined it. Every door of every house was wide to the wall. Out on the cobbles, women clasped babes to their breasts or, with toddlers tucked under their arms, hobbled forward like cripples into the centre of the road. Men grouped a little way off. The younger ones, not long in from the night shift, peered blearily through heavy lids and fumbled to buckle on their broad leather belts again. Elderly colliers, with the narrow chests and shrunken legs they had won from a lifetime's work on their knees, had a hard knowledge of mines and explosions. With the worst of the visions locked away deep in their memories, they had no inclination ever to talk of them with man or woman. Full well, though, they understood what the acrid canopy of smoke and barrage of cannon-like sounds meant.

'That'll be the Number Two,' someone called.

No matter what their age or sex, everyone began to run towards the reek.

Skirts caught up, Kate gripped her mother's elbow and attempted to keep her from falling on the muddy road. The lunatic blare of the hooter fluctuated, rising and lowering, finally withering away. They could hear the babble of voices already drifting up from the vicinity of the mine, and, soon after, caught sight of the crowds from close houses and the surviving pit blocks.

'Mam! Kate!'

Craning her neck, Kate caught sight of her sister through the press.

She waved. 'Mirrin! Here!'

'Who ... who's that?'

'It's Mirrin, Mother.' Kate gently squeezed her mother's arm. 'At least she's ...'

The woman raised her hand and brushed back hair from her eyes. She seemed to indicate by that gesture that Mirrin, picking coal at the pit-head troughs, had never been in serious danger and so had no call on her concern.

Kate released her mother's arm, lifting on tip-toe to signal again to Mirrin. Her upraised hand was caught at the wrist and painfully dragged down, turning her. She was confronted by Joe McCausland, a retired ganger and a close crony of her father's.

'Your good-sister's been took bad,' he wheezed. 'God, but it's a desperate time for a bairn to be strugglin' into the world. Still, I've been sent for one o'you, so you'd best hasten down there, Katie.'

Kate moaned. Lily! How could she have forgotten her

brother's wife, eight months pregnant and all alone in her house. The dread in her own bosom had driven all thought of Lily's plight out of her mind.

Mirrin burrowed through the crowd and reached them. They were not close to the shafts yet, and would not, for a while at least, venture closer and perhaps impede the rescuers. Kate pulled her sister into the lee of the pub gallery. The girl's eyes were wide and unblinking. A stiff white ring all round her mouth made the question almost unnecessary.

'How bad, Mirrin?'

'Bad: awful bad.' Her fingers locked on Kate's shoulder for emphasis. 'Know what they're saying already? Fire-damp. Hear that: fire-damp! An' just how long is it since Daddy and the Ewings complained that there was damp in the mine? Two months. Even reported two spurts; och, no, nothin' serious . . .'

The girl choked with angry tears.

'They were told, and they did nothing, nothing. The rotten bosses just ignored . . . Now, my old man and m'brothers are . . .'

'Stop it, Mirrin.'

Intentionally Kate made her tone harsh. She had no time to spare for Mirrin's tantrums. Her mother had wandered on and should not be left without a member of the family, not so close to the pit. Then there was Lily – and Betsy and Drew at school. They all had to be looked after; she couldn't do it by herself.

She caught Mirrin as the younger girl had caught her, and gave her a vigorous shake. 'Time for that kind of talk later. Right now, there's too many things to be done. D'you hear me?'

'Aye, I hear.' Mirrin's voice was calmer, but bitterness still made her lips tight and hard. 'What d'you want me to do, Kate?'

'Stay with mother.'

'Where are you . . .?'

'Lily's been taken bad.'

'Lily? But James isn't . . .'

'He signed for an extra shift, for the cash, because the baby was coming.'

28

'Hell,' said Mirrin. 'James too, then. Poor Lily.'

Aye, poor Lily, and poor James. Poor Alex and Flora Stalker. Poor Dougie and his mate, Nick. Poor folk of Blacklaw.

Kate gave her sister a push. 'Find Mother an' don't leave her.'

Mirrin nodded, and thrust into the back of the crowd which had grown and congealed even in the minute's conversation.

Kate watched her go, gathering herself. She was shaking now with the aftermath of shock, and with cold. She had thought of the shawl for her mother but had not realized her own need of protection against the keen March bluster. Hugging her arms across her breast, she hurried back down Main Street in search of the youngest Stalkers.

School pupils were milling up from the kirk lane, some sobbing with fear and lack of comprehension. But the older ones, girls as well as boys, *they* knew. Denied the release of childhood, they loitered or wandered in clannish groups, growing up in the season of a single morning.

Drew and Betsy found her at the same moment, each running to her from a different direction. Betsy's black ringlets jiggled prettily on her shoulders and her eyes had the lustre of tears. Drew, though paler than usual, was calmer than she would have anticipated. His only sign of distress was the manner in which he kneaded and clicked the lid of his shiny tin pencil box, and a fleck of blood on his lip. The boy and girl were twins, sharing a likeness of colouring and feature, but, in many ways, were of opposite temperament.

Betsy threw herself into Kate's arms, craving selfish attention for her own emotions. Drew stood back a pace, waiting, silent.

Kate allowed Betsy only a moment, then carefully disentangled the girl. 'No time for crying, Betsy,' she said firmly. 'So give over. We don't know what's happened yet.'

'Mr McCausland told me,' said Drew grimly. 'The word's out that Number Two pit's gone up and everyone in it.'

His fingers laboured frantically over the edges of the pencil box.

'Is he *sure?*' Kate said.

Drew shook his head.

Keeping a rein on her mounting panic, Kate slipped her arms round the twins' waists and steered them along the street away from the smoke.

'Well,' she said, almost lightly. 'McCausland's an old blether, an' always was. So, come on, I've something special for you two to do.'

'What?' asked Drew.

'I want you to stay with your Auntie Lily an' keep her company.'

'Where's James?' Betsy enquired.

'He's ...'

'All right, Kate,' said Drew quickly. 'We'll stay with her.'

'Oh, Kate,' Betsy complained tearfully. 'I don't want to leave you.'

Kate raised her forefinger as a signal of authority. 'No arguing. Aunt Lily just can't be left by herself.'

'What if the baby starts?' asked Drew.

How had he known that it could happen under stress? It was not a subject in which the lads of her day had ever displayed much knowledge. She had never been able to evaluate the depths of Drew's intelligence, or come close to him in the mutual warmth she shared with her other brothers.

'I'll come an' have a look at her,' Kate said.

'What if it starts after you've gone?'

'It won't,' said Kate; and prayed to God that she was right.

*

The neighbour who had served a kindly turn as nurse stood now with Kate in the shadowy corner near the door of Lily's kitchen, speaking in a murmurous tone which belied her optimism.

'Och, she's not so bad; just a wee turn. She'll be right as rain soon. Eight months is not near as chancy as four or five.'

'Thanks, Mrs Dow,' Kate said.

'I suppose there's been no official word about your kinfolk?'

'I'm on my way up there now.' Kate smiled stiffly. 'It's good of you to give Lily your time.'

The woman shrugged.

'Time,' she said. 'What's time t'me, lass?'

Eighteen years ago this woman's husband and two sons had been crushed by a rock fall over in Northrigg. She was safe now from intimate pain and grief, with only the ghosts of that old sorrow to help her share the agony of other wives and mothers.

Kate saw her out, and returned to the kitchen where Betsy was already spooning tea from the caddy into the pot.

'You'll be wantin' a cup, Kate?' said Betsy.

'No.'

'Lily's going to try t'eat a wee bit of toast,' Betsy went on chirpily.

'That's fine.'

The girl, who looked hardly older than fourteen-year-old Betsy, was in the big knobbly chair by the side of the fire, her limbs tucked snugly under a hodden blanket, her swollen stomach making the cloth tight. Her eyes were dry but had that vague out-of-focus slant which disturbed Kate more than tears would have done.

Kneeling by the chair, Kate said gently, 'Try to be brave, Lily. Nobody's sure of anythin' yet. I'll away up there now, an' as soon as there's any sort of news at all, I'll come right back here with it.'

The girl did not answer. Fear and pregnancy had robbed Lily of the last of her prettiness. Now, enveloped in the coarse blanket, she looked like nothing other than a stray tabby brought in out of the wet.

'Betsy'll stay with you,' Kate said. 'Drew'll keep Edward amused.'

Sitting back on her heels, Kate glanced at the eighteen-month-old toddler who, gingerly taunted by Drew, was scrambling to reach a ragged clooty ball. In spite of his indifference, Drew was a great favourite with his wee nephew.

'Babby-clouts.' Lilly spoke clearly and distinctly, but with puzzlement, questions in her inflection. 'It was babby-clouts we wanted.'

'Aye,' said Kate.

'James'd done his shift: he wanted the extra for babby-clouts.'

'Are you positive he was underground?'

Lily wrinkled her brow. She had not once looked directly at her good-sister, but continued to stare at the hummock of the blanket as if it was a burden of which she had no knowledge at all.

'Lily, are you *sure* James was below?'

'He ... never ... No, he never ... never said.'

The girl lifted her chin, head cocked.

'D'you think ... ?'

'I don't know.' Kate got to her feet and smoothed down the front of her skirt. 'I think it's best if I get up there and find out.'

Lily nodded eagerly, struggled with the blanket and freed one frail arm. She gave her hand to her good-sister who squeezed it briefly.

'Go on,' Lily said.

'Will you be all right?'

'With Betsy here, an' that handsome Drew,' Lily declared: she swallowed, 'I'll be fine.'

Betsy followed Kate to the street door.

'Why did you do that?'

'Do what?'

'Tell her a lie,' said Betsy. 'You know fine James's below with Daddy and Douglas.'

'Don't tell Lily yet; not yet,' said Kate. 'Promise now.'

Betsy's lips pursed, trembling. 'James's our brother as well as bein' her man. An' he's not the only one of ours down there.'

'Maybe so,' said Kate severely. 'But just you remember that you've got me and Mirrin and Mam and Drew. Lily's got nobody – except us.'

'Sorry,' said Betsy. 'I am, I'm sorry. I won't tell.'

Kate hugged her, then slipped out of the house into the empty main street.

A fine mist of rain had come with the wind again, varnishing the cobbles and slates. It was quiet and peaceful there when she did not look up at the pinnacles of smoke. Something told her that this would be the last moment's solitude she would know for quite a while. Though her urge to reach the pit-head was strong, she hesitated, reluctant to give herself up to all the demands which would be made on her in the days ahead.

Then she heard the sound. Walking a few quick paces she peered curiously down the tunnel between the rows into the backyards. The tune was sweet and harmonious for a casual phrase or two, the trenchant pathos of the daftie given a bit of voice by the tines and tin reeds of the mouth organ.

A young, broad-shouldered man, with bulging thighs in his soiled breeks and a face as frank as ham, Lauchlan Abercorn sat on the midden-heap like a king on his throne, entranced by the music he blew for himself. But when he saw her spying on him, his mood changed. His features contorted and he leaned from the waist and played *at* her, not a melody now but a ranting two-note complaint which mocked the call of the pit-head hooter.

Poor Loony Lachie, the butt of many village jokes, never savage, seldom sad, just prone to be vexed at intrusions on his privacy. What would he make of today's events?

Not much, Kate thought, though at least for a time he would rule over Blacklaw and make of it his daft and innocent estate.

With the noise of the mouth-organ sawing in her ears, Kate turned and ran to submerge her fears in those of the multitude who waited at the mouth of the colliery shaft.

2

Blacklaw Colliery lay a half mile north of the village. It was one of a hundred similar mines sunk down to tap the rich coal seams which slanted west from Fife and the Lothians, and earned for Lanarkshire the doubtful crown as the blackest county in Scotland.

Situated wide of the main Glasgow–Hamilton road, the workings were divided into two principal sections, known simply as Pits One and Two. An ancient bypath, which staggered in from Claypark and lost itself in a patch of wilderness half-roads to Hamilton, divided Lamont's property yet again. Seventy yards apart, the pits both opened from the north section beyond the bypath. Offices, workshops and other essential sheds sprawled south of it. The pits themselves were linked by a spur of the Hamilton Branch line which stemmed in turn from an artery of the Caledonian Railway.

Among the colliers there had been talk, some months before, of incipient fire-damp. Minor injuries caused by spurt explosions were not rare, and Alex Stalker, among others, had been loud in his assertions that a dangerous condition existed in Lamont's seams.

Lamont was not unaware of the complaints, nor was he confident enough to let them pass unchallenged. Only that morning, at 4.30 a.m., firemen and the underground manager had descended the pit for the express purpose of giving it clearance prior to the arrival of the men.

No trace of gas had been found.

At 6 a.m. a full day-shift had started work.

At 11.5 a.m. an explosion of great magnitude had ripped the guts from Number Two pit, destroying it totally and projecting a jet of smoke, sparks and ignited coal two hundred-odd feet through the shaft and into the sky.

The source of the blast was unquestionably fire-damp.

The toll obtained from the pay-office put the number of colliers underground at the time at one hundred and fifteen.

*

The reality of the pit-head was more horrifying than Kate's imaginings.

Bursting out of the shaft, the shock wave had wrecked the cage, hurling boulders and showers of coal-warped girders and lethal stumps of wood-shoring over a wide area. Roof, walls and windows of the managers' office were holed and speared with debris. Many of the workshops too had suffered the brunt of the first detonation.

Worst of all, though, was the fate of a squad of surface-men. Engaged in drawing hutches from the pit-head to the wagon coups, their route had placed them directly in the path of the blast. It had ripped the line asunder and tossed workers like straw dolls over the scorched ground or into the rocking metal hutches. A few survivors, dazed and injured, were still stumbling aimlessly around, oblivious to the origins of the calamity.

Railway crews had rushed down the embankment to lend their aid and the first organized platoons from adjoining villages had arrived to swell the ranks.

Numb with terror, Kate stared at the scene.

Everything, animate and inanimate, was coated with oily black dust. She could taste it in her mouth. It clogged her nostrils and made her eyes smart like salt.

She was in the thick of it now.

A boy not much older than Drew swayed past her, his face covered by his hands. Blood welled stickily through his fingers. Impulsively, she stepped towards him, but he thrust her roughly away, cursing, and blundered on in search of his own relief.

'Dinna stand gawping, girl.' A coal-black figure waved angrily. 'Away y'go up t'the joiners' shop and help the doctors.'

Kate spun round.

There were hummocks and mounds all about her.

She could hardly have identified them had it not been for the stretcher carriers who bent over them, digging and prying with their hands and found implements. Ashen-faced women hurried from mound to mound, anxious, yet desperately afraid, to see the faces which emerged from the mud.

'M'laddie; just a wee laddie, wi' red hair : have y'seen a laddie wi' red hair?'

Many of the women had gathered by the wreckage of the managers' office. From there they could view Number Two's splintered shaft-top and the preparations underway to support the first search party. Kate drifted up towards them, glimpsed Mirrin's black hair, then lost her again as a sweeping surge in the crowd closed the gap.

The wives were keening and crying like beggars.

As a raucous shout went up – 'All out of Number One. Number One's all cleared.' – Kate caught sight of another of her father's mates, and pushed her way over to him.

'How many in Two, Mr Pritchard?'

'Ach, Katie.' He took the stumpy clay pipe from his mouth and spat disgustedly. 'It's a sorry day, lass, a sorry day.'

'But, Mr Pritchard . . .'

'They'll be postin' lists, shortly. That's all the dirty black-guards are good for – postin' bloody lists.'

'How many?' she pleaded.

'Sixty, nigh on.'

'In Two?'

'Aye, lass.'

He turned away, spitting again.

A slight figure with bright red hair was rolled on to a blanket-stretcher. A clean sack was drawn over him, up over the crusted face.

From the back of the crowd, she could still hear the mother's appeal; 'Have y'not seen m'laddie, a wee laddie, wi' red . . .'

Weeping, Kate moved on.

Mirrin had found a place for her mother, a seat on a broken barrow against the workshop wall. The woman's face was chalk-white but composed. She looked enquiringly at Kate, who, stooping, told her rapidly of how things were with the younger children and Lily.

Her mother nodded.

Mirrin said, 'You'll have heard : none of our folk came out of Number One.'

A little fretful crease appeared between Flora Stalker's brows. 'Funny! You'd have thought . . .' Her words dribbled out and ceased.

'Don't think about it, Mam,' said Mirrin. 'We'll know nothin' for sure 'til the rescue crew comes up.'

'What have you heard, Mirrin?' Kate asked.

'A crew's headed in through Number One,' Mirrin answered. 'Seems they were hardly on the level before they caught a whiff of foul. They sent up to the surface for instructions just ten minutes ago. Manager Wyld gave them the go-ahead, but told them to take precautions.'

'Are they breakin' into Two?'

'They're goin' to try,' said Mirrin. 'They're talkin' about puttin' down a kettle if they can clear the shaft enough.'

Miners' argot came easily to Mirrin. Kate understood enough of it to follow the gist, though she had never seen the barrel-shaped contrivance in which three men could be lowered into places where a cage would have foundered – the 'kettle'.

Shaking her thick black hair free of her eyes, Mirrin rattled on, 'Old man Ewing was set on goin' down personally, but Rob got a couple of cronies to hold him back.'

There was a trace of derision in Mirrin's voice when she mentioned Rob Ewing's name. The odd love-hate relationship between them was a source of irritation to the rest of the Stalkers. Flora in particular could not understand Mirrin's taunting, derisive attitude towards young Rob, who was a catch worth the reeling on any lass's hook.

Even now, in the storm centre of disaster, there was something so bold and challenging in Mirrin's stance that Kate was glad they held her with them at the rear of the crowd. Mirrin's chin was tilted defiantly, her fists planted in the small of her back like a prop-orator's. Her generous breasts pressed full against the stuff of her blouse which, as always, was open by one button more than was considered decent. Scorn mingled with sorrow in her. Clearly she despised the trivial, pompous details with which Lamont's minor officials adulterated this tragedy.

On this day of all days Kate prayed that Mirrin would not shame them with her outspokenness.

But Mirrin did nothing, said nothing. She stood motionless for the quarter hour it took the cage to descend the Number

One shaft and for news to be siphoned back to the surface.

Two men had been found right at the bottom of the shaft. It was assumed that they had crawled there in the wake of the holocaust.

'Who are they?'

'Have they news of Two?'

Shouting incoherently, the crowd surged forward. Children shrieked as the force of the press lifted them from their feet or separated them from their mothers' sides.

'For the love of God, *stand back.*'

Donald Wyld wagged his hands in the air like a chorus-master. Men, already drawn for the full-scale search party, linked arms and, like strike-pickets, shouldered the mob into the semblance of order.

'Give us room to fetch them out,' Wyld pleaded. 'We'll post the names all the quicker. Christ, it's a living hell down there. *Don't go makin' it worse for them.*'

His appeal was heeded.

The crowd hushed and receded ten or fifteen yards, though every person in it craned and strained to watch the raising of the cage gate.

Two of the rescue squad slouched out, followed by two more. The sight of them sucked a growl of disappointment from the watchers. Where were the rescued men? They had seen the brave rescuers. Only the underground shift bore the dark secrets of the morning and its aftermath. Then the growl altered into a strange, fluting sound, like peewits flighting over a field. Each pair of rescuers bent and lifted. Awkwardly hunched, their fists twisted at the blankets on which lay mud-fouled, black-charred objects, things that had recently been men.

The Stalkers did not crush forward with the throng. Even so, the odour reached Kate's nostrils before she could cover them with her wrist. With sickness welling in her throat, she wrenched away from it. Involuntarily Mirrin too stepped back and, for an instant, Kate saw the signature of age scrawled over her sister's face.

'I thought ... I thought they meant ... *alive*,' said Mirrin softly: 'Oh, God! They must *all* be dead.'

'Shush, girl!' her mother said.

Flora Stalker was still seated, hands clasped tightly in the lap of her dress. She did not look at the bodies as they were filed through the crowd. Instead she canted her head to catch the oversman's announcement.

An uncle of Davy Henderson, the oversman was but lately made up to the post.

Hoarsely, he called out, 'I've made identification. By a ring. It's ... it's m'own brother, Joe. Joseph Henderson. The other ...'

He hesitated, unable to go on.

'*Who?*'

The oversman steeled himself. 'The wrights' shop'll serve as the death-house.'

Every villager understood – there the bodies would be laid out, trinkets carefully removed, shoes, knives, belt-buckles, tobacco cases, anything which would help put a name to the loved ones.

Kate sat by her mother, arm around the woman, hair against her mother's hair, waiting, not watching now, just waiting and listening, hope dimmed by tangible evidence of catastrophe. With three of the Stalker family submerged in Pit Two, the odds that even one had survived were very slender. To bring up all three to breathe again the moist air of that Monday afternoon would need a miracle of God.

Four times the cage descended.

Four times it rose, grinding to the surface. Four times it disgorged a grisly cargo.

Mirrin spoke only once, relaying a fragment of news back to Kate. 'They've started on the brattice. When it's clear, they'll sink the kettle direct into Two.'

Kate contrived to ignore other shouts and wild-fire rumours.

For hours, the clangour went on. Whiles it smirred with rain, and whiles it was only damp, then the first of the lists was posted: the worst period of all had arrived.

Hand-printed papers were tacked to the walls of the joiners' shop. Women went forth with the crowd, some flying, some lagging, and ready, and groaned or wept, and turned away, remote in the knowledge that their waiting turn was over – or waiting still.

By late afternoon the convocation round the pit-head had been increased by hundreds of miners from neighbouring collieries. Choke-damp, that noxious, clinging gas which was the inevitable legacy of a fire-damp explosion, had taken a sad toll of the rescuers. It denied them the weary dignity which heroes deserved, brought them scrabbling out of the cage to roll and writhe in the wet earth, to rid their skins of the deadly film.

In spite of Kate's urgings, Flora Stalker would not leave the site. She had to share in every act, every scene of the drama, though on her seat by the quiet wall she apparently remained aloof from it.

As lists, or amendments to lists, went up, Mirrin would go across to them, elbow herself to the front, would read, return, and grimly shake her head.

Articles brought to the surface, or gingerly stolen from the dead, were clerically processed and put, like forfeit charms, into a green tin cash-box which Henderson or Wyld periodically brought out into the crowd.

'If anybody can ... put a name.'

'*Holy Mary, Mother of God! Holy Mary, Mother ...*'

'Knife; tip of the blade broke. The letter B in poker-work ...'

'*An' her youngest only nine months.*'

'Merchant navy button; from the breeks ...'

'*Peter!*'

'A buckle ...'

'*John!*'

'A brown boot, wi' four star studs ...'

'*Willie Lomax!*'

'It canny be true.'

'*Holy Mary, Mother of God!*'

Kate closed her eyes. Tears rivered her cheeks. She was left only with an acrid compassion for all of them, and the resolution that she would not nurture false hopes – though she did, in spite of herself.

'Kate!'

She looked up.

Mirrin was before her, an older Mirrin, no longer brave and bold.

'Mam,' the girl said. 'It's James an' Douglas.'

Flora Stalker sighed.

'They're named,' Mirrin said. 'On the last bit list. Our James, an' our Dougie.'

Flora sagged. Placing her hand on Kate's arm, she confided, 'Douglas was just sixteen, y'know.'

Kate nodded.

'Just a wee lad.'

Kate nodded again. It wasn't strictly true, though. Douglas was no lad: he was a man, a collier. He had been proud when he reached the age to crawl to the face on his brother's heels. They always thought of Dougie as being boy-young; perhaps because his hair was fair and wavy and because, when he swung along in step with big, brawny James, he still showed the litheness of childhood.

'Daddy?' asked Kate.

'Can't be sure,' Mirrin answered. 'The last lot up were ... so ... bad.'

'I want my Alex,' said Flora Stalker firmly. She got to her feet. '*I want my man.*'

*

Two hours later rescue operations ground to a halt. Members of the rescue squads were collapsing from exhaustion and the effects of choke-damp. Vast pockets of the gas had gathered in the levels and seeped along the lines of the seams.

Word of this hazard was brought to Wyld who, in the absence of Houston Lamont, was cudgelled into making decisions. Though Donald Wyld had never lived through a disaster of this scale before, he had been tutored well in the techniques of rescue. He arranged for the pouring of hundreds of gallons of water down the pit-shaft, a prospect which filled the still-waiting womenfolk with dread.

Wyld took it upon himself to explain the nature of this measure to the crowd. Any collier worth his candle would have done the same. Water, the manager told them, was the only agent capable of counteracting choke-damp. Volumes of it would be pumped into the shaft where, by the time it reached the bottom, it would have sifted out into a fine rain. He did not await the crowd's approval of the plan, but hurried off to superintend the haulage of pumps and hoses.

Meanwhile, work continued on clearing the main shaft, the pulley apparatus and brattices.

Fresh teams of rescuers were recruited and briefed. Word of the disaster had spread out of Lanarkshire. Many spectators had already arrived on foot. More came by cart, horse, omnibus and even by train.

The squads were fed with hot soup and tea from big copper urns. In a makeshift hospital, local doctors worked feverishly to patch up the injured or, in the worst cases, to calm the agony of wounds which would never properly heal. A few relatives were permitted brief visits, and came out weeping.

No one, however, was admitted to the wheelwrights' shop.

In her heart, Kate was now convinced that in that sullen place she would find all that remained of her father.

Flora Stalker swayed, staggered and leaned her weight on her eldest daughter's shoulder. There was no despair in her expression. The remoteness brought out her resemblance to Drew very strongly at that moment.

Perhaps Mirrin noticed it too.

'Go down to Lily's,' Mirrin said. 'Drew and Betsy have been alone long enough.'

'I won't leave 'til I know the truth,' said Flora Stalker.

'You're bein' selfish, Mother,' said Mirrin. 'Lily'll have heard word by this time, an' she'll be in sore need of you both. The young 'uns can't cope.'

'It's true, Mother,' said Kate.

'There's nothin' here for you now,' Mirrin said.

'Mirrin, don't.'

'They're all gone,' Mirrin snapped. 'All the Stalker menfolk – except Drew.'

'Perhaps you're wrong.'

'I'm not wrong, Kate,' said Mirrin. 'For God's sake, get her

42

out of here. Take her to Lily's; that's where the life is now.'

'But what if . . . ?'

'I'll wait,' Mirrin said.

'But why?'

'It's where I belong,' Mirrin answered.

3

Now that her sister and her mother were gone, Mirrin concentrated on ridding her mind of sentiment. She had no patience with weepers. The proper time for womanly grief was in the dark of the night, secret minutes, precious as pearls, wrested from the day to be weathered or enjoyed, touched with pleasure or endured in sorrow, the lot of dutiful wives.

But Mirrin was neither wife nor maiden. She worked with men at the pit-head, argued and laughed and traded insults with them. Her good looks and womanly figure, matched to a mind tempered by her father's philosophies, made her disconcertingly different. Mirrin didn't care.

When Kate had coaxed her mother away to comfort Lily, Mirrin steeled herself and, for the tenth time that afternoon, pushed across to the lists.

Dusk was near now.

Two slush-lamps and a brass bullseye had been lighted and hung on nails over and by the wall. Rain had made the names run. Some were already almost illegible. Another example of official stupidity, Mirrin thought; were there no wax pencils in the racks?

James Stalker.

Douglas Stalker.

The ink had blotted. The names of her lovely brothers seemed to merge and form a single unit separate from the scores of others.

'Ach, James!' she murmured, for she had loved him most dearly of all the family. 'James, James, it was hardly the time to be goin', love.'

Behind her, she could hear torrents of water spouting from the hoses, the medley of creaks and whinnies which the pumps made, and the familiar slapping of the cage-cable in the girders above the working shaft.

The wheel was turning.

No matter what befell the men, that wheel seldom ceased.

44

Though it might sleep or ail for a spell, it was never dormant long. That symbol of the coalmaster's power, the fetter of all colliers.

Mirrin moved away quickly from the joiners' shop. She marched as if she had a purpose and a destination. In reality she had neither.

She tramped the back rows, circled abandoned sheds and headed out by the sorting troughs. All work had ceased there at the moment of the first earth-shaking. Some of the tables had been thrown over, spilling the coal.

It was in her mind that perhaps she would encounter Rob Ewing. Logically, she supposed he would be below with one of the rescue parties. She would have welcomed masculine company then. An argument would soon hoist her from her misery. Who, though, had time to spare for politics, or to listen to her condemnation of a system which failed to protect its most valuable commodity – its workers?

She came round again closer to the shaft.

Look at them! Fancy-dans up from Hamilton and Glasgow, warm and snug in their nap overcoats, uniform in curly-brimmed hats. Look at the townies gawping, newspapermen ferreting for sensation to pile up in columns of grey print. Mountains of reporters' scribbles would not bury the shame of Blacklaw.

And where was the coalmaster, the grand man, God on High? Where was Houston Lamont, then? Cowering in the neuk of some posh club in the city; or, even now, before he had cast his mollie eyes on his ruined pit, even now was he off canvassing his powerful committee pals with excuses?

She walked faster, her boots biting at the crust of coal-dust which carpeted the area.

It was nowhere properly dark, save far out in the slags. She could not bring herself to go there, to forsake the periphery of the lanterns and temporary lamps which had been rigged up to stave off the horrors of the night. She was like a moth battened to its wayward courses round the flame.

On the fifth perambulation of the pit area, her stamina finally flagged. Her feet became suddenly leaden and her back ached.

She eased her fierce pace. A hundred yards from the frieze of swart shapes round the pit-shafts, she halted and rested her shoulder on the wall of a docking hut.

The unplaned timber exuded a piny fragrance. She rubbed the resin scars with her fingernail, and sniffed the faint perfume of the fresh, green woods from which the living tree had been hewn. At long last, she found the weakness which allowed her to weep for her brothers.

The spasm did not last. She wept with her brow against the timber and her hands slack by her sides. There was nobody in the vicinity – so she thought. She did not notice the man leave his companions in the silent group in the avenue between the sheds and cross over to her.

For a tall man, he moved lightly and without a sound. He held himself very straight. Inside the cape of the Ulster, his shoulders were as broad as those of any dross-heaver. The stand-collar was up, framing his face. He had removed the bowler and held it in his gloved left hand.

When he touched Mirrin, she whirled, ashamed to be caught weeping. In the reflected light from the distant lamps she could not, just at first, discern who he was, though the dress and the barbering of the hair and side-whiskers left her in no doubt that he was a gentleman.

Now that he had made the gesture, the man seemed tongue-tied. Mirrin wiped her eyes with the corners of her shawl, tried to square up and put on a bold front once more.

It was only when he spoke that she recognized him.

Instantly her self-pity turned to anger.

'A ... a dear one lost?' the man said, formally.

She opened her lips to reply, then, furious, found so many things crowding on to the tip of her tongue that she remained speechless.

'Your ... husband?'

'I ... I have no husband, Mr Lamont.'

'Ah!'

'If you must know,' Mirrin said, 'it was two brothers. Nothin' important; just two brothers.'

'I am sorry.'

'I'll wager you are,' Mirrin said.

Lamont raised one eyebrow.

'I did not mean to intrude.'

'It's a bit late for that, *Mister* Lamont,' said Mirrin. 'If you'd intruded a month ago, when . . .'

'May I have one of my men escort you home?'

'Hah!' Mirrin laughed. 'Home! God Almighty, this *is* home. Don't you see that yet, *Mister* Lamont?'

'Miss . . .'

She was already walking away from him, marching at a great rate, her body outlined against the gaseous glow of the workings.

Mirrin did not think of how she appeared, or of the rudeness of her outburst. It was not half, not a tenth, of all the things she had wanted to shout at him. Prudence, product of distress, had stayed her, had censored her rage and her desire to impress upon him that he was no better than an assassin.

One second longer in his company and she would have called him a murderer to his face.

Tears blinded her again, blurring the tallow-coloured dabs of light, the red licks of the torches and the sudden ripple of activity which stirred through the watchers ahead of her.

Abruptly she stopped again, bowing her head.

She knew she *had* to control herself. It was not the time yet, nor the proper setting. Anger would avail her nothing. She couldn't have cared less about revenge. But there were others to consider – Mam, and Lily, Kate and the twins. No saying what Lamont might do, if she riled him sufficiently.

Shouts brought her to her senses.

Voices were raised up in unison. They had that quality which a good field-minister could wring from his congregation, a kind of sceptical jubilation.

'Alive.' Mirrin lifted her head. 'Some of them alive.'

She gathered her skirts and ran.

Excited shouts, loud prayers, and the crying of loved ones' names greeted the news.

The forefront of the crowd was still largely composed of women and older children. They were jammed forward against the hurdles of saw-horses which had been erected in the immediate area of the shaft. The motion of the mob was like that of the sea when the tide shifts from ebb to flood, a massive surge, not harried, but forceful. Out on the flanks were newspaper writers and artists, their paper tablets the whitest spots in the scene. On a rack of girders the last squad slumped, too utterly spent to share in the triumph to which their efforts had contributed.

'They're bringin' them up. They're bringin' them up *alive*!'

Mirrin elbowed her way into the crowd, caring nothing for the curses and thumps she received. She felt dizzy with relief. In examining her motive, however, she could find no real hope that one of the saved miners might be her father. It was enough, for the moment, that the black, brittle earth had been persuaded to yield up a little of the life it had claimed, to relinquish the prisoners of wet low levels and bottom seams.

She came up hard against the bar of the saw-horse. The trestle wobbled under the weight of the crowd. A dozen men, mostly hatted, stood agitatedly on the platform boards at the lip of the shaft. Light lay in great pallid wedges across the shoring. Shadows of the overhead beams, solidly cleaving the pit, were cut again by the shadowgraphs of cables and spokes.

When the lid of the cage lifted into sight, the crowd hushed. Cables twanged and drums shrieked and grated. Slowly the fretwork cage hoisted level with the boards and, rocking, stopped.

Within it, like cloth dolls in a candle-theatre, were a dozen men.

The gate lifted.

Mirrin stuffed her knuckles into her mouth and bit on them, bit until the skin bruised.

She could hear something, something that made her heart race and her breath catch in her throat. She could hear it, not clearly yet, but audibly enough.

First out was a wounded collier, hobbling between two rescuers. Doctors were on hand, two surgeons from Glasgow, still in frock-coats and tile hats.

Next was a blanket-stretcher with a young man in it. Wrapped tightly, blood stained the fabric scarlet.

Still she could hear it.

Then she saw.

She closed her eyes, and uttered a wail.

No stretcher this, but a shoring plank held up by two of the relief squad. As they edged it gingerly out of the cage, she heard the words come clear, the snarling, vigorous phrases which had so often filled the Stalker house.

'Told the bloody-minded bastards ... told them months ago ... Oh, Christ *Jesus*! One man's greed ... I ... Ah, *God*! ... Listen, *listen* .. Lamont, y'murderin' *swine*.'

Mirrin pushed the trestle barrier with all her might and clambered over it as it fell. She ran towards him, calling out, 'Daddy: Daddy. I'm here.'

Alex Stalker was propped up on the plank, chest and head bolstered on the thighs of the bearer. There was nothing much of him to see. He was coal-black, all black, a charred effigy. Mirrin would not have taken him for mortal if it had not been for the open pink mouth and the glorious volume of his shouting.

Bowler hats stood back from him. He reclined on his plank seat, watery eyes scanning the rows of faces in search of the one face he wanted to see – not his wife, nor his daughter, but Houston Lamont in person.

Mirrin restrained herself, did not throw herself upon him, as was her impulse.

Garments and flesh were knitted together by the suppurations of his burns. His face was blistered and blasted with dust. Silvery scales of scalded flesh made his fist seem like a mailed gauntlet as he raised it up and bellowed his curses on the coalmaster and the hell's brigade of petty officials whose negligence had destroyed so many comrades in the layers below ground.

Mirrin knelt beside the plank.

'Da!' she said. 'Daddy?'

Eyebrows, lashes, most of his hair had gone. His lips drew back in a grimace that parodied a smile. He peered down at her.

'It's me; Mirrin.'

'Hullo, chick,' he said, gruffly. 'Where's ... your ... Mam?'

'At Lily's. She'll be here any minute.'

He struggled to sit up.

'Listen, chick, listen . . .'

Mirrin sobbed. 'Don't talk, Da. Please.'

'Ach, let'm talk,' said a voice above her.

She glanced up and saw that one of the bearers was Rob Ewing, hardly recognizable under layers of grime. His feathery moustache, fair no longer, stuck out like a piece of flint.

'He should be bloody dead, Mirrin,' Rob told her. 'He's livin' on hate, that's all.'

'Lamont . . .' her father growled.

'Move aside.'

Mirrin was lifted by the elbows and hauled a few feet clear of the plank. The doctor was not one of the gentlemanly surgeons, but a bones from the poors' hospital in Waygate. He had a whey-face, a bush of cropped grey hair, and wore a rubber apron.

Two officials, not locals, stood behind him.

The doctor bent over Alex Stalker. Mirrin winced as her father cried out.

'Take him up to the shop,' the doctor told Rob. 'I'll do what I can for him there.'

Rob Ewing and his mate steered the plank away, running a course along the front of the crowd. Mirrin walked by her father's side. He had flopped down gasping, but he could not still the protests that were in him.

Struggling fiercely, he got himself up again, fist clenched, the forefinger, like a stump of charcoal, pointed accusingly at the crowd.

'You . . . all . . . know him.'

'Da, please, no.'

'You *find* . . . him. Make'm pay.'

'Rest yourself, Mr Stalker.'

His voice was louder. 'Houston Lamont must . . . face the *law*. The law's on . . . *our* side.'

They were moving up in a cautious procession towards the open lanes which led directly to the joiners' shed.

The crowd shuffled restlessly.

They had no eyes for the other rescued men, only for Alex Stalker. His ruined body seemed to epitomize all that the miners had suffered. His words were like the accusations of a martyr newly taken from a cross. But his strength had almost gone. His efforts had split the crisp, rucked skin on his chest. His eyes closed, his head fell back, and the words bubbled weakly from his lips.

Mirrin gripped the plank, and lifted herself on tip-toe so that all could recognize her.

'Hear him?' she cried. 'Hear what my father says? It's Houston Lamont's fault. We'll find him, by God, an' we'll make him pay.'

It was as though the utterance of Lamont's name had at last freed their tongues. For the first time there was anger. Indignation drowned out the sounds of grief. Shouts of approval, good wishes, whole-hearted assurances, rolled out of the crowd and confronted Mirrin and – if he heard them – eased the awfulness of her father's agony.

'In the name of God, girl, have you taken leave of your senses?' The doctor caught hold of her elbow. 'This fellow's in a serious crisis, might even be dying. Don't you understand?'

'Aye, I understand,' said Mirrin. 'I understand that it would better suit the bosses' purpose if he had come *dead* out of that cage.'

'It'll be Glasgow for him,' the doctor said. 'We haven't the facilities here. I'll arrange to have him sent to a Glasgow hospital immediately. There's a train standing by . . .'

They were close to the door of the joiners' shop. She could smell the hideous stink of it, a fusion of balms and ointments and disinfectants and the reek of burned flesh.

Mirrin stepped in front of the stretcher.

'No,' she said.

'Look, girl, he's . . .'

'Then he'll not die here,' said Mirrin. 'Rob, see if you can find a hand cart.'

'Miss,' said the doctor grimly, 'if you don't leave this man in my care . . .'

'I'll risk it,' said Mirrin. 'My father's a Blacklaw collier. He's ducked it once, down on the level with his sons. If he's chalked up t'die now, then it'll not be in Lamont's shed, or some smelly Glasgow hospital. If anywhere, he'll die at home.'

The doctor pounded his fist against his thigh.

'I never met folk like you damned miners!' he exclaimed. 'In all my born days I never met such a pig-headed bunch. Very well! If that's the way of it. Keep him warm and give him quantities of fluid, but no alcohol and no food. I'll come in when I can, when this is ...'

He wagged his hand expressively at the scenes around him.

'The last house in the main street,' Mirrin said. 'That's where he'll be.'

Rob came hurrying out of the gloom behind the shed. He trundled a slaters' long hand-cart behind him.

'Mirrin,' he said. 'Are you sure?'

'I'm sure,' she said; though in truth she was not.

Later she could not be certain that her impetuous gesture had not deprived her father of many, many days of life.

*

Not much of a man was Alex Stalker, what was left of him, transferred like a puckle of old furniture from the slaters' cart and carried ben the house to the back room bed: not much of anything, now that his speeches were all discharged and his mouth pinched shut. But he was theirs still, and worth more to them than a hutchful of sovereigns. The care and nursing required to hold him on the right side of living would take the women's minds off the loss of Dougie and James.

It was bad with James's wife, so Rob had heard. She had been smitten with a madness of grief, so fitful and violent that it was feared it would damage the bairn in her womb, if not do for the innocent mite altogether, and herself with it.

The Ewings had been lucky: they had lost none of their family. But then there was no great clan of them, as there was with so many of the miners in Blacklaw. The Ewing household numbered three – Rob himself, his Da and his Ma. He had an elder brother, nine years his senior, but Dave had packed up and cleared out years ago, was working on the railway now, down in Sunderland. They seldom heard from him. Old man

Ewing and Dave had never hit it off, and there had been bad blood before the parting.

In a sense, the Stalker household was a constant warning to Rob as to the fate to which he might fall – unless he was crafty and evaded matrimony, or got himself promoted to an overs-man or a position with a jingle of silver more than a humble digger brought home in his pouch. He did not feel comfortable there in the kitchen, cramped in with all the Stalker women, haunted, like them, by memories of sons who would never again stoop under the lintel or pack themselves into the corner at the table.

Besides, Rob was foul with mud and could not prevent pit-dirt brushing off on the spotless floor. None of them would be caring much about that sort of wifely nonsense – but it bothered him nonetheless.

He said, 'I'll be away back then.'

Kate said, 'When did you last eat, Rob?'

'Ach, I'd a bit of sausage a while ago.'

'There's soup here,' Kate said.

'I'm not wantin' t'intrude.'

'Sit yourself down.'

She was calm enough. Kate was always the strong one, stronger even than the boys.

Rob had known James all his life. They had been lads in school together, full of pranks, and had gone up, eight years syne, on that first clear warm summer's day to sue Andrew McIntosh – who was the manager then – for employment. They had signed one name over the other on the register tally and had drawn their first week's pay together. Then they had gone with the money and chinned an elderly miner into carrying out a quart-pail of ale from the *Lantern*, had half-hidden themselves in the evening sunlight behind the dyke and had drunk it, passing the can back and forth until the amber brew was all gone, and a buzzing, pleasant, free feeling had overcome them both. They had laughed and capered uproariously, and both got their lugs clipped from their mothers for staggering home with their wages broken into, and clouted again from their fathers while being read a lesson on the evils of strong drink. They had been as close as kin for many years, James Stalker and he – until the lassies came between them. James had been smitten into an ardent wooing of Lily Dawson and, in spite of better judgement, Rob had been drawn into a relationship with Mirrin Stalker which was more like pugilism than courting.

Though Rob would never admit it, he was half afraid of Mirrin, afraid of the hunger he had for her which he could not declare lest she laughed in his face. Oh, he could handle girls who were prim and moral, he could deal with them fine. But Mirrin Stalker was as unlike them as keg-rum from sugary beer. She suffered no coyness about her own attractions.

Kate put the plate before him on the table. He wiped his hands on his trousers, and lifted a spoon. He did not feel right, eating there, seated in Dougie's chair and maybe even using the lad's big spoon. But that was the underside of every tragedy, one of the wee fragments of sorrow which, lumped together, made the huge leaden lump of grief.

'Who's stayin' with Lily?' he asked.

'A Salvation Army lass,' Kate answered.

She was filling a kettle from the water tub, setting it on the hob. He reminded himself to fetch coal from the backheap and to stoke up the fire and draw more water for her before he left. The soup was thick mutton broth, almost the texture of porridge. He sapped up some on the heel of bread the girl had put out for him. Now that he had begun to eat, he found that he was ravenously hungry.

'Will she . . . will she be all right?'

'I hope so,' said Kate. 'She's not strong.'

'No.'

Kate's eyes were red. The tip of her nose was red too, which did not make her any prettier. She had the same dark hair as Mirrin, as all the Stalkers, but she was more angular and had more bones in her face. Eldest of the family, she would be a couple of years older than him. In a year or two, past the watershed of twenty-five, she would be lucky if she could claim a man of her own. Too many bonnie lassies lived in the

54

area and a man, unless he was a widower or a kirk minister, preferred a girl who was young and strong. In the pub, sometimes, to hear the lads talk of women was like listening to farmers at a cattle market.

In Kate was a quiet and comforting thing, a quality which Rob could not quite define, a streak in which Mirrin was sadly lacking. Had Kate Stalker, he wondered, already reconciled herself to spinsterhood, a condition not altogether uncommon to the eldest daughters of miners' families? It would be a pitiful waste if she had, Rob thought. Perhaps the tragic loss of her brothers would change things for her. In the confusion of that night he could not decide whether it would make things easier or more difficult. A family could be a comfort, but also a trap — especially for women.

He said, 'It'll not be easy for you all.'

'It never was,' Kate said.

They were alone in the kitchen.

Upstairs in the tiny attic room which some of the houses had, Betsy and Drew had been put to bed in separate cots with a blanket rigged up between them. That room usually belonged to Drew and Dougie. Kate, Mirrin and Betsy shared the bigger back bedroom, and old man Stalker and his wife cosied down in the hole-in-the-wall bed in the kitchen itself. Now, though, Alex would need a room and a bed to himself, maybe for as long as he lived. Even without Dougie, the family would have to shift for a while. Rob reckoned that Mirrin would fare worst, having to sleep on a palliasse on the floor.

He had a big soft double bed in his room at the pit-end of Main Street. The thought tickled him like blasphemy and made him guilty. He swabbed up the last of the soup, and would have risen and taken his leave if Kate had not set the tea mug by him.

From the back room there was no sound. Mirrin and Mam Stalker had done what they could for Alex, would be sitting with him now, soothing him. It was good that he was still, making no audible groans — or was it?

Kate poured tea for herself. She replaced the pot on the

range and seated herself on a chair at the table. In the silence the old ratchet-clock on the wall ticked, tin hands showing the hour as near nine.

Rob sipped tea. His moustache was wet about the fringes and seeped the filthy taste of sweat and coal-grit into his mouth. He wiped it with his fingertips.

'Rob,' said Kate. 'Do you think he'll die?'

'Not him,' Rob replied. 'D'you know how we found him? I'll tell you. He was off the gallery, in a tight place. The damned props had near burnt through. There was tons of chip rubble down afore him, steaming an' like to ignite, a leg an' a foot stickin' out of it.'

He hesitated, debating with himself if the girl was ready for such details.

'Go on,' Kate said.

'Hot as hell, an' reekin' with choke-damp,' Rob continued. 'Your old man was lyin' on his back, his neb an inch from the roof, a big crack right above him. You could hardly tell him from the rubble. I was first in. I'd never have spotted him, even with the safety lamp, but, my God, I could hear'm.'

Kate grinned crookedly.

'Givin' Lamont big licks, he was,' Rob said. 'Down there under a million tons of rock an' coal, cursin' Lamont blind. It wasn't me got your father out of that pit alive, it was that bugger Houston Lamont.'

'He's only a man,' said Kate.

'Who?'

'Lamont.'

'Aye,' said Rob. 'He'll be havin' nightmares this night.'

'He can't be without feelin'.'

'I didn't mean that,' said Rob. 'I mean, lest there's an inquiry, an' he's found guilty of criminal negligence.'

'It won't happen.'

'It might,' said Rob. 'If your father an' his cronies have anythin' t'do with it, certain facts will not be allowed to pass unnoticed.'

'Lamont has the power.'

'Hm?'

'He can put us out.'

'If that's what's worryin' you, Kate, you can rest assured that Lamont'll not dare pitch your family out of the house, not for a year or more, an' not while your father's alive.'

'It's the rule,' said Kate. 'We'll not have a man workin' in the pit – not 'til Drew reaches age.'

'Even so,' said Rob, 'Lamont's no fool. He'll not risk puttin' himself in bad odour with the community or out of sympathy with the public in general by slingin' an injured collier into the gutter.'

'But after the inquiry?'

'If there is an inquiry.'

'Mirrin said . . .'

'Mirrin's an idealist,' said Rob, whispering. 'But I agree with her for once. I don't really see how Lamont can prevent it. For a while you'll at least have a roof over your heads.'

'But no money comin' in.'

Rob nodded.

He could not offer to help. There was little to spare in the Ewing coffers. Though he would willingly have donated some small pittance to the Stalkers each week, natural pride would not allow them to accept. He respected that pride and would not insult Kate by offering financial help.

Kate finished her tea, and got to her feet.

Her weariness was palpable, of a different order from that of the menfolk of the village. There would be many like her in Blacklaw, girls and women forced by their innate strength to carry heavy burdens of responsibility and suppress their own sorrow for the sake of others in need.

'I'll need to away in,' Kate said.

'I'll be goin' then,' Rob said. 'If there's anythin' . . .'

'No, Rob,' Kate said. 'You've been . . .'

Mirrin came quietly out of the bedroom door. She had been weeping. Her cheeks were flushed and her eyes glittered. Tears seemed to add to her beauty, a trick of temperament which cheated her of sympathy.

'Mam needs you now,' said Mirrin. 'I . . . I can't do it. It's the breeks . . . they're . . . stickin'.'

'He's fair quiet?' said Rob.

'So would you be if you'd a rag-roll stuck in your mouth.'

Kate held a finger to her lips to hush her sister, then with a quick nod of goodnight to Rob Ewing slipped into the back room.

'I'll see you out,' Mirrin said.

They stood for a moment by the outer door. The glow of the pit-head showed yellow against the underside of the cloud. It was raining heavily again, but the wind had backed and the drops fell straight, rods of silver and gold against the lit windows of the row opposite. All the houses were lighted, no niggardly saving of dips and candles and oil-lamps on this night. Some doors were open, as at Hogmanay, as if to let spirits of ministration flit freely through the village.

Main Street only gave the impression of life. The *Lantern* was lighted up but there were no men clustered outside it. A priest walked rapidly up the cobbles, knocked on a closed house door and, without waiting, entered. Two Salvation Army women and a wee old man hurried across the street.

A baby was yelling far up, near Rob's own house; the Mc-Garrety bairn, maybe. Like an echo of that hungry sound, there was an impression of other cries and wailings in the wet night air.

Rob felt like weeping himself.

For once when he touched her Mirrin did not flirt away, nor did he experience any measure of desire for her. He put his arms about her waist and kissed her on the brow. She was wet through, soaked, shivering.

'You'll catch your death, Mirrin.'

'God! As if that mattered.'

'Mirrin!'

'I'm goin' to get that man,' she said softly.

'Now, Mirrin . . .'

'Go on,' she said, still softly. 'Away back t'the pit. You'll be needed again, Rob Ewing.'

He tried to kiss her once more, to console himself as much as the girl. But she held her arm across her face and gave him a demure little push with her fingertips.

Rob turned away and set off up the street. He had gone twenty yards when instinct made him pause and glance back over his shoulder.

She was still standing out from the shelter of the eaves, rain drumming down on her. She did not wave, but, with one quick, graceful movement, passed the palms of her hands back over her hair, squeezing the water out of it, then, with odd deliberation, rid her hands of the moisture by stroking them down the front of her thighs from hip to knee. She pointed, not at Rob, not for Rob, but up at the highest arc of the pit-wheel cowling which showed in silhouette against the smoke-yellow cloud.

'Houston Lamont,' she shouted. 'That's who I mean. Bloody Houston Lamont.'

Then she went inside and slammed the door.

*

'How does it appear, Mr Wyld?'

The colliery manager pushed the papers across the deal table away from him. He peeped into the enamel mug beside him and, finding it empty, yawned. It did not seem fitting to yawn, but he could not prevent it.

'My figures make no mention of the eighty-three men who returned from Number One pit, you understand? They weren't actually involved in the explosion.'

All three of the other men at the table in the temporary office grunted assent.

'Of the one hundred and twenty-seven men below ground in pit Number Two,' Wyld went on, 'one hundred and eighteen have been brought to the surface.'

'Nine . . . ah, unaccounted?'

'I think,' said Wyld, 'that we may take them for dead.'

Nobody even bothered to agree.

'Of that one hundred and eighteen, ninety-four were dead on recovery by the squads. Of the twenty-four still alive, less than half can reasonably be expected to survive their injuries.'

'In other words,' said one of the sleek, bewhiskered gentlemen, 'virtually the whole shift was wiped out?'

'Aye,' said Wyld. 'Yes, sir, a whole shift gone.'

For over a minute there was a complete silence in the room. It was broken at length by the thump of a fist on the table. The man had a rubicund complexion which made his anger seem more intense.

'Bad : bad : *bad*!' he declared.

The colliery manager gathered his papers together and got to his feet. He studied the others, his gaze shifting from face to face.

'May I take it, gentlemen, that there will be an inquiry?'

He had his answer at once.

'Without question, Mr Wyld, there *will* be an inquiry.'

Donald Wyld bowed and walked stiffly out into the grey and granular dawn.

4

Edith Lamont did not raise her eyes from the letter in her hand. Her pale, perfectly oval face showed no dismay at the ominous crack which the Sheraton chair made when her husband slumped into it. Common sense informed her that reprimands were not in order. Patiently, thoroughly, she completed the reading of her formal correspondence, sipping up the stilted phrases as if imbibing thimblefuls of lemon juice. When she finally chose to glance at Houston, she did it with calmness and resignation.

He had been less careful than usual in shaving. Traces of dark stubble showed under his chin and at the corners of his whiskers. His eyes were dull, red-rimmed, and his whole face seemed puffy. She wondered if this was some sign of ageing which she had failed to remark before. She did not often study him with such attention.

Placing the letter by the side of her plate, she reached out for the silver bell which stood poised between butter dish and honey jar.

'Anne will make you fresh tea.'

Houston Lamont tugged at the corners of his eyes with his thumbs in an effort to dispel some of his weariness.

'She's doing it now,' he said. 'I looked into the kitchen on the way down.'

'You didn't come to bed at all last night?'

'No.'

Edith allowed her fingers to rest lightly on the edge of the table and bent slightly forward in an attitude of restrained concern.

'What is the position at the pit, my dear?'

'Grave.'

'How many ... passed on?'

'Ninety-four.'

It was Lamont's turn to study his wife and the effect of his news on her.

'Edith,' he said, more distinctly. 'Ninety-four men died yesterday.'

'We have been too long associated with the colliery,' she said, 'to be unaware of its dangers. Have you determined the cause?'

'Fire-damp.'

Edith's eyes narrowed a little.

She said, 'The explosion which injured several youths last month, was that not also attributed to fire-damp?'

'Edith, I've no stomach for debate this morning,' Lamont said. 'Most pits are rife with damp – as you well know.'

'I am concerned with the implications, Houston,' she said. 'If that earlier mishap showed the presence of the damp, and, further, that insufficient measures for safety...'

'Rank carelessness caused the tragedy,' Houston interrupted. 'One, or more, of the day shift neglected to observe the rules laid down for their protection.'

'Have you proof of that, dear?'

Lamont shoved back his chair, thrusting up runnels in the soft-pile carpet.

'Damn it all, I can't be expected to hound them, molly-coddle them every minute of every shift. I can't...'

'Hush!'

Edith raised her hand.

A girl of thirteen cautiously elbowed round the dining room door, trying not to tilt the tray. On the tray was a cup, saucer and plate to match the fine, forget-me-not sprigged china already on the table.

The little servant crept across the room, eyes on the carpet, thin back as straight as she could manage despite her nervousness. Annie – Anne as his wife insisted on calling her – appeared closer than ever to the verge of collapse.

As a rule the child's awkwardness irked Lamont, but the cause was not hard to find that morning.

'Anne?' he said. 'Annie, did you lose someone?'

'Aye, sir.'

'Your father?'

'M'brother.'

Gently Lamont removed the tray from her hands and slid it on to the table.

The girl's features were streaked with tears. She could not rid herself of the embarrassment of betraying emotion in the august presence of her employers.

'Well, Annie!' said Lamont. 'You'll have to try to be brave.'

'Weeping will not help, child,' Edith Lamont said.

Annie said, 'I'm all that's left.'

'Your father?' Lamont asked.

'Been gone this long while, sir.'

'Ah, I see.'

'Weeping will not help,' Edith repeated, adding, 'but work will. The wages you earn here will be more important than ever to your mother now that your brother is no longer a breadwinner.'

Stick-like wrists and bony fingers, a pinched and narrow face; Lamont might have offered the girl comfort if Edith's rule of the domestics had been more flexible.

'Bear that in mind, Anne,' Edith said. 'It will give you strength and add to your fortitude. Off you go now. Wash your face. You may boil yourself one of the brown eggs, and warm a cup of milk; then busy yourself with the door-brasses.'

The girl dropped a curtsey.

'Oh, Anne?'

'Aye, ma'am?'

'Do be sure to offer my sincere condolences to your bereaved mother.'

Lamont doubted if the girl would know the meaning of the word 'condolences'.

'Aye, ma'am.'

Wiping her tears with her apron, the servant left the room.

Lamont seated himself at the table, and buttered toast. He had no appetite for a cooked breakfast today.

'Milk and brown eggs won't mend a broken heart,' he remarked.

'Food will coax her thoughts from morbid matters,' Edith

said. 'Besides, she will be better for the nourishment.'

Lamont did not speak again, merely nodding when she asked him if he wished tea poured.

In times of stress it was possible to see people with clarity. Edith had not always been so cold, so distant, as she was now. There were many questions he wished to ask her but the opportunity for intimate dialogue never seemed to arise.

It had been different before their young son had died during the measles epidemic which had swept Glasgow seven or eight years before. There had been few outbreaks in the county and Lamont could only suppose that he had carried the infection back with him from the city, though there was no proof to give fuel to the smoulder of guilt in him.

Edith had been so warm and yielding in the early days of their marriage. But even before little Gordon had fallen ill and died six years ago, she had begun to grow away from her husband. In some slight ways he had resented the child, or, if not the child, at least the attention Edith lavished on her son. She had been happy then, selfishly happy. He could never be sure that she had not regarded marriage merely as a necessary step towards motherhood; could never be sure of the veracity of his memories.

Afterwards? How could he really blame her? She had not been seasoned in suffering and loss as he had been.

Suddenly, the sight of her there at table, prim and neat and contained, fell into contrast with the vivid scenes of last night. Hurriedly he put down the cup and got to his feet once more.

'You've eaten nothing, Houston.'

'I've a meeting in a quarter of an hour.'

The woman rose too.

'Wait, Houston.'

'What is it?'

'We can, I imagine, assume that last night's events will lead to an investigation and an inquiry?'

'Probably,' Lamont conceded.

'Feelings will run high in Blacklaw.'

'They're bereft, if that's what you . . .'

'Resentment,' said Edith. 'Hatred.'

'I've nothing to be . . .'

'Would you consider leaving Blacklaw for a few days' . . . rest?'

'Leave?' He blinked. 'Leave, now?'

The woman lifted the letter from beside her plate. 'Joanna Cunningham has cordially invited us to visit with her in Cramond. Roger is home from India. You've always considered the Cunninghams an agreeable couple and Cramond is delightful in spring.'

Lamont snorted ruefully, almost amused.

'You are unique, Edith,' he said. 'Quite unique.'

'Am I to take it that you don't wish to go?'

'Of course, I *wish* to go,' said Lamont. 'But I won't. I can't. I *daren't*.'

'I don't understand why . . .'

Curtly, he touched her forehead with his lips, and headed towards the door.

'Then I'll endeavour to explain at dinner – *if* I manage home for dinner, that is.'

'Houston . . .?'

The door closed.

When her husband had gone, Edith Lamont replaced the letter in its envelope and put it into the pocket of her dress. From the adjacent pocket she removed the second letter which had been delivered by the morning post. It was not addressed to the household but exclusively to her husband. The slanting script was unsteady, the capital letters overly decorative, like floral sketches.

Immediately she recognized the hand as that of her husband's sister.

As proof, the embossing on the back flap of the envelope stated:

Miss Dorothy Allerton Lamont,
Woodbank House,
Marleford,
Kent.

Crossing to the hearth, Edith dropped the letter on to the

burning coals. She watched it ignite and lethargically char, then with a brass poker she broke down the sheets of ash into fragments.

That done to her satisfaction, she rang a silver bell to summon Anne to clear away the breakfast things.

*

The climate relented. A pale sun shone down on Blacklaw and its near fields, on slag and coal rees and grey stone kirk. Rain, though, might have been better, holding the village to itself, drowning the land's desolate emptiness and rinsing away the coal dust which clung like shroud-ribbons to gutters and eaves.

There was still concentrated activity at the pit. Efforts were being made to reach the nine miners in the spur-tunnel. They were reckoned to be dead. Nobody nurtured the faintest hope that even one of them might have survived the blast, choke gas and slumping rock falls which still made that level dangerous.

Protestant and Catholic services were held in the church and the nearby chapel. Friends of many years had the demeanour of strangers in their stiff, unfamiliar black clothes. A train waited in the siding for families who possessed lairs in Hamilton or Glasgow. The majority of the processions wended up to the local kirk-yard. For those who had not been able to afford a lair, a long trench – dug at the parish's expense – waited now to receive fifty plain-wood coffins.

It seemed as if every man and woman in the county had turned up. Many carried parcels of foodstuffs and clothing which, with downcast eyes, they pressed into the hands of the widows and orphans. Others dropped coins into a barrel which had been set up at the colliery gate to contribute to the distress fund.

Newspapermen were out in force. Even urbane reporters sent from London and the hard mining towns of the North of England had grim faces as they went about their work. The radical presses' representatives were somewhat less solemn. Quietly but persistently, they badgered mining and civic officials in the hope of winning an inflammatory quotation about the source of the explosion. Hounded by an impudent youth from a Glasgow rag, Houston Lamont demonstrated his opinion of the whole publicity pack by using his walking stick to shift the offensive young cub from his path.

Northrigg Colliery Band was stationed on the cobbles opposite the church. As the first of the coffins was carried across the cobbles from the church gate, it rendered *Abide with Me* very softly and sweetly. The musicians played verse after verse as groups of mourners and shouldered coffins came, endlessly it seemed, from kirk and chapel. The whole of the back-yard acre was packed with black-clad families.

The Stalkers, however, had places in a quiet corner which fronted the street. Kate was glad of that, glad that the boys would be buried side by side. Their one small raw stone tablet stood out among the weathered monuments.

At the graveside were her mother, Mirrin, Betsy and herself. Rob Ewing and his father assisted in the lowering of the coffins. For some reason, Drew stood with them. He looked tall now, as tall as Douglas had been – but not like a collier.

Sun glinted on slates and on the brass instruments of the band who, with caps off and heads bowed, listened to the murmurs of the interment services.

The Stalkers had no minister to read for their boys or offer a prayer. Rob Ewing did the one and his father did the other. It was soon over and Kate led her mother away, first out of the gate into the deserted main street.

There were no dogs, no cats, not even daft Lachie Abercorn, only a few nesting sparrows and the sun pale on the cobbles and dusty house walls. The proprietor of the *Lantern* had covered his sign with black crepe cloth and had lit a wax candle in every window for the souls of the clients he had lost.

The band played again, distantly now. Pit cables and wheels and all the grimy metal guardians of the colliery were silent and still – not, Mirrin thought from shame or respect, but cunningly, waiting in stealth for their time to come again as it would with tomorrow's hooter.

Drew and Betsy walked at the rear of the Stalkers' file.

Betsy had cried herself out. Drew had not cried at all, not even into his pillow in the comforting privacy of the night.

He walked with his head up, lips pursed shut, an ember of almost disdainful annoyance in his eyes, the Mirrin-thing which he shared only with his bold older sister.

Betsy clutched his arm.

'Promise me, Drew,' she said. 'That you'll not let them make you a collier.'

'I don't have to promise.'

'They'll put you to it,' she said. 'We'll be needing the money.'

'No,' he said harshly. 'I'm better than that.'

'Drew!'

'You know it, Betsy; don't you?'

'Aye.'

'I'm better than that,' he said, nodding. 'And before long I'll prove it.'

'You don't have to prove it to me,' she said.

Drew did not answer. Absently, he patted her hand and, lifting his head, continued to stare past the end of the main street at the handsome stand of oaks showing green round Lamont's mansion.

*

Two days after the funerals, the last of the bodies were recovered from the pit and the feeling of the folk of Blacklaw changed. Grief was reserved for curtained rooms, a matter, like conspiracy, for locked doors. Between shifts, groups of miners gathered at street corners and in the yard of the *Lantern*, growling rebellion against coalmasters and examining, in the light of their own knowledge, the conditions which led to the explosion.

A notice finally posted on the colliery gate did nothing to lessen the tension.

The Secretary of State has directed that a Public Inquiry
into the causes of the Blacklaw Colliery explosion shall be held
by Mister Ian Hutchison and an appointed legal assessor.
Please make known.
(Signed) Ian K. Hutchison,
Chief Inspector of Mines

The Ewings brought word of this development to the Stalker household.

Even in so short a time, the changes which the tragedy had wrought seemed deep-rooted. Flora had little to say to anyone now. Most of her day was spent seated on a wooden chair by the kitchen window staring listlessly at the houses opposite. Knitting pins, a hank of coarse blue wool and a few rows of some anonymous garment lay virtually untouched in her lap. Very occasionally she would glance up at the figure propped in the alcove bed and give a faint, vague smile as if to acknowledge the presence of some casual acquaintance. Cooking, nursing, all domestic routines she left now to Kate or Mirrin.

'Go on, Mother, have a wee blether with Daddy,' Kate would whisper, and the woman would smile faintly and give a dutiful nod in the direction of the bed.

Mirrin would say, anxiously, 'What's wrong with you, Mam? God; my Father shows more life than you do.'

That statement held more than a grain of truth. Alex Stalker refused to languish in the privacy of the back-bedroom. He had had himself transferred to the set-in bed in the kitchen from which he could observe the routines of daily life and, if he felt strong enough, could find an audience for his conversation.

According to the local doctor, Flora Stalker was suffering from shock. He gave other fancy names to it too, but the labelling of the condition did not make it easier for the daughters to bear. Their only comfort came from the doctor's assurance that, gradually, the woman would emerge from her trance-like state and resume an interest in living.

Though Alex was ill and suffered great bouts of pain, he was the healing force in the household. He had screwed himself up to active involvement in the wave of rebellion which was spreading throughout the mining communities. Any miner was welcome at any hour of the day or night, and the kettle was seldom off the hob.

Favourite moments came with the visits of Rob and Callum Ewing, old friends, fingers of the fist which would crush the tyranny of the employers and wring justice from the whole corrupt system, justice and fair play for the common working man.

It was a Saturday morning, almost four weeks after the disaster, when Rob and Callum arrived with the good news that a public inquiry had at last been announced.

During the early days of his illness, visitors had crouched close to Alex's bed, murmuring condolences and answering his questions indulgently. Lately, however, the visitations had become so frequent and Alex's health seemingly so improved that the whole kitchen was put to use as a committee room. Arguments and imprecations were hurled about, regardless of the daughters or the mute old woman by the window.

Rob was by the range in the lugged armchair, Callum by the table, drinking tea. Shoulders supported by pillows, Alex leaned on his elbow half out of the alcove. Mirrin, too, was present. Now that April was come and the working days were longer, her shift at the coal troughs did not begin until noon.

Alex's words were thick and slurred, for his lips were still blistered and warped by burns.

He said, 'An inquiry was inevitable.'

'It'll place the blame square on Lamont,' Rob Ewing predicted.

'Aye, but will it?' Alex said. 'An inquiry could hardly be prevented, but there's nothin' cut an' dried about its findings.'

Callum Ewing was of Stalker's vintage; a grizzled, lumpy-featured man, leathery and scarred as a smith's apron, though hardly bigger than a dwarf.

'Aye, man,' he said, 'there's been a wheen of inquiries afore now, an' I don't recollect them improvin' the colliers' lot much.'

'I'm more confident this time,' said Alex. 'We're not as we were, Callum. The miner's learnin' he has a voice, an' he's learnin' how t'use it.'

'Aye, but who's t'listen?' said Callum.

'They'll listen,' said Alex. 'Tell me about the last evenin', about the meetin'.'

Rob extracted a batch of leaflets from his pocket and took

them to the bed. Alex glanced over the blotchy blocks of print and rebellious headings, nodding approval. The hand of the honest militant was evident in their composition, but he wished some bugger would teach the pamphleteer to spell properly.

'Education's the thing,' he said.

Callum agreed; Rob was less sure; and Mirrin, peeling potatoes into a tin by the sink, snorted her opinion without bothering to define it or back it with reasons.

'Education costs money,' said Kate.

She too was working close to the sink on the scrubbed board by the pot rack. The knife had been honed away almost to the proportions of a darning-needle and it made a brisk *snecking* sound on the board as she trimmed leeks with it and shredded down the shrivelled piece of mutton which was all that the family budget would allow by way of meat.

'It's a privilege,' Mirrin said.

Rob swung in his chair to look at her, as if her statement was a pearl of sagacity and observation.

Alex said, 'Define privilege, lass.'

Mirrin said, 'You know fine well what privilege is – somethin' that's the right of everybody an' isn't. Somethin' that's gathered an' held by a stupid entitlement an' protected by laws an' rules.'

Rob said, 'Class.'

'Aye, class,' said Mirrin. 'An accident of history that's become a law as immutable as ... as gravity.'

Alex said, 'Laws're never immutable, chick. Never.'

'Then how can we change them?'

'By process of law.'

'Rubbish!'

The girl flung the potato into the basin so hard that it skated out again and rolled across the floor. She chased it and gathered it and wiped it on her skirt.

'So, lass, you think we're stuck?' Callum Ewing asked, mildly.

'Force built the walls round the rich,' Mirrin said. 'An' force'll knock them down.'

'The minister would not be agreein' with you,' said Kate.

'The kirk!' said Mirrin. She sliced the potato expertly, viciously. 'The kirk are the worst of the lot, Ministers and priests've always been hand-in-glove with the ruling establishment. No, none of that pratin' about how good it'll be in the next world if you do what you're told in this.'

'Then what *do* you advocate, lass?' asked Callum Ewing.

'Revolution!' Rob stroked his feathery moustache smugly. 'She'd have us all armed wi' picks and shovels chargin' up the hill t'lay waste t'Lamont's gardens.'

'Shut up, you!'

'Free speech's the right of everybody,' said Rob, turning again. 'Even humble young colliers, like me.'

'Revolution doesn't necessarily lead to reform,' said Alex, soberly.

'Even so,' said Callum. 'Even so, the bosses're encounterin' a new breed of collier . . .'

'It'll take years, maybe centuries,' said Alex.

'That's defeatist talk,' Mirrin said.

'I'm no defeatist,' said Alex. 'But *I'll* not live t'see it.'

There was a sudden appalled silence in the room. Even the chitter of the knife on the board stopped as Kate glanced round at the bandaged figure in the bed.

Alex Stalker stared back at them, then laughed wheezily, painfully, at the effect his words had had on them.

'My, now, that's not what I was meanin',' he said. 'I'll not be a Methusalum, an' neither will none of you, I doubt. God, how many men in history have been privileged to be in at the endin' of anythin' they've started? We're the first batch of a new breed, an' we must work, aye, an' live, in the shadow of the knowledge that we'll not be here when all's right with the world, when the Golden Age of labour comes.'

The explanation was logical. Even so, his statement had stilled the flow of conversation. Not even Mirrin could bring herself to stir up another argument.

'Now, Callum,' Alex said. 'Will you be tellin' me about that meetin' an' leave the young folk t'their idealistic blethers.'

Callum Ewing took his chair close to the bed. Alex lay back, content for a while to be a listener, to rest and gather his strength. He would need it in the months to come when conflict between coalmaster and colliers found its true channel, and philosophy degenerated into feud.

5

March, which had come in like a lion, went out without learning humility. April's early sunshine lasted only a day or two then wavered into squally showers and finally, by the middle of the month, settled to rain. Great herds of cloud drove in from the west and browsed round the low hills of Lanarkshire. Blacklaw was less bleak than desolate.

With Number Two pit closed, work in Number One was shared among the surviving miners. Reduction in hours of work meant a reduction in money. Before long the proprietors of the two shops which served the village were regretfully obliged to conduct their business on a 'cash only' basis. In the *Lantern*, too, 'tick' was strictly limited to clerical and professional workers. Ministers of religion, Catholic and Protestant, united to relieve extreme cases of need by providing lines of credit acceptable in both shops; fixed sums to be repaid when Lamont's settlements were finally doled out. Lack of nourishment resulted in a general lowering of health, accentuated by miserable weather. Influenza and enteritis claimed the very young and very old; easy victims. More than one family walked the path from kirk to graveyard yet again in the six weeks following the disaster.

Lamont's name was seldom off folks' tongues, though the man himself was little enough to be seen abroad in the street or round the pit-head.

'O'er wet for his lordship t'day. He'll be feart t'get his feet wet.'

'He'll get his feet wet enough wi' meltit brimstone when he's dancin' in Hell, the bugger.'

Little else was talked about but Lamont and settlements, and, ironically, brands of insurrection which were quite at odds with charity and the nature of its deliverance.

Kate Stalker was caught in a whirlpool of tensions. Even her rota of nursing – both her father *and* Lily – and household chores did not muffle her awareness of the anomalies of the situation which the colliers were creating for themselves and of which, she felt sure, Houston Lamont was fully appraised.

So much *had* happened : so much *was* happening.

The houses were the same; smoke purling from chimneys, mother-of-thousands and star-of-Bethlehem in pots by the doors, curtains no longer closed in daylight hours, the smell of kail and pea-broth and baking bannocks in the air – all much as it had been; but not quite.

As she walked up Main Street to shop or to visit Lily, Kate tried to visualize the place as it had been before; the back-shift coming through the gates, James and Douglas and their young mates joking and laughing, and her father, pick on shoulder, amid a group of his cronies. And James would wink and make sarcastic comments about 'the old men up front there', and her father would *grumph* and retort, 'I could be takin' on any four o'you afore breakfast an' never break sweat.' Then there would be ribald banter all the way down the cobbles until, one by one, the miners entered their own doors and the street would settle to quiet again. But it was a contented, secure quiet, not forlorn like it was now.

When the present quiet was disturbed, it was by unwholesome ranting, the shouting and jeering of angry crowds. Impromptu meetings had become commonplace, and were no longer limited to weekends. They would accumulate from the idlers and restless militants, women from the troughs, men unlucky enough not to be on shift. Any corner was a suitable stance. Any rowdy orator was welcome to the step on the dross-box which gave him – or her – the right to vocalize popular sentiments of the day.

On several occasions, Kate had witnessed Mirrin on the box, gesturing and shouting like a man, egged on by Christy Moran who was as close to a professional rebel as Blacklaw was ever liable to draw. Moran frightened Kate. He had served a penal term for bashing an official at Wellbrig pit in Ayrshire before that county got too hot to hold him.

On Sunday the agitators were out in force, hardly waiting until kirk services and schools were over and dinners gulped down. Kate had left her father asleep and her mother drowsing in her chair by the window. Betsy was shaping sugar rolls with some dough left from the Saturday baking and Drew was up in his room labouring at his studies. Kate did not have to pass through the forty-strong crowd to reach Lily's door. But she could see Mirrin clearly in the forefront, her face lifted to follow every radical syllable of the speech.

'Our rights, that's all us colliers want,' Moran was bellowing, him that had never been below ground in the past ten years. 'An' we're willin' to fight for them, ain't we now? The sooner the bloody coalmasters take heed, the sooner they realize their day is near done, the sooner . . .'

Cheering drowned him out.

'We don't want their bloody charity. Let 'em keep their paltry handouts, their salves for a guilty conscience, their blood money . . .'

Kate's fingers closed on the two florins she had in her pocket. Rights and justices were fine, but bairns couldn't sup on words. While men, and some girls like Mirrin, squabbled about the division of responsibility, most wives and mothers were only too glad of the few shillings that would ladle a little extra food on the plates.

Kate's annoyance fixed on Mirrin. What was a girl of eighteen doing shouting on a street corner? She was almost the only girl in that horde of men, and her with her coat flying and her blouse near half unbuttoned. Kate experienced a matronly sense of outrage which her fondness for Mirrin could not quell.

She was full of indignation when she reached Lily's house. For once, she vented her temper in a tirade to her sister-in-law, as if poor Lily did not have enough to cope with as it was.

Lily, though, seemed quite amused by the outburst. Of all the Stalkers she seemed to have recovered most rapidly from the shock of James's death. Perhaps the new life growing in her womb helped, or perhaps she had just suffered too much privation and grief in her young days. With some help from neighbours and much from in-laws, Lily had pulled herself together and had moved on in anticipation of the day when her second child and James Stalker's last would decide to come into the world. She did not dwell on the future beyond that point, nor did she choose to live in the past.

She spooned the last of the bread and milk into Edward's mouth, and wiped the child's cheeks with a cloth.

'I thought you'd have realized by this time, Kate,' she said, 'that your Mirrin's cut from a different cloth from the rest of us. She'll gang her own route. James was forever sayin' that nothin' but an act of God could prevent Mirrin havin' her own way.'

Kate took the empty bowl and wooden spoon and rattled them to amuse Edward.

'My father could manage her,' she said. 'But he's ... he's not able now. It's not just Mirrin, it's Daddy and Mam, an' everything ...'

She broke off, cheeks flushed.

'Would you hark at me!' she said, guiltily. 'Here I come to cheer you an' Edward up, an' all I can do is complain.'

'It's a relief to complain, whiles,' said Lily.

Kate regarded her good-sister affectionately. 'Lily, how are you, really?'

'Fine.'

'You're a bit paler today.'

'I told you, Kate; it's the dress. Black always did make me look like a ghost.'

'Is it ... sore?' asked Kate, curiously.

'No, no; I'm just tired. It happens at this stage. I wish the wee beggar would hurry. Edward could hardly wait, but ... this one ...'

'How long are you overdue?'

'A week.'

'What does Doctor Mackay say?'

'Nothin' to fret about.'

'Are you eatin' properly?'

'Aye.'

'There'll be a handsome settlement for widows soon,' Kate said.

'I doubt it,' said Lily.

'Lamont'll have to pay up,' Kate said.

'James never had any faith in the boss's duty.'

'Rest assured,' said Kate, 'Houston Lamont's no fool. A mean task-master he may be – though there's those as say it's that wife of his who calls the tune – but he won't antagonize his own colliers too much.'

'We'll see,' said Lily.

She got up from the kneeling position by the fire, and handed Edward over to Kate. Kate watched the young woman hobble slowly across the kitchen to fill a cup with milk and water. She was younger than Kate herself, yet seemed much older and wiser in many respects. Kate felt awe for the enclave to which this slip of a girl had been admitted and to which she herself would perhaps always remain an outsider, the mysteries of being loved by a man and of motherhood, the act of giving birth. Would she ever have a child of her own, she wondered?

The wee boy in her lap was so like her brother, fair and stocky and alert, responsive to fun. She played pat a-cake with him, much to his delight, while his mother flavoured the milk with a drop of treacle.

'Mirrin needs a man,' Lily said.

'She's attractive enough looking,' said Kate. 'But she scares all the lads off with her headstrong ways and her outspokenness.'

'I thought Rob Ewing was interested?'

'Aye, he is that,' said Kate. 'But he's a decent, conventional type. Mirrin's too much for him.'

'She'll change,' said Lily.

'For better or for worse, though?'

'With a man to look after an' two or three bairns clamourin' for her attention,' said Lily, 'Mirrin'll have no time left t'cherish these daft ideas of hers.'

'I'm not so sure that they are daft,' Kate admitted.

'It's not the principle, James used t'say, but the method that has flaws. Anyway, Mirrin'd be better leavin' all that t'the menfolk.'

'Don't let her catch you sayin' so,' said Kate. 'It's my father's fault, really. He stuffed us all with too much respect for our rights.'

'I don't know what I'll do when the baby comes,' Lily said, matter-of-factly. 'I can't think about it yet. You'll not be in much better circumstances yourself financially.'

'Och, not so bad,' said Kate. 'Mirrin's still employed. In a couple of months Drew and Betsy'll be leavin' school. They'll not earn much but it'll help. I'll start up at the sortin' troughs with Mirrin as soon as the old man's on the mend. It'll be fine, I'm sure.'

Her optimism was forced. She did not really believe that all would be well. She questioned if her father would ever be strong enough to look after himself, and her mother would hardly be capable of it unless she snapped out of her melancholic depression. Still, she could not lay her fears before Lily, and went chattily on with feigned joviality.

'Aye,' said Lily, pretending too, 'if only this wee mite would get up the courage t'jump, I'd fine too.'

'Why don't you lie down an' rest for a while, Lily?' said Kate. 'I'll look after Edward.'

Lily agreed. She was on the point of settling herself on the alcove bed when a disturbance close outside the window brought her to her feet again.

'What's that?'

'The meetin' breakin' up.'

Kate carried Edward to the window to satisfy his curiosity and let him look out at the people. The child's eye could discern the comedy of it all but not the wrath and the despair. The crowd was dispersing reluctantly, gathered in groups of four or five, still arguing heatedly. She could not see Mirrin, or Moran, but the Ewings were there, Rob and Callum, coming round the gable from the direction of the pit gate. Come to think of it, she had not noticed them in the crowd.

Edward giggled and pointed with his soft round fist.

She saw what had caught his attention and made him laugh. A dozen children had brought Loonie Abercorn out of hiding and had taunted him into mimicking the orators. He was conducting a council of his own now, flinging his arms about and shouting unintelligible phrases, becoming more and more excited by the people around him.

With unwitting cruelty, the children leapt and cavorted round him, chanting, 'Hurrah! Hurrah! Loonie for provost. Loonie for provost. Come on, Loonie, give's a speech. Tell's the school's closed!'

Loonie had never received the benefits of education, much to the envy of the children. The man's boyish countenance was distorted now, ruddy and glowing with earnestness. The past week's events had obviously made an impact on him. Perhaps, Kate thought, he was seriously outlining his own programme of reform. Was he inviting them to share the answers to all their problems stored in his brain and just too tangled to be clear? Loonie Lachie was not the only one to think that words were enough to change the world, but he was the only one in Blacklaw whom everyone labelled daft.

At least Edward enjoyed the show.

Suddenly, out of the corner of her eye, Kate saw Rob and Callum again. They were with Mirrin now, and Mirrin was distraught with rage. Temper was no stranger to the girl, but this fury was beyond anything Kate had seen in her sister before. Her black hair was shaken out. Her hands were bunched into fists and she was shaking her fists and stamping her feet and shouting straight at Rob Ewing.

A tremor of apprehension tickled Kate's spine.

Other men, friends of her father's mainly, were drawing into the group now. Rob was shouting. He too seemed to be stirred to rage.

A string of men and women broke and ran, running for their own homes. The Ewings and Mirrin bunched and ran too, round the gable and round the backs of the muddy short-cut which would lead them either to the pit or back to the Stalker house.

Kate was afraid now. All the folk in Blacklaw had a sensitive region in them which trembled with panic at any unusual event, no matter how minor.

She tried not to show her apprehension to Lily.

'I ... I'd forgotten,' she said, lamely. 'I've left loaves in the oven. Listen, I'll come back soon.'

Lily had got out of bed again, nodding. She was too astute to be deceived by the lie, but she did not question Kate. Perhaps she imagined it was some bad news brought from the Stalker house concerning Daddy. She took Edward again, still nodding.

From her pocket, Kate brought out one florin. She put it on the table top. Before Lily could protest, she said, 'Take it. We can spare it. Honest!'

As Kate went out of the door, she heard Lily calling 'You'll tell me, won't you? You'll tell me as soon as you can?'

Kate did did not pause to give an answer.

She was full of panic now. She ran through the scattering groups towards the end of the row where she would find the cause of Mirrin's fit and Rob Ewing's unusual vehemence.

*

Kate tried to reach the bed to assist her father. He had himself raised up on his knees, the bandages from his chest and belly trailing and his pustuled flesh revealed. Flora had been in the process of changing the dressings when the Ewings burst in with the news. The bowl of healing lotion had been knocked over. The soft new-washed pads, still sopping, had been dropped and trampled underfoot. The whole kitchen seemed to be full of men, a Bedlam of them, all fighting to reach the bed, to see Stalker, symbol of their passive uprising and balanced champion of their rights.

There was no evidence of passivity in the room that evening, nor could her father be considered balanced. He was howling like a wolf, beating away the hands which reached to help him. The sight of his blistered and lacerated body appalled many of the men, yet they were conscious of a terrible pity for him only below the immediate concern for communal safety. Stalker himself appeared to be unaware of his own leaking wounds. It was the courage of disregard.

Kate recognized the Pritchard brothers, and George McNeillage, Donald Ormond, Ormond's eldest son, and four or five more of the men. Rob and Callum Ewing and Mirrin had the front gallery, pressed against the mattress in the alcove.

'The black-hearted bastard!' her father shouted.

'By God, he'll not get away with this,' Mirrin stormed.

'It's happened afore, remember,' said Callum. 'In Carron and Eastlagg, only a year syne. It's colliery law.'

'*Law!*' Mirrin screamed. 'You call it law?'

'If Lamont's a mind to . . .' began Rob Ewing, but his remark was quashed by the general hubbub.

Kate wriggled past her sister and caught Alex as he slumped sideways, almost tumbling from the bed. By now, she knew the places on his body where her hands would not cause too much pain and she held him there, like a big squawking baby.

'What is it?' she said. 'Tell me what's happened.'

'We're to be put out,' Flora Stalker said.

'What!'

'Out of this house; evicted!'

'Oh, God. Oh, no!'

'Aye, it's the truth,' said Rob. 'You an' twenty more families.'

Mirrin called, 'Just because he doesn't work in the pit any more.'

It was law, the invidious law which coalmasters in most mining areas had invented for their own protection. They built the houses, and 'tied' the tenure of the dwelling to the job in the pit. Almost without exception, every house in Blacklaw belonged to Houston Lamont and was bound by shackles of iron to the coal pits.

Eviction! Kate could hardly credit it. Was he so much of a fool, so much of a tyrant, this Houston Lamont? Was he so confident of his power over them that he could blatantly flout public opinion? Did nothing in the world matter to him but the tonnage drawn up from underground and the silver into which his tradings converted it? Her brothers, and ninety other colliers, had given their lives to Lamont's workings – and he could not even stay his greedy hand and keep it away from the properties.

'Nothin' the likes of us can do,' whined George McNeillage, his voice rising waspishly over the babble. 'They get the measure of the likes of us every bloody time. What about your precious settlement now, Stalker?'

'Shut your mouth, McNeillage,' Mirrin shouted.

'What'll you do, then?' McNeillage went on. 'Get Lamont to send it to you in the poors' hoose?'

Mirrin shoved the rodent-faced little miner. McNeillage was known for his low opinion of women and his even lower opinion of the Stalkers.

'Get your hands off me, Mirrin Stalker,' he squealed. 'It's not right for a chit of a lass t'be tellin' a man t'shut up.'

Mirrin's hand moved towards the brass-knobbed poker on the hob but Rob Ewing caught her wrist and pulled her back.

'I'll brain him,' Mirrin promised. 'Give me one chance an' I'll bash the old lip.'

It was apparent that she had transferred her spleen at Lamont on to McNeillage. Rob continued to hold her, his arms over her arms while she struggled and shouted.

Kate felt her father's strength. He flexed his tattered body against her and sat upright.

'Mirrin!' he snapped. 'Hold your tongue. You're not too spunky yet to fetch a taste of my belt.'

That was the voice Mirrin knew, the threat she understood. She went slack in Rob's grip, nodding, grim-lipped.

'Now,' said Alex Stalker, 'sit yourselves down, those of you that want, an' we'll talk this out among us like sane an' sensible folk.'

He was still half naked and in the struggle his belly and thighs too had become exposed. Kate realized how hideous the sight must be to those who had not seen it before. She looked at the extent of his burns and wounds with fresh insight into the pain her father must suffer. She felt her eyes fill with tears. She had the urge to turn to them, and point out the incongruity of the expectation of leadership from a man who was less than half alive. She wanted to say, 'Have you ever seen anything like it? Have you ever seen such pride?' But she could not embarrass him by doing so, and contented herself with bathing and dressing his injuries there before his workmates while, like the natural leader he was, the old man conducted the meeting.

It was a meeting full of heat and anger, emotions which covered a root pessimism and an inclination to bow once more before the system. In fact, Kate thought, there was no way out of the plight – not for the Stalkers, nor any of the families on whom the notices of eviction had been posted. In Eastlagg, in another county, they had brought out the soldiers to enforce the owner's right to take back his houses when he wanted them. There was a grain of right on the employers' side, too, though she did not dare mention it in that inflammable company. Pits were places of work, and workers needed homes, and homes were the carrots a coalmaster dangled to keep his shifts staffed with strong and willing men. It was slavery, sure enough, but the articles of the bond were steeped in age-old acceptance and the tacit acknowledgement of privileges whose origins were lost in the mists of feudal serfdoms, buried like the stumps of the ancient Scottish forests out of which the hard black coal was formed.

When she had finished with the nursing, she went to the hob, edging through the arguing men, to help her mother brew tea for the assembly. One good thing had come out of that day; at least her mother had been startled out of her shock. Flora Stalker had emerged again from her stupor and, now that the family was threatened, had regained some of her former competence.

Mirrin sat carefully on the bed-edge, holding her father's hand. It was a sign that she aligned herself with his authority and, in spite of her proclaimed freedom, would support him as long as he lived. Duty and discipline were best fostered out of love.

Kate only half listened to the debates.

'A strike!' Jock Pritchard declared. 'A strike's the thing Lamont'll understand.'

'Aye, or a brick-hod on his nut next time he sets foot in the yard,' Mirrin suggested speculatively.

The talk grew slack and inconsequential, as the men sought release from their fears and tensions in words. Alex Stalker allowed them to ramble on. He was silent now, brooding. Kate wondered if the pain was deep in him. His eyes were sunken, sullen and distant, and his hand in Mirrin's was slack.

Tea was dispensed. Only in the lull which briefly overcame

the company did Alex Stalker find the quietness he required to declare his opinion and make his point.

He raised his fist, fingers spread.

'Start talkin' about a strike,' he said.

Strike action had been mooted but the topic had gone sliding down amid the dross of idle suggestions. Now the old man had brought it up again.

'Are you serious, Alex?' asked Donald Ormond.

'Aye.'

'But a strike at this time...'

'I said, start *talking* about strike action.'

The men glanced at each other nervously.

'Get the word around,' Stalker went on. 'Stir it up a wee bit, but avoid all trouble. No more of this street-corner militancy.'

'But Da...?'

'You heard me, Mirrin; no more of it. Leave rowdyism t'Christy Moran an' his like. Fat lot they've ever done for us, except create useless unrest.'

'What's in your mind, Alex?' Colin Pritchard asked.

'Lamont's on shaky ground, an' he knows it,' Alex Stalker explained. 'He's givin' the village a fright. He's like a laddie playin' at bogeyman, makin' a sudden jump at us all.'

Mirrin grinned, and slapped her knee.

'Two can play at that game,' she said.

'Aye,' said her father. 'No doubt we'll be heaved out eventually, those of us not fit t'work or widows with no man on the books. But that's a situation Lamont can come to when he's done right by us all, when he's made a settlement for his negligence.'

'He won't want a strike before the public inquiry,' said Rob. 'You're right there, Mr Stalker!'

'Of course he's right,' said Mirrin, proudly.

'You really think he'll back down on the evictions, Alex?' Ormond asked.

'I'm sure of it.'

They were most of them grinning now, chuckling.

'We'll put the word out on the night-shift,' Callum promised. 'Threaten strike-action.'

Mirrin slid from the bed and raised her arms, giving them all a good look at her bosom.

'Bogeyman!' she said. '*Boo* to bloody Houston Lamont!'

The men laughed.

Kate turned and saw, with a melting heart, that her mother was laughing too.

6

Labour began shortly after two o'clock in the morning, three days after the serving of the eviction notices. The movement in her body was heavy but, for the first hour, the pain was slight and irregular. Lily, who had been up to attend to her first-born, could not be sure that her second child had at last decided to make his entry into the world, ten days overdue, as far as the doctor could calculate.

She sat deep in the chair, James's chair, by the banked fire and hugged the vague ache as a remembrance of the times that were past now and would never come again. Consciously and without sentiment, she thought of her first meetings with James, and of the manner in which the Stalker family had accepted her and taken her into their guarded fold. She thought of the fun of courtship, the daftness, and the softness of her feelings, that indescribable quality in life which made even the drudgery of the pit-head troughs seem sweet. She thought of the excitement of the preparations for the wedding and the breath-stopping nervousness of her walk to the kirk and of the restorative calm of the service, the high-spirited fun of the celebrations, thirty folk or more packed into the Stalkers' house, spilling out into the street to dance to the music of the piper, the fiddler and the wee melodion-man. She thought of the marriage bed, still there, still tangible in the corner of the kitchen, and of how gentle James had been with her, how understanding. She thought of the forty months thereafter, the fluctuations of love, the hardships, and the few quarrels, the pain and the joy of giving birth to Edward, of James's great pride in her and in his son. She appreciated too late the security of life in the village of one street, with the hours of the day marked off by the colliery hooter, more regular than sunrise or dusk, more sure than the ebb and flow of the seasons. She thought of the dawn of the day, the last day, and how he had come to her where she lay in bed, groaning and crabbit with the weight of the child in her belly, and how he had kissed her

and put the mug of tea on the chair arm and had told her, with
another kiss and a bit of a dunt on the tip of her nose, told her
to cheer up and bear up and be glad she wasn't an elephant
who carried their kids for twenty-four months. She had crabbed at him and pulled the blanket over her face, and he had
gone off, not minding, whistling a quiet, cheerful tune, and the
latch had clacked, and the hooter had sounded and she had
never seen him again.

Now it was April, a raw, chill night, and she could not deny
to herself that the pains were bad, that her time had come. She
held it for a half hour more, rocking herself over her forearms,
yet not afraid, still unwilling to share her distress with others,
not even the Stalkers.

Abdomen, back and the bones of her hips were racked with
pain before she cracked under it, gave up her selfish exculpa-
tion, dragged herself to the door of the house and screamed.

*

'What is it?'

'Lily, your Lily,' the neighbour said.

'Her time?' said Kate.

'Aye. She's took real bad.'

'Kate, is it Lily?'

'It is, Mother.'

'Fetch the clean blankets from the chest.'

'I'll get them now. You dress yourself.'

'Is it Father?' Mirrin said.

'Lily.'

'Right: I'll stay with Daddy.'

'You'd better come quick, lass,' the neighbour said.

Lily Stalker was in the bed in the kitchen.

'Och, your face is no bigger than a farthin', love,' Flora
Stalker said. 'How is it with the babby?'

'It's . . . fine.'

'Edward's next door,' Kate said. 'Don't fret about him. He
never even woke up. He'll have a wee brother or sister to play
with soon. He'll like that.'

Lily's eyes crinkled, then widened. She reared convulsively
on the bed, head arched.

Another neighbour brought the news; Doctor Mackay had been called out to attend to old Mrs Flood, and would be along as soon as he could.

Kate filled the big pot and the iron kettle and set them on the range. The fire burned well, a collier's fire, banked high at the back, sloping evenly down at the front. It gave more light than either the candle or the oil lamp.

Lily arched again, and a shriek broke from her lips.

After that, there was no talking to her, only the holding and the soothing and the helpless ordeal of giving sympathy in lieu of relief. It worried Kate that her mother was so solemn, for Flora, who had assisted at many births, was always exuberant and encouraging even when the pain was worst.

It was almost four o'clock before Doctor Mackay arrived.

Gravely he examined Lily.

Opening his bag he removed a trumpet-shaped instrument, poked one end in his ear and listened with the bell against the mound of Lily's stomach.

When he raised his head, he said nothing.

There was a low wooden chair which James had cut down to give Lily more comfort when working with Edward. The Doctor drew it to the bedside to stand on, for he was a short man and the mattress was high. He cooled the girl's brow with damp compresses and examined her again with his fingers, crooning to her, the voice low but harsh, instructing her how to help herself and her infant.

For an hour, Mackay kept it up.

His shirt was taut and pale over his elderly back. Two canvas straps held his sleeves furled almost to his shoulders. His bald crown glistened as if he had anointed it with almond oil. When he judged that the minute was near, he stripped the bed of its clothing and pulled the girl this way and that, roughly but with expert assurance. Flora Stalker was there, too, and Kate could see little.

One glimpse of Lily's face, in repose, showed such a dreadful awareness in the eyes that Kate did not dare to look again.

The birth itself was rapid.

Lily fell back against the pillows.

Mackay turned.

The baby was tiny, gnarled, like a waxed doll laid there on the linen cloth: a male, another Stalker boy. But he had no temper, and did not cry. He lay curled in the position in which he had made his journey, twitching his tiny fists and imperfect feet, noiseless, as if he did not wish to be noticed.

Kate held him, rocking him gently, gently, until life flickered and ebbed away again and the last-born of her brother's sons returned to the pleasant place from which he had come.

Outside, at exactly that moment, the colliery hooter lowed and the night-shift cage ground to a halt with the weary miners from underground.

Mackay coaxed the bundle from Kate's lap and folded the linen neatly over the infant's still and fragile limbs.

He sighed.

Kate said, 'Lily?'

Mackay nodded.

'Och, she'll live,' he said bitterly. 'At least 'til her next lying in.'

Outside, in the grey daylight, the colliers trudged home.

7

Kate was alone in the house with her father when Houston Lamont called. For a week now her mother had been staying with Lily, attending to Edward while the poor girl recovered from her ordeal. Drew and Betsy were at school, and Mirrin, thank God, was on shift at the picking tables. Kate shuddered to imagine what her middle sister's reaction might have been to the sight of the tall, dark-clad, sober figure there on the door-step.

Lamont did not feel the need to identify himself.

'Miss Stalker?'

Kate nodded, hand still on the latch.

'May I come in?'

'What . . . what for?'

The carriage was drawn up just a yard down the street, the big glossy-black horse snickering and champing a little against the tie-rein. On the bow of the coach door, varnished into the veneer, was a gilded circle of letters – *Blacklaw Colliery: Proprietor Houston Lamont*. In the windows of the opposite houses curtains shifted slyly and the few pedestrians in the street slowed their steps in order to glance side-long at the visitor.

Lamont cleared his throat. 'I wish to speak with your father.'

Kate stood back.

'Come in,' she said. 'I'll see if he's awake.'

Fine well she knew he would be awake. So long had he been bedbound now that he did little more than doze intermittently. The rumble of that unfamiliar voice would have brought him out of his cat-nap instantly.

'It's Mr Lamont, father.'

'Aye, so I heard. Help me up, lass.'

She eased a pillow under his back and straightened the collar of his nightshirt. The action was prompted solely by habit. Nothing could improve the grotesque and pitiful spectacle her father made. She stepped back and signalled for Lamont to approach from the kitchen door, murmuring as he passed her, 'He's still very ill, an' should not be overtaxed.'

'My business here will not take long.'

Kate hesitated, then took herself to the window and deliberately turned her back on the two men. She questioned if Lamont would bully her father, but she had no intention of leaving the room while the coalmaster was there.

She had seldom heard Lamont's voice before, only a dozen times in her life, in fact, when he had found the need to speechify up at the pit-head and the whole village had turned out to listen. She could not even recall what the substance of his addresses had been, only that he had sounded solemn and pompous, more like a minister than any minister she'd ever heard in a pulpit.

In conversation some of that tone was still present, but the accent was more gentle, clipped, cultured.

'How is your health, Stalker?'

'Fair.'

'I'm glad to hear that.'

'The ... rumour I heard about being flung out of my house wasn't exactly the best sort of medicine, though,' Alex Stalker said.

Lamont did not seat himself on the chair Kate had provided. Instead he remained standing, towering over the wizened little miner, head a bare half inch from the roof. He could not, Kate thought inconsequentially, have put his tile-hat on without stooping. Collier's cottages were not built for men in tiles.

'Perhaps not,' Lamont said. 'I presume, however, that you would accept that all that has been said and done in Blacklaw this past month or so has not been truthful or rational?'

Kate wondered exactly what that long, involved sentence meant.

Her father answered, 'Not everythin', sir : no.'

'We're both colliers, Stalker,' Lamont went on. 'Different ends of the scale, admittedly. It would be hypocritical of me to pretend otherwise. But we *are* both colliers. Each of us has the industry at heart; particularly that portion of the industry which affects us most – namely, Blacklaw Colliery.'

'Aye, I wouldn't argue too much with that, sir.'

After a pause, Lamont said, 'Bad feeling, Stalker.'

Across the street, Kate noticed, quite a crowd of women and toddlers had gathered to admire the polished carriage and the big, polished horse. Mercifully there were no militants abroad that morning, none who might be tempted to defile or damage the coach, or cut the horse free from its traces. She did not know why she felt responsible for Lamont's property.

Behind her, Lamont said again, 'Bad feeling.'

'Inevitable at a time like this, sir.'

'Is it?' said Lamont. 'I've caught wind of meetings, threats to withdraw labour from the pits. What's the truth behind it?'

'How would I know?' Alex Stalker asked.

'Come now, Stalker. I'm in no mood for verbal shilly-shallying.'

'Right,' Alex Stalker said. 'There *has* been talk of a strike.'

'How serious?'

'You know colliers, Mr Lamont.'

'Will a strike solve anybody's problems?'

'Maybe not,' Alex said. 'But it's the only weapon folk like us have in the armoury.'

'A dangerous weapon.'

'We're aware of that.'

'I'd be obliged if you would remind your ... your cronies, your associates, just how dangerous strikes can be.'

'They'll not take much heed of an old wreck like me.'

Lamont said, 'I had deemed you an honest man, Stalker. Are you afraid to admit your part in this unrest?'

'I'm not afraid of anythin',' retorted the collier.

'Then will you ... pass word that I will not be blackmailed?' Lamont said.

'You took me for an honest man, sir,' Alex Stalker said. 'But y'failed to specify just where my loyalties lie. Honesty and loyalty go hand-in-glove, as I'm sure you'd be the first t'admit.'

'You have influence with the agitators, Stalker,' said Lamont drily. 'I would be grateful if you would exercise that influence to ascertain that there are no outbreaks of labour unrest in this village at this time. Request them to have patience until results of the inquiry are officially announced.'

'An' then, Mr Lamont?'

'I'll review the situation thoroughly.'

'How long will that take?'

'Not long.'

'Just long enough for a few more families t'famish?'

'Nobody need starve these days.'

'Maybe not directly,' said Stalker. 'But . . .'

'It's not my task to right all the social evils of the day,' said Lamont. 'I came to invite your help in the matter of averting a strike which could only be detrimental to the community as a whole.'

'An' you especially, Mr Lamont.'

'I doubt,' said Lamont distinctly, 'if I will ever find myself in the parish poor-house, Stalker. Profit and loss – like honesty and loyalty – are relative. I have less to lose than any of you. *Will* you speak to your friends?'

'I'll . . . ah, give the matter consideration.'

Lamont tapped his hat-brim thoughtfully on the back of the chair. It made a noise like a papier-mâché drum.

'Believe it or not,' he said slowly. 'I do have the welfare of this village at heart. I'm not stamped with the old mores, though you may think I am.'

'Then pull in the eviction orders.'

Lamont laughed, a nasal sound, shorn off.

'So that's it?'

'Aye.'

'Of course,' said Lamont, 'there would be no question of your being put out into the street, Stalker, not in your condition.'

'An' the others?'

'I *need* the houses.'

'Not with one pit closed, y'don't.'

'Are we bargaining, Stalker?'

'Aye, it would seem so, sir.'

'How many houses?'

'Twenty-three,' Alex Stalker said quickly. 'Widows, mostly. Some injured miners like myself.'

'I will need those properties.'

'In the future tense now, Mr Lamont?'

'Number Two pit will be in operating order inside a month.'

'An' the public inquiry will announce its findings sooner than that . . .'

'You're setting a great deal of store by the public inquiry.'

'I've still a wee bit of belief in justice.'

'*Very* well, I will withdraw the eviction notices temporarily.'

'An' the rental dues?'

'Stalker, really . . .'

The last score had been a calculated attempt to rile the coalmaster. Alex Stalker did not push the point. There were societies, and kirk and chapel funds to aid the truly destitute, those families in which nobody was of an age to work; a mere dozen in all. The rest of the village houses all had somebody, a woman or a boy, booked to the pit, a wage from which the tithe-due could be extracted.

'I'll be seein' some of my friends the night, sir,' Stalker said. 'If the talk comes round t'the subject of its own accord, I'll mention your kindness an' make fittin' suggestions.'

Houston Lamont grunted.

With no more to say, he turned away from the bed and walked to the door. Kate opened it for him. He hesitated on the threshold, bowed under the lintel, and looked back at her father.

'Take care, Stalker,' he said. 'You're a sick man.'

Was it a veiled threat, or some stiff and formal benediction? Kate wondered. Lamont went out of the house, leaving the street door open behind him. She stood by it, watching him climb up on to the seat of the carriage and untie the rein. He clicked his tongue and flicked the strap across the animal's rump. It snickered and trotted forward. The huge painted wheels of the carriage bounced and vibrated on the cobbles. He did not look round at her or at the crowd of women and toddlers who had remained, not shy now, to gawk at the great man. He did not even spare a glance at Lachie Abercorn who stood to attention like a soldier and fashioned a salute with his mouth-organ.

Kate went indoors again.

Her father was kneeling on the bed, chuckling to himself.

'You'll be pleased?' Kate said.

'Aye, I'm pleased, chick. Pleased as a tinker's spaniel. Now, see's a wee cup of tea t'wash the taste of all that dirty dealin' out of m'throat.'

'Then lie down an' rest yourself,' Kate said. 'Even Houston Lamont says you're a sick man.'

'Aye, I may be sick,' Stalker said. 'But he's scared, scared t'bloody death – at last.'

'Lie down,' Kate said. 'You look terrible.'

Still chuckling, Alex Stalker lay back.

Kate wondered what Mirrin would say.

*

'Here? Him? Lamont? In this house!' Mirrin exploded. 'The bloody gall of him. What did he want, then?'

'Came t'see you, Mirrin, like Rob Ewing does,' said Betsy. She giggled and bent over her exercise book.

'An' maybe I'll give you a clip on the lug, Miss Cheeky,' said Mirrin. 'Come on, Daddy; tell me what Lamont wanted.'

'Trade an' barter,' said Alex Stalker smugly. He was propped on a clean pillow in a clean nightshirt, the blankets drawn up over his chest. In spite of his glee at the triumphs of the afternoon, pain was riding him hard and only his indifference to it hid the fact from his daughters. He had been relishing this moment all day long, and took his time in explaining to Mirrin what had transpired. Kate noted that her father gave an honest account of his dealings with the coalmaster, and did not embellish or exaggerate the extent of the victory.

'One month's reprieve,' said Mirrin. 'Is that all?'

'The settlements'll be through by then,' said her father.

'Depending on the results of the inquiry.'

'They can't fail t'find liability.'

'They're an official body,' said Mirrin. 'They can twist the facts as they like.'

'A month's better than a week,' Kate said.

'Anyway, as soon's you've had your tea,' Alex Stalker said, 'away up the street an' find Callum Ewing. He'll have heard that the boss was here an' he'll be all agog t'learn the reason for the illustrious visitation. Besides, I've a need t'talk with him.'

'I'll go now,' said Mirrin.

'Have your tea first, chicken.'

'Keep it warm,' Mirrin told Kate.

'What's your hurry, Mirrin?' Betsy asked. 'Rob Ewing?'

'I'm just doin' what my Daddy told me,' said Mirrin. 'I'm lookin' for Callum Ewing. I might even have to go right into the pub t'find him.'

'Oh, Mirrin Stalker!' said Betsy. 'You wouldn't dare!'

'Why not?'

Betsy squealed in pleasurable outrage as Mirrin caught up her skirts and, flirting them from side to side above her knees, executed a quick impromptu jig across the kitchen. With a grossly suggestive wink, she exited into the hall and closed the door behind her.

'That girl,' Kate said, half seriously, 'will come to a bad end.'

'Not her,' said Alex Stalker. 'Not my Mirrin.'

*

Mirrin's spasm of jollity was soon extinguished by the chill evening air. Spring was well advanced by the almanac but there had been little sun and no warmth at all. Tonight the air was as cold as October, the grass of the distant fields was a deep, dark, sodden green. The sun was over by Lamont's mansion, caught in the trees like a sugary peardrop, neither red nor yellow, but a translucent acid green colour which, given the appropriate mood, would have struck Mirrin as sinister in the extreme. Her thoughts were fastened on her father, and on Lamont's visit. The outer core of Alex Stalker was eroding, decaying like a nut. Inside herself the girl knew that it was only a matter of time before it would be all over with him and his raw courage too would be corrupted by the diseases of his wounds.

Mackay has as good as predicted it, though the doctor never gave up hope of miracles. Medicine had done what it could; the rest was up to God. Mirrin did not believe in God, not the kirk God, Saviour of Men. She did not believe that Houston Lamont was a saviour of men either, and did not hold the deal forged by her father and the coalmaster in much esteem. If it had been up to her, she would have placated the boss, lulled him into a sense of security, then she would have attacked – brought out the whole village, maybe Eastlagg too, on strike. The angry impetus which the disaster had given them was dwindling. Well Lamont was aware of it; time was his ally.

God, she thought, how generous he was to let them stay on in their two, damp, draughty little rooms.

'Well, would y'look at *her* face.'

'Who's done it to you, Mirrin?'

Two companions of the picking troughs had stopped before her. Their eyes were bright with a malicious curiosity, their mouths full of giggles.

Mirrin pulled herself down from her morbid speculations.

She was close to the entrance to the *Lantern*'s yard.

Maggie Fox and Jean McCrae were forever hanging about this quarter, hopeful that some young buck, too drunk to be fastidious, would give them the eye.

Mirrin lowered her eyelids suggestively.

'Since you're nosy enough t'ask, Maggie,' she said, 'nobody's done it to me yet, but when somebody does I'll be sure t'let you know.'

'Impudent bitch.'

'Bitch yourself.'

With an airy wave, Mirrin swung round the corner of the public house and entered the rear yard.

Rob Ewing was seated on a bench near the open door. There were four other youngish men with him, two of whom were bachelors. All had tankards in their fists. No matter how short cash was in the village, the *Lantern*'s pumps were never idle.

All five, including Rob, straightened slowly as Mirrin approached. As a rule, women did not venture into the precincts of the public house; even disreputable tinkers' jennies would not enter the tap-room or bar parlour. Now here was Mirrin Stalker, daughter of one of the most respected miners in the county, striding up bold as brass. The young men eyed her appraisingly.

Mirrin let them gaze their fill. She knew how she appeared, with her thick black hair and her good figure, and was considerably less embarrassed by their reactions than Rob was.

One man, George Laverty, belched loudly.

Cheeks flushed, Rob set aside his tankard and came quickly forward to greet her.

'What d'you want here, Mirrin?'

'My father's after a few words with your father.' She jerked her head. 'Is he inside?'

'Aye.' Without turning his head, Rob said, 'Pat, fetch the old man.'

'I'll do that,' Pat Marshall said.

He drained his tankard, then nudged his companions left and right. 'C'mon, lads, it'll be warmer inside.'

With some ribald droning under their breaths, the four men left the yard to Rob and Mirrin.

Neither spoke, standing face to face, until the back door of the pub opened again and Callum Ewing hurried out.

'What's wrong, Mirrin?' he asked anxiously.

'Just the opposite of wrong, Mr Ewing,' Mirrin said. 'Lamont had it out with Daddy today, about the strike-threat . . .'

'And?'

'The evictions've been withdrawn for the time being.'

Callum cackled and patted the girl's shoulder. 'Eh, but that's a grand bit of news. What else?'

'I wouldn't be spoilin' the old man's fun by tellin' you.'

'Well, I'll away down then,' Callum said. He glanced speculatively at his son and the girl, hiding his grin. 'You'll follow at your leisure, I take it?'

'Aye, Da.'

The old collier went off through the gap in the wall, taking the back track to save himself time.

Rob and Mirrin remained.

The light had all gone from the yard now, though it still laid a band of scarlet on the claybrick of the walltop and touched the stunted buds of the beech which grew beyond the wall with a green which suggested growth. In the corner, under the adventurous boughs of the ancient tree, was a wheel-less flat-cart. To this secluded spot Rob and Mirrin gravitated.

Once a family of lovely red squirrels had inhabited the tree but it was assumed that they had been trapped and eaten during a hard winter when the prices of pork and mutton had been exorbitantly high. In the twilight years the beech seemed lonely without the company of lively little animals.

Rob said, 'So we've put the wind up Houston Lamont, have we?'

'Somethin' did.'

'He'll have heard about the meetings.'

'He admitted as much,' said Mirrin.

'Now he's tryin' t'shut your old man up. It'll not be so easy.'

'God!' said Mirrin. 'D'you imagine that he got t'be a coal-master with no more brains in his skull than a cutter or a cableboy? Lamont's up t'somethin'.'

'Well, we'll forestall him,' said Rob. 'We'll call an official meetin' . . .'

'A meetin'!' Mirrin threw her hands in the air. 'Honest to God, Rob Ewing! If you heard the Last Trump soundin' you'd scurry away t'call a meetin' t'petition the Almighty for fair shares.'

'What would you have me do, Mirrin?' Rob demanded. 'Throw in my lot with hot-headed trouble makers like Moran? D'you really want t'see Blacklaw shut?'

'If it got the colliers justice . . .'

'That's not the way; not with the settlements in the pipeline.'

'What if there is no settlement?'

'We'll . . . we'll take proper action then.'

'An' what's "proper action" – kneelin' in the muck t'kiss Houston Lamont's boots?'

Rob caught her, hands closing on her shoulders, his face

thrust so close that she could see the stubble coarse under his jaw and the grain of dust in his pores. 'One of these days, Mirrin, that tongue of yours is goin' t'get you into deep trouble.'

She tried to pull away, but her reaction only increased his anger. He gripped her chin with one hand, snaking the other hand about her waist, pulling her even closer, so that their bodies touched. She could smell tobacco and beer from him and male sweat, but it was not that which caused her to struggle so furiously.

'Have you . . . taken . . . leave of your . . . senses, Rob Ewing?' she panted. 'Damn you t'hell! Let me go.'

'When I'm ready: not afore.'

'What's got into you?'

'I could ask you the same question.'

'An' what's that supposed t'mean?'

'Fine well you know, Mirrin.'

'You can't go talkin' t'me like that!'

'So you're a lady now, are you? You want freedom on one hand an' "respectable" treatment on the other. You can't have both, love. The way you're carryin' on these past weeks, you'll be lucky to have either.'

'Are y'goin' t'let me go?'

'No.'

She tried to go limp in his arms, but he only hugged her tighter. The flush was dusky red on his cheeks, and his eyes were slitted. The passion in him was not political now, not cerebral, but wholly physical.

At any moment the rear door of the pub might open and a gang of his mates come rolling out. That possibility did not appear to stay Rob. All his speculations about 'decency' had gone out of him at the intimate touch of her body.

If he pushed her, she would fall back across the flat-cart, and would be an easy conquest. A great sob broke from Mirrin's throat. It was not fear but realization, almost anticipation, which prompted her. She inclined her face, waiting for him to kiss her on the mouth.

But Rob did not respond. Instead, he held her, forcing her to listen. That was all he forced on her, words, rationalizations of his own hunger.

'It's a man you need,' he said. 'You might not be aware of it, but it's ... it's ...'

'Yes,' she said. 'What? Tell me!'

'I'm sick of the way you behave,' he said. 'I'm sick of hearin' how the lads talk of you.'

'How?'

'Sayin' ... things about your ... your chest, an' just what they'd do if you weren't Alex Stalker's kin. God, I tell you, Mirrin, it chokes me sore t'hear how they soil your name.'

'An' what about you, Rob, what do you think when they talk like that about me?'

'I think it cheapens you, an' makes me small, too.'

'Makes *you* small!'

'It's no secret, Mirrin. I want t'marry you,' he declared. 'A decent husband, an' a weddin' ring an' a couple of bairns, an' you'll be fine, love.'

'Are you ...?'

He released her a little, pushing her to arms' length.

'I am,' he said, soberly. 'I'm askin' you t'marry me, Mirrin.'

'So my "good name" will not be ruined?' she said, quietly. 'It's so kind, Rob, so ... so noble of you t'consider my reputation.'

'It can't go on any longer.'

'Aye, but it can.'

'Mirrin, marry me.'

'Oh, Rob,' she murmured. 'Oh, Rob!'

He made to draw her to him once again, but she held him, fingers against his broad chest and her body swayed back from him. 'Oh, Rob! You stupid, bumptious, conceited idiot.'

'Mirrin?'

'So you'd marry me just t'save my reputation, would you; just t'make an honest woman out of me, t'still the dirty tongues of a bunch of black-eared coal-grubbers? You'd sacrifice yourself for that, would you?'

'Mirrin, I don't understand.'

'No,' she said. 'No, you wouldn't.'

She calmed herself. He looked so astonished and hurt that she almost regretted her outburst – not that it was unjustified. But Rob was not a wicked man, just too earnest for his own good. She remembered how he had come up out of the hell-pit and taken her father on the board, how he had tended her old man, and his affection and loyalty when the road had been at its roughest. Suddenly, she saw herself as Rob Ewing must see her, and repented of her blistering invective.

'Rob,' she said, softly now. 'I can't marry you, because I don't love you; because I'm not ready t'marry anybody yet. I've seen what it can do, an' it's not for me. Some day, maybe, but not now, not yet.'

'You're in the prime . . .'

'Aye, I'm ripe enough,' Mirrin said. 'Ripe t'be plucked and squeezed like a grape by some man or other, turned into a dried-up raisin with child-bearin', an' cookin' an' worry. I'll see you all in Hades before I'll sell myself into that slavery.'

'I never knew you felt . . .'

Another rapid change of mood came over her. She smiled, 'See, Rob, you're already beginnin' to think you've had a fortunate escape. Away y'go an' have a drink with your mates.'

'I'm feared for you, Mirrin.'

'You are? Why?'

'You draw trouble the way jam draws wasps.'

'D'you say?'

'Troubles'll be the plague of your life.'

She smiled again, crookedly, and touched the centre of his feathery moustache with her forefinger. 'You don't mean troubles, Rob; you mean men. Men like m'father, like you, like Lamont. Aye, you're right. Life's full of troubles. But I'll square up t'them as they come – provided they're of my own choosing.'

'Mirrin, if I ask . . .'

'No, Rob,' she said, emphatically.

'Is there no chance you'll change your mind?'

She had already begun to drift away from him, backing

across the yard. He stood by the flat-cart under the dark boughs of the beech tree, big and forlorn in the dusk. She did feel sorry for him; but not flattered by his proposal, as most other girls would feel. For all that, she could not add further hurt to that which she had already inflicted. Awareness of her own power came to her in that twilit moment. She hung in awe of it, conscious of her own lack of understanding of its potency.

'No possible chance, Mirrin?'

'No, Rob,' she said, very gently. 'None.'

'God! I'm a fool!' he said.

Mirrin did not disagree. She wheeled and hurried out of the yard, just as the rear door opened, spilling light and the sounds of laughter into the gloomy evening air.

It was not until she was almost home that she realized that, for some peculiar reason, her eyes were swimming with tears.

*

There were many in Blacklaw who, like Mirrin and Kate, secretly believed that Houston Lamont had capitulated only to gain time in which to work out some demonic ruse to crush rebellion in 'his' village. Others, more frank about it, did not linger in the hope of a settlement which, so they thought, was but a fond dream of idealists like Stalker and Ewing and the Christy Moran brigade. The realists were all women, of course – widows robbed of loved ones, mothers cheated of the comfort of sons, spinster sisters deprived of breadwinning brethren. Those concerned had known it was coming. Defraying the sad day would not help matters in the long run. A job with a tied house was the acme of security – provided times were good. But when coal prices were low and production cut, when fatal accidents marred the tenor of life, the womenfolk were faced with the tragedy of uprooting their homes and going off in search of new seams of life elsewhere.

Lily Stalker was one of ten who elected to leave Blacklaw.

She confided her intention to Flora only a few days before her departure. Nothing anyone could say would dissuade her from her intention. Alex was angered by the girl's decision. It seemed to hint at a lack of faith in his ability to deal with

Lamont and the weight of official authority. Though Lily was in and out of the Stalkers' house all that week, Alex would not talk to her. He sulked miserably in his bed, feigning sleep or taking refuge in the hurts of his body.

It was a pretty, bright, late-April morning. The breeze cracked the laundry on the ropes stretched along the backs, and whipped the streamers on Edward's sailor cap as he stood on the pavement before the Stalker doorstep, brought there by his mother to say a final goodbye.

The little boy regarded the promise of the trip with excitement and enthusiasm. It did not occur to him that he would never again return to Blacklaw, to Granny and Granpa Stalker's kitchen, to be petted and spoiled by his aunts and his uncle. The young were so innocent of endings, seeing life obliquely as a circle of narrow paths, each leading back into each. His mother was now his guide; he trusted her, but the vague memory of his father's strength was already in him, bred deep and immutable.

It was hardest for Flora.

'I don't see why you have t'go, dear,' she said. 'There's plenty room here for you an' Edward. James would've wanted you to stay.'

'Perhaps,' said Lily. 'But I can't continue to live my life under James's sway. I've got t'do what's best for Edward.'

'Would it be so bad for him t'stay here with us?' Flora asked.

'I'll be needin' a job an' you'd have to look after him.'

'I'd do that willingly.'

'Aye, I know you would,' said Lily. 'But at the end of it, in ten years, what would there be for Edward – only the pits.'

'But Yorkshire,' said Flora. 'It's so far away, Lily. When will we see you again?'

Lily shrugged by way of an answer.

Since the death of her infant, Lily had changed in subtle ways. Physically she was healthy enough and, indeed, had gained weight during her convalescence. The changes were not obvious, but a quality of toughness – almost of ruthlessness – lay under her calm.

'My parents'll be pleased to have me back,' she said. 'My father's already spoken for me at the mill.'

'We'll miss you, Lily,' Kate said.

'An' I'll miss you,' said Lily. 'What frightens me most about going home is that before very long all my years in Blacklaw will be as if they'd never happened. I'll be back in Yorkshire, in the same town, working at the same job – just the way it was before I met James.'

'Except that you'll have Edward,' said Mirrin.

'My Mam'll be lookin' after him,' said Lily. 'Folk will forget. I'll maybe forget myself. People will go back to callin' me Lily Dawson. It'll be as if none of it ever happened.'

'Lily?'

Alex Stalker beckoned to her from the bed. New skin had grown in pinkish freckles on brow and cheeks, but most of his flesh was still puckered and black. He pretended not to notice Lily's reluctance to come too close to him, and she in turn did her best to disguise her revulsion.

'Listen, lass,' he said, gruffly. 'Stop bletherin' about your memories. Of course, y'had a fine marriage, an' those years are part of your life from now on. None of us are allocated that much time on earth, so much that we can allow even one sweet memory t'slip away.'

His hand was shaking as he signalled her to come closer still. 'You're a collier's widow, Lily. I've always thought colliers' widows are a breed of woman who stands head an' shoulders above the rest. Mind you that when you're back in your mill-town. Mind too that you're a Stalker. Stalkers are fighters, Lily. They don't give up.'

She leaned forward and kissed him, lingeringly, on the brow. Alex closed his eyes tight so that she could not see his tears.

'Come on,' said Mirrin, briskly. 'You'll miss your train, Lily. I'll walk you t'the station.'

'No.'

'But yes,' said Mirrin. Without waiting for an answer she swept up her nephew and set him on her shoulders just as his father used to do with him.

From the door, Kate and Flora watched Lily hurry up Main

Street. Two stuffed canvas bags in her fists and the little boy in the sailor suit were all that she took away as record of her sojourn in pit-head country, and forty months of marriage to collier James Stalker.

There were no false hopes in Kate and Flora; they knew that they would never see Lily, or James's son, again.

8

The gardens were bright with late-spring flowers, a brilliant peepshow embedded in the leaded-glass of the drawing room windows. So clotted, still and fresh were the flowerbeds that they might have been painted by some eminent academic only that morning. Houston Lamont stared at them for ten minutes, stared with such intensity that he could almost imagine the warp and woof of canvas under the colours and decipher brushstrokes in the fronds of the tall cedars.

Cool and prim, the drawing-room held nothing to engage his attention, not even a copy of *The Times*.

When Miss Emerson entered, he turned reluctantly from the floral display.

Short and matronly, pure white hair parted and smoothed down over her ears, Regina Emerson was as English as her name. Lamont could think of no person more suited by demeanour to found a residence specifically for 'Gentlewomen Desirous of Care and Seclusion'.

'Ah, Mr Lamont,' the woman said. 'I do apologize for keeping you waiting.'

'Not at all,' Lamont bowed slightly. 'I trust you are in good health, ma'am.'

'I am quite well, thank you.' She indicated a chair a little distance from the one in which she seated herself. 'Please . . .'

Lamont sat. He was strangely relieved by the woman's formality, by the fact that he no longer had to stare out into the hot, gaudy garden. He could still see a corner of it, the only spot of colour in the room, imprinted on the bevel of an ebony-framed mirror above the matron's head.

'And you, Mr Lamont?' Miss Emerson said. 'Are you still engaged with your coal mine, up there in Scotland?'

Lamont nodded shortly, and did not take up that thread. On his previous visits he had not been averse to a half hour of preliminary conversation with Miss Emerson, or to sipping a cup of delicate jasmine-flower tea. Today, however, he did not feel up to social niceties; the pressure of affairs in Blacklaw, four hundred-odd miles north, sat ponderously upon him.

He came directly to the point. 'Your letter requesting me to call had something of the nature of an urgent summons, ma'am. Since you assured me that my sister is not involved, I am filled with curiosity.'

'I deliberated for some time before penning my letter,' the woman said. 'And my declaration that it did not concern Dorothy was rather ... rather untrue.'

'Has her condition worsened?'

'Not ... no, not greatly.'

Lamont drew in a deep breath and released it slowly.

'Would you care for tea, sir?'

'No,' he said. 'Thank you.'

'Do you recall our last conversation, Mr Lamont?'

'I do.'

'Have you considered my suggestion?'

'I have.'

'And your decision?'

'I would prefer, under the circumstances, not to remove my sister from your care.'

Miss Emerson sucked in her underlip and gnawed it for a moment, a lapse in ladylike serenity, and one of the few tell-tale mannerisms which indicated that her vocation was not without its stresses.

'Mendacity and hypocrisy are not the sources of my involvement with my clients,' she said carefully. 'I leave such motivations for charitable societies and parish governors. My concern is for the well-being of my guests.'

'I have always understood it to be so,' said Lamont, with equal caution.

'As I hinted on the occasion of your last visit, Dorothy is undergoing change. It is not uncommon in a woman of her age.'

'But she has been here for so long,' said Lamont. 'I thought she considered this place her home.'

'The ... condition which necessitated her seclusion is not dormant, you know.'

'What's happened?'

'She endeavoured to run away.'

'How did that happen?'

'As you know, she has free access to the gardens,' Miss Emerson explained. 'Eight weeks ago, she found an unlocked gate near the potting shed and ... wandered off.'

'Why was I not informed?'

'I did not deem it necessary,' said Miss Emerson. 'Your sister did not stray far. Indeed, she was discovered within the hour.'

'But in that hour ...?'

'She had gone to the pond.'

'The pond!' said Lamont. 'Good God!'

'No, no, sir,' said Miss Emerson quickly. 'There was no sinister intent in it; besides, the water is only a few inches deep. She had gone there to play with the village children. They had a little frog circus ...'

'I see,' said Lamont. 'Yes, I understand.'

'I assure you, she came to no harm.'

'But is that sufficient cause for asking me to remove her from your residence?'

'I do not insist on it, Mr Lamont,' said Miss Emerson. 'I merely suggest that Dorothy might be better cared for ... elsewhere. You see, her ... well, her "escape", if you will pardon the word, was not an isolated incident. She has tried again to leave the privacy of the grounds – several times, to be truthful.'

'After ... what, twelve years? It seems incredible!'

'Change, Mr Lamont; tilts and shifts in the equilibrium of the brain,' said Miss Emerson. 'I cannot watch her day and night.'

'Where is she now?'

'I regret to inform you that I've been obliged to board her on the second floor.'

Initially the full significance of the statement did not strike Lamont. It had never quite occurred to him before that this residence was other than a pleasant private hotel, a haven from the churlishness of a world too self-concerned to condone naivety in a grown woman.

He blinked, 'The second ...?'

It came to him: the second floor was a prison, a level

reserved for those who had drifted beyond mere feyness, the stratum where the demented and fitfully violent were incarcerated. He had difficulty in reconciling the woman in the chair before him with the image of a Mistress of Lunatics. Hair rose on the nape of his neck at the very thought of Dorothy's confinement in such a repellent place.

'Yes,' said Miss Emerson, sympathetically. 'Four such ladies occupy rooms there.'

'Chained to the wall, I suppose!'

'Mr Lamont, *sir*!'

Confused, ashamed of his outburst, Lamont blushed and apologized.

Miss Emerson said, 'I do not "take on" ladies of violent temperament. But on rare occasions there is a deterioration, a weakening, which makes such a floor essential, both for the protection of the poor creatures themselves, and for the peace of mind of the majority of my charges.'

'Why do you keep them?'

'What choice have I?' said Miss Emerson. 'The ladies are settled with me under bonds of contract or life-long annuities. Their relatives are abroad or have abandoned them, forgetting their very existence. Few are as fortunate as Dorothy, you see. At least you care enough to call two or three times per annum, and to write to her between whiles. The others ... would you have me throw them out, or deliver them into the parish bedlam?'

'Why has Dorothy changed?' said Lamont. 'Why?'

'She is no longer a young woman,' said Miss Emerson. 'Her wayward fantasies do not preclude feelings and thoughts common to many normal women of her age and station, In short, Mr Lamont, she senses that life has passed her by.'

'What is the cure?'

'There is no cure.'

'But something ... something?'

'Love,' said Miss Emerson: the word did not falter on her spinster's lips. 'Love and understanding.'

'She receives that from you.'

'She is but one of twenty-seven residents,' said Miss Emerson.

'I select my staff with great care, but we cannot be expected to offer the equivalent of a home, a real home.'

Lamont got to his feet.

'I take your meaning, ma'am.'

'And your answer, sir?'

'It's ... it's not possible,' Lamont said. 'I would prefer to have you continue your ministrations as best you can. I will pay more ...'

'There is no question of that, Mr Lamont.'

'*Can* you take care of her?'

'We can ensure her safety, but we cannot guarantee her happiness.'

Lamont rubbed his face with his palm. He had shaved on the train that forenoon but already his beard was beginning to sprout, dark and rough, on his jowls. The drawing room did not seem cool now; he was sweating heavily inside the morning coat.

He said, 'Miss Emerson, I do appreciate your concern for my sister's happiness and welfare. And I am grateful to you for sending for me. At this time however, professional and domestic circumstances prohibit the possibility of taking Dorothy home with me.'

'Is Scotland so inhospitable, then?'

'At the present juncture – yes.'

Miss Emerson made no attempt to disguise her disappointment.

'May I see my sister now?' said Lamont. 'I must leave by the evening train, I fear. Regrettably I am involved in the complexities of a public inquiry and cannot spare more time.'

The matron rose.

'More time,' she said. 'Of course.'

'Miss Emerson ...'

'This way, Mr Lamont. I will escort you immediately to your sister's room.'

Lamont bit back further excuses, and silently followed the voluminous grey skirts across the hallway and up two flights of stairs to the shadowed corridors of the second floor.

*

Stalker could not sit in the sun. On that point Mackay was adamant. The sun's rays would eat into his scabs like acid and might, if he loitered outside, cause him lethal illness. When summer was young and ripening, the scents of the fields overpowered the noxious reeks of the colliery. Stalker had always loved this season of the year, and the strong yellow sunlight.

Now he was a prisoner of four walls.

Contamination threatened him from the very source of life, the sun, which all miners worshipped and regarded as pure and beneficient and good. Bounty had turned cankerous, changed by the tragedy, mildewed by the black, porous damp of the underground depths. Now he could do no more than look longingly out at the sunshine from the confines of the big lugged armchair close to the side of his sick-bed in the stifling kitchen.

It said much for the loyalty of his friends that they were willing to forgo the restorative blink of sunlight on their faces to keep their ailing work-mate company. Four of them were seated on uncomfortable wood chairs facing Alex who faced towards the open doors to catch a glimpse of the sizzling street and the gilded wall of the house opposite.

'Aye, I'd like fine t'see a bit of the sky.'

'You're doin' well to be in that chair, man,' said Callum Ewing. 'It'll be a fair while yet before you're allowed out.'

'Aye, you're right, Callum.' Donald Pritchard puffed at his blunt clay pipe. Like his companions, he was dressed in a clean, faded flannel shirt, open at the round collar. His sleeves were rolled up, and his skin was flushed where he had scrubbed himself earlier that day at the wash tub in the back yard.

Colin Pritchard said, 'I know fine what Alex means. Rain or shine I never get tired of lookin' at the sky. God, but I hate havin' t'climb into the cage on the back shift in the fat of the year; them nights when the sky's still blue and the clouds like thistle-spume, y'know.'

'T'tell the truth,' said Callum. 'I never like climbin' int'the cage at any season; even at night.'

'I've seen some bonnie sunsets over Blacklaw,' mused Alex Stalker. 'An' some bonnie dawns as well. I mind one, near the back end of last November, right at the finish of the night-shift : dark, dark, dark, shinin' blue, an' hundreds of stars, like a cartload of silver buttons tipped up an' spread...'

The wheeze of his breathing was the only sound in the room.

He coughed, then went on, 'It brought t'mind a yarn m'old father used t'tell about how the stars were the lights from the lamps of all the colliers that were dead an' gone t'heaven. I tell you, I could've believed the tale that night.'

McNeillage said, 'Ach, I've never subscribed t'ministers' promises that we're all bound for Paradise wi' wings on wur backs an' harps in wur hands. I'd feel a sight more comfortable wi' a tin hat an' a lamp an' a bit pick for balance.'

'No imagination,' Callum said.

'Ach, well, I can wait t'find out if I'm wrong,' said McNeillage. 'I'm in no rush t'get there, thanks.'

'What's the time?' asked Stalker suddenly.

'Near three o'clock,' Colin Pritchard answered.

'When'll they be done?' Stalker shifted his buttocks restlessly in the armchair, groaning a little, unusually petulant. 'When'll they come through with a verdict?'

'When they're good an' ready,' said McNeillage. 'Not all them angels in heaven could hurry along an inquiry.'

'What I'm wantin' t'know is where Lamont went?' said Donald Pritchard. 'He was spotted leavin' by the train yesterday, y'know.'

'He'll have booked passage for the Americas rather than pay out his dues t'the likes of us,' McNeillage said.

Callum said, 'Maybe he's petitionin' in Glasgow or Midlothian.'

'Petitionin'?' said Colin Pritchard; he glanced at his brother for an explanation.

'Drawin' the big traders and coalmasters t'his aid in case the decision goes against him,' Callum said.

'Aye, or hirin' a regiment o'the Black Watch t'put us all in wur places,' McNeillage predicted.

'It makes no matter,' said Alex Stalker. 'Na, na; the boss'll not be needed 'til the shoutin' dies an' the verdict's posted. Even then ... Aye, we've fought an' we've achieved somethin'. Those as died in the bottom level didn't die in vain. I say it now an' will say it again no matter what verdict comes from the offices of the Inspector and his clan.'

Murmurs of agreement went up, like tobacco smoke, from his companions.

'Since lyin' here,' said Stalker, 'I've come t'realize what our wee fight's really about, what worth it is. We've taken a step, moved an inch or two out of the hole. The next step, whatever it is, can only drag us further towards the air, towards the sunshine.'

Donald Pritchard slapped his thigh.

'By God, Alex!' he declared. 'If they had you up there at their big town rallies, they'd hear some sense.'

Stalker shook his head. 'I've no stomach for meetings now.'

'Get awa' wi' you, Alex!' said Callum. 'You'll be back on the dross-box before Christmastide.'

'I've spoken m'last in public,' said Alex Stalker, quietly. 'I've attended m'last rally.'

'Na, na, Alex.'

'It's dishonest t'blind yourself t'facts,' said Stalker. 'I've never been dishonest in m'life an' I'm not startin' now. I've got things in mind, plans. They'll have t'stand in my stead soon enough.'

'Are y'weary, Alex? Will we go now?'

'Stay,' he said. 'I'm not tired, just ... just ...'

Quickly Callum Ewing said, 'What's your plans then? Tell us that.'

'Kate can go out t'the sortin' troughs, join Mirrin there. Betsy'll be leavin' the school an' she's pretty enough t'do better. She'll get a position in a shop, maybe in Hamilton.'

'An' there's Drew,' Colin Pritchard said. 'He'll be on a full wage in three or four years.'

'Drew!' Stalker was motionless now, sunken, chin on chest, his claw-like hands clutched on the knobs of the chair's arms. 'Aye, Drew!'

'We'll make a collier of the lad, never fear,' Callum Ewing said.

'That you will not,' said Stalker. 'Not Drew, not him.'

'Then what?'

'He's what I've struggled for,' Stalker growled. 'Drew's the one, the face I'll put towards the future. Even ... even if I'm not here he'll do for us what we can't do for ourselves.'

'What's that, then?' McNeillage asked.

'Fight the bosses in their parlours,' said Stalker. He lifted his face now, burned and bitten flesh tight to the bone. 'Fight them where they stand, shoulder t'shoulder with them; on equal footing, in their bloody councils an' secret chambers, in the courts of law.'

'But ...'

Stalker grinned malevolently.

'Aye,' he said. 'Drew'll do it.'

'If he can.'

'Can?' said Stalker. 'You forget, man, Drew Stalker is my son. The last, maybe, but the best of the whole sad bunch.'

*

High on the gable wall, the room was screened from the sunlight for most of the day. A tall window gave a limited view of the garden, a view impeded by vertical iron bars and a meshwork grid screwed into the wood. The chamber itself was quite large and the appointments, though sparse, were comfortable and clean. The faint odour, Lamont guessed, came from the water-closet which adjoined the room and was closed not by a door but only by a plum-velvet drape hung on a brass rail.

'Leave us, please,' Lamont said.

Miss Emerson stepped out into the corridor and closed the door behind her, leaving Houston Lamont and his sister, Dorothy, alone in the room.

Eight years his senior, Dorothy had Lamont colouring. She too was tall but, where her brother was broad and hard muscled, the woman was gaunt. The bones of her wrists were like ivory and the structure of her features showed under taut white skin. Her hair, which only a year ago had been sloe-black, was now thickly streaked with grey.

She stood motionless by the window, watching him uncertainly.

With an expression of love and tenderness which nobody but Dorothy had ever been privileged to see, the coalmaster hurried across to her and took her in his arms.

116

'Dorothy,' he said. 'Dorothy, dearest. Let me look at you.'

He held her at arms' length. Her wide mouth curved and the smile was as beautiful as it was unexpected. She fidgeted under his scrutiny like a schoolchild.

'Dorothy,' he said. 'You look lovely.'

'Oh, Houston!'

'What is it about you . . . ?' He snapped his fingers. 'I know: you're wearing a new gown.'

The smile slipped from her face, replaced by bewilderment. 'Am I?'

She fingered the collar of the day-dress with jerky, plucking motions. Distress gathered like shadows in her eyes. Lamont cursed himself for tactlessness. He should not have blurted out the compliments, but waited for her to tell him, surprise him. Now her painstaking preparations with unfashionable flounces, ribbons and laces had all been for naught; the very fact of the garment's newness had filtered through the mesh of her memory, leaving her discomfited.

She glanced up at him again, head angled.

'Am I, Houston?'

Someday she would not even remember him: the thought chilled him.

'You always look so attractive,' he said. 'More beautiful every time I see you.'

He drew her to a satinwood and brocade sofa, away from the window, close to the tall and narrow hearth with its basket of crushed paper roses in lieu of coals.

'I do like your hair in that style,' he said.

Pleased and flattered, and made girlishly vain, she patted the coils of her hair gently.

'One of the ladies did it for me,' she said. 'I . . . I . . .'

'Yes, Dorothy?'

'It's . . . it's . . .'

'Yes?'

'Will you stay with me today: since I look so nice?'

'For a little while.'

'Today, all day?'

'Dorothy, I . . . yes, of course.'

'Have tea with me? I will ring the bell like Mama used to do and a servant will come with the service. She won't be as nice as Nursie, but she ain't so bad.'

Lamont listened to her chatter on. It pleased him that she was so bright; the brittle quality in her tone did not unduly distress him. In the light of the Emerson woman's prologue he had expected a greater degree of deterioration in Dorothy's condition. It was difficult for him not to talk of his own affairs, to rationally explain why, after an hour in her company, he would be obliged to take his leave. How could Dorothy be expected to grasp the significance of a public inquiry into his competence? He doubted if she recalled Blacklaw at all, save perhaps as a dim nightmare which troubled her sleeping mind.

It was unfortunate that Miss Emerson had chosen to write to him at this time: he had troubles enough at home. On Monday he had been questioned – interrogated would be a more fitting word – on the clauses in his deposition. Hutchison and McCallien had drilled away at his statements as if they believed him guilty of culpable negligence. The board of inquiry was not a court of law, of course. It did not need accurate proof of anything and would not bring a verdict, *per se*, only make recommendations on their findings – as good, or as bad, as a verdict, though. The damned colliers regarded the issue of pronouncement as roughly similar to Moses' descent from Sinai with the Tablets of the Lord.

Dorothy and Blacklaw had become entirely divorced in his mind. In a sense he was glad of the opportunity to escape the oppressive atmosphere of the mining village for a while. Even the day-long trip by various trains had seemed a holiday from the tension of waiting, and from Edith's oddly glorying attitude to his predicament. Wyld knew only that he had gone south on business, and Hutchison had assured him that there would be no official release of 'the verdict' before Thursday at the earliest. Often Lamont wished that he could be free of Edith and the mansion and Blacklaw and the legacy of coal. If only he could escape, as Dorothy had escaped, to exist in an orderly, unassuming little town, in a small cottage, with his sister for company and no other demanding responsibilities. He did not believe that her madness was totally without grace.

'Houston?'

At last she had realized that his attention was not wholly devoted to her; that was a woman's instinct, no product of the intelligence.

'Yes, dearest?'

'I am a ... prisoner.'

'No, Dorothy: here you are free.'

'The flowers are my only friends.'

'What?'

'The flowers and the shrubs; I am being kept from my friends. She keeps me from them. If I do not ... converse ... converse with them, they will shrivel up and die.'

'If you look from that window,' Lamont said, 'you will see that the flowers are hale and hearty and blooming. In the autumn, as you know, they will sleep.'

'Yes, but I ... I cannot talk with them.'

'Shall I ask Miss Emerson to bring some in a vase?'

'No,' she shouted. 'Then they are dying. I hear them whimpering and crying as they die, Houston. Only in the earth are they alive, as we are alive.'

'Do not excite yourself, Dorothy, please.'

'I cannot ... *get out.*'

'Perhaps ...'

'Why will they not let me *out?*'

Confronted by such logical agitation, Lamont was faced with a decision between fact and falsehood. It was many years since he had been obliged to spin fantasies for her, to make promises which he knew he could not keep, to cheat her. He hated himself for doing it, yet there was no help for it. Her mind was not stable enough to take blunt truths.

He caught her hands and held them to make her still.

'Soon,' he said. 'Soon, you will have a garden.'

'When?'

'Soon, Dorothy.'

'A garden?'

'You will have a garden of your own.'

'The dust will smother it.'

She had remembered the acrid smoke from the chimneys and the coal dust from the pit-head which had rendered the soil infertile at the house where they had been children together, an angular house much closer to the colliery than his present dwelling. How much other refuse was buried in her brain?

'There will be no dust in your garden,' he said. 'Now, Dorothy, tell me what you will grow there.'

She frowned, smiled, then furrowed her brow in complete concentration, nibbling the tip of her little finger.

'Not large flowers. Only little ones. Sweetly scented. Scent is the voice of the flower, do you know?'

'I didn't know that,' said Lamont in soft amazement.

'Oh, yes, vapours of perfume are how flowers put out words to each other ... and to me.' Her fingers smoothed her skirt with delicate brushing motions.

'What will you grow?'

'Lily-of-the-Valley. Violets. Columbines. Carnations. Pansies. Honeysuckle. Irises. Tall blue lupins. Roses, of course. Marigolds, and Michaelmas daisies.'

On and on, she repetitively listed flowers and shrubs, even trees, all in a jumble, yet with a poetic sense of the rhythmic beauty of the names.

'Hyacinth; quince; poppy; juniper; holly-berry; and pimpernel ...'

Few of these flowers had she seen for herself. In the main they were culled from the large, expensive folios of floral paintings and drawings which he sent her from time to time.

Lamont listened with mingled delight and apprehension. He was conscious of the weight of the fob-watch in the pocket of his vest and the image of the station arch and the steam and smoke of the train. He was impatient with her, yet intrigued.

For an hour he sat with her, occasionally prompting her or stilling the anxieties which came upon her as suddenly as April rains. He told her lies. He made her false promises and let her wander unchecked through the confusion of colourful visions which massed in her mind.

He did not need to consult his watch surreptitiously – an inner clock told him that he had no time left.

He squeezed her hands and lifted himself slowly to his feet, inching away from her, slowly, slowly.

'I must go now, Dorothy.'

The flow of words cut off abruptly. Her chin was pointed up at him, a spark of emotion akin to anger in her vacant eyes.

'It is not a day.'

'Almost a day, Dorothy.'

'No. The sun is still in the garden.'

'I will come again,' he said. 'Very soon.'

'Make them ... make them let me *out*.'

'Dorothy ...'

She jerked her hands from his and, twisting away from him, cowered into a corner of the swan-backed sofa.

'Shall I send you another picture book?' he asked.

'You promised ...'

'Pictures of flowers, of gardens?'

'You did not answer my last letter.'

Under the stress of disappointment, she had become almost rational. He had witnessed this phenomenon in her many times before. It disconcerted him more than her gibberish. He could never be sure how much she *really* understood.

'Did I not?' he said, seriously. 'But you have not written to me lately, my love.'

'I did. I wrote when they ... when ...'

She leapt to her feet, clutching at him.

'Houston, I have dreamed. I dreamed that you'd forgotten me; didn't come and didn't write. That I'm all alone.'

Lamont was still.

He held her tightly.

'Dorothy, do you remember Scotland?'

'The place with the dust?'

'Think hard, Dorothy: more than the dust.'

'Hills.'

'Surely you remember Mama and Papa, and Nursie and Mrs Tindall?'

'I *think* so.'

'Do you ...?'

She smiled beamingly, inspired.

'Home, you mean?' she said.

'Yes.'

'Where *you* live?'

'Yes.'

'I know the address I write on your letters.'

'That is the place.'

'Are there flowers?'

'There are lawns and trees, oaks, but not many flowers.'

'I will grow flowers for you, Houston.'

'Yes.'

'Take me home.'

'I will, Dorothy,' he said. 'Soon.'

'Soon, soon, soon, soon,' she said. '*Today!*'

'Watch the flowers from the window, Dorothy,' said Lamont, though he could hardly speak for the thick sorrow in his throat. 'When the flowers waken from their next long sleep, perhaps then I will take you . . . home.'

'Tomorrow?'

'Yes,' he lied. 'Tomorrow.'

On the strength of that promise, she allowed him to leave, calmed by her faith in his ability to right all wrongs and bring happiness back once more to colour her innocent days.

*

The big wrought-iron gates at the avenue's end were open. The chaise was already waiting on the gravel forecourt. It swayed under Lamont's weight as he climbed in. The driver peered round, awaiting a signal to flick the whip and set the pair of horses trotting.

Lamont knew that he had missed the local train. He would pay the driver to gallop the twenty miles to London, a dusty and detestable journey. Pray that he was not too late to catch the Scottish connection in the capital.

Miss Emerson stood close by the painted wheel.

She wore a bonnet which matched the hue of her dress. The strong sunlight cast a lattice of grey shadows over her face, concealing her expression.

She did not release her hold upon the board-rail, however, and in that impediment was her unspoken question.

Pointedly, Lamont fished out his watch and studied it.

'Miss Emerson . . .'

'Yes, Mr Lamont?'

'Dorothy seems well enough,' he said, curtly. 'Keep her here.'

He tapped his cane on the end of the rail. Responsively, the driver switched his whip.

Miss Emerson stepped hastily back as the carriage wheels rolled and chuckled forward through the deep, raked gravel.

As the chaise bowled through the gates, Lamont leaned out and looked back. The flowerbeds were blindingly colourful and the lawns so green. High on the wall, he could see the slot of the window of Dorothy's room and, so he imagined, the wraith-like shape of his sister standing close against the grid.

The road opened before him.

He whacked the cane hard on the rail to attract the driver's attention.

Holding up a golden sovereign, he said, 'This is for you if I reach London by five.'

The countryman grunted, and switched the whip again.

Behind Lamont, the residence dropped rapidly out of sight, and, for the time being, out of his thoughts.

What concerned him now was the coalmaster's world, the world of black dust, slag and rebellious colliers, the results of Hutchison's probe into the workings of Blacklaw.

Dorothy, flowers and rash promises were all swallowed up in his urgent need to be home.

9

The managers' office had it first. It came there in the form of a meek, slope-shouldered ambassador from the inquiry rooms. Snug in the inner pocket of his tweed jacket he bore a sealed envelope containing a resumé of the Report of the Findings of the Inspector of Mines Committee on the Blacklaw Colliery Explosion.

The news was too potent to be contained for long. As the crankshaft wound up the hooter to signal the end of the day-shift, clerks debouched excitedly from four separate exits in the office to carry the tidings out into the workshops. From that source, it spread like wildfire throughout the yards and down, mysteriously, to the lower levels. Colliers in the first cage up from the coal-face heard the word in stunned silence. Instead of heading for home in noisy confusion, they hung together until their ranks were swelled by the rest of the shift drawn up from underground.

Snippets of fresh information leaked out from the office. Each clerk who had actually read the contents of the paper became for a while an oracle of stature whose pronouncements were avidly absorbed.

It took some fifteen minutes for the rumbles of complaint to grow into rage.

'Whitewash; bloody whitewash.'

'Old excuses again.'

'Just like it happened in Eastlagg.'

'I told y'all this's what would happen.'

'Exposed lights: some poor dead collier's fault. Our damn' carelessness.'

'What about Wyld's inspection, then?'

'He was cleared.'

'Holy God! How?'

'Took his word for it!'

'What'd they say?'

'Quantity of foul air accumulatin' in a short period of time.'

'Christ!'

'Claimed precedents.'

'Jesus!'

'Contact with naked lights.'

'Blethers: pure bloody blethers.'

'Assume that somebody slipped up the safety mesh on the lamp.'

'Never heard the like!'

'An' Lamont?'

'Exonerated.'

'On what grounds?'

'Took all reasonable precautions.'

'Us t'blame, in other words.'

'It's always us t'blame.'

'What about the claims?'

'No case t'answer in a court.'

'God! The poor bastards!'

'What d'we get, then? Compensation?'

'Nothin': not a bloody brass farthin'.'

'I told ye, did I not?'

'Nothin'?'

'That's it. All for nothin'.'

'What's the next step, then?'

'Strike!'

A sorter named Edna Brown brought the news to Mirrin. She was a shambling, rufus-haired woman, in ragged skirt and bodice. Her canvas apron dropped and trailed in the mud.

'True,' she cried. 'True's I'm standin' here.'

'They found *no* blame?' Mirrin said.

Edna Brown had the habit of closing her mouth by bringing her full lower lip up over her broken teeth. She did this now, giving the impression that she was forcibly restraining herself from saying more.

'Speak, y'bitch, or I'll brain you,' Mirrin shouted, raising a great lump of coal in her fist.

'I've telt you, Mirrin: the inquiry cleared 'im.'

Mirrin Stalker pivoted, jabbing the mud with the heels of her boots. She swung once, then twice and released the coal lump.

It curved away high over the store sheds and thudded on the roof of the joiners' shop. When she turned again, Edna Brown cowered in fear of her life.

But Mirrin had expanded the first sick fever of wrath in casting the coal far into the yard. She was cool now, and dangerously composed.

'Who told you?'

'The gaffer.'

'Who told him?'

'It's all over the yard.'

'So,' said Mirrin. 'It's official, is it?'

'Aye.'

'Mirrin, don't . . .'

The girl had swung away again, as another bout of blind rage rocked her. She shoved her hips against the frame of the narrow, plank-walled trough, strained, heaving and grunting, with incredible strength until the bracket which held the trough to its neighbour bent and the weight of the coal caused the table to list. Stooping, the girl put her back under the planks. Fists pressed on thighs she gradually straightened until the scoop shifted again and canted clean over, spilling coal out into the mud.

'Mirrin, you'll get arrested.'

'They can hang me, if they like,' the girl said. 'I don't give a damn now.'

Once more, she seemed completely collected and in control of herself.

The hooter lowed again; an unusual occurrence, since it had sounded not ten minutes ago for the end of the day shift.

Rounding on Edna Brown, Mirrin demanded, 'Is Lamont here yet?'

'Na, na, not him.'

'Who is? Wyld?'

'Na.'

'Then I'll wait.'

'Wait, Mirrin?' said Maggie Fox. 'For what?'

'T'murder one'r the other – or maybe both.'

'Mirrin Stalker: you're . . .'

But Mirrin did not wait to hear Maggie Fox's opinion of her character. She marched off in the direction of the manager's office, leaving her work-mates to right the twisted table as best they could, in fear that her rash act would implicate them and bring the sack from the jobs they so desperately needed.

It was all right for Mirrin Stalker; she would never starve, not with that figure.

New bricks and slates, used to repair the damage done by the explosion, stood out boldly from the weathered fabric. The door, at the top of a raw-pine step, was new too. It had been daubed with scarlet paint, fresh but already blistered by the week's hot sun.

Mirrin strode up to the office and mounted the step. She knocked on the door, and waited.

A gaffer called Inglis opened it.

'Miss Stalker?' he said.

'Aye, Miss Stalker. Is Wyld here yet?'

'He's been in attendance at the inquiry rooms all week.'

'Davy Dunlop, then?'

'Aye, he's here.'

'Let me talk t'him.'

'Davy!'

In his forties, Dunlop had reached his personal pinnacle of success. He was plump and pompous, fancied himself as an expert on mining matters and a confidant of Donald Wyld's. In effect, Wyld despised him and would not have tolerated him one hour but for Lamont's peculiar favouring of the man.

Dunlop had his thumbs in his vest pockets. His hat was a half-crown flat from Hamilton Haberdashery, brushed almost bald of nap, perched far back on his crown.

'An' what d'you want, missy?'

'I want a look at that report.'

'That's managerial business.'

'It's everybody's business,' said Mirrin. 'Do I get a look'r not?'

'Certainly not!'

'Stand out of my way, y'fat bag of tripe, or I'll skelp your mouth.'

'Wha'?'

'What does she want?' Jock Baird, gaffer of the night-shift crew, demanded. A widower and father of four rapscallion sons, he spent all his time on shift or off drinking tea in the office. Mirrin knew him for a fair and forthright man. Even her father respected him.

'She . . . she *insulted* me,' gasped Dunlop.

'Mr Baird,' said Mirrin quietly. 'I want a look at the inquiry report. Please.'

'It'll be in the *Advertiser* in full tomorrow, lass.'

'That slu . . .'

'Davy, hold your tongue, man.'

'Please, Mr Baird; just one look, that's all.'

'For why, lass?'

'To tell m'father it's fact.'

Baird nodded. 'Come in.'

Mirrin entered.

'There.' Baird pointed to a document lying on the table, two long paper pages covered in script. 'Read it, but be quick.'

There were a dozen men in the room, all associated in some way with the running of the pit or the administration of trading accounts. Most Mirrin recognized, a few she did not. Clerks' tables, breast-high deal-wood boxes with brass ink-pots lined along them and sprays of pen-holders neatly arranged, were deserted. Clouds of tobacco smoke made bilious auras round the four main oil lamps hung from the rafters. Light from the windows hardly penetrated the haze.

'That slut insulted . . .'

'Davy, will y'please haud your tongue.'

Silence descended on the men.

They watched her, some furtively, some with apparent ire, as she lifted the paper in one hand and scanned the itemized contents, nodding and frowning, like a parody of a lawyer in female garb.

Baird stood protectively by her side, arm outstretched to hold back the fuming Dunlop whose wattles were red like a turkey's at this outrageous breach of rank.

Mirrin turned the page, her eye skipping over the points,

selecting the most pertinent, until she reached the signature of Mister Ian Hutchison, Her Majesty's Inspector of Mines.

Carefully she laid the paper down on the table again, and smoothed it with one hand, leaving an appropriate smear of coal-dust across it.

'Thank you, Mr Baird,' she said.

'You see, it's true,' Baird said.

'Aye: it is.'

Baird opened the door for her. She went down the step and turned right.

Behind her a buzz of conversation rose loudly within the office quarters, Dunlop's whine rising out of it, 'D'you know what that bitch called me . . .?'

Walking fast, Mirrin skirted away from the knot of miners gathered at the shaft-head. She took the lanes between the stores and shops ignoring the tradesmen there, and slipped unnoticed out of the gate, walking on, into the head of Main Street.

She did not know why she walked so hurriedly, or what clamp held down all that rage in her. All she knew was that she had to be home first, home with the correct account of the commission's treachery, bearer of the news which in all likelihood would bring her father to his grave.

*

Stalker could see them. He could hear himself talking. But he was not clearly aware of what his words meant now or of what the men and women in the room wanted from him. The lugged armchair was like a leaf in a blizzard, whirling up and round. Try as he might, he could not hold it steady. If only it would settle, come to rest again upon the kitchen floor, he might be able to adjust to the din and confusion which had descended on him out of the evening light.

Mirrin had been first home; he could remember that. He could remember Mirrin and the words she had spoken, telling him of the failure of the Inspector to find the boss to blame. He had listened to all that the girl had to say. She had knelt beside him, holding him as if he was a bairn, one arm about his shoulders, the other holding on to his wrist. Handsome Mirrin, soft in shape but strong and durable as a new pit-prop.

Then there was Kate, trying to stop him talking, and Flora shouting that they should send for Mackay. He did not really understand the need for Mackay; he wasn't in pain now. Indeed, he was free of the burning for the first time in weeks. He closed his eyes and shouted at them not to touch him, then the chair began its dithering-withering leaf-like flight up and round the kitchen, and he fought and fought to force it down. But he had no weight and no strength left.

At the instant of the blast, he had been stooped on his knees in the spur, not crawling, but worming his way forward after James and Douglas in that waddling gait which wee men found natural but which hurt the husky big lads and wearied them.

The shawl from his knees had fallen on the floor. Kate and Flora and Mirrin and Rob Ewing were arguing, trying to transfer him from the chair to the bed, trying to keep him upright on the chair itself. He could feel their hands on his body.

'Leave me ... leave me be!'

Betsy and Drew were at the end of a long tunnel, framed against lavender daylight, like gaffers at the shaft exit at the end of the shift; two wee gaffers; two wee Stalkers.

Rob Ewing's face was black with pit-dirt, his moustache filthy. Only his eyes and lips had colour.

'What in the name of God d'you think a man in your condition can do now?' he was saying. 'Leave Lamont to us, Mr Stalker. Leave it all t'us.'

There had been heat, terrible heat. James had splayed back, the lamp and the short-pick flying out of his hands. Douglas had gone down, plunging forward. He had picked up the boy's piercing cry in the split-second before the tide of scorching heat had hit him too and the ear-numbing thunder of the explosion had deafened him.

'Give him peace, Rob, for God's sake,' Mirrin pleaded. 'Can't y'see how bad he is?'

Stalker called out.

His throat was raw and his skin felt tacky.

Some sensation returned to him, spluttering through his nerves.

130

'Just tell'm we'll back him t'the hilt,' somebody shouted.

He had caught James's leg. He could remember the strange jerking and twitching of it as if the lad had been filled with panic at the grasp of his father's fist. The lamp canister at his side had a dim glow left on the surface of the wire barrel, just enough for him to make out the state of the flesh on his arm.

'We're all bankin' on a settlement, Alex. So what are y'goin' t'do about Lamont now?'

The flesh was all burned away. He could see the meaty, fatty raw-red stump of his forearm up close before his eyes. There were more blasts and thunders, and a noise like rain-floods pouring through a drain, a hollow, hurrying sound; then the massive crackings and flinty reports of rocks and props and great rich layers of honest coal all shifting the stance of centuries. Rubble, fine as dross, cascaded down from in front of him. The last of the light was soaked up. He had waited then, waited for the grains to absorb and drown him, for air to be crushed out of his lungs, but that had not happened. Instead the black comber had broken and splashed out against the narrow roof, had carried him on its breast, still clinging to somebody's leg. He could not be sure that it was James or that his sons had been with him at all.

'For what?' he said clearly. 'Not justice?'

Above him the men were open-mouthed.

'Fight!' he cried.

'Christ, this's bloody terrible. I'm gettin' out of here.'

In the darkness, under the earth, he had lain for an eternity, his body leaping and writhing in agony and his mind, like the barrel of a tin lamp, glowing with intelligent rage.

'No more, Daddy.' Kate was sobbing. 'No more, now, please.'

Her pleadings were like echoes out of the dark rooms of the pit-bottom, out of the splint-seams of his memory.

Somebody always cried, 'No more.'

Why? Why did they not see that life was chalked against the scale of excess, a trial between endurance and capitulation? All of it was superfluous to them but vital to their sons and their sons' sons and the poor, lovely, loving women who would marry them.

Ach, they would not call *No more* if they had lain in the lather of their own juices, buried in sma'coal for an age of hours.

'Look at him! Can y'not see he's killin' himself?' Mirrin kicked at the wedge which held the kitchen door open to the cool evening air.

'Black ... deep ... curse'm into a hell ... the one they fashion ... for us,' he said.

Aye, the pain was back now. It was not on the surface but far down in the sumps and lowest workings of his body. He had a picture in his mind of a mine-shaft caving, ponderously shutting in on itself, filling up with the stuff from which it had been dug. Equivalent occurrences ruined the zones within him. He reared and arched and went rigid, bowed up from the arm-chair, fighting it to the last.

Murmuring, the spasm passed through him. He felt the blackness coming again. He slumped and sagged forward and fell to the floor.

'Where's Mackay?' Mirrin shouted. 'Somebody get that bastard here.'

Two figures bent over him, big lads on their knees.

'It's too late, Mirrin,' Rob Ewing said.

He could not move, nothing would move. He laboured with the muscles of his jaw and tongue and, even as they lifted him and laid him on the bed, managed to enunciate the words, '*Not yet*'.

After that, there was nothing but the soothing dark, and rest.

*

The kitchen was shining clean. The black panes of the range had the sheen of velvet, its brass edgings gleaming like more precious metal. The square straw mat and round patchwork rug had been washed. The rug's yellow flecks resembled pollen fallen from the pussywillows in the jug on the dresser. The sink surround and table top were bone white with cold-water scrubbing. The red and green coverlet of the chair and the bed's Alhambra spread fell across into obedient folds and creases.

In the centre of the bed, arms stretched by his sides, Alex

132

Stalker went about the quiet and lonely business of dying.

From her chair in the neuk by the hearth, Kate stared unseeing across the kitchen. A woollen sock, strung on four wires, lay in her lap. The heel needed turning, but her mind shrank from the effort of concentration the task required.

The house was so quiet: not silent, though, for her mother's gentle purring snores came from the back room, the fire in the grate crackled softly and her father's breathing was quite perceptible in the lapses of other small sounds.

Kate ached with weariness.

Mackay had been blunt.

'Heart,' he said. 'Nothing to be done.'

There were few men who could have stood up to the horrors of the past season and survived as long as her father. She should not now grudge him a gentle passing.

It was all done, the cleaning and the scrubbing, the washing and the polishing, that ritual of excessive neatness with which her mother met every crisis, and by which she staved off the realization that before the week was out she would have lost her husband as she had lost her sons.

Now they slept – Mirrin and Mam in the back room bed, cramped together, each comforted by the other's nearness; Drew and Betsy in the attic, just overhead.

And her father – he slept too, a tranquil rest at last.

Outside, the streets of Blacklaw were deserted. Only the familiar and unceasing *churr* of some wheel or steam-machine up at the pit-head suggested that the pit was breathing too, gently in the dark of the morning.

A stirring, a halt in the pulse of her father's breathing, brought Kate upright.

She moved instantly to the chair by the bed.

His eyes were open.

'Hello, Daddy.'

'Kate?'

'Aye.'

'Is it mornin'?'

'Nearly.'

'Is it fair outside?'

'Clear skies,' she said. 'Can I get you something?'

'No.'

'I'll fetch Mother.'

'No,' he said. 'Wait.'

'They're ... they're all asleep.'

'Good,' he murmured. 'Good.'

'D'you feel any better?'

Nothing moved but his lips and his eyes. His gaze searched her face, not for sympathy but for a last sign of her loyalty to him.

'Promise me, Kate.'

'What, Daddy?'

'Drew ...'

'What about Drew?'

She inclined her head closer to his mouth. His jaw was set firm, dogged, held in control by sheer strength of will. His voice was a husky whisper far back in his chest.

'Promise me ... you'll see he's kept at the school ...'

'Aye.'

'... that he goes on t'a university.'

'But ...'

'Kate!'

'I promise, Father.'

'Listen ... University, then a study of the Law. A lawyer ... that's Drew's trade ... lawyer.'

Kate said, 'Our Drew?'

'Listen, listen, lass, m'mind's not ... not rotted yet. I see things so clear. Education, words, law, those must be the weapons ...'

'It'll cost a lot of money ...'

'Find it, Kate; earn it.'

'I will,' she said firmly.

'Your hand, love.'

She gave him her hand. The dry hardness of the skin surprised her.

'It'll ... not be easy, nothin' is ever easy, but ... you'll do it, will y'not? You'll see that it's done, just as I ask?'

'I'll see that it's done – somehow.'

'Promise?'

'Solemn,' she said. 'I've never broken m'word t'you as long as
... you've lived, Daddy. Not now, not now.'

'Give's a kiss, chick.'

Gently, she kissed him on the brow, still clasping his hand in
hers.

He sighed, settled back against the pillow, and closed his
eyes.

For an hour, Kate sat with him while he slept, then she
returned to the chair by the hearth, for the summer night was
chill.

The bold-faced clock on the wall above the mantel ticked
away the minutes of the night and brought at last the stirring
of the day to the houses of Blacklaw. When, at dawn, Kate
crossed again to the alcove bed, she found that her father was
peacefully dead.

Even though she had watched with care and love, she could
not say with certainty at what hour the last breath had fluttered through the old collier's throat and the last Stalker, bar
one, had passed beyond her aid.

10

It was a nice hat: the blocked crown gave it a pleasing shape, and the wings of moiré ribbon at the sides added height and style. Flora Stalker's fingers caressed the pliant felt. It was only the second hat she had ever owned and both had been bought by Alex.

The one she'd worn on honeymoon had been cherry-red with a big bead ornament hanging on the side. That had been Alex's favourite. Saucy, he had said, in a colour that matched her lips. He had been a rare one with the compliments when he was young. Their honeymoon had lasted three whole days, far from the dust and slag of Blacklaw. Hard to believe that Portobello existed before they'd stepped down from the funny fat train on its toy rails – or that it existed still. She considered it a magical place, created for a young bride and her husband, then, when they were done with it, mysteriously wiped away again. All that blue-green water, the salt breeze whipping it into snowy peaks like icing in a bowl. Daringly, they had gone out in a rowing boat. She had not known what to cling to – Alex or her hat. When she had reminded him of their perilous escapade on the face of the deep, he had always laughed and told her the hat was worth more than him. On the third evening, their last in the seacoast town, he had unearthed from the sand a fan-shaped shell, fluted, silvery and rough like the sea itself. This keepsake was still in her box in the dresser drawer. Many times during the years she had taken it out to remind her that there were more things to life than dirt and poverty, grief and fear.

Today, she had no need of the shell.

Every single moment of those long-gone happy days was sharp and clear in her memory.

At the grave, she had not shed a tear. It puzzled her, for many emotions churned inside her. Manifestations of sorrow, though, were diluted by the peacefulness of Alex's expression and the comforting assurance that at last he was free from pain and struggle.

The clink of tea cups ben the house reminded her that her duties were not over. In a moment one of the girls would come to make sure that she was all right. She would go through now, and drink a cup of strong dark tea from the china pot, which, like her hat, was reserved for special occasions.

She thought seriously about herself: a widow.

She still had the girls, and Drew. She was not all alone like some of the poor wives in the village. Even today, she had much to be thankful for.

Crossing to the table by the bed, she unfolded a faded piece of lace curtaining. In it she wrapped the black hat and placed it on the high top shelf of the wardrobe. She would wear it, perhaps, at other funerals, at weddings and christenings. But the cherry-cloth hat with the beaded ornament, safe in its wrap on the same high shelf, she would never wear again.

*

Throughout the evening, the residents of Blacklaw called in little groups to offer their condolences to the Stalker family and to wistfully sing the praises of the collier who had been buried that day. Kate kept a wary eye on her mother, but the woman seemed settled and composed and talked freely with the neighbours and friends of thirty years.

Mirrin and Betsy were kept occupied with kettles and tea-pots and endless chains of cups.

'How is it that the kindest folk are always the drouthiest?'

'Here, Mirrin, scald this cup out. Old Granny Malcolm's dipped that many bannocks in it, it's like a basin of gruel.'

'Save some of that pie for Drew.'

'He can look after himself.'

'Where is he?'

'In our room.'

'Is he all right?'

'He's fine; he's readin'.'

'Right, Betsy, take supper up, and get ready for bed.'

'Better give'm a knock first: he's that modest.'

'Bit of modesty would do no harm, Miss Cheeky.'

'Ach, what's wrong with him? I've seen more scuddy bums than he's had hot dinners.'

'It'll only be for a night or two,' said Kate. 'He can have the attic to himself then.'

'Huh! Why should *he* get it t'himself?'

' 'Cause he needs it t'himself.'

'What's so special about him? Just 'cause he's a man.'

'You'll learn!' said Mirrin. 'Men are always special. Lords of the dance, that's what they are. In halls or hovels, they're the real privileged class.'

'Mirrin, please!'

'All right.'

'Betsy, off up t'your bed.'

'Can I not...?'

'Shoo!'

When the last of the visitors had gone and the dishes had been washed for the final time that evening and the three Stalker women were left alone in the kitchen, Kate seized her opportunity.

Throughout the day, the memory of her promise had troubled her considerably. At first, she had been tempted to lock the vow away in her heart, never to mention it again. But that would have been too dishonest and corroding a thing for her conscience to endure. The promise had been made and sealed; she must find a way of keeping it, no matter what the cost.

There was no immediate urgency for what she had to say. Mirrin and her mother were both tired and in no real state to make vital decisions. Against that had to be balanced the insidious power of routine. In a few days or weeks, without their being aware of it, they would slip into new patterns of living, not so dissimilar from the old.

How difficult would it be then to speak of the promise she'd made to her father?

'Before we go t'bed,' she said. 'There's a matter we must discuss.'

'Och, not tonight, Kate,' said Mirrin.

'Yes; tonight.'

In appearance Kate was akin to her mother and sister, but it was only in flashes that her innate strength of character became evident and marked her irrefutably as a Stalker woman.

Flora was seated in her husband's armchair. She filled it better than he had ever done, solidly.

'Please,' Kate said. 'It won't take long.'

Mirrin sighed and flopped into a wooden chair, skirts bunched up to expose her long, smooth legs to the heat of the last embers.

'It's a queer time for mysteries, Kate,' she said. 'But if you must . . . fire up, then.'

'That night,' Kate said, speaking of it as if it had been months ago, 'that night Daddy died, I was here with him. We had a bit of a talk . . .'

'You didn't tell me that, Kate,' Flora said, sitting forward.

'I'm tellin' you both now,' Kate said. 'He didn't say very much, but he made me promise, a solemn promise, that I would see Drew through school.'

'Aye, Daddy would,' said Mirrin. 'He was a great one for education.'

'Can we manage without Drew's wages for a whole year?' Flora asked anxiously.

'That's not all,' Kate went on. 'Father made me promise that we would find the money to put Drew to a university.'

'Our Drew!' Flora exclaimed.

'What did Daddy want him t'study?' Mirrin said.

'Law.'

'Our Drew – a lawyer!' Plainly, the whole idea was so new to Flora Stalker that the boldness of it struck her as ludicrous. 'Och, no, Kate! That's not for the likes of us.'

Kate had expected this reaction from her mother; it was Mirrin she watched most closely.

Mirrin snorted: 'Did Daddy, by any chance, tell you how we were t'find the money for this . . . this venture?'

'Earn it,' said Kate.

'Four women!' said Mirrin. 'How can four women earn . . .?'

'Your Daddy must have been wanderin' in his mind,' said Flora, firmly.

'Not him.' Mirrin threw herself back in the chair, arms raised and her hands behind her head. 'Old Alex was never more foxy than when he wheedled that promise out of you, Kate.'

'Mirrin, don't you speak ill of your father,' Flora said. 'An' him not cold.'

'If he were here,' said Mirrin, 'he would take it as flattery, Mam. No, he knew what he was saying. He's right, of course. That's what we *should* do – send Drew t'university.'

'It's ... it's unthinkable!' said Flora Stalker. 'Our Drew!'

Mirrin sat forward now, pointing her finger at her mother. 'Don't ever talk like that again, Mother. What's wrong with you? Don't you think Drew's got the brains for it?'

'He's clever enough, no doubt...'

'But he's "not good enough"?' said Mirrin. 'Is that it?'

'I never meant...'

Mirrin glanced at Kate. 'He has the intelligence: what he lacks is opportunity. Can we give him that? Can the four of us give him that?'

'I ... I promised Father we'd try.'

'But what would it cost?' asked Flora.

'I don't know yet.'

'There's a lot of it,' Mirrin said. 'We'll need to find out so many things – about the proper courses of study, an' the expense of the whole thing – board and lodgin', books, clothes ...'

'The dominie might be able t'tell us,' Kate said.

'Then go an' talk with the dominie,' said Mirrin. 'He'll tell you if Drew's got brains enough, an' inform you of the qualifications he'll need, an' how long it's liable t'take.'

'But ... but a lawyer!' said Flora again, her protest less adamant now.

'If it's to be managed at all,' said Kate, 'it'll mean sacrifices, dreadful sacrifices, from all of us.'

Mirrin shot to her feet. 'But, by God, Katie, wouldn't it be worth it? A collier's son in legal robes. That's what Daddy had in mind, y'know. Change: radical change in our thinkin', that's what's needed now. Why not our Drew?'

'Will Drew agree?' asked Flora.

'He'll agree,' said Mirrin. 'That lad knows what it's about: he'll leap at the chance.'

Kate said, 'I'll find work at the colliery. You have your job, Mirrin. Betsy'll go up t'Hamilton, or maybe into service . . .'

'I suppose,' said Flora Stalker, glancing at her hands, 'I suppose my fingers still have their skill with a needle. If I could find sewing work t'do at home . . .'

'Find out just what it will require, Kate,' Mirrin said. 'If colliery wages aren't enough, we'll discover a means of earnin' more. Daddy left his instructions, plain as plain. We're not goin' to ignore them, are we? I mean, we're Stalkers: we're not goin' down without a fight.'

'Is it agreed then?' Kate asked.

'Of course, it's agreed,' said Mirrin.

'Mother?'

'I'd like t'think it possible, but . . .'

'Don't be afraid, Mother,' Mirrin said.

'I'm thinking of Mr Lamont,' Flora said. 'He'll want us out of this house now that your father's gone.'

'Know what Daddy used t'talk about – he talked about putting a face towards the future,' said Mirrin. 'I see now just what he meant.'

'But Mother's right,' said Kate, anxiously. 'What will we do about a house?'

Mirrin stared down into the dying embers in the grate for a moment, then glanced first at her mother and then at Kate. She grinned, reflectively, mischievously. 'Leave that to me,' she said. 'I'll handle Houston Lamont. By God, I will.'

*

Eavesdroppers, so the dominie said, never heard any good of themselves. But, Drew felt, he had disproved the truth of the old adage that night. It was difficult not to listen in on the conversation which, latterly, had become quite heated and loud. Mirrin's voice in particular could be heard half way across the yard, never mind just over the kitchen, through one thickness of wood and plaster.

The news had come as a shock to Drew, but the substance of his older sister's' debate thrilled him to the core. It had come as a shock to Betsy as well. From the corner of his eye. Drew glanced distastefully at his sister. He had only recently discovered that his twin was every bit as selfish and self-centred as all the other girls in Blacklaw.

Her whispered, furious arguments had been peevish, feeble and without logical foundation.

'I've to have the chance for two reasons,' Drew had explained. 'One: I've earned it. Two: only men can become lawyers.'

'I want to stay at school too.'

'We can't both stay at school, that's obvious.'

'Why should it be you, then, *why*?'

'I've just told you. Besides, it takes you all your time to sit at your desk from Monday to Friday, as it is. Another "besides" – I question if you'll be invited into the senior school.'

'It's so *unfair*.'

'I can hardly wait t'see their faces.'

'Faces?'

'Henderson, McLaren, big Tom Reilly's faces, I mean. They'll hate me.'

'They don't exactly like you just now.'

'They're jealous of me.'

'Mister Big Shirt!'

'I work for it.'

'An' I suppose I'll be expected to work for you?'

'If Kate says so.'

'*It's not fair!*'

'It's what Daddy wanted, Betsy.'

'I *knew* you'd say that.'

'The law! Lord, won't it be wonderful! Me, in Glasgow, or Edinburgh perhaps...'

'It's not your dull old studies I covet. I just want t'get out of this place, out of Blacklaw. I hate it so much.'

'You'll be workin' in Hamilton: or at some grand mansion.'

'I don't want t'be a *servant*!'

'What do you want t'be?'

'I don't know, Drew.'

'A lady?'

'You're makin' fun of me.'

'No, I'm not.'

'What'll I do without you? I can't talk t'them the way I talk t'you.'

'That's 'cause we're twins. Anyway, I won't be going anywhere for a long while yet. I'm not old enough.'

'You'll go to university?'

'Oh, aye! But listen, listen, Betsy, it's a chance for you too.'

'You're only sayin' that to make me shut up.'

'I mean it. Listen, once I get settled in . . . in Edinburgh, say, with rooms of my own, you can come an' stay, if you like.'

'Will they let me?'

'You won't be a wee lassie, then: you'll be a grown-up workin' girl. You'll be able t'do what you choose.'

'Edinburgh?'

'I would think Edinburgh. All in all, I've heard some rather good things about the colleges there.'

'Stop it, Drew.'

'Hm?'

'Puttin' on that swank voice.'

'I'll have t'practise how to speak properly: not like a collier.'

'Will you really let me stay in Edinburgh with you?'

'Aye, of course.'

'I'll clear out of here anyway. There's nothin' in this slag-heap good enough for me.'

'Nor me.'

'Is that a promise, Drew?'

'Hm?'

'That you'll take me t'Edinburgh when the time comes.'

'I said I would, did I not?'

'But d'you mean it?'

'Aye, of course I mean it.'

'Oh, Drew! It's goin' to be wonderful!'

'I'm not there yet.'

'But you will be. I know you. You will be.'

Long after the rustlings of undressing had ceased and tired bodies had settled into their beds, Drew Stalker lay wide awake.

As far back as he could recall, he had wanted to be somebody of importance, not just the youngest Stalker son. James

had all the attention from the girls. James had been their hero –
but James was dead now. The pit had killed him. Drew had
always dreaded the pit, now he hated it, and, by a warped
process of association, despised those lads who would work
there, giving up their lives to its darkness and dampness, all for
a few miserable shillings a week.

A tacit understanding had long existed between Drew and
his father. There had been little genuine liking between them,
even when Drew was small, but they had respected each other,
had forged a bond out of intangibles, a subtle understanding.

It seemed to Drew, though he could not explain it clearly,
that his father's whole life, and death, had been but a series of
object lessons designed to spur his youngest on towards a better
mode of living. It was a grasp of the old man's principles
which, from a remarkably early age, had chained Drew to his
studies. Now his father was dead, and, in dying, had set the
final seal on the contrast between them.

Kate would back him. Mirrin was on his side.

Between them, that formidable pair would handle all the
worrying details which would be needed to put him through
senior form and pack him on his way, like a gentleman's son,
into the faculty of law in some grand college in the capital.

To be a lawyer was better than aiming to be a colliery
manager, or even a doctor. He would have fine chambers in the
city; his own circle of friends, not snot-nosed tykes like Henderson, but gentlemen of intellectual persuasion, titled companions, maybe. The highest in the land would come to respect
him.

Betsy? He had fobbed her off well enough. Women were so
easily satisfied with hopeful promises. She would be content to
leave school next month, to seek employment fitted to her
station, in a shop in the town, most like. She would probably
be courting a poor clerk or journeyman and eager to get married long before he went up to the city.

Even so, he hadn't much cared for her assumption that she
had an equal share in the plans they had heard discussed that
evening. The future was being built for him; whatever part his
twin sister might have in it would depend wholly on his whim

and his evaluation of the circumstances. After all, it might not suit him to have the likes of Betsy, a rough-mannered little shop assistant, with him in Edinburgh.

Time enough to worry about that eventually.

He would find a way to put her off. If it came to the bit, he would be as cruel and blunt with her as she would be with him had the roles been reversed.

He would simply inform her that he didn't want her.

Cheered by this resolution, Drew turned on his side and tucked the blanket round his ears to close out the sound of Mirrin's muffled weeping which filtered up from the alcove bed below.

Within minutes, he was fast asleep.

Part Two

Servants and Masters

I

Under the canopy of oaks the humid air was filled with the murmurous industry of big, brown, pollen-laden bees working the routes from the rhododendron shrubs to the hives by the old walled garden. The morning's scents were sweet and aromatic, heavy with summer and long days of sun; it seemed a far cry from the bleak, bitter weather of the day of the explosion. So much had been packed into the time that many months might have passed, not just a dozen weeks. A turn of the path brought Mirrin from the shadows of the trees. The packed earth gave way to a broad sweeping avenue of washed sea-pebbles, raked and glittering, which led up to the front court of Lamont's house.

Mirrin paused and pressed her handkerchief to her cheeks, swabbing away rivulets of perspiration, then flapped her skirts in an attempt to diminish the heat contained within the tent of petticoats and skirts and the black serge overcoat.

Kate had insisted on her wearing the coat, had brushed it, sponged it, brushed it again, and, against Mirrin's protests, had held it up and buttoned it firmly. The overcoat was a symbol of respect and respectability; Kate would not condone a visit to the most important man in Blacklaw – the minister excepted – in less than 'decent' dress. Mirrin had given in. She was apprehensive enough about the visit, though she herself had proposed it, to put up no serious argument. Besides, the lines of the coat did serve to emphasize the soft curves of her breast and the narrowness of her waist; she just wished that the material had been finer and more suited to a brilliant June forenoon.

Dry, but not one bit cooler, Mirrin walked on again up the branch of the avenue which led to the main front door.

Above the house the sky was pure, pale blue, as flawless as a bolt of best South Sea silk. The broad steps which climbed to the door were pipe-clayed to snowy whiteness and the brass furnishings on the woodwork gleamed like molten gold. Flat

rectangular windows flanked the portico, matching the un-
broken line of windows which stretched across the breadth of
the house and made it seem, from that angle, like one of the
Queen's grand palaces.

Mirrin wiped her palms on the damp handkerchief and
tucked the cloth away into her pocket. She squared her
shoulders, lifted her hand and rapped on the brass lion's-head
knocker. The sound, muted but impudently demanding, echoed
inside the hall.

Mirrin did not dare knock again.

She waited, more nervous than she would care to admit.

The girl was scrawny, whey-faced and wrapped in a coarse
canvas apron. Smuts of blacklead on her cheekbones and the
tip of her nose told Mirrin which chore she had interrupted.

'Good morning, Annie,' Mirrin said. 'Is Mr Lamont at home?'

Stupidly, the girl stared at her.

'Aye.'

'Well, can I see him then?' Mirrin asked.

The childish mouth gaped.

'Eh?'

'I want a word with Mr Lamont.'

'You can't come here askin' for the master, like that, Mirrin
Stalker: an' at the front door too.' The girl darted a quick
panicky glance back into the hall, then made shooing motions
with her bony hands. 'Away y'go, Mirrin: away y'go afore
somebody sees you. I've enough trouble as it is.'

'Go on, Annie, tell your Mr Lamont I'm asking to see him.
There's no trouble in it for you.'

The little skivvy shuffled uncertainly, then, with a whimper
of apprehension, turned, scuttled back across the hall and
vanished round the newel-post at the bottom of the staircase.

Mirrin stepped up on to the threshold and peered curiously
into the cool and sober depths of the coalmaster's mansion.

She could not resist the opportunity. Never before had she
been this close though, like most of the village children, she
had climbed the overhanging bough of an elm by the back wall
once or twice and spied on the kitchen yards and rear bedroom
windows. What was known of Lamont's residence had been

carried to the villagers by servants like Annie, and the exaggerations of the servant-kind had made it sound like a treasure-house or a potentate's castle.

Now Mirrin saw that it was just a house, bigger, neater, and more ornate than the manse but still disappointingly small. The shiny linoleum which covered the boards of the hall was the brownish colour of cold pease-brose and the panelled doors were old and rusty-coloured, though their white china finger-plates painted with rosebuds were pretty enough.

Between the doors on the left side crouched a huge, carved hallstand. The mirror in its paws reflected clearly a framed portrait of a grim, bearded man whose visage reminded Mirrin of the engravings of wrathful prophets in the Sunday School Bible.

Mirrin craned further round the post, studying the painting's likeness. The moulding of the nose and brooding eyes suggested an ancestor of Houston Lamont's; grandfather or father perhaps.

Footsteps on the linoleum caused her to draw rapidly back.

A familiar voice boomed out, 'Go on about your duties, Annie, I'll deal with this.'

This: Mirrin screwed up her nose – was she just a *this*, an annoyance to be 'dealt with' like a choked-up drain or a wasps' byke in the attic? She wondered if Lamont would so much as recognize her. They were hardly on social terms, and had met face to face only three or four times.

That question was soon answered. He recognized her instantly. A flicker of something – interest, amusement? – showed in his expression before being suppressed by natural annoyance at the intrusion. In the shadow of the hall he halted a half dozen paces from her, and she noted with surprise that his face was stronger and coarser than she remembered it to be and that his hair was streaked with grey.

In turn, Lamont scrutinized her, and gave no hint of his conclusions.

When he finally spoke, his tone was clipped but not hostile. 'Why have you come here, young woman?'

'To discuss business,' said Mirrin, then, thinking better of it, added, 'sir.'

'I conduct my business in my manager's office, not on the doorstep of my home.'

'Yes, sir, but within ten minutes of a talk in your office, our business would be known to half of Blacklaw.'

Lamont grunted.

Encouraged, Mirrin went on, 'What I have to say won't take long, Mr Lamont. And we needn't loiter on the step if it bothers you.'

Had she already gone too far? Her heartbeat quickened. Suddenly, it seemed overwhelmingly important to her to be invited indoors and ushered into one of those closed rooms. Why this should be, Mirrin did not know. Swiftly she rejected the notion that it was pride in her, the daft idea that admittance to the coalmaster's drawing-room would raise her to a level nearer his own. The urgency of her wish was absurd: the absurdity of it made her uncomfortable. Even so, when Lamont stepped back and reached for the handle of the nearest door. Mirrin experienced deep-rooted excitement and the intense satisfaction of achievement.

'Five minutes,' Lamont said. 'I've little time to spare today.'

Head high, Mirrin entered the house, crossed the hall with as much grace as she could muster and passed through the imposing panelled door.

She had expected plush and velvet, walnut and mahogany, ankle-deep Indian carpets. Her elation immediately waned and died.

The spartan chamber was furnished with only a long deal table and ten back-breaking yew-wood chairs. No carpet, not even linoleum, covered the dusty floorboards. It was apparently a disused office or occasional board room. Turning, Mirrin realized that Lamont had seen through her snobbish little ploy and had derived amusement from it.

Her cheeks coloured. It cost effort to speak evenly and calmly.

'Since you're busy today, Mr Lamont, I'll ask straight out – will you give me your assurance that my family will not be put out of our cottage, that we can hold on to the tenancy?'

The coalmaster scowled.

'Your name is . . . ?'

'Stalker.'

'Ah, yes!'

Fine well Lamont had known her name: it was as if he had extracted it from her maliciously, like a confession.

Impulsively, she blurted out, 'A wee while ago you could have looked us up in the pay-ledger. But you'll have to trail down to the kirkyard now. You'll find it worthwhile, sir, I'm sure, there being three of us there – Alex, James and Douglas: three Stalkers.'

Lamont was no longer scowling. Head tilted slightly, he regarded her steadily, then lifted his shoulders in a gesture that was not indifferent but merely helpless.

'I honestly do regret your loss, Miss Stalker,' he said. 'However, you are no doubt aware of the regulations attached to a tied house. There's nothing I can do: to make a single exception is to court . . .'

'I'm not begging for favours,' Mirrin snapped. 'I'm willin' to work for the entitlement to the house.'

'But you work already at the troughs, and the troughs have never been classed as a householder's post: never.'

'Then *give* me a householder's post, sir.'

'How can I?'

'Because you're the boss, Mr Lamont,' Mirrin said. 'Just give me the chance, an' I'll pull a hutch or coup bogies – anything a man can do.'

'And what, Miss Stalker, would the men have to say about that?'

'I don't care what they say.'

'Really?' Lamont said, innocently. 'You don't care about the others, only about yourself?'

'That's not what I meant.'

'It sounded suspiciously like it.'

'Listen, Mr Lamont,' said Mirrin, 'it's not so long since women worked a bloody sight harder than their menfolk to earn bread for their bairns. There's plenty in this village can still remember when wee lassies and old grannies hauled coal-sleds through two feet of stinkin' slime . . .'

'No doubt,' Lamont said.

'If they were considered fit for hard labour . . .'

Abruptly, the coalmaster lifted his fist, the index finger stiff, hushing her. Mirrin felt all the weight of authority and an attendant stir of interest in the man. She had struggled against her own impetuosity too long not to appreciate the self-control Lamont now showed. At least he did her the honour of crushing her with reason and logic.

He said, 'Yes, Miss Stalker, children and women slaved for centuries, but it was the men who struggled for laws to prevent it, to legally debar them from the seams. Is that not so?'

Mirrin bit her lip.

She had no answer to his question: the truth of the statement was too blatant. Her grandfather, so she had been told, had fought for parliamentary injunctions at ground-level, seeking the Queen's protection for females and children. The colliers had rejoiced when the statutes were made law.

'Now you're pleading with me to flout the law of the land just to suit you and your family,' Lamont said.

He did not press home the point smugly as Rob or one of the other young debaters would have done, and he tempered his victory with a sympathetic smile.

Self-control again, thought Mirrin, and supposed that it was an attribute essential to the conducting of the pit's day to day affairs, a quality acquired over the years, part of the inheritance of the masters.

Once she had overheard the dominie tell the minister that where there was restraint there was sensuality too; she had understood the statement better than either of the learned gentlemen might have imagined. Did the teacher's remark apply itself to Houston Lamont, she wondered; the possibility made her a little afraid of him.

She reined her mind back to more urgent things.

'Find me *something*, Mr Lamont,' she said. 'Something I can do that'll let us hold to the house.'

'Impossible, I'm afraid.'

'Don't you owe us that at least? It's not much of a price to pay for three lives, is it?'

Lamont's head jerked as if she had pricked him with a knife.

He said, 'I owe your family nothing, young woman. Official adjudicators of the law established beyond doubt that I was in no way responsible for the accident. You have no claim on me, you know, none at all.'

'You hated my father, didn't you?'

The coalmaster's surprise was perfectly genuine.

'I hardly knew him.'

'But you knew of him.'

'Yes, and I respected his ... his rights.'

'What rights? You chalked him up as a trouble-maker.'

'On the contrary,' Lamont retorted. 'Your father served me well.'

'He hated you.'

'Be that as it may : he gave service for his pay,' said Lamont, 'and that's all I ask. Besides, your father was a *practical* idealist. One always knows exactly where one stands with a man of principle.'

'He would have stood you against a wall an'—'. Hastily, Mirrin bit off the sentence.

'Go on.'

'My sister's workin' at the troughs too, now,' said Mirrin, cautiously. 'Do two women not equal one man?'

'No,' Lamont said: he hesitated, then added, 'But you do have a brother, a younger brother, do you not, Miss Stalker?'

'Aye, but Drew's not for the pit.'

'Why not?' said Lamont.

Mirrin regretted her rashness: it was too soon to air their plans for Drew.

She said, 'It was my father's wish that Drew be kept at school.'

'Indeed!'

Mirrin flushed: Lamont injected so much into that isolated word, filling it with incredulity, tolerance and a touch of derision. She clenched her fingers into her palms. It had been a fond notion in the first place that she might find sympathy in this quarter, or be able to bully such an autocrat as Houston Lamont into granting them a favour. The whole breed of bosses and masters was tarred with the same pitch. All she could do now was retreat from the situation with as much dignity as she could muster.

'I won't keep you any longer, sir,' she said, moving to pass him.

'Wait.'

He looked down at the table and, with his forefinger, described an uneven circle in the fine layer of dust. His tone was no longer authoritative, but oddly bemused as if he was puzzled by his own presumption.

'I'm not without feeling, Miss Stalker, whatever popular opinion may charge to the contrary. I appreciate the confusion caused by the tragedy in our midst, and the suffering it's brought to my workers.'

He paused, still not looking at her, his finger outlining other geometric forms in the dust now, a triangle, a rectangle and a square.

'As you say, two women in the Stalker family work under my employ,' the coalmaster continued. 'Provided your sister retains her position at the pit-head, and you agree to work for me, then I will grant you tenancy of the Main Street house.'

She stared at him, astonished at his sudden capitulation. The realization that she had won out against the system, and against Lamont, caused her such overwhelming relief that laughter rose in her throat.

'But I *do* work for you,' said Mirrin. 'I've been three years at the troughs. Two for the price of one.'

'As you say.' Lamont glanced up at her. 'You *will* continue to work for me, then?'

'Aye, of course I will.'

'Good!' Lamont extracted a handkerchief from his cuff and dusted his hands with it. 'As Annie will be leaving our service in a week's time, you will make your first duty as housekeeper the engaging of a young girl from the village to replace her.'

In spite of herself, Mirrin goggled, the remnants of her smile frozen on her lips.

'House . . . keeper?'

'Housekeeper.'

'Where? Here?'

'Naturally.'

'But . . . but I wouldn't know what t'do. I never had *any* domestic training.'

'You will learn,' Lamont told her. 'When Mrs Lamont returns from Edinburgh I am sure she will organize your instruction.'

'But I know . . . nothing!'

'You underestimate yourself, Miss Stalker,' said Lamont. 'You are energetic, almost certainly conscientious, and, I'm sure, have your share of your father's principles. In addition, you know the villagers. They will work well for you. You will manage them better than I can, or Mrs Lamont can, for that matter.'

'So that's it!' Mirrin exclaimed. 'You want me to crack the whip just to make life easier for you.'

'Not entirely,' said Lamont. She could no longer tell if he was making sport of her or meant the caution seriously. 'I want to keep a close eye on you. As you've already pointed out, your father would've stood me against a wall and shot me: and you are your father's daughter. The best place for you, Miss Stalker, is here, under my nose.'

'You're not suggesting I . . . I spy for you?'

'I have more sense than to ask that of you,' Lamont answered sharply. 'Loyalty is a quality I respect, wherever it falls due.'

Mirrin let out her breath in a harsh sigh. She had not yet agreed to his unexpected terms.

If it had not been for Kate's rash promise to their father, she would not have agreed at all – or would she? There would be wagging tongues in Blacklaw, but gossip worried her not one bit. What worried her was her urge to grab this opportunity. Housekeeper to Houston Lamont, the mine owner, was an elevation in status beyond her wildest dreams.

If he really was engaging her to report back on her fellow villagers, then he would be doomed to disappointment.

She stepped to the window to make her decision without the disconcerting penetration of his gaze.

A green sward separated the house from a mass of scarlet-blooming shrubs above which clouds of bees hovered and hummed in the motionless heat. There were so many things she wanted to ask him, so many imponderables involved in his offer. But she sensed that he would not allow her to hold off her answer.

Did he realize that she would take the side of the colliers and would fill his ears with things which no boss liked to hear – assuming he gave her half a chance? Did he realize that she would never waver in her loyalty to her own people? All his other conjectures, though, were accurate and showed him as a man of shrewdness and understanding. Yet there were so many issues on which they could never see eye to eye.

She sighed again and dabbed at her brow with her wrist.

Perhaps it *would* be possible to let Alex Stalker rest quiet, for Lamont's trouble-maker to remain a trouble-maker and her hero a hero.

She turned back to the room.

'Our house would be safe? You'd promise that?'

'For the duration of your employment, yes.'

'How long have I got to make up my mind?'

'I'd like your answer now, please.'

'I need some time to think it over.'

'Why?'

Mirrin shook her head, freeing the bunch of soft dark hair from under her overcoat collar.

'I need the job badly, Mr Lamont, but I don't quite trust you.'

Lamont nodded, not apparently put out by her frankness.

'I'll give you one day, Miss Stalker. One day, that's all. I must have a decision by noon tomorrow.'

'Very well, sir,' Mirrin said.

*

From the mansion's doorway Houston Lamont watched the young woman make her way briskly down the avenue of washed pebbles. Once, her heel turned on the loose surface and she stumbled and regained her balance with an irritable toss of her head which indicated that she was fully aware of his attention.

The overcoat was trim-fitting on her full figure. The cut of it suited her build, though no woman of his acquaintance would have ventured out in serge material on such a day as this. The coat, of course, was kirk garb, as much a symbol of respect and gravity as a herald's plume. It was wrong of him to criticize, even privately, the mores of folk whose natures he did not *quite* understand.

Edith viewed the miners' families as landed gentry regarded game birds – useful adjuncts to the income, valuable but dispensable. He too had been conditioned to regard them collectively, and recalled his father's dicta that the colliers' unity was both their strength and their weakness, that there were just too damned many of them and not enough willing to shoulder responsibility for their own conditions.

But his father's simplifications were erroneous, taking no account of the tides of circumstance or the individual characteristics of the men and women whom he employed. Alex Stalker, for example, the young woman's father, had had more wit than many a Queen's Bench Lord, more fire in his belly than a taproom full of agents, traders and their slyly humble clerks.

The girl entered the mouth of the tunnel under the oaks. Her drab overcoat was absorbed into the charred paths of shadow which the boughs and leaves made. He lost sight of her.

Closing the door he made his way to his study at the rear of the house.

On the littered desk stood a railed tray of decanters containing whisky, brandy and port, the bottles balancing the coal-oil lamp on the adjacent wing, like lighthouses across a channel of paperwork.

Behind the desk the tall windows opened to a cool enclosure of rye grass which, on his instructions, was not shorn down but left to ripple in the wind and give shelter to dormice and hares and small creatures from the woods. The kitchen cats had good hunting there and often of a night he would listen to the dolorous wails of their mating songs and the fierce wild snarling of their scraps.

He seated himself in the creaking leather chair behind the desk and debated whether it was too early in the day to quench his thirst with an alcoholic beverage. He decided that it was too early and, having little enough taste for spirits, reached back and tugged the bell-pull to summon Annie from the kitchen to fetch him a pot of tea.

The tall, coffin-like grandfather clock, made by Brighouse of Halifax, ticked loudly in the silence.

On the clock's face were two tiny tin miners who, on the stroke of the hour, swung their pickaxes in jerky unison while a sma' barrow, also of painted tin, travelled on a wire round the crown of the dial. He had never liked the piece, but Edith found it 'amusing'.

Until that moment he had not seriously considered Edith's possible reactions to an unexpected addition to her household staff. She would be surprised and probably disquieted, at least until the girl had proved herself capable of performing her duties. It did not occur to Houston Lamont that his wife would be made uneasy by the fact that she would be contrasted daily with a woman less than half her age and with twice her capacity for enjoyment of living.

He did not harbour any doubts that Mirrin Stalker would accept his offer. She was in no position to refuse. The assurance brought him a sense of satisfaction which he neglected to analyse fully. She was an attractive lass : a shade fiery, perhaps, but spirit was always preferable to insipidity. He was weary of Edith's choice of staff : tired, shabby, ugly little things without a brain in their heads, who crept about the house in terror of being spoken to, as if he was an ogre who ate servants instead of chops for breakfast every morning.

For all that good domestic positions were scarce in the county, it seemed that he could not keep servants for any length of time, though he paid them as much as any Edinburgh merchant and did not starve them.

As if to personify his thoughts, Annie knocked.

'Enter,' he said, automatically.

She stood by the door.

It was difficult to think of her as a child, a mere thirteen years old. She did not even look at him but kept her eyes glued to the carpet a yard in front of him, her thin, bloodless lips pinched nervously together.

From observation, he knew that not all young girls in Blacklaw were as puny as Annie. Though dog-labour at the pits and the hardships of home-making and child-bearing tended to age them early, there were many strong, healthy females in the region.

'You're leaving us, then, Annie?'

'Aye, sir.'

'Do you intend to travel far?'

'M'mither an' me are goin' t'Ayr, sir.'

'Do you have relatives there?'

'M'uncle's a shoe-mender. He'll take us in for a whiles, 'til we can find work.'

Odd, thought Lamont, how a single spark deep under the earth could so thoroughly blast away the foundations of folks' lives. The roots of two or three generations had been effectively stunted. Annie and her mother and brother had probably dwelled under one of his roofs all of their lives. Now they were on the footpath to vagrancy, setting out in search of a lost security which, God knows, had been frail enough in the first place.

How precarious an existence they eked out, his colliers – or was their condition evidence of a flaw in the mineral of the human soul, the erosion of weakness, fear and despair? After all, was his life so much better, so much more secure?

On sudden impulse, he drew open the lowest drawer of the desk pedestal, reached into its rear compartment and, with a key from his watch-fob ring, opened a stout green metal cashbox. From it, he removed a sovereign and held it out across the desk between finger and thumb.

Dumbly, without comprehension, Annie blinked at the coin.

'Take it,' Lamont said.

'What . . . what for, sir?'

'As a token of your good service.'

'But . . . Mr Lamont . . .'

161

'Come, Annie, I'm waiting for my pot of tea: now take the sovereign and put it away safe. Don't tell anyone, except your mother. It will aid your journey and give you something to spend in Ayr. Come.'

Hesitant and unsure, Annie approached the desk and stood staring at the large round coin.

'Here, damn' it, take it.'

Impatiently, gruffly, Lamont thrust it into her hand.

'See me before you leave on Friday week,' he said. 'I will furnish you with a letter of recommendation which you will keep by you in case you ever wish to apply for another domestic post.'

'Oh ... sir!'

'Now, off with you, and fetch my tea.'

'Oh, Mr Lamont, sir!'

'Be quick about it.'

'Aye, sir.'

Expressing her gratitude in a sudden flood of tears, Annie scuttled out of the study, leaving the door ajar behind her.

Houston Lamont sat back and linked his fingers behind his head. The generous gesture should have made him feel self-satisfied, but it did not.

The open drawer and cashbox were too potent a reminder of the irrationality of his impulse, and he could not relax in the knowledge of his charity. Stooping, he locked up the reserve, and closed the drawer with his boot heel.

He could not understand why he had given the child a sovereign: a shilling would have been quite sufficient.

It did not strike him until many months later that Mirrin Stalker's influence had already begun to make itself felt in his house and in his heart.

*

Mirrin wakened from shallow sleep and lay listening to Kate's soft snoring from the pillow beside her. She could see nothing of her sister save a few wisps of hair, and the sound had a weird disembodied quality which, in the first instant of wakening, frightened her a little and caused her to prop herself up immediately on her elbow.

Kate's face was slack and lumpy but comfortingly familiar, and Mirrin sank back against the bolster, rubbing her tired eyes with her thumbs.

Outside, the starlings were already twittering and the paper blind had taken on the speckled grey pallor which signified dawn.

In the long cot in the corner, Betsy lay on her back, her profile as fine as porcelain in the gelid light and her breathing a gentle, ladylike purr which only a spiteful rival would have dared define as a snore.

Drew was upstairs, all alone in the attic room, like a young anchorite to whom the luxury of solitude had been granted as a sacred right.

Flora Stalker had the kitchen bed to herself, the coolest berth in the summer and the warmest in winter. Of course, she had protested, but Kate had been adamant that their mother's comfort was their prime concern now that Alex was gone.

It had been a short night for all the Stalkers, the twins excepted. Long after the youngsters had been packed off to bed, the sisters and their mother had huddled round the grate in anxious discussion of Houston Lamont's startling proposition.

Worn out by indecision, Mirrin went over the principal points of the argument again, seeking, even now, a kernel of advice which might sway her away from acceptance of the housekeeper's post.

'But they've never had a housekeeper before,' her mother said. 'There was Alice Scott for a while t'do the cooking, and some bits of lassies for the scrubbing an' the washing an' the polishing. When they left, McVane's wife was in the job for a year while old McVane was working' away down in Durham. Then there was Peggy Blyth and her old sister, just the two of them t'run yon big place...'

'Annie's quitting next week,' Mirrin had interrupted. 'Who does that leave still there?'

'Nelly Burns in the kitchen, an' the McCormick cousins,' Flora had promptly answered.

'Three good reasons for Lamont wanting a change,' Mirrin had remarked.

'Do you really want to take the job?' Kate had asked.

'I'm not sure.'

'Working for Houston Lamont at the pit is one thing,' Flora had said, sourly, 'an' working in his house is another. I'm not keen for you to go there, Mirrin.'

'If I don't, we'll be flung out on the street, like the others,' Mirrin had said. 'We'll have to find another house, then what'll happen to Drew an' all Da's grand plans for him?'

'What'll folk say about a daughter of Alex Stalker rubbing shoulders with the likes of Houston Lamont?'

'They can say what they like,' Mirrin had retorted. 'That's no reason for cutting our own throats.'

'You do want t'take it,' Kate had said.

'Aye, it's the sane thing t'do,' Mirrin had admitted. 'But I can't help feeling that there's something at the back of it all, something that'll benefit Lamont.'

'What could it be?'

'I can't pin it down, Kate.'

Flora Stalker had snorted contemptuously, and Mirrin had been all too aware of the implications in her mother's mind.

'Well,' Mirrin had said, 'he's as good as told me he wants me where he can keep his eye on me; but I don't give much credit to that story. A coalmaster's not worried about the bother a chit of a girl like me could cause, not even if I am Alex Stalker's daughter.'

'Perhaps he's wanting you to keep him informed of what's happening among the men,' Kate had suggested.

'Aye, that was mentioned too,' Mirrin had said. 'I told him straight out he'd never manage to make a spy of me.'

'There's no sayin' what he'll manage to make out of you,' Flora had remarked.

'Mother!'

'Do you think that's it, Mirrin?' Kate had asked.

'No,' Mirrin had quickly replied. 'Lamont's not like that at all. He's a master born an' bred an' he'd hang himself before he'd lose dignity over a collier's lass.'

Flora Stalker had uttered a derisive 'Huh!' and took no further part in the conversation, glowering sulkily into the embers of the fire as they waned and fell cold into the ash-pan.

For an hour or more after, Kate and Mirrin had debated the situation and studied it from every angle, until at length Kate could not stifle her yawns.

'What will you tell him tomorrow?' Kate had said.

'I still can't decide.'

'Well, whatever it is,' Kate had said, reassuringly, 'I'm sure you'll know exactly what you're doing.'

'Aye!' Flora Stalker had the last word. 'She'll know what she's doing, the way a mouse knows when it runs out in front of the cat.'

'I'll sleep on it,' Mirrin had said.

Now she had slept on it, and common sense had not provided an answer during the short hours of darkness. She was as un-certain as she had been yesterday and all last night. For all that, her indecision was not honest and did not lie close to her heart. Her nerves were tingling with excitement, and her instinct had already driven her to a choice which her logical mind would not quite accept.

She let her gaze stray over the room, from the window to the damp stain on the ceiling, to the cupboard door with its row of skirts and scarves hanging from nails, to Kate's plain features drugged with sleep, and to pretty, vain little Betsy's curls on the pillow.

She had seen all this a thousand times before and would see it all again, no doubt – but never quite in the same light.

Suddenly she knew that she must take the position in Houston Lamont's grand house.

Must: must: must.

Even a temporary exposure to a manner of living so vastly different from her own could not fail to have an effect on her. With startling clarity she realized that she hungered for change, craved it with every fibre of her being; the second half of 1875 must be made more fruitful than the first.

She swung herself soundlessly from the bed, gathered her best clothes from the hooks and the chair and crept out of the bedroom.

In a dark corner of the kitchen, hidden from the alcove bed in which her mother slept, Mirrin dressed and combed her hair, then quickly, silently and resolutely left the collier's cramped cottage to climb the long path to the house behind the oaks.

2

'Kate, I'm scared.'

Kate turned sideways on the bench and peered into her brother's face. Save for the constriction and paling of the skin around his mouth, he did not appear apprehensive; but then Drew had long had the knack of concealing his feelings behind a diffident mask which all the family, including her father, had found disconcertingly precocious. Dressed now in his neatest, newest clothes, shiny, round-ended collar and all, with his face scrubbed and his hair slicked down with a sprinkling of Betsy's precious toilet water, he seemed far too adult and composed to be undergoing torments of anxiety. His complexion was unmarked by adolescent pimples and his beard did not sprout a comical down as with the other lads of his generation; it was hardly evident at all except as a darkening on the chin and upper lip. Kate had long ago lost the habit of regarding Drew as a child, in need of her care and understanding.

'Scared of the dominie who's been your teacher for so long a while?' she said, smiling. 'I thought you'd be past that.'

'I'm not scared of Guthrie in the ordinary way,' said Drew. 'I'm afraid he won't be able to help me, that I won't make it to the university.'

'It means a lot to you, doesn't it?'

'It means *everything*.'

'Calm yourself, love,' Kate said, a little startled by his vehemence. 'It'll be all right; you'll see.'

Their voices echoed in the bleak, narrow corridor which separated the classroom areas and, by a series of right-angled corners, penned out the headmaster's study – the dominie's parlour, as it was commonly called – from the droning, chanting herd. The illusion of privacy in term-time was totally false, as every pupil who had ever trembled before the dominie's desk realized; the parlour lay centre to currents of sound from all quarters of the school and, huddled at the root of the tower, vibrated regularly to the clang of the clock and the tolling of the bell. The miracle was that Dominie Guthrie had not gone deaf years ago.

From the 'culprit's bench', however, the only view was to the parlour door, a relic of a former age, battened with iron bands, rivets and knobbly bolts like the siege gate of a castle keep. As a waggish jest at the expense of his impressionable charges the dominie saw to it that the door was regularly painted black. Memories of that door, just as funereal and awesome now as in her day, moved Kate to empathy with her brother. She slid her arm along the benchback and administered a comforting hug.

'Wheesh now,' she whispered. 'We don't want to disturb Mr Guthrie and the Officer from Hamilton. Sit quiet and don't worry. I'm sure it'll work out just fine.'

For once Drew did not evade the gesture of sisterly affection, even inclined himself an inch or two closer. He sat stiffly against her, his fingers clenching his knees, listening to the dull, monotonous murmur of the men's voices in the unnatural evening stillness, trying, and failing, to make out the substance of their discussion.

In herself, Kate was confident. Since the tenancy of their home had been re-secured, she had taken stock of the future with fresh heart. The long hours of labour at the pit-head troughs caused her no concern at all: she was well used to work. With her mother in command of the household routines and doing a bit of sewing in the evenings, and with Mirrin also earning, it seemed as if the improbable dream which Alex Stalker had willed to her might be transformed into a reality after all.

The only cloud presently on the horizon was not in Mr Guthrie's pronouncement on Drew's capabilities but had to do with Mirrin's role as Lamont's housekeeper.

For the first day or two, Flora Stalker had descended into a deep, brooding sulk, the like of which Kate had never encountered in her mother before. This in-turned anger was perhaps due to the wounds she had suffered over the loss of her sons and husband, or simply the result of the encroachment of the years. More and more, the big, stolid woman met reverses with a hurt and sullen silence, not, as before, with frank and honest temper.

After the mood had passed, Flora was voluble enough and had given Mirrin a piece of her mind, nagging the girl persistently and without real reason until Mirrin had rebelled and raged back. After the outburst, the women had declared a truce and Flora had even shown some signs of curiosity as to what went on in the coalmaster's house, though she was careful not to capitulate too readily.

As the weeks passed, however, Kate found herself becoming more uneasy, possessed of the suspicion that trouble was brewing, though she could not begin to guess at its nature or direction. All she knew was that putting Mirrin in Lamont's household was like waving a lit taper close to a pocket of gas. She prayed that the explosion would be long enough delayed to see Drew out of Blacklaw and settled to his legal studies in Edinburgh.

The voices grew louder on the other side of the parlour door and the handle rattled and dipped. Kate gave a final encouraging hug to her brother and withdrew her arm.

The Representative Officer of the Parish Schools Committee of Hamilton and District had a physique as stern and imposing as his official appellation. He was massively tall and barrel-chested. A swart spade-beard covered his cravat. He walked with his lum-hat in one hand and his other hand thrust under his coat-tails, a stiff, formal pose which – had his secret been known – he had perfected by many private rehearsals before his dressing-room mirror. He cast a single withering glance at the young woman and the boy who had risen from the bench, nodded curtly to Mr Guthrie, and stalked out of the side door into the playground, still with fist on hip and hat in hand.

Mr Forbes Guthrie puffed out his cheeks and let the relief whistle out of him like steam from a kettle. He looked at the rigid figures by the bench, winked, smiled and beckoned them to enter, waiting by the door to close it in their wake.

The study smelled of damp paper, calfskin and tobacco. Mr Guthrie's collection of charred and chipped clay pipes filled several earthenware dishes on shelves and ledges around the walls, dishes which also served as bookends, paperweights and receptacles for pins, chalks, sealing wax, matches, pen-nibs, and wriggly rubber bands.

A stone jar which had once contained one pound net of Reevers' Best Quality Orange Marmalade bristled now with a posy of pencils and penholders. Three glass ink pots on a stained blotting pad caught a mote of sunlight from the upper edge of the frame and cast a rainbow oval of red, green and blue across the open attendance ledgers on the desk.

Mr Guthrie lurked by the square window and watched the parish official pass out of the Infants' gate.

Audibly, the dominie remarked, 'He who discommendeth others obliquely commendeth himself,' then, turning, casually invited Drew to identify the author of the quotation.

Drew swallowed and shook his head.

'Sir Thomas Browne,' said Mr Guthrie. 'A marvellous lad with epigrams but a wee bit of a bore nonetheless.'

Drawing out his chair, he seated himself, slapped the ledgers shut and pushed them aside, leaned on his elbows and peered with disconcerting attention at his visitors.

The passage of years had left few imprints on Dominie Guthrie. He had looked middleaged since his graduation from Glasgow University thirty-odd years before, and his progress from infant master to head of Blacklaw School, through the morass of local and national regulations which had come into force in that period of reform, had served only to increase the wrinkles which webbed his eyes and make his patrician nose a little more gaunt. He had also slipped back into boyish untidiness and each succeeding generation found him just a shade more dishevelled in habit and environs than its predecessor. This carelessness disguised a brain which had become proportionally more perceptive and astute as he grew older and more acrimoniously disposed towards the strictures of the bodies who governed him from afar.

'Kate, isn't it?'

'Yes, Mr Guthrie.'

His eyes were very pale, like mother-of-pearl buttons.

'Well, what can I do for you?'

A discreet nudge from Drew forced Kate to collect herself and embark on the matter which had brought her.

'It was my father's wish, Dominie, that my brother here should find a place at the university and undertake the studies which would make him int' a lawyer.'

The phrases were stilted and she had spoken them as correctly as her tongue could manage, sounding false and affected as a result. The dominie, the doctor and the minister were used to this strained form of address which occasionally reached heights of verbosity close to unintelligibility. Dominie Guthrie made no attempt to correct the young woman, or to hurry her along.

'You'll know the procedures for such a course,' Kate went on, 'an' we hoped you'd see your way to giving us the boon of your advice.'

'The . . . ah, the boon of my advice, Kate.' Guthrie stroked his nose, which was perhaps why it had sharpened over the years, and considered his reply.

Drew's rigidity was palpable and on the verge of causing him tremors.

'Make Drew a lawyer,' said the dominie at length. 'That's a tall order, Kate Stalker, a very tall order, indeed.'

'What do you advise, Mr Guthrie?' the young woman inquired.

'I'll admit that your father's ambition for his son is highly praiseworthy but . . .' Guthrie hesitated. 'But, Kate, my advice is to put the idea firmly out of your head.'

'But why, sir?' Drew blurted out.

'Because it's impractical : it can't be done.'

'Why can't it be done?' Drew demanded.

'That's enough, Drew,' Kate reprimanded.

The dominie checked her, and addressed himself to Drew, fixing the boy genially with his eye. 'You're disappointed?'

'Yes, Mr Guthrie.'

'Ah, well, you're a bright lad, Stalker, and you shouldn't have associated yourself with such a singular idea in the first place; though I suspect your father must take a wee share of the blame for that.'

171

'But what's to . . . ?'

The pale gaze hardened perceptibly and Drew obediently closed his mouth.

'I've always been impressed by your intelligence, Stalker, and by your appetite for work. You've a stability in you which is at variance with your . . . ah, less responsible contemporaries. I'll tell you what I'll do; I've heard that Mr Crawford, the executive manager up at Northrigg, is on the look-out for a suitable young chap to train as a clerk. It's a foot on the ladder to a manager's job, if you apply yourself diligently. I'd have no hesitation in recommending you for . . .'

'I don't want to be a clerk: I want to study law.'

'Drew, don't talk to Mr Guthrie . . .'

'No, Kate, let the lad have his say.'

Drew pulled back his stooped shoulders and straightened himself until he seemed as tall as the dominie himself. He was pale as tallow and his eyes had widened dangerously, and yet his voice was as grave and steady and controlled as a kirk elder's.

'I've studied hard, Mr Guthrie,' he declared. 'My father forced me to it at first, but for a year or more now I've buckled down because I understood the sense in it. I'm not cut out for a pit job, not even a manager's job. I thank you for your offer, though, sir, and I'm grateful for your interest.'

'But you won't even consider it?'

'Even if my father had never had this idea, I would've wanted more than what's to be had in Blacklaw.'

'More, Stalker? In what way, more?'

'I don't mean money, Mr Guthrie. I mean more . . . more opportunity.'

'Many lads of your age cant on about "opportunity".'

'Aye, Dominie, but how many are willing to do something about finding it?'

The schoolmaster's eyes crinkled, not with mirth, but speculatively, as if he was weighing up the experiences which had lifted the boy to such a level of perspicacity.

'Will you, at least, tell me what I'd have to do?' Drew went on. 'Do I have to apply for entrance to a university, or will I be needing special classes?'

'What age are you?'

'I'll be fifteen in a month.'

'You'd have a year to work for the examination,' Mr Guthrie said. 'There would be an examination, a stiff one. You'd need tutoring.'

'Would you tutor me, sir?'

Kate almost intervened: she felt that her brother had discarded respect for his headmaster and had strayed into impertinence. The dominie, however, forestalled her interruption by holding up his hand, though his gaze did not for an instant leave the boy's face. Drew did not flinch. To Kate, it was like watching a stranger perform some strange ceremony, a legal ritual, cold and verbal and astonishingly mature.

'What if I say no?' the dominie asked.

'Then, sir, I'd make my own way to Edinburgh and find a job, any sort of job – emptying slops in a pub if I could do no better – and I would earn enough to pay for the necessary lessons and find a cheap tutor to make me proficient in the subjects and I would, *somehow*, contrive to become a law student.'

'You could apprentice yourself to a law firm?'

'That's only another sort of clerking.'

'True,' Guthrie admitted. 'However, your other plan – doing it on your own – is admirable in theory but would never work in practice.'

Kate said, 'We ... we have some money saved.'

'Have you the faintest idea of the costs of this venture?' the dominie asked.

Kate shook her head.

'Or how long it takes?'

'Five years,' Drew said.

'Or how much grinding, blinding work is involved?'

'I'll work,' Drew said.

'An' we'll meet the costs,' said Kate. 'However much it takes, we'd see to that side of it.'

The dominie pursed his lips.

He honed his nose with forefinger and thumb.

He looked away from them and surveyed the racks and

shelves of books around the walls for two or three minutes, running his eye along the titles. In that agonizing pause, neither Kate nor Drew moved: they sat before the shabby, middle aged man as if mesmerized.

At length the dominie blinked, stroked his hand over his thinning hair, making it more spiky and unruly, and almost petulantly declared, 'All right, Stalker, if that's the way of it. I still have grave doubts as to the wisdom and the outcome of such a course, but you're so *damned* ... pardon me, Miss Stalker ... you're so devilishly determined that I will undertake to tutor you for a preparatory examination.'

'An entry exam?' said Drew.

'The entrance examination for Edinburgh University, aye,' the dominie replied; sarcastically adding, 'would you have it in writing, sealed by a notary?'

Drew sank gradually back, slouching against the chair.

Kate leapt to her feet, eyes shining and cheeks rubicund with delight. 'Oh, Mr Guthrie, how can I thank you? If you only knew what it means t'us all, an' what it would've meant t'my father.'

'If the plan comes to grief,' Mr Guthrie said, 'I trust that you won't blame me.' He stood up and clapped his hands as if to call a rowdy class to attention. 'Now, I wish to state the terms of our agreement. I will give you, Stalker, a full course in Latin and Greek, starting from scratch. In addition to the major subjects, you will be expected to increase your proficiency in Mathematics, History, and the elements of English Grammar. We will work in the evening, at times suitable to me, and you will make yourself available at those times; not less than six hours per week, beginning on Thursday evening at seven o'clock. At the end of each period I will set work which you will complete in time for correction at our next class.'

Drew had risen too now, and was nodding solemnly. His splenetic tension had been replaced by ardour, a hungry concentration on every word which passed from the dominie's lips.

'The fee for my services,' said Mr Guthrie, raising his voice a little, 'will be two shillings per week, paid in advance, please.'

'I can pay you now, sir,' said Kate, eagerly.

'No, no, no, no,' said Mr Guthrie, embarrassed by his own mendicity. 'Bring it along on Thursday, Drew.'

'I just don't know what t'say, Mr Guthrie,' Kate told him, beaming.

'Thank you, sir,' said Drew quietly.

'Aye, well, I hope you still have cause to thank me a year hence,' said the pessimist in Mr Guthrie's bosom.

*

They walked out together by the main door into the playground. Now that her initial elation was over, Kate was overwhelmed by the enormity of the task that Drew had taken upon himself. Latin, Greek, Mathematics: and the dominie had not really given them hope, in spite of his proffered assistance. She knew enough of the man to be sure that he would put everything he had into the lessons and would not stint encouragement and advice: but still – he thought it would come to nothing in the long run. That tacit opinion disturbed Kate and made her wonder again at the prudence of pushing on into the hardships and economies of the winter ahead all for the sake of a promise to a dying man.

'Drew,' she said quietly, 'what d'you think?'

The boy did not answer immediately.

He was staring out over the low schoolyard wall to the rising ground beyond Poulter's burn, where the gap left by the chestnut tree still seemed to cause an imbalance in the landscape, and the hole – deep enough for a man to stand up in – had not quite healed over with the summer's growths.

Believing that he was brooding and melancholy, Kate slipped an arm through his and tried to hug him again. This time he would have none of it and discreetly disengaged his elbow.

'Your Daddy would be proud of you, Drew,' Kate said.

'Not yet,' said her brother. 'Anyhow, it's too late for him.'

'Perhaps, he'll . . . know.'

'I don't believe that nonsense,' Drew said. 'It doesn't matter, anyhow.'

'What doesn't matter?'

'The past.'

'It's the past that makes us all what we are,' said Kate. 'You'd do well to remember that, love, in the months to come.'

'No, I think I'd do better to remember that it's the present as makes the future.'

'Away with you, Drew Stalker,' said Kate, trying to restore some jollity to the occasion. 'Don't try your twisty arguments on me.'

Drew laughed.

'At least we talked old Guthrie out of putting me into the Northrigg clerking job,' he said. 'You know, it's just as well I planned on studying law, not theology or ... or music, or somethin'.'

'Och, we'd have found another tutor if that had been your bent.'

'But Guthrie was right, Kate,' Drew said. 'It's a harebrained impractical sort of idea. If he hadn't once wanted t'be a lawyer himself ...'

'Who? The dominie?' Kate said in surprise.

'Years ago, when he was young,' Drew said. 'It was the law that called him, too. But he never succeeded.'

'How d'you know all this, Drew: did he tell you?'

'Not him,' the boy replied. 'Da told me.'

'When?'

'A wee while before he died.'

'You should've said.'

'No need,' Drew explained. 'But it was a help today. You just have t'look at the books on Guthrie's shelves to see for yourself.'

'I never noticed.'

'He sent me to the parlour for chalk one day an' I took a quick squint round.'

'That wasn't right, Drew.'

'There was no harm in it,' the boy said. 'He's got all those bashed old law books stacked up on the top shelf, covered in dust. Inside one of them, it says – "To my beloved son, Forbes, on the occasion of his acceptance into the Faculty of Law of the University of Glasgow, this year of 1836." That's what it says.'

'I wonder what happened?' Kate mused.

They were out of the playground now and walking along the narrow lane by the kirkyard wall heading for the path by the backs of the houses. The summer night was still and fragrant and the sun still winey across the farmlands and the stooped hills away towards the Lothians.

Drew chopped at the purple heads of a clump of flame weed which flourished beside the verge.

'I expect he failed,' he said.

'The dominie failed?'

Drew shrugged and glanced back at her, his left hand full of the stalks and heads of the bright, tousled weed.

'That's why he'll help me all he can,' the boy said. 'But it's also why he doesn't like me very much.'

'You're imaginin' things, Drew Stalker.'

'Perhaps,' Drew said. 'But, you see, he knows I'll do it. He knows fine well that, with or without his help, I won't fail.'

'Sometimes . . .' Kate began, but he grinned at her, and she discarded most of what he had said as boastful blethers.

'Run on ahead,' she said, 'an' tell Mam t'put the kettle on.'

'Right.'

He tossed the bunch of weeds aside and, taking to his heels, ran swiftly ahead of her, around the corner behind the backs.

Kate lifted the tattered flowering weeds and arranged them into a little posy to carry home for the jar in the bedroom. She was bewildered now and devoid of the jubilation which the dominie's generous offer had brought her not ten minutes ago.

Drew had that effect on her. His confidence was inherited from his father. James had had it in small measure, and Mirrin was full of it. But the quality of Mirrin's self-assurance was gentler and more kindly, though often maddeningly frank. With Drew, recklessness and kindliness had been melted down and beaten out thin by the wheels of his ambition. As the dominie had remarked, her father was really responsible for this trait in his youngest son, and Alex was no longer there to guide the boy. All that was left to Drew was Alex's legacy of single-mindedness, aimed at one purpose.

She never doubted Drew when he proclaimed his intentions

forthrightly, but, for all her belief in him, it shamed her that he should treat Mr Guthrie with such arrogance and contempt.

The lessons would be good for her brother in more ways than one. The dominie's ability to shape decent young men was more proven than his ability to make a lawyer out of a collier's son.

However it turned out a year hence, Kate reckoned that the two shillings paid out each week would be money well spent.

3

'There!'

Mirrin sagged against the broad end of the kitchen dresser and, flushed and profusely sweating, fanned her face with her hand. She was stripped to a bodice and petticoat, her bare feet black with dust from the unscrubbed regions of the stone-flagged floor which the shifting of the massive dresser had exposed.

The shorter of the girls who had assisted in the major task of haulage was also scarlet-cheeked with effort, though she was more decorously and less comfortably dressed.

'Mirrin Stalker,' she tittered, 'you should see what y'look like.'

'No, thanks.' Mirrin shook her damp hair back from her brow. 'Right now I've no inclination t'admire myself – beautiful though I am. So stop snitterin', Mattie, an' hand me a towel.'

'Have we finished then?' asked young Mattie hopefully.

'Now that we've made a start,' said Mirrin, 'we'll just see what else could do with rearrangin'.'

Mattie groaned.

Towel in hand, Mirrin mopped her neck and shoulders and thrust a corner of the material down between her breasts which swelled well above the rucked edge of her bodice.

'Do you not think that's more convenient, Mrs Burns?' Mirrin waved the towel in the direction of the dresser. 'Will it not be much easier to reach your crocks and pots now?'

Mrs Burns sniffed.

'I liked it fine where it was.'

Mrs Burns was a stout, bulbous-nosed woman in her mid forties. She had been married once to a sergeant in the 21st Regiment of the Royal Scots Fusiliers but he had died twenty-one years ago, only a few months after taking a bride, run through by a Russian bayonet in the fogs of Inkerman in the far-off Crimea. Since then Mrs Burns had remained defiantly widowed, flaunting her rusty weeds and speaking frequently of 'her Hector' and how handsome he looked in his bearskin cap and crimson sash, though the truth was that she could now only remember the uniform and not the man at all.

'But,' said Mirrin, 'you could hardly see there in yon dark corner.'

Mrs Burns tucked her fists under her cook's apron. 'Maybe – but upstairs would not have approved of the likes of me duntin' their furniture about.'

'Aye, but if you'd ladled sugar instead of salt into the porridge some mornin' they might just have decided t'dunt you right out the door.'

'Well, it's done now.' Mrs Burns withdrew from the argument.

'An' the better for it,' said Mirrin.

The cook took three deliberate steps back from the long spotless iron stove, slapped her palm experimentally on the workledge of the dresser, and walked back.

Though the woman gave no sign of approval, Mirrin sensed her pleasure at the simple reorganization of her kitchen furniture. The big dresser, where the everyday utensils and foodstuffs were ranked on open shelves, was now ready to hand, a turn and step from the cooking range and brightly lit by the lamp hooked to the main beam overhead. It had been as sensible an adjustment as she had yet made, and she had made several. Perhaps she *should* have asked permission but it was probable that Mrs Edith, out of spite, would have refused. As it was, it might be weeks before the mistress of the house as much as noticed the change.

'I'll say this,' Mrs Burns remarked, 'you're not a shirker, Mirrin Stalker, not above rollin' up your sleeves like some better-bred housekeepers I've known in my time.'

Mirrin hitched up her petticoat and flicked the towel at her ankles and shins. She had changed in the past weeks, had shed seven or eight pounds in weight for one thing, so that the planes of her face were sharper and her petticoat hung more smoothly over her hips and thighs. Then too, she was happy, happier than she had been since she had left the safety of the school. The variety of chores checked any fear of boredom, and regular routines gave her established points through which to navigate her day. She also took pleasure in the innovations she had made which had resulted in better service for the family and a lightening of work for the servants.

There would soon come a time, however, when all that was done and she would be obliged to start work in earnest on herself, to set about the difficult business of acquiring poise and discretion such as befitted the housekeeper of a largish establishment.

Mirrin had no notion of how long this process might take and had put it to the very back of her mind until the mechanics of running the household had been mastered. Indeed, if it had not been for Edith Lamont, she would never have contemplated the need for self-improvement at all. Try as she would, Lamont's wife could find little fault with Mirrin's 'new-broom' policies and had so far criticized her only on rights and wrongs of manners and fashions and proper attitudes to her superiors, demanding – unfairly – everything at once from her unwanted employee.

The house, or mansion – the term of reference varied according to the status of the speaker – was managed by a peculiar hotchpotch of styles and customs. Some were borrowed from the housekeeping manuals, others dithered along in the traditional lackadaisical patterns, fostered by Lamont's grandmother, who had been a manager's daughter and not quite up to scratch socially.

In spite of its apparent size there were only a dozen rooms within the house itself. None of them were particularly imposing – according to Mrs Burns, who had had much experience in Glasgow 'cooking for the very best folk'. Why the cook had ever left the plush pastures of the city to take up this provincial position, Mirrin never did discover.

In addition to the cook, who had a comfortable basement room all to herself in the warm warren behind the stoves and boilers, the McCormick cousins were the only other resident servants within the house itself. Lamont had never 'risen' to a butler or footman, in spite of Edith's occasional hints. The cousins' chamber was a garret high under the eaves of the west wing, over the tomb-like room which had once been a nursery.

So far no arrangement had been made regarding Mirrin's residence, and she finished each night at nine and tramped back down to the family house in Main Street. She knew that very soon she would be obliged to take up residence on the premises, that even the most casual of housekeepers was expected to be on call at the end of a bell-wire twenty-four hours each day and for six and one half days in the week. To do less would not be proper, and Mirrin, unwittingly, had become considerably interested in doing that which was right according to the genteel traditions outlined by the expert, Mrs Burns.

The aged groom and lame boy who cared for Lamont's four horses and three carriages lived in an attic over the stable court. The gardener was even older than the groom. He had come down from the Isle of Lewis fifty years ago and still spoke English reluctantly and with a correctness which the dominie himself might have envied. He was responsible only for the plots which supplied the house with fresh fruit and vegetables. Though his name linked him to the great musical family of the north-west, Pibroch McCrimmond was no piper. He lived as shy as a hermit in a ramshackle lean-to hut in the wilderness beyond the dry-stone wall, with only two blind collies for company. It seemed to Mirrin that McCrimmond performed his arts by incantation, for he was seldom to be seen about the rows and bushes. His sole communication with the house came in the form of great wicker baskets brimful of carrots, turnips, cabbages, peas, apples, rasps, currants, and other succulent seasonal fare, which appeared daily on the stoup of the kitchen door.

Casual day labour, in the shape of wheezy old miners, tended the lawns and flowerbeds. Considering that they were grossly underpaid and totally ignored, they kept the grounds of the miniature estate remarkably spick and span.

Annie's position as an upstairs maid and general servant to the family had not been filled after the girl's departure. The duties of attending to the wants of the master and mistress had been equally divided between the two complaining cousins who, until then, had kept well out of the Lamonts' sight.

All in all, Mirrin soon came to appreciate the force of Mrs Burns's pronouncement that Lamont's house was 'neither one thing nor much of t'other'. Edith Lamont's struggle to pattern her home on the Edinburgh model failed dismally because of her husband's indifference and her own inability to coax experienced domestic staff away from the respectable middle-class citadels of Glasgow where openings were fairly plentiful and servants had quite a tightly-knit community of their own.

But there was more to it than that, a more subtle reason than the makeshift gentility of the place.

Mirrin had felt it already and an instinct told her that even child-like maids like Annie must have been aware of the pre-vailing atmosphere of bitterness and burgeoning hatred which tainted the air like a bad smell.

Servants, no matter how ignorant or how desperate for employment, could not long endure that contagious morbidity.

What the house needed was not more and better servants, but a bit of laughter about it, occupants for its shrouded guest-rooms, and children to run over its tidy lawns and slide shriek-ing on the polished floors of its hall and corridors.

All that space wasted, all that nourishing food spent on two sad people, all that green sweet grass and the gaudy perfumed flowers – the contrast with the cramped homes of the colliers was almost too much for Mirrin to bear, even though she now had a share of the coalmaster's luxuries for herself. Ach, and they didn't even have enough sense to shift a dresser in the kitchen to make life just an iota better for the poor cook!

'Mirrin, had you not better put somethin' on: you're half unclad like that.'

Hannah McCormick had sidled up beside her and spoke in an urgent, outraged hiss as if she had just entered the room and discovered Mirrin's state of dress.

It was typical of Hannah to feign dreadful offence, while peeping enviously down her bodice at her full breasts. If Hannah ever graduated to the august rank of housekeeper, God help the poor scullions under her charge.

The McCormick girls did not hail from Blacklaw. Their home was a tiny hamlet clustered round a brickwork near Carron, thirty miles away. Just at first Mirrin had had difficulty remembering which cousin was which: the shorter and younger fussed about her chores singing sonorous snatches of *Nearer My God to Thee* like a drowning mariner, while the taller, Hannah, was the true religious fanatic and spent every spare hour in kirk or at a meeting house.

To help her memory, Mirrin had composed a silly wee jingle:

'Hannah, tall, goes to church.
Mattie, short, sings too much.'

If ever they pushed her temper too far she might shock them by reciting it aloud one day.

'I'll dress in a minute,' Mirrin said. 'I'll want the pair of you t'help me shove that broom locker over into the dark corner.'

'Aaaawwww!' whined Mattie. 'What for?'

'So we can put the small table in its place, close by the door, a place for you to rest the breakfast tray, Mattie, while you open the door. Then Mrs Lamont will have no cause t'complain about spillings on the cloth, will she?'

'She'll find somethin' else to moan about, no doubt,' said Mrs Burns.

'If it keeps her happy,' said Mirrin, 'then let her moan away all day: some folk are like that.'

'Meanin' me?' said Mrs Burns, testily.

'*Not* meanin' you,' Mirrin said. 'Come on, girls, let's put our rumps t'this cupboard and shift it over t'the corner.'

Mrs Burns took a step closer to the stove, as if to disassociate herself from the actions of the housekeeper, while Hannah and Mattie, grumbling under their breaths, braced themselves against the squat cupboard.

'Right,' said Mirrin. 'Heave awa', m'hearties.'

Creaking and swaying and grating on the flagstones, the cupboard was duly pushed across the kitchen and aligned with the corner walls. The effort left the girls winded and sore and only Mirrin took sufficient pride in the little achievement to stand and admire the cupboard's new location.

She opened the door several times, testing its clearance, and, in pantomime, took out brooms and shovels and stuck them back in again, smiling as she did so. The whisperings behind her did not distract her attention from her innocent experiments and she did not realize that the cousins and the cook had discreetly abandoned the kitchen to the mistress of the house.

'And why, may I enquire, Miss Stalker, are you parading yourself in my kitchen in a state of undress?'

Mirrin swung round.

In contrast to herself, Edith Lamont was encased in the silks and velours of a fashionable day-dress and its frilly appurtenances. The weight and mass of the fabrics seemed to project her through the doorway on a comber of lavender cloth, and the indignation of her tone was enhanced by a sinister rustling and hissing from the pleats of the dress itself.

Mirrin said, 'Because it's hot an' dirty work, madam.'

She never used the contraction, but enunciated the title in full, even emphasizing the *dee* with her tongue to impart a special drollery to the separate parts of the word. According to the tenor of the confrontation, Mirrin could then make the address either insulting or respectful, and could even ambiguously mix the two.

Mistress and maid had met by design on a half dozen occasions during the weeks of Mirrin's employment; on each occasion Mirrin's dislike and mistrust of the woman increased. They faced each other now like two of the Highland wrestlers who performed at the Hamilton Fair, each sizing up the other's weaknesses and seeking the best point of attack.

Without undue haste, Mirrin reached her blouse and skirt from the chair and buttoned them on.

'My husband is seldom down here,' Edith Lamont said.

The innuendo was not lost on Mirrin, but she ignored it, or rather, reversed it against the enemy.

'I know that, madam, otherwise I wouldn't have taken my stuff off in the first place.'

'You will not do such a thing again,' Edith said, quietly. 'May I remind you that this is a gentleman's residence and not some miners' slum where such lax habits are commonplace.'

Aye, thought Mirrin, the knives were out at last.

Had there been an argument with the coalmaster over her continued captaincy of the domestics? By now, Edith Lamont must have broached the subject of getting rid of such village 'trash'.

Mirrin smiled, and said sweetly, 'I will endeavour to correct my acquaintances in the village, madam, and to train them in less ... "slummy" habits.'

Edith could find no answer to such submissiveness, though the barb struck home. She glanced round the kitchen.

'By whose authority has the furniture been moved?'

'By my authority, madam,' said Mirrin.

'*Your* authority, indeed?'

'Mr Lamont requested me t'attend the welfare of the staff.'

'By causing upheaval?'

'Everything's squared away, madam,' Mirrin explained, using the tone she had once used to Betsy when the girl was only a child and did not understand the simplest things. 'It is so much more handy for Mrs Burns and for the maids this way. As you'll see here.'

A demonstration of the workings of a cupboard door and the placement of pots was not Edith's idea of entertainment and certainly did not feature in her list of wifely duties.

If she had assumed from her husband's report on the new housekeeper's character that she could bait her into an outburst of temper, then she had sadly underestimated Mirrin's intelligence. With every jibe, every snobbish insult, Mirrin's resolve to remain calm and outwardly cooperative received an added boost. Tractability was her most potent weapon at this stage in the contest of wills, and her unctuousness was so patently false that Edith Lamont could not fail to detect the glint of impudence behind it. Any tale which Edith might carry to the master of the house, however, would lack the niceties of inflexion and seem merely petty in the telling.

'Now that you have squandered the morning in the effort, I suppose it had better stay as it is,' Edith Lamont said.

'Yes, madam.'

Edith's gaze now fixed itself on Mirrin's dark and tangled hair.

'In addition to remaining decently dressed,' she said, 'might I also suggest that you wear a cap while engaged upon your household duties. A strong cotton one with an elastic edge may be purchased with your next order to Dalzells'. In fact, in the cause of hygiene, you will dispatch one of the gels to fetch it this afternoon. Purchase two caps against the account. Please see that they are kept scrupulously clean and that you never appear without one.'

'Very well, madam, but ...'

'But?'

'Am I to appear before guests that way, too?'

'Of course.'

'Hmmmmm,' said Mirrin.

Stirring like a small ornamental conifer in a cold blast of wind, Edith Lamont rustled her skirts.

'Do you have an objection?'

'I don't mind at all, madam,' Mirrin said. 'I'm just wonderin' what the guests'll think of us, though.'

The point was rather moot, for the Lamonts entertained only rarely, when the necessity to reciprocate a season's social calls forced them to it. Edith appeared to have forgotten this fact in her urge to unravel the source of the girl's mysterious reluctance to wear a cap, a hesitation which did not seem to have anything to do with shallow vanity.

'The guests?' Edith asked, lightly.

'I wouldn't want them t'think us countrified.'

'*Countrified!*' Edith was shocked. 'What on earth do you mean?'

'Well, according to Lady Peacock's *Cyclopaedia of Domestic Duty, Decorum and Accounts*, only housekeepers of low farmers ever cover their hair – except in kirk, that is.'

'I don't believe you.'

'It's there in black an' white, madam. Mr Lamont gave me the book himself an' told me t'study it up. Lady Peacock says it's quite improper for a housekeeper t'attire herself like an

187

ordinary maid; says it's a vulgarity not t'be tolerated, an' a sign of ... gaucheness – would that be right?'

Edith was tempted to ask the girl to fetch down the volume and show her the reference. On the other hand, she did not imagine that the Stalker girl would be foolish enough to bluff on this question and, now that she thought of it, she could not recall ever having seen a housekeeper with an elasticated cap on before, and certainly not in any of her Edinburgh friends' houses.

The disagreement was not now about vanity or the wearing of a cotton cap: it had to do with social propriety and the establishment of the girl's precise status in the household.

Houston had employed her as a housekeeper and if she was to be presented as such then she would have to conform, to some degree at least, with the fashionably accepted image of a housekeeper. Edith had pressed her husband for several years now to acquire either a butler or a steward to enhance their presentable staff. Houston's solution had been to employ this insolent, ill-bred creature and paste an inappropriate label on her.

Edith considered: the girl had obviously outsmarted her. Compromise was required to save face.

Edith said, 'You will wear a cap below stairs.'

'Just below stairs?'

'Yes.'

'Aye, madam: thank you for your advice.'

A suppressed giggle came from the vault of the still-room, and Edith's mouth closed to a wire-like line.

Mirrin raised her voice.

'Mattie, Hannah, less of that noise: get on with washin' those bottles, like I told you.' She dropped an incomplete curtsey to Edith. 'If you'll pardon me, madam, I'll have t'see that the water's warm enough.'

Edith Lamont inclined her head graciously, though Mirrin knew that she was seething with indignation inside her whalebone stays.

'Very well, Miss Stalker.'

With a slapping motion of her hands to clamp the skirts of the day-dress to her hips, she backed out of the door and closed it behind her, not loudly.

Mirrin noted the restraint, and marked it down for emulation.

She tip-toed to the still-room door and then leapt forward, slithering a little on the damp and soapy stone.

As she suspected, Mattie and Hannah were hugging each other tightly, half doubled over and with their sleeves stuffed into their mouths to hold back laughter. In spite of their fear of Edith Lamont's temper, and their inherent stuffiness, the cousins had at last found something to tickle their funnybones, and Mirrin, while feigning sternness, could not seriously rebuke them for it.

'A . . . a vulgarity not t'be . . . tolerated . . .' Mattie gasped.

'A . . . a . . . a sign of – what's it?' Hannah panted.

From the door behind, Mrs Burns asked, 'Does it really say that in the book, Mirrin?'

'Hmmmm!' Mirrin answered. 'If it doesn't, it should – don't y'think?'

The cousins collapsed once more, and it was quite ten minutes before Mirrin could bring herself to chivvy them back to their chores.

*

'Lady Peacock's *Cyclopaedia*?'

Houston Lamont lowered his paper an inch.

'What of it, my dear?' he said.

'Did you present a copy to the Stalker girl?'

'I did: together with a copy of Beeton's *Household Management*.'

Edith continued with her sewing in silence.

Houston said, 'Has she been discussing the volumes with you?'

'After a fashion.'

'I'm glad that she shows such interest in her work.'

'To my mind, Houston, she is not suitable material for a housekeeper.'

'She is young and totally inexperienced. In time she will acquire proficiency – and some of the airs and graces which seem to be the starch in a housekeeper's composition.'

'I doubt it.'

'You don't like the girl, Edith, do you?'

'She is . . . impudent.'

'Has she given you cheek, then?'

'Obliquely,' said Edith.

'Perhaps you are a little oversensitive,' said Lamont.

'Why do we need a housekeeper?'

'To ease the burden on you, dear.'

'Have you found my housekeeping unsatisfactory?'

'Not at all,' Lamont said. 'But it chains you so.'

'A steward or butler would be more in keeping . . .'

'A man servant of that calibre would have to be brought from Edinburgh or Glasgow and would cost the earth.' Lamont turned the pages of the *Hamilton Advertiser* and settled a little more deeply into his chair.

'But a male servant would be more dignified,' Edith persisted.

'In a quarter, the Stalker girl will be less uncouth; by Christmas she will be presiding like an expert, mark my words,' Lamont said. 'I did not select her at random, you know.'

'No,' said Edith, pointedly. 'I am sure you did not.'

'She is nimble-witted, and keen to learn.'

'And pretty.'

'Certainly prettier than any other servant we have ever had.' Lamont spread the paper on his knee and looked across the drawing-room at his wife.

'Ah,' he said. 'Is that the crux of your complaint?'

Edith plied her fine needle without response.

'If she was ugly would you be less antagonistic?' he asked.

'Are you implying that I'm envious of a collier's brat?'

'Not at all,' said Lamont. 'Why should you envy a mere chit of a girl, who lives in a narrow house among a host of callous-mannered miners?'

Edith laid down the sewing-frame.

'If I asked you to dismiss her, Houston, would you do so?'

'No, my dear, I would not.'

'If she was insubordinate...?'

'I would need proof.'

'My word would not be enough?'

'Edith, I have a use for this girl, an interest in her...'

'I thought as much.'

'Guard your tongue, Edith,' he said.

'You sneaked her in here behind my back...'

'Nonsense!' said Lamont who, though careful to hide it, was rather enjoying his wife's display of female jealousy. He had intended to explain his purpose to her in full and thus allay some of her silly fears, but now he checked himself. Let her think what she liked about his motives. Let her carp and connive against the Stalker girl for a while: it would keep her from becoming bored and from sharpening her tongue on him.

He was in closer communication with the kitchen than Edith imagined, and had discreetly questioned Mrs Burns on the subject of Mirrin Stalker's proficiency. His faith in her had so far been rewarded; she had improved the standards below stairs. Soon he would instruct her in keeping the domestic accounts: he felt he knew the Stalkers' reputation well enough to have no doubts as to her honesty. Mirrin Stalker would never tinker with the flour stocks or the tea-canisters or 'come to an arrangement' with a local vendor and pocket profit for herself.

'Have you found a suitable room for her yet?'

Edith's eyes widened. 'To live in the house?'

'Housekeepers customarily do, you know.'

'I thought it had been agreed...'

'I informed her that she may continue to sleep at her own home until the beginning of the winter quarter.'

'We have no room here,' Edith snapped.

'The attics...'

'The attics are damp and draughty.'

'But surely good enough for a servant?'

'I... I suppose so.'

'We could put her in the nurse's room.'

'How can you suggest such a thing!'

'It's time we used those chambers.'

'How... how... *unfeeling* you are!'

'Not the nursery, Edith: no, not the nursery itself,' said Lamont. 'But what harm can there be in reopening the side bedroom? It's decently removed from our quarters.'

She tossed the sewing-frame to the carpet, and leapt to her feet. Lamont had seldom seen her so roused.

'*I will not have it!*' she cried.

'Gordon has been dead so long,' said Lamont, using the boy's name for the first time in many, many months.

'How *dare* you bring my son's name into this conversation. *How dare you!*'

'We will discuss it again when you are in a calmer state of mind.' Lamont reached out his hand to the bell-pull. 'Shall I ring?'

'For her?'

'No,' said Lamont. 'For brandy.'

His wife's face had the brittleness and the tint of ivory, and her eyes were feverish with the fury which raged in her breast and which he, for once, did nothing to appease. Why was it that he had no hard knot of pity in his stomach tonight? He regarded her with perfect aplomb, relaxed and detached, watching her battle to bring herself back into that unnatural state of inhibition which was the seal of good breeding in a lady.

'I . . . I have a slight indisposition,' she said, as if reading from a manual on etiquette. 'I will retire early, if you have no objection.'

Lamont rose from the armchair and crossed to the door and opened it for her. She glided towards him and paused while he kissed her dutifully on the brow.

'Goodnight.'

'Goodnight, my dear,' he said. 'I trust you will have recovered by morning.'

He watched her cross the hall and make her slow, sedate way up the staircase, then he closed the drawing-room door, returned to his armchair by the fire and rang the servants' bell.

Within a minute a knock sounded.

He did not lower the *Advertiser*.

'Enter.'

She wore the black serge overcoat and no hat and her dark hair, freshly combed by the sheen of it, hung in a bunch over her left shoulder.

'Is it nine o'clock, Mirrin?'

'A few minutes after, sir.'

'Even so,' he said, 'if you choose to answer the bell you must not appear in your overcoat. It takes only a moment to slip it off, and that is the proper thing to do.'

'Aye, sir: I'm sorry. I was just on my way out.'

'Off you go home, then,' Lamont said. 'But ask one of the maids to bring in the decanter as you leave.'

'Brandy, sir?'

'Yes.'

She held the door with her knee and gestured out into the hall where he caught a glimpse of both the young maids each with a tray in hand. The taller of the two stepped forward and carefully gave the tray over to Mirrin who then turned and, closing the door with her left hand as she had been taught to do, brought the tray over to him. She shifted the wine-table with her left hand and brought it closer to the armchair, then laid the tray down upon it and deftly unstoppered the square, cut-glass decanter.

'A half-glass, sir?'

'Thank you.'

She poured with great deliberation, doling out the measure exactly – according to Lady Peacock's recommendations, he supposed.

On the tray were two glasses, a small flagon of water and a dish of sliced lemon. She stoppered the decanter again and set it down, then offered him the glass.

'Just put it where I may reach it, Mirrin.'

'Yes, sir.'

'You may go home now.'

'Thank you, sir.'

Lamont watched her go, then, just as she turned to close the door behind her, said, 'Mirrin, what was on the other tray?'

'Port, Mr Lamont.'

'What if I'd asked for whisky?'

'Then that would've been your hard ...' She caught herself just in time. 'That would have taken a little longer, sir.'

'Goodnight, Mirrin.'

'Goodnight, sir,' she said, cheerily. 'Sleep tight.'

4

A fortnight's true summer weather broke at last and when the colliery hooter blared to signal the end of the day shift, the corrugated tin roofs of the workshops rattled under the onslaught of heavy rain, and the dust of the yard had pitted and crumbled into runnels of rust-coloured mud.

Miserably Kate knotted the scarf about her head and contemplated the downpour from under the scant shelter of the trough bills. She drew her shawl up over her head too and sniffed and shivered as its damp hems brushed her cheeks.

A persistent cold had drained her of energy, left her nostrils raw and her head aching. She was afraid of what the wet might do and examined her responses cautiously, praying that the infection would not slip down into her lungs and roost there. She could ill afford to be laid up with the wheeze in midsummer, not with Drew's lessons to be paid for and a tidy sum to be put by each week out of the family's collective earnings.

The tang of an orange cut through her clogged senses, and made her feel both squeamish and thirsty.

She sneezed, and gulped air through her open mouth.

Beside her, Peggy Rudkin finished ripping the peel from the fruit and thrust her thumbs into the pithy flesh.

'My, my, Kate!' the woman remarked, matter-of-factly. 'You look like death warmed up.'

'God the code.'

'Aye, so I notice: still, so long's it stays out o' your tubes you'll live t'see the winter, like as not. Here, have a bit o'orange.'

'Wooden mind,' said Kate, gratefully.

The woman halved the small and almost juiceless fruit with her fingernails, coating it in the process with a generous helping of grime. She passed a segment to Kate who put the leaf in her mouth and sucked on the acid flesh gladly.

'Looks like y'haven't seen food in days,' Peggy Rudkin remarked.

'Nod hungry.'

'You're a right martyr, Kate Stalker, starvin' yourself for yon brother o'yours.'

Kate tugged the shawl tighter and took a pace towards the drowned landscape of the pithead, through which, sooner or later, she would have to make her way.

'Mind your own business, Peggy, an' I'll mind mine.'

'Makes me damned mad, though,' Peggy Rudkin went on, 't'see you an' your Mam doin' without just so's that stuck-up wee brat can swank himself b'goin' t'a university.'

Kate spat out the orange pith.

'If I were you, Peggy, I'd nod be sayin' too much about families: you're nod one t'talk.'

The woman's face coloured under the dirt. She knew only too well that Kate was making a reference to the regularity with which Tom Rudkin was conveyed home in a barrow from the public house. So much a part of Blacklaw's routine had Rudkin's alcoholic collapses become that nobody would think of approaching the publican for a loan of the barrow on Fridays, Saturdays, or Mondays, and the vehicle in question was openly referred to as *Rudkin's Express*.

'Well, mark my words, Kate Stalker, it's a mistake educatin' that boy past what's natural.'

Full of spleen and misery at her workmate's outspokenness, Kate broke from the shelter of the trough bills without waiting for the rain to ease.

Her boots splashed in the runnels and puddles soaked the hems of her skirts so that, as she ran, the material wrapped itself wetly around her bare calves and ankles.

Though not prone to self-pity, she felt sorry for herself that evening. Tears welled up and rolled down her cheeks as she scurried from the colliery gate and set off across the cobbled square towards the upper reaches of the main street.

Peggy Rudkin's criticism was typical of much of the comment which had been levelled at the Stalkers in past weeks. Deflated by the head cold and the wet weather, Kate no longer had the gumption to shake off the villagers' slanders. She was close to admitting that there might be a grain of truth in what they said about Drew's aloofness and ambitiousness.

She had deluded herself into thinking that the family's numerous small economies had gone unremarked. She should have known better: nothing went unremarked in Blacklaw. God knows, there had been chatter enough when news leaked out that Drew Stalker had been enrolled for private lessons from the dominie and that his ultimate goal was a place in a university. For a day or two there had been signs of grudging respect for the lad's cleverness, born out of the assumption that Mr Guthrie would not tutor a dunderhead. But 'scholar' was soon equated with 'gentleman', and gentlemen as a class were publicly despised in the mining community – though, in private, the upper classes were regarded with considerable respect. Those who held education and ambition in greatest awe were, of course, the most vociferous in their condemnation of the Stalkers' intentions.

Drew had never been popular; his quiet, studious manner and reserve had long ago been interpreted as arrogance. Now Kate could not quite separate herself from the general opinion, and the disloyalty to her brother added to the confusion in her heart.

Head bent against the driving sheets of rain, she hobbled on to the pavement and covered a hundred yards past the doors of the public house. Blurred and bleary lamps showed already in the windows of the houses, dips to cheer the gloom; little tin lanterns swinging in neuks by the doors were relics of a bygone age, an age addicted to such homely symbols.

The melancholy evening and her own discomforts and confusions caused Kate's tears to fall faster. She tried to convince herself that the local gossip was based on ignorance and the jealousy of people who lived without dreams, but Peggy Rudkin had spoken with something akin to pity, and pity had a sharp, flinty edge which chipped away pride much faster than scorn ever did.

Sobbing, hugging her elbows to her sides, Kate rushed over the shallow summit and on down the pavement towards the bottom rows.

When she collided with the man, the blow was almost hard enough to send her reeling. Only Rob's quick action prevented her from being flung to the ground. He caught her round the waist and cradled her for a moment against the black, crackling oilskins. Thus clad, the young man seemed larger than ever, like some coal-giant newly escaped from the shaft.

''Strewth, Kate, are y'practisin' for the Eastlagg Sprint, or runnin' after the Hamilton train?'

'I'm just code an' wet an' wantin' home.'

Not releasing her, he peered more closely at her features.

She did not raise her head.

'God, Kate, y'look like . . .'

'Aye, I've heard,' she snapped.

'An' you've been sheddin' tears,' he said. He swiftly unbuttoned the breast and skirts of the big oilskin coat and spread it out. 'Here, come inside.'

'Ach, Rob, I'm wed through as it is.'

'I'll give y'a paddy as far as your house. Y'look as if you could do with it.'

It was easier to give in than to argue with him and she snuggled under the shelter of the oilskin, her arm about his waist, leaning on him. Step for step they tramped on down to the last house, and he stooped with her and entered the closet-like hall, shaking the coat behind him as a crow shakes its wet wings.

'Mrs Stalker,' he called, as Kate went on into the living-room.

'She's out,' Kate said.

'Kettle's boilin',' Rob said. 'She can't be far. Look, lass, you get those wet clothes off ben the house an' I'll brew up the tea.'

'Scrounger,' said Kate, cheered by his company.

'Aye, always was,' Rob said, reaching down the tea-caddy from its place of honour on the overmantel shelf.

In dry clothes, with a blanket wrapped around her and her chair drawn close to the fire which Rob had poked and coaxed into vivid life, she felt much better. The depression and uncertainty which had marred the latter hours of the shift had lifted and even her head seemed less stuffy now.

Rob handed her a steaming mug of sweet tea.

As she gulped it down, she sighed and told herself that perhaps life was worth living after all.

'Better?' Rob asked.

'Much better,' she said. 'I'll say this, y'make a braw cup of tea, Rob Ewing.'

'It's more than an infusion of the leaf you're needin', Kate. Have y'not a bottle in the house?'

'Can't afford it just now.'

'Aye, I heard,' he said, embarrassed.

He seated himself in the armchair which had once been her father's, spreading his knees and inclining himself forward, huge in the narrow room.

Kate said, 'My mother'll be in soon, I expect. She'll be down at the Henderson's house, helpin' to lay out the old lady. She died, y'know.'

Rod nodded: he didn't have much interest in the demise of Granma Henderson who, after all, was well into her seventies and had been ailing for the best part of a decade.

'Come on, Rob, what's on your mind?' said Kate. 'Out with it.'

'Well . . .'

'Is it Mirrin?'

'Aye, it is,' the young man admitted. 'I haven't clapped an eye on her for weeks. Is she livin' up at that bloody house now?'

'No, she sleeps here,' said Kate. 'But she works long hours; longer than the rest of us.'

'What does she do there, Kate?'

'Everythin', I suppose.'

'There's a rumour . . .'

'Are you givin' credence t'rumours too, Rob Ewing?'

'She's the housekeeper, is she?'

'That's what she calls herself.'

Rob's lips twisted and for an instant he too looked hostile.

'Old Alex wouldn't never've stood for it,' he said.

Kate filled her mouth with tea from the mug and swallowed.

So, Rob was as unkindly disposed to the family as the rest of the village. Still, the Ewings had always been close friends of the Stalkers and she valued that friendship enough not to fly off the handle with him at the first sign of a change in his attitude.

'Mirrin has more of m'father in her than you realize, Rob,' she explained. 'What she's doin' is hurryin' on the day m'father dreamed about, *died* dreamin' about.'

'I don't set much store by dreams, Kate.'

'Maybe that's why you're still . . .'

'Still a collier?'

'I'm sorry, Rob: I shouldn't have said that.'

'I know all about the dominie's lessons and what Alex wanted for Drew: but it'll be years before the lad's in a position t'fend for himself, bloody years. And I don't want Mirrin workin' that long in that man's house.'

'It's her choice.'

'Some damned choice.'

'That's enough, Rob.'

'Look, Kate, you know what I want. It's no big secret. I don't want her in Lamont's house, because I want her in mine – as my wife.'

Kate rubbed her hand across her brow. She had been glad enough of his company when he had been cheerful and hearty, but she had not the strength to cope with his bitterness.

'You've been into that with her, Rob, haven't you?'

''Course I have, a dozen times.'

'An' she gave you an answer?'

'Aye.'

'Then there's nothin' I can do.'

'You could talk to her.'

'It would only make matters worse, she has a mind of her own, our Mirrin,' said Kate.

Crestfallen, he stared at her for a minute.

Suddenly she realized to what extent this large, good-looking young man had fallen under the spell which Mirrin cast about her. The independence which was so much a part of Mirrin's personality was the very facet of her character with which Rob Ewing could not come to terms. He slapped his thighs, got to his feet and lifted his oilskin from the sink where he had put it to drip.

'Rob,' said Kate. 'Listen. I'll tell Mirrin you were askin' after her. If you really want t'see her, then she's here most nights by half past nine. I'll ... I'll have a quiet word in her ear. But I can't promise it'll do much good.'

'I'll take my chances on that,' said Rob, happily. 'It's all I can ask: thanks, Kate.'

As he buttoned on the oilskin again, the door opened and Flora Stalker entered. Her shawl was pearled with rain. In one hand she carried a small package wrapped in stiff white paper.

Kate jumped immediately to her feet.

'Come over t'the fire, mother, an' take off that wet shawl. The tea's still hot in the pot.'

Flora paused, looking up at Rob.

'Dreich day, Mrs Stalker.'

'It is that, Rob. How's your father's health?'

'Fine, fine.'

'We haven't seen much of either of you lately.'

'No, Mrs Stalker: we've ... we've been workin' extra shifts when we can.'

Though there was no real reason for it, Kate noticed that her mother's friendly inquiry struck Rob as some sort of rebuke; perhaps he felt a little bit guilty at not having called more often on the Stalkers since Alex's death. Mam could hardly expect it now, though.

'Thanks for the tea, Kate,' Rob said. With a half-hearted smile at the elder woman he took his leave, closing the outer door behind him.

Flora Stalker seated herself on the chair by the table, shook off her damp shawl and, stooping, picked at the swollen leather laces of her boots, puffing a little with the effort.

'What a day!' she said. 'I suppose you got soaked too, Kate?'

'Aye,' Kate answered. She knelt on the floor and worried at the laces with her strong fingers, unthreading the leather from its knots. 'Could the Hendersons not have kept you 'til the rain eased?'

'I wasn't at the Hendersons.'

Kate glanced up.

'I thought ...'

'It seems I wasn't needed.'

'But you've been friendly with Alice Henderson since you were girls.'

'There was nothin' said.'

'Then – what?'

'I could see that my company wasn't welcome.'

'Oh, Mam! Not the Hendersons, too.'

Flora nodded, grim-lipped.

Kate drew off the boot and put it by the hob, then rolled down the black stocking. Her mother's calves were still smooth and pale and firm, like those of the country girl she had been thirty years ago, the foot small and dainty for such a large woman.

'It seems,' Flora said, slowly, 'that we've lost our friends as well as our menfolk.'

'It'll pass,' said Kate. 'You'll see; once they get used to the idea, they'll come chappin' at our door again.'

'Drew, and now Mirrin,' Flora said. 'There's even those that look down their snoots at us for puttin' Betsy to the Hamilton shop instead of up t'the pit.'

Kate discarded the second boot and stocking.

Flora wriggled her toes towards the flames, forcing a sad, embittered smile on to her lips.

'It doesn't pay t'be different, Kate.'

'Aye, it does,' Kate said, emphatically. 'Father knew that: he was never like the others, though he pretended t'be.'

'Maybe we're not pretendin' hard enough.'

'Don't worry about them,' said Kate, who could think of no other comfort to offer. 'You've got us, an' that should be enough.'

'Aye.'

Kate poured tea and gave the cup to her mother, then, feigning a cheerfulness she did not feel, said, 'Betsy'll be home soon. Maybe she'll mind t'bring the *Advertiser*. I'm told there's t'be pictures of the Queen and the visiting foreign dignitaries.'

'That'll be nice.'

'An' a picture of Balmoral, too.'

'Aye.'

But her mother was not listening. She sat, slumped and bare-legged with the teacup in one hand and her eyes fastened on the spluttering flames in the grate, lost once more in nostalgia for the days of her youth and the happy years when Alex and her boys were alive and the Stalkers were admired and respected by everyone in Blacklaw.

Suddenly, Kate found that she had no patience with her mother's inclination to take refuge in the past. It was the future which held the best promises, and the goals for which they must all aim.

'What's in the wee packet?' asked Kate, lifting it from the table.

'Hm?' said Flora, distantly. 'Oh, that! Powders from the chemist for your cold.'

Even as she slit the wrapping and extracted the plain cardboard box, Kate realized with delight that she had not sniffled or sneezed in almost an hour.

At last, her cold had broken and would probably be gone by the weekend. With luck, she might live to see the winter after all.

*

Mirrin replaced the pile of white Turkish towels on the upper shelf of the linen cupboard and patted into place the column of folded sheets which still smelled warm from the smoothing irons. She glanced round at the girl who was perched on the corner of the table with a notebook propped on her knees.

'How does that leave us, Hannah?'

Hannah McCormick crouched over the book, licked the stub of her pencil for inspiration, then announced, 'Pillow slips – low. Bolsters – we could do with a few more. Sheets – plenty.'

'Silk *and* flannel?'

'Aye, a wheen o' both.'

'Fine.'

Mirrin closed the cupboard and pegged the wooden bars top and bottom of the double doors. From Hannah she took the notebook, checked down the row of childishly formed figures, then tucked the volume into the deep pocket of her skirt.

'I'll give it t'the mistress tomorrow,' she said, looking round the kitchen. 'That's us all stocked up with linen.'

203

'Exceptin' for the pillow slips and bolsters.'

'I'll suggest we purchase a dozen pairs of each,' said Mirrin. 'Anyway, that's the linen, the store cupboard, the crockery, china an' cutlery – the lot, in fact, for another half year. I wonder when it was last done so thoroughly?'

Hannah did not answer and Mirrin noted with mild surprise that the girl, who had not moved from her post, was abstractedly pecking at the table with her pencil stump.

'What's wrong with you, Hannah?'

'Ach, I was just thinkin' about all the stuff crammed int' this house, cupboards bulgin' with it; so much we've t'take stock twice a year like it was an emporium. All for just two folk.'

'That's the way of it,' said Mirrin.

'Do y'not think it's . . . unfair, Mirrin?'

'Aye,' Mirrin reluctantly agreed. 'If y'must know, Hannah, I think it's close t'bein' immoral. But that's just my humble opinion, an' the brush I've been tarred with. I thought you'd been in domestic service long enough t'have got over it.'

'I thought I *was* over it, an' all,' said Hannah. 'But takin' tally o'all them sheets – twenty-two pairs! Well, that got me t'thinkin' again. Y'know, Mirrin, 'til I came here I'd never slept in a bed wi' sheets on it; not even in the last big house where I was scullery maid. I had two hodden blankets an' an old scabby greatcoat the master forked out t'put across the cot in place o' a quilt – that was one blanket less than I managed at home.'

'At least we all sleep on sheets here, even if they are patched an' a bit on the yellowish side,' Mirrin said.

'But it's not the same.'

'The same as what?'

'Havin' them on your own bed.'

'I never heard you talk this way before, Hannah. What's got int' you?'

'I dunno.' Hannah shrugged.

'You'll have a fine set of sheets for your honeymoon, never fear.'

'I don't plan t'marry,' the girl primly retorted.

She hopped off the table.

'How can y'say that, Hannah?' Mirrin asked in surprise. 'Every girl wants t'marry.'

'*You* don't.'

'Not yet, that's true,' said Mirrin. 'But someday, if the right lad comes along, maybe I will.'

'The right lad? You'll wait long enough for one o'those.'

'I'm surprised at you, Hannah.'

'What way?'

'Do y'not believe in love?'

'God's love – aye.'

'I wasn't thinkin' about God's love.'

'If y'mean the other kind, I can do very well without that, thanks very much.'

Sudden pity for the girl enveloped Mirrin and she had to struggle hard not to offer advice which, coming from her, could only have sounded patronizing.

'Maybe you'll change your mind,' she said, lamely.

'They're all after one thing from us poor feeble women.'

'Och, you're haverin',' said Mirrin. 'There's plenty decent lads in Blacklaw an' Northrigg, even in Hamilton.'

'I've yet t'meet one.'

'Wouldn't y'marry a preacher?' asked Mirrin.

Hannah's brows rose, and a faint blush suffused her already ruddy cheeks. 'That would be . . . aye, that would be different.'

'What would be different about it?'

'That'd be sort o' spiritual: a union under God.'

'As far as my knowledge of theology goes,' said Mirrin, 'there's nothin' in the Presbytery laws that forbids a minister sleepin' in the same bed as his wife.'

'That's dirty talk,' said Hannah, indignantly. 'I'll not listen t'any more.'

'I didn't mean t'offend you, Hannah.'

'Oh, I've heard about you, Mirrin Stalker,' the girl blurted out.

'An' what have y'heard?'

'That you were . . . loose.'

'Where did y'hear that?'

'Places.'

'The Evangelists' Halls, maybe?'

'No, not there: other places.'

Mirrin experienced a surge of anger, but managed to curtail it before it found expression in harsh words. Instead of chiding the servant, she said, mildly, 'Aye, but I've put all that behind me now, Hannah.'

Such a reply caught the girl unaware.

She blinked. 'Renounced the Devil, y'mean?'

'In a manner of speaking.'

'Oh, I'm glad, Mirrin,' said Hannah with unfeigned sincerity.

'Mind you,' Mirrin added, 'there's devils and devils.'

Hannah considered this remark, then winked: 'I know just what's behind that, Mirrin; I know exactly what y'mean.'

How the conversation would have developed Mirrin did not discover. At that moment, Mattie appeared in the kitchen doorway, breathlessly bearing news.

'The master's home.'

'He's early,' said Mirrin. 'I'll fetch his dinner.'

'He'll maybe not want it,' said Mattie. 'By the looks o'him he's got the fever.'

'The fever?' said Mirrin. 'Where's Mrs Lamont?'

'Out at a ladies' meetin' in Hamilton: Sandy's t'collect her at ten prompt.'

'That's three hours yet,' Mirrin said. 'Are y'sure it's the fever?'

'Aye.'

'Maybe he'll die,' said Hannah. 'Maybe we'll all catch it from him, an' we'll all . . .'

'Is Mrs Burns not back yet?' Mirrin demanded.

'Not yet.'

'Right: you'll find a basket of lemons in the back of the cupboard over there. Pick out the four best, wash them, then slice them, peel an' all, into the biggest jug y'can find. Boil water, fill the jug half full, an' add four big spoons o' tacky sugar.'

'Should we not send for the missus?' said Hannah. 'Under the circumstances, she should be here.'

'First I'll see what's ailin' him,' Mirrin said. 'Now get on with what I told you – an' stop jumpin' t'morbid conclusions.'

'I've witnessed all this before,' droned Hannah, dolefully. 'Many's the buddy I've seen just slip away like . . .'

Leaving the cousins to entertain themselves with gloomy predictions, Mirrin hurried up to the hall, ascended the main staircase, trotted along the corridor and halted, a little breathlessly, outside Lamont's bedroom. She tidied her hair and checked the buttons of her bodice. She was not neat enough to pass muster with Edith Lamont, but the coalmaster, in poor health, would hardly be likely to notice her dishevelled state.

The bedroom door was painted black, a rich, glossy, funeral-plume black. Sudden dread overwhelmed her as the thought crossed her mind that Hannah might be right. Hale and healthy men in the prime of life did sometimes die of simple fevers. Fever was the scourge of every class, a reaper much respected in hall and hovel alike. Just what would happen if Lamont passed away? Edith Lamont would have her out in the gutter in a trice, that was certain – but what of all those families in Blacklaw who depended on Lamont for their livelihood? Probably the colliery would be sold. A new owner would descend on them, and scour the place out. It was almost inevitable; no new owner could have the traditional attachments of the Lamont clan, or Lamont's responsibility towards colliers he did not know from Chinamen.

Strong rumours had been brought into the village that Blacklaw was a little Eden compared with most other mining areas, that the coal market was glutted, the paying price from regular sources dipping by the month. Naturally, no citizen of Blacklaw believed a word of such tales. But her father had once confided in her, almost shamefacedly, that Lamont was no worse a master than most in Scotland, and a bloody sight better than some he'd heard of not twenty miles off as the crow flies.

So what if Houston Lamont did succumb to fever? What would become of them all?

Snorting loudly, sceptical of her own imaginative fancies, Mirrin knocked on the bedroom door.

'Who is that?' came the croaked response.

'Stalker.'

'Come.'

As the master had not been expected home so early in the evening, the fire had not been lit and this, along with the sombre mauve-patterned wallpaper, made the room cheerless and uninviting. Lamont stood close to the hearth, caught by his overcoat sleeves which, so impatiently had he tried to haul off the garment, had become entangled by the buttons on the half-belt and had locked him as effectively as a convict's straight-jacket. To add to his plight, he was presently convulsed by a series of gargantuan sneezes which seemed to paste a label on his illness and brought Mirrin out of her cloud of apprehension.

'Did that fool of a girl not tell you to come immediately?' Lamont snapped, still struggling with the overcoat, and punctu-ating every other word with a sneeze. 'Or did ... you ... decide ... not to come ... until it ... suited you?'

Only her employer's rheumy eyes and rubicund nose won him sufficient sympathy to check Mirrin's impulse to walk straight out of the door again.

She said, 'Short of poppin' through the floorboards like a genie, sir, I couldn't have got here much quicker.'

Coming forward, side-stepping the blast of his sneezes, she tripped the buttons from the half-belt's snare and tugged the coat from his arms and shoulders. As he hunched and stretched his aching bones, Mirrin hung the overcoat in the wardrobe and brought out in its place his quilted myrtle-green smoking-jacket.

'What do I want with that?' he demanded.

'It's warmer than your gown, sir.'

Still grousing, clearing his tubes with a croaking noise like a mating rook, Lamont plucked the jacket from the girl's grasp and shrugged himself into it.

'I suppose it will do.'

'Shall I put a warmin' brick in the bed?'

'Bed?'

'If you're unwell, Mr Lamont, should y'not be in bed?'

'Bed?' he repeated, outraged. 'I cannot afford to take to my bed. No, no: I have correspondence to answer, urgent reports to read.'

'Then I'll light the fire at once.'

'It should have been lit before now.'

'Aye, sir.'

'Pull that sofa closer to the hearth. Give me some heat to warm this mausoleum.' He dropped into a chair, stretched his legs and glowered threateningly at Mirrin. 'And help me off with my boots.'

Mirrin took a deep breath. Kneeling before him, she deftly unlaced the stylish leather boots. At any other time she would have instantly rebelled against his tyrannical attitude, but instinct directed her to avoid a confrontation. Her mother had often warned her that a man with a head cold was like a boar with toothache, and she decided to act on the principle that Lamont was not himself on this occasion. She removed the boots and placed them by the door ready to take downstairs for drying and polishing. Prompted by another bout of sneezing and coughing, she hurried across to his dressing-table and opened one of the bow-fronted drawers. From it she removed six handkerchiefs, put one directly into his hand and laid the other five on top of the castored table which she then pushed close to his chair.

'Will you *please* stop fidgeting about my bedroom, Stalker,' he cried. 'I'm about to undress. I expect you back here in five minutes to move the sofa and light the fire. Then you will leave me in peace. Now go.'

Mirrin retreated to the door, dropped a full curtsey that would have done a courtier proud, picked up the boots en route, and left the coalmaster's bedroom.

She loitered for a moment on the landing, grinning to herself. In every way Lamont was a superior being, the great landowner and coalmaster, lord of his wee sooty kingdom. But every now and again the image crumbled a bit and she glimpsed the ordinary mortal beneath the dictatorial disguise. He certainly didn't look like a lord and master now, not with his eyes all puffy, his nose like a railway beacon and his hair straggling. She *almost* felt sorry for him.

Running downstairs, she burst into the kitchen with a speed which startled the McCormick cousins, and Mrs Burns, who had just returned from a rare afternoon's freedom.

'He's dead,' cried Hannah, clasping her hands to her bosom. 'Oh, God! I knew it. He's . . .'

'He's no more dead than I am,' said Mirrin. 'In fact, he's lyin' in state up there, issuin' orders like Napoleon Bonaparte.'

Mrs Burns had just time to remove her overcoat and hat but had not yet put them away. 'I've returned this very minute from a friend's house,' she said, 'an' her man's lyin' gravely ill. I doubt if he'll last the week. Young he is, too; not much older than the master.'

Mattie asked, 'What's takin' him?'

'The fever.'

'God spare us,' Hannah prayed.

'I tell you, Mr Lamont doesn't *have* the damn' fever,' Mirrin said. 'Are y'all daft? I can recognize a cold when I see it. But it hasn't helped his temper any, so you'd better disband this wake an' get on with makin' him comfortable. Where's that hot lemon water?'

'Kettle's not quite boiled yet.'

'I'll see t'that, Mirrin,' the cook promised.

Unclipping a small key from the bunch on the chain at her waist, Mirrin handed it to Mrs Burns.

'Whisky, rum or brandy?'

'Rum, I reckon,' Mirrin answered. 'Two measures of the silver cup from the bottle in the cabinet in the study: no, make it three.'

'Aye, a hot rum toddy'll soon sweat it out of him,' the cook said.

'Mattie,' said Mirrin. 'You come with me: we've orders t'shift the big sofa.'

Leading the servant, Mirrin returned to the first floor.

Inside a quarter of an hour the bedroom and its occupant presented a much changed picture. With curtains drawn, the gas mantels lit, the sofa close to the hearth, and the heavy ugly furniture wrapped in shadow, the chamber seemed smaller and more comfortable. Coals burned brightly in the grate, casting flickering light on the Delft tiles which surrounded the hearth and on the high brass fender.

In warm woollen breeks, a flannel shirt and smoking-jacket, the coalmaster was propped against pillows on the sofa which the combined efforts of Mattie and Mirrin had contrived to push close to the fire. A blanket was wrapped round his legs. The castored table had been stationed close at hand. It was littered with administrative files and letters which Lamont had instructed Mirrin to fetch up from the study. But the coalmaster seemed uninterested in the material now, being more obsessed with the proper positioning of the table itself.

'Closer.'

Mirrin pushed the table closer.

'Do not smother me.'

Mirrin edged the table back.

'I cannot reach it there.'

Mirrin readjusted it.

'Now lower the height of it.'

Impatiently, Lamont caught hold of the flap and, twisting his body, groped for the brass ratchet by which the table could be reduced to a convenient height.

His movements were so abrupt that he caused the little table to rock and topple over, cascading papers and handkerchiefs across the carpet.

'Now look what you've done,' he shouted.

The Stalkers would have recognized the meaning of the whiteness which appeared round Mirrin's compressed lips and would have had sense enough to shift away.

'Pick them up, Stalker,' Lamont growled, coughing into the back of his hand. 'Pick them up, will you, girl?'

Familiar enough with colds to appreciate how miserable her employer was feeling, Mirrin nevertheless marked off mentally the boundary of irascibility which was permissible under the circumstances. It was not just the discomfort of the symptoms which was making the master so vile-tempered; it was the fact that illness had attacked and conquered *him*. Colds for colliers, chills for kitchen maids, colic for cooks – but *not* for coalmasters!

Mirrin replaced the table in an upright position with a

thump. Plucking up the scattered handkerchiefs she slapped them down, then whisked up the papers and deposited them in an untidy pile by the man's elbow.

He watched her, scowling.

'Will that be all?' she demanded.

Before Lamont could answer, a faint shuffling outside the bedroom door sent Mirrin to open it. Hannah's plump little hands gripped a tray on which stood a steaming pewter tankard. The servant's eyes were round with apprehension: no doubt Mattie had suitably embellished Mirrin's account of the master's mood.

'I'll take it,' Mirrin said.

'Thanks, Mirrin,' Hannah whispered.

'The reading tonight's from the Book of Daniel,' Mirrin said softly, and closed the door on Hannah's bewildered expression.

There was a look of hostile suspicion on the coalmaster's face as she carried the tray across to the table. Continuing her Biblical terms of reference, Mirrin imagined that she might be Jezebel trotting in the butter. The image amused her and lessened her angry mood.

She smiled to herself.

'Do you find some entertainment in my being ill?'

Without answering, Mirrin brushed the papers aside and put the tray down gingerly.

'Well?'

'No, Mr Lamont.'

'Then why do you smile?'

'That was sympathy, Mr Lamont.'

Head craned back, he squinted up at her. She could see that the posture made his head swim a little. Theatrically he bridged his forehead with his fingers.

'Sit, sit down: I cannot bear to have you towering over me.'

Obediently, Mirrin lowered herself into the round chair on the other side of the hearth and demurely folded her hands in her lap.

She waited.

The coalmaster peered at the steaming tankard.

'Is that alcohol?'

'Rum and lemon, sir.'

Stretching, he triggered the pewter lid and sniffed the steam. Cupping the hot tankard, he sipped experimentally. Still cradling the vessel, he leaned back against the pillows visibly relaxing and contemplated the housekeeper.

'So,' he said, 'you consider my bedroom to be a lions' den?'

'Well, you did frighten them a bit,' said Mirrin boldly.

If her employer wanted to amuse himself with some sharp conversation, she thought, she was not averse to providing opposition.

Lamont grunted, and sipped the rum toddy. 'But I do not ... ah, frighten you?'

'No.'

'Not even a little?'

'No, Mr Lamont.'

'You don't have much patience with illness, Stalker?'

'On the contrary, Mr Lamont.'

'Then why are you so amused by my present condition?'

'Because it's just a head cold.'

'I am suffering, Miss Stalker.'

'Aye.'

'That means nothing to you?'

'With the things I've seen, a head cold's not much more than a joke.'

'And what ... "horrors" have you witnessed, tell me?'

'At least you don't have t'drag yourself out of bed tomorrow mornin' at five o'clock, sick or not, t'get yourself ...'

'I must work too.'

Mirrin's patience evaporated. She sat forward.

'Listen, I've seen men an' women crawlin' out of their beds when they were hardly fit t'stand: doctorin' themselves with axle grease, an' poultices made from bread that should've been in their bairns' hungry bellies ...'

'Oh, really! I'm in no mood for radicalism.'

'... because they knew that if they didn't turn up for the shift they wouldn't get their pittance, an' might even be paid off.'

'I've never paid off a sick man yet – malingerers excepted.'

'Would you class yourself as a malingerer?'

'I am unwell,' Lamont said.

'Aye, an' sorry for yourself.'

'Do not be insolent.'

'*You* invited me t'converse.'

'Concerning my colliers,' Lamont said: 'do you not realize how prominently cold hard cash figures in the things an owner has to do?'

'Too well, I realize.'

'For your information, a coalmaster is tied to his capital investment. What do you imagine would happen if I were spendthrift? I would run into trouble with the lending banks. My credit would be cut off. And if I thus failed to honour my commitments, by God, there would be no work of any kind for any miner in these parts. Your collier friends would not be able to heal *that* sickness with axle grease and dough poultices.'

'But it wouldn't hurt you,' Mirrin snapped.

'I would lose face . . .'

'*Face!*'

'. . . and my colliery.'

'Have you ever been in a parish workhouse?'

'Naturally, I have visited . . .'

'Try stayin' in one. Aye, your "terrible" cold would be a more serious thing if you were made t'sleep in a box bed with forty other souls wheezin' round you.'

'Believe it or not, Stalker, I want that for no man or woman.' Lamont clanked down the tankard.

'It never happens t'the masters, though, does it?' At last Mirrin's temper had broken. Her voice was shrill, and she had risen to her feet. 'For the proof of it just try walkin' round the kirkyard – not just the new graves where the men an' the boys lie buried – but the other ones, the old ones. Read them, Mr Lamont; read them, then think about how bloody good the life the masters offer us is; read – In Loving Memory of Andrew, aged two years, and his sister, Mary, ten months, and Jeannie, beloved wife, and her infant son . . . an' count the years, the bad years, the hard years, Mr Lamont; the years when the damned masters . . .'

She caught herself, and with an effort brought her voice down to a normal pitch.

'No, Mr Lamont,' she said, 'all things considered I'm afraid I can't feel much concern about your head cold.'

'Nor about your position here either, I presume?'

'You'd do that? Push me, goad me into speakin' my mind, then sling me out for it?' A flush rushed to her cheeks. 'Then, Mr Lamont, all that's left for me t'say is ...'

'Nothing.' He held up his hand warningly. 'Say nothing, Miss Stalker.'

'It's all been said.'

'No, you leap too rapidly to conclusions, and attach too great importance to your opinions. For the moment, Mirrin Stalker, I have had quite enough of both.'

'I thought ...'

'You thought that because I am a coalmaster, I am immune from all the things that scar you and your kind. You thought that because I am the coalmaster I profess to *own* you – soul, body and mind. Ah, no, Mirrin, that's not the tenet of my belief, however much it strikes you so. I own land, seams, winding engines, trucks, bolts, rivets and all. But I do not *own* any man or woman. I am responsible for them, to some degree, and I expect – nay, I demand, where I must – their responsibility in return. But own them – never.'

'Mr Lamont ...'

'My head spins,' he growled. 'See what you have done. Go away, please.'

Mirrin hesitated.

He had what he wanted from her. She could not be sure that he had not somehow trapped her into feeling genuinely sorry for him. The thought was incredible: her, Alex Stalker's daughter, not only deigning to work in the coalmaster's den, but actually feeling for him the same kind of sympathy which she would extend to any coughing collier.

She lifted the tankard and found it empty.

Quietly, meekly, she said, 'Shall I bring you more, sir?'

Lamont sighed.

'Please,' he said, then as she turned towards the door with

the tray, added, 'but send Hannah with it. She, thank God, is too much afraid of the lion to stick her arm in his mouth.'

Relief that there were to be no repercussions as a result of her outspokenness, added to the humour of Lamont's request, almost caused Mirrin to burst out laughing. But a smile had almost cost her her job, and she was wary now, too wary to respond. She nodded and carried the tray out into the corridor, then, turning to close the door, said, 'I . . . hope you feel better tomorrow.'

Lamont grunted, sneezed, and dismissed her with a wave of his hand.

*

To Betsy Stalker, Dalzells' Emporium in High Street, Hamilton, was the wonder of creation and the treasure-house of the civilized world. Its imposing façade dominated the High Street's western approach, an edifice of mullioned glass, brass plate, striped blinds, gilded legends and beautifully fluted gas lamps. Its huge, smoothly-oiled doors were guarded by a former cavalry sergeant whose moustaches alone were sufficiently grand to scare off the scruffy urchins who begged along the beat, and to set the hearts of not-so-young matrons fluttering with memories of romance. His uniform was cut from Prussian blue worsted, decorated with gold braid and pinwheel buttons. On his head, he wore an incongruous but enormously raffish astrakhan to which, when the weather was chill, he pinned a magnificent scarf of peacock silk to keep his whiskers warm.

Only the common people of the town ever laughed at Sergeant Walters, and few patrons of Dalzells' fell into that class.

There was money in the county now and a sufficient number of folk with 'pretensions to suit their purses' to allow the Dalzell Brothers' experiment in multiple storekeeping to catch on. Within a couple of years of opening, their emporium had become incorporated into the fabric of Hamilton's social life.

Randolph and Anstruther Dalzell had learned their trading methods in London. After their father's death, they had returned to Scotland to expand and reshape the cosy corner drapery into its present form, epitomizing its exotic cosmopolitan appeal by hiring and costuming the doorman.

Behind the sergeant's ramrod back, the ground floor opened spaciously into the warm and carpeted regions of what had once been a weavers' sweatshop. Here was a salon of wickerwork models sumptuously clad in the very height of fashion. Tea-dresses, day-dresses, evening gowns, ball gowns, Dolly Vardens and even an example of the latest Princess Polonaise – each was mounted on appropriate undergarments, with matching accessories placed on the plinth at its base.

Gowns and Mantles, Children's and Ladies' Footwear, Gloves and Haberdashery led on to an intimate alcove guarded by a palm tree in a copper pot and an oriental screen behind which the secret monitors of femininity were tucked away – tight-lacing corsets, sheaths and chemisettes, crinolettes, bustles and a paradise of petticoats and drawers. For some reason too modest to imagine, veils, reticules, and tennis shoes with India-rubber soles were also displayed only behind the potted palm.

The upstairs floors proffered a wide and varied choice of Floor Coverings, Bed Linen, Napery, Curtain Fabrics, Blinds, Blankets, Furs and Muffs, as well as directing pampered customers towards Retiring Rooms in which, in addition to the usual offices, individual hand towels and pellets of lavender soap were to be found.

Betsy loved every square yard of the sprawling building and, in particular, her own department – Haberdashery. Satin ribbons, lace frettings, tortoiseshell combs, dainty silver buckles and tiny china-headed pins all might have been stocked just for her pleasure.

It wasn't the existence of such gorgeous trifles which astonished her. She had always known that they were available somewhere, reserved for those who had nothing better to do with their money: but the scope and variety of the stuffs stunned her into a dreamy euphoria which lasted throughout the whole of her first week's employ and never quite wore off during her apprentice years. If she could not possess the items which transformed a girl into a lady, at least she could move freely among them every working day and hope that some of the quality might rub off on her.

It was wholly through her own efforts that she had side-stepped the colliery troughs and the vacancy which Annie's departure had left in Mr Lamont's domestic staff. Mirrin had been overbearingly keen to have her up at the mansion as one of the servants, and, for a day or two, it had been touch and go for Betsy.

To gain a stay on making a decision, she had thrown several frantic tantrums, screaming, kicking and writhing on the living room floor. Though calculated, the spasms had seemed like the last childish fling she would ever have. She had climbed out of them almost ready to face the inevitable, then May Gilles had come to call on her granny who lived four doors up from the Stalkers. Betsy and May had known each other at school in the days before May's Dad had found a job as a drayman in the town and shifted the family there. By chance, Betsy and May had met in Main Street and had struck up a conversation which led quickly to May's hymn of praise to urban living and depiction of the wonders of Hamilton's principal store – Dalzells'.

Next morning, telling no one, Betsy left Blacklaw early and tramped the miles to Hamilton, carrying her best clothes in a bag under her arm. May's mother provided soap and water and a room in which to change.

At eleven o'clock in the morning, Betsy timidly presented herself before Dalzells' Assistant Supervisor who, fortunately for Miss Stalker, was not too old to be impervious to a pretty face and trim figure.

At noon, Betsy was interviewed by no less a person than Albert Sutton, Deputy Manager of the Emporium. Though less susceptible to coy charm than his underling, Mr Sutton too saw 'makings' in Miss Stalker. After consultation with his female counterpart in charge of trainees, he instructed Betsy to solve some simple arithmetical problems and to copy out in her best hand a lengthy goods' invoice. That done to his satisfaction, he then offered her 'terms of eight shillings per week of six days duration'. Betsy accepted on the proviso that her family agreed. As eight shillings per week was more than she could have earned as Lamont's maid-of-all-work, the employment was settled the following morning, and Monday, bright and early, found Betsy a passenger on the horse-drawn 'penny' omnibus which rumbled through Blacklaw at seven o'clock.

Her mother did not approve – which was to be expected.

Mirrin was disappointed that she had failed to persuade her young sister to give her support up at the mansion in the oaks. But Kate, at least, was happy for her and, perhaps, relieved that yet another Stalker had evaded the clutches of the colliery.

At first, Drew was non-committal, too absorbed in his Latin and Greek primers to pay much attention to his twin's accounts of the wonders of Dalzells'. It was not until summer had passed its peak and the leaves were turning tobacco-yellow, that he gave her any hint of his interest in the course she had chosen, or delivered himself of the opinion that her situation was ideally suited to his plans for her future.

The trappings of Dalzells' Emporium, and contact with upper-class customers, added substance to Betsy's dreams. Luxury was all around her; she had ample opportunity to dwell on its finer shades, to equate wealth with cosseting, and cosseting with respect. Where else but in a rich ladies' store would one find plump velvet cushions for the customer to rest her wrist and elbow on while fitting gloves? Where else would an assistant manager flit through the departments twice a day sweetening the air with Attar of Roses squeezed from a little rubber bulb attached to an elegant china bottle? Life, Betsy realized, should be like that, constantly soft and warm and scented; a far cry from the sour-smelling, hard-angled, cold and gloomy kitchens in which miners and their families spent their days.

But there was more to the dream, much more; one quality which Betsy could not have anticipated and which revealed itself to her suddenly one afternoon in Gentlemen's Modes.

The moment was impossible to define, yet its ramifications were so important that in the course of a month Betsy changed from a child in a gigantic toybox of possessions into a young woman alive to the realities upon which the whole expensive structure of trade and commerce were founded.

The Breakfast Jacket, of maroon velvet lined with quilted satin was quite the most elegant and useless item of apparel in the store – or so Betsy thought. She took the label literally and tried to imagine Rob Ewing exchanging his grubby vest for the opulent garment simply to sup his porridge before the start of the day-shift.

The vision was so ridiculous that she giggled to herself and received a stern reprimanding sniff from the haughty young man – a husband and father and pillar of the church, alas – who stood behind the short, teak-topped counter like one of his own dummies.

The failure of her imagination in fitting Rob into the Breakfast Jacket did not daunt her and she mentally stuffed the big young miner into a Dressing Gown of Berlin wool, a Top Frock Coat, and an Ulster with Detachable Cape. In all of them, she thought, Rob Ewing would still look like a coarse collier : then, instantly, her mind made the intuitive leap which was shortly to bring her to the verge of ruin.

What sort of man *would* fit into Dalzells' best?

What sort of man, indeed?

It did not take Betsy long to find out.

*

During the two days of Haberdashery's Unrepeatable Offer of Genuine French Camisole Lace at Greatly Reduced Prices, Betsy had been rushed off her feet. It was close to eight o'clock closing before the endless parade of customers dwindled and she had cleared from the floor behind the counter the mountains of paper, wrapping-bands and boxes and had stolen a moment to indulge herself at an adjacent roundabout of new English ribbons.

There was more than idle fancy involved in her viewing that evening. She draped ribbons over her hand and formed them into loops with all the meticulous indecision of a purchasing customer.

Phyllis Rose McBean, a junior assistant of two years' standing, sidled up to her younger companion, and said, 'Can't afford that quality on your wages, Betsy Stalker.'

Nonchalantly, Betsy touched the clustered ribbons to her hair. 'Suit me, don't they, Phyllis Rose? Don't they bring out the colour in my hair?'

'Give them here,' said Phyllis Rose.

'Hold the cuddy a minute,' Betsy said, drawing the bunch away. 'I think I might just have these three; if you'd be good enough to put them in the bottom drawer for me 'til Friday.'

'Three at a shillin' an' two pence each?'

'Three an' sixpence,' said Betsy, airily. 'Oh, yes, I think so. Do set them aside, Phyllis dear.'

'I'm not supposed t'do that for juniors.'

'I'll pay on Friday.'

'Your Mam'll skin you for breakin' into your wages,' warned Phyllis Rose, in the kirkyard tone of one who has frequently undergone maternal skinning. '*Three an' six!*'

'It'll be quite all right,' said Betsy, folding the three ribbons neatly. 'She won't know.'

Phyllis Rose placed her hand on Betsy's arm and, squinting curiously at the girl, said, 'Is it him, then?'

'Who?'

'Him: the lad?'

Betsy affected an indulgent tinkle of mirth. 'Oh, he's hardly a lad, Phyllis Rose.'

'All right, then: is it the gentleman I saw you talkin' to on Monday night when we closed?'

'He *may* wish to make me a little present.'

'Ooooooooh,' exclaimed Phyllis Rose in admiration. 'It *is* him. An' he's *so* goodlookin'.'

'Yes, isn't he?' said Betsy, casually. 'He's only an acquaintance, of course; nothin' more.'

But the light in her deep blue eyes and the winsome smile at the corner of her lips defied poor Phyllis Rose to believe it.

5

There were four letters on the wooden tray which Mirrin Stalker carried into the study and, to Lamont's astonishment, withheld from him by the simple expedient of drawing back her elbows. It was bad enough the mail being an hour overdue without his servant conspiring to keep it from him. He reached across the desk for the tray but the damned girl cocked it out of his grasp. He glanced up at her angrily. Her defiant, pursed-lipped mood so accurately matched his own, however, that he elected to avoid an encounter and sat back again in the chair.

'My letters, Miss Stalker?'

'Can I have the evening off, sir?'

'Ah!' said Lamont. 'Have you asked Mrs Lamont?'

'She says I can't.'

'Then you mustn't expect me to contradict her.'

'I haven't had an evening off in the six weeks I've been here.'

'Haven't you?' said Lamont.

'No, sir.'

'Why do you wish to have this evening off, Mirrin? Is it important?'

'There's a wedding in the village.'

'A close friend, or a relative, perhaps?'

'Just a friend, sir, kind of. She used t'work at the troughs with me. I ... I'd like t'see the poor fish she managed t'land.'

'When do the celebrations begin?'

'Seven o'clock, sir.'

'Did you tell the mistress your reason?'

'She ... Mrs Lamont did not ask, sir.'

Lamont considered. Of course, the girl was entitled to three hours off. If he remembered correctly, there were rules which governed servants' hours – recommendations, at least – but he could not for the life of him recall specific items. Probably an evening each week, or a half day, in addition to the Sabbath.

The problem would have been easily solved had it not been

for Edith. Obviously if he countermanded her refusal she would make his life a misery for the next week or more. Ruefully, he considered that she would probably do that without an excuse.

'No, Mirrin,' he said, 'if Mrs Lamont has refused you an evening off, then that must be the way of it. On the other hand, you *may* leave early tonight; at a quarter past six, say, provided you organize the serving of the dinner before you go.'

Mirrin did not grin. She would have done so a month or a fortnight ago but now she was learning to conceal her triumphs as well as her tempers. She swung the tray out, lifted the letters from it and placed them neatly on the sheets and scraps on the desktop, the one flat surface in the house which the servants were forbidden to touch, on pain of instant dismissal.

'May I inform the mistress, sir?'

'No, I will do that,' Lamont said. 'Later this evening.'

'Very good, sir,' Mirrin said. 'Will that be all?'

Lamont nodded.

He hardly noticed her leave, his attention caught by the scrawled writing on the long plain buff envelope before him.

Deliberately he left it until last.

The rest of the post was inconsequential. It took him but a moment to open, scan and discard the three other letters, then to slit open Dorothy's epistle and, with a sinking sad heart, cast his eyes over the illegible scribble which was her notion of a long, informative, and loving communication.

Far back, during her first months in Miss Emerson's care, her letters had been like this, scrawls and scribbles and elaborate leafy designs standing in lieu of handwriting. It seemed that she had reverted again, had slunk back into the menacing shadows of madness.

Was it, he wondered, a symptom of her age, as Miss Emerson suggested: or was it, somehow, his fault? He thought of the narrow window in the upper floor behind the gable of Woodbank House in far off Kent, and the gaudy blossoms of the gardens which Dorothy could no longer see. Her view of the outside world was now divided into squares by the bars and the meshwork grid which contained her as if she was a wild and dangerous creature and not just a poor, bewildered woman.

Bending over the paper, he deciphered a few ill-formed words – book, dust, while, lady, sister, rabbit, loving. No more : a jumble of illogicalities. Had his last letter to her, written only a week ago, been as meaningless? He must send her something. He would be in Hamilton tomorrow to meet with an iron-master to negotiate for a contract on small coal. He would take time off to browse in Strachan's Bookshop, would find some-thing really nice to send her, with his love. Something really nice? Pictures flatly printed! Mere substitutes.

Thrusting himself to his feet, he pushed back the chair and crumpled the letter and its envelope in his fist.

The fire in the study hearth had not been lit that morning, though it was set for the match. He crushed the paper ball tightly and, hand in pocket, walked out of the study and across the hall in search of some ready flame upon which to cast the letter and so be rid of the pain and guilt which it carried like a curse from Dorothy's locked prison in the south.

The dining-room was hardly ever used, yet it was maintained diligently and almost lovingly by the staff who, for some peculiar reason, seemed to find it as attractive as a magnet. Perhaps, Lamont suddenly realized, they preferred to work there because it was safe and quiet and far from his wife's habitual domain of parlour and drawing-room.

Certainly it was the most formal room in the house. The heavy mahogany articles glowed with lavender oil and bees-wax, the scents mingling with that of the camphor blocks under the sideboards and corner service cupboards.

The girl's cherry-red smock was a suitable counter to the soberness of the room's appointments, colourful but not flip-pant. The light reflected from the polished surface of the long dining table gave her face a luminous quality. He had not noticed before how clear her skin had become, losing the granular coarseness which daily work at the troughs imparted. She hummed contentedly as she swirled the knots of rags across the velveteen surface of the table top, smoothing into the pores of the wood the soft little nuggets of perfumed wax which she had previously applied from the tub in her smock pocket.

The fire had been lighted in the hearth but the coals had not spurted into vivid flame yet, and Lamont, hesitating, thumbed the paper deeper into the corner of his pocket.

A little startled, Mirrin looked up at him.

'Go on with your work,' he said.

She applied herself once more to polishing.

'You like this room?'

'I do that, Mr Lamont.'

'Why?'

'I'm not sure, sir.'

'Because it's removed from the main part of the house?'

'Not really.' Mirrin stroked the polish into the mahogany thoughtfully. 'It's got an air of history about it, I suppose.'

'That's very perceptive of you, Mirrin,' said Lamont. 'It is, in effect, the only room in the house to remain completely unaltered since my great-grandfather's day.'

'How long would that be, sir?'

'A hundred years,' said Lamont. 'No, no, much longer, I suppose. My great-grandfather purchased the place from the Earl of Blacklaw, whose own grandfather had had the misfortune to be a supporter of Charlie and had been dispossessed of the entitlement by the Crown.'

'But it was restored to him?' asked Mirrin.

'A generous gesture by the Duke of Hamilton: the Earl was in desperate straits, apparently. There are histories in the library in my study which you may borrow if you're interested.'

'Thank you, Mr Lamont. I'd like that fine, to learn about the gentry.'

'You're well versed in proletarian history, I take it?'

'Aye, my father dinned enough of that into me.'

'Then,' said Lamont, 'perhaps I should adjust the balance. See here.'

The coalmaster came forward and took the girl's hand in his and led her fingers across the table top, guiding them to a long shallow scar in the mahogany, a scar which a century of wax and elbow-grease had failed to heal completely.

'Feel the indentation,' Lamont said.

'Aye, I'd wondered about that,' said Mirrin.

'That's part of my history, the history of my family and this house.'

He released her hand and she continued to explore the furrow gingerly with her fingertips.

'Can you guess what made such an enduring mark?'

'Tell me, Mr Lamont.'

'An axe.'

Mirrin's eyes widened with astonishment.

Good-humouredly, the coalmaster continued the story.

'The axe was intended to cleave my great-grandfather from tip to tail, like a herring,' he said. 'Fortunately, the young man's aim was a shade wide of the mark.'

'What young man?'

'A suitor to my grandmother, the favourite daughter.'

'Why could he not just marry her?'

'My great-grandfather did not approve of the match.'

'Why not?'

'The young man was not considered . . . stable enough to take into the family.'

'You mean, he was a miner?' asked Mirrin in disgust.

'Not at all,' Lamont answered. 'As it happens he was a tenant farmer. I imagine that that occupation might not have damned him in my great-grandfather's eyes, for he was, by all accounts, a shrewd judge of men. He was opposed to the match on more personal grounds.'

'So the farmer tried t'do your forebear t'death?'

Lamont had positioned himself at the head of the table, back to the door. In playing both roles of victim and attacker he showed more animation than Mirrin had ever seen in him before, as if the dramas of his ancestors had so engrossed him that he had forgotten the pettiness of his own immediate problems.

'Can you imagine it, Mirrin: the table set with all its finery, a dozen glittering guests, my grandmother in her evening dress, my great-grandfather presiding at the head of his board, here where I'm standing. Suddenly, the door bursts open and the wild-eyed young farmer lunges into the room, a hewer's axe upraised and madness twisting his handsome features. My great-grandfather hardly glances round, just sways an inch or two and lets the big, ugly blade come hacking down, shattering the crystal glasses and the fine plate and burying itself deep into the table.'

'Go on : go on.'

Lamont's arm, imitating the axe, was stretched across the gleaming mahogany, his chest upon the table's edge.

'Swiftly, without flinching, my great-grandfather snares the young man's neck. He was as strong as a bull. He pins his assailant face down in the spilled wine and broken glass, and holds him with one hand, waving away servants and guests who would have rushed to his assistance.'

'Until the constables arrived t'cart the poor lad off to the clink, no doubt,' said Mirrin.

'The enforcers of law and order were not summoned,' said Lamont, unfolding himself from the pose. 'No, there was to be no more violence, and no retribution – at least not that evening. My great-grandfather had his own way of dealing with the situation. Being a shrewd judge of character, as I've said, he knew how to turn the incident to his advantage and prove his point to his daughter.'

'What did he do, then?'

'He allowed the young man to sit up a little, to talk, to explain his reasons for the murderous assault. Then my great-grandfather sent his steward to fetch a purse of five golden guineas, and offered the purse to the young farmer on condition that he left the county that night and did not show his face in Lanarkshire ever again.'

'Of all the patronizing...'

'The young farmer accepted with alacrity. By midnight he had fled the county, lock, stock and barrel.'

'I'd rather have gone t'prison,' Mirrin declared.

'And so, I think, should I,' said Lamont.

His agreement surprised her.

In the moment they stood facing each other, the coalmaster saw that suspicion and much of her antagonism had drained from her eyes.

In sudden confusion, Mirrin gathered the cloths and stuffed them down into the smock's broad pocket.

'I ... I'd better go, sir. There's things to be done in the kitchen.'

'But Mírrin,' he said, 'I thought you would have shown some curiosity concerning my grandmother, the young lady abandoned in favour of five golden guineas.'

Mirrin shrugged. 'I suppose she married somebody "suitable", picked by her father, and they lived happily enough and had bairns.'

'Oh, yes,' said Lamont. 'She married: she married a not-so-young coalmaster from Fife. He had, so I believe, capital and much experience in the trade and wished to expand his interests by securing a lease of ownership in Lanarkshire.'

'So *he* got himself the guineas *and* the lady.'

'And the son he needed to clinch the contract,' said Lamont. 'My grandmother soon presented her husband with a male heir – my father.'

'Just as well for you, then, Mr Lamont.'

'Four months after the birth, however,' the coalmaster continued, 'she came down into this very room in the dark of an October midnight, came very silently, dressed in the gown she had worn on the eve of her jilting. From God knows what source, she had acquired a vial of laudanum. Carefully, she poured the drug into a wine glass and drank every drop. Early next morning, the maids found her sprawled across the table, just there: she was dead.'

Mirrin's cheeks drained of colour. For a second or two she said nothing, then, harshly and abruptly, laughed.

'Poor woman,' she said. 'I suppose they blamed the strain of childbirth, and salved their conscience that way.'

'I expect they tried,' said Lamont. 'But even the consciences of coalmasters cannot be easily salved. My great-grandfather suffered a spasm of the heart and died a year later.'

'He deserved it.'

'I daresay: but I cannot help considering what I might have done if I'd been faced with his decision.'

'It's maybe lucky you've no . . .'

Mirrin looked at the floor, wishing that it would open into an abyss and swallow her up. The remark had been tactless, unintentionally cruel.

'I must go, sir,' she murmured and, backing away from him, went out into the hall and fled in shame to the safety of the kitchens.

Lamont felt no animosity towards her. Tactlessness and honesty had the same stem; she had spoken her mind to him without regard for the niceties of rank which divided them. The fact that she could now feel regret at having touched the quick of his heart spoke well for the girl and for their relationship.

He walked down the length of the table, running his hand along its surface. The piece of history had amused her: would she be as amused if he had told her of his own childhood in this house, if he had spoken to her of Dorothy? He talked to no one about Dorothy. Edith would not listen: her impatience was more cruel than the girl's frankness could ever be.

The sun had swung round from behind the oaks and laid a wedge of colour across the rock garden, pin-pointing the star-flowers and tiny herbaceous leaves of the plant collection.

Quite plainly he could see Dorothy again upon the lawn by the stones, a young girl, willowy and graceful and brimful of laughter – in the happy days before the axe had fallen across her reason and split it as the farmer's blade had indelibly scored the table top so many years ago.

Digging the crumpled letter from his pocket, he smoothed out its folds and once more scanned the childish scrawl.

Ciphers of feeling, pared away from logic, intellect and the grammar of restraint, the random words seemed to shout aloud and plead for understanding – *book, dust, while, lady, sister, rabbit, loving.*

Loving!

Loving sister.

Folding the sheet with care, he pressed it into his velvet pocket.

To burn the letter now would serve no purpose. His loneliness made him vulnerable to the ghosts of yesterday. Now that the past was unsealed, he would be haunted by memories, sad and sweet, throughout the rest of the day. Alas, there were no vials of laudanum, no murderous axes, and no occlusions of the heart to give his conscience ease.

*

The shelf creaked. Drew heard shouting, laughter and the slamming of doors.

Obviously Mirrin was home early.

There was excitement in her voice tonight, not weariness, ire or complaint. During the past few weeks his sister had become calmer and quieter and much less aggressively boisterous. He assumed that the work up at Lamont's place imposed stresses upon her which tapped off her abundant energy during the long day. Whatever the cause, she tended to leave him to his own devices, and for that mercy, Drew was heartily thankful.

The shelf groaned again.

A slim, stained copy of Platt's *Primer of Roots and Derivations* gently collapsed under the mustard-cloth cover of *Antiquities of Classical Greek*. The beam from the tin-shaded candle-lamp quivered, and Drew, lying on the cot mattress in his best clothes, reached out with a sigh and steadied the sand-filled base.

Warily, he surveyed the shelf. He had erected it himself from a couple of found planks as an essential repository for the collection of books with which old Guthrie had deluged him since lessons began. He was less sure of the shelf's ability to contain the physical manifestations of learning than of his brain's capacity to store and arrange its intangible facts.

The books settled. Drew lay back against the bolster and inclined the book page towards the light.

On the little table placed under the neuk of the sky-light, his exercises lay finished. His handwriting had become neater but more crabbed and had taken on the guise of maturity, being legible but unexpressive, showing no sign at all of the irregular rhythm at which he worked – a blend of confident haste and pedantic uncertainty.

Already in the room, however, were all the reference works he required to polish and perfect his written work and he had acquired – as the dominie no doubt intended – that habit of painstaking thoroughness which would become the bedrock of a legal career. His enthusiasm for knowledge had already been flattened by the sheer weight of matter which he was required to absorb, and by the grindingly dull meticulousness of the dominie's tutorials.

Compensations were few but important, the luxury of privacy, and the comparative comfort of his attic room listed high among them. He had no compunction about milking the family for any items which he felt would increase the cosiness of his study. He had wheedled the candle-lamp out of Kate, and had informed her that, come the autumn frosts, he would expect to be provided with some form of heating, preferably a coal-oil stove, and an adequate supply of fuel. His mother had been ordered to knit him an ankle-length robe with a tall collar, styled like that which saints and martyrs wore in picture-book engravings. He had left to her, without a qualm of conscience, the problem of finding cash with which to buy wool. After all – or so ran the thread of his argument – a place at university would be of little use to him if he was too sick to take it up.

Even Betsy had contributed to his welfare by presenting him with a hunting coat of bright scarlet melton. She claimed that the extraordinary garment had only cost her a penny at Dalzells' last clearance sale. Kate and his mother accepted the explanation at face value, but Drew was not convinced. Though the coat was not new, its condition could not be faulted, and it had obviously cost a great deal originally. From what he had heard of Dalzells', it seemed improbable that the coat had been relinquished at under ten shillings, if it had ever been out for clearance at all. At the time he offered no comment, thanked Betsy for her generosity, and now wore the coat constantly to protect his thin shoulders from the invidious draughts which assailed him as he pored over his books.

The monotony of his routine would have driven any one of his former school companions mad in a week, but Drew found security in it, and ample opportunity to evade the petty responsibilities which fell on most boys of his age. His dedication made his life incredibly compact and, oddly, free.

He had little real contact with his family and even during supper exempted himself from conversation by devouring the contents of the *Hamilton Advertiser* or, if Betsy had been fortunate enough to find a discarded copy, the *Glasgow Herald*. Occasionally, he would take a stroll before bed: more often than not he read himself to sleep and left Kate or his mother to snuff out the candle.

This evening, however, he had taken a half hour off to wash himself and don his Sunday clothes. Shortly before seven, he would accompany his sisters across the backs and up to the allotment at the top of the row to partake of a little social frolic with the folk of the village. He did not view the celebration of Maggie Fox's nuptials with any great relish but felt that it was his duty, as the man of the house, to at least show his face. Besides Henderson and McLaren were sure to be there, aching from a hard shift at the pit, and he would not pass up an encounter with his 'old chums' for worlds.

Caesar's account of his conquests could not compete with his sisters' bellowings below.

Drew recorded his place with a spill of paper, laid the book aside and rolled over on to his elbow, listening.

'Dumplin' and treacle scones,' Mirrin cried. 'I can smell them.'

'They're not for you,' Kate answered.

'Mam, were you at the kirk this mornin'?' said Betsy.

'Aye.'

'Was Maggie bonnie?' asked Kate.

'Maggie Fox couldn't be bonnie if she was coated wi' sugar violets,' Mirrin declared from the back bedroom.

Betsy, who had also been granted the dispensation of an evening off, asked, 'What did she wear?'

'The white dress,' his mother said.

'Same one as her sisters wore?'

'Aye, but wi' new trimmin'.'

'I heard McRobbie near tore yon dress off Letty in his anxiety to be at her,' said Mirrin.

Betsy's giggle echoed quite clearly in the attic.

Drew smiled indulgently at the lewdness in it.

'Wheeesht!' Mam said, and he knew that she had pointed at the ceiling.

'Och, him,' said Mirrin. 'It's time Drew got an education that didn't come from books. God, but I could do with a slice o' that dumpling.'

Mirrin was in the living room now, probably preening her hair. Drew, too, could smell the spicy aroma which indicated that the clootie dumpling had at last been removed from the pot and, drained, would soon be in the process of being wrapped in greased paper for transportation to the communal feast.

Drew had never really understood colliers' celebrations and the verve with which such entertainments were broached. Reticent by nature, he could see no need for spirited gatherings or appreciate that marriages were the best of all excuses to bring out the villagers from their drab rows and instil some cheerful anticipation and festivity into their lives.

'I can't believe that Maggie Fox's actually wedded,' said Mirrin, from below.

'You said some terrible things about that lassie,' his mother reminded Mirrin. 'You'll have t'be changin' your tune now that she's a marrit woman.'

'Not me,' said Mirrin. 'Maggie Fox poked her fingers in enough eyes before she got one poor wretch blinded enough to haul t'the altar.'

'Mirrin!' The reprimand was not stern.

'Well, it's true enough. That's how half of them trap husbands, an' fine you know it, Mam.'

'I just hope it's not in your mind.'

Mirrin wailed with laughter.

'Me? D'you think I'm daft? I don't intend to be a bondserf to any man.'

Betsy whispered something which Drew failed to catch.

The remark, whatever its import, riled Mirrin.

'Mind your tongue, Betsy,' she snapped. 'I want no more of that, or I'll skelp your lug. I might be housekeeper to a gentleman and you might be a fancy shop assistant, but I'm still your big sister and capable of deliverin' a fast clip yet.'

There was silence below for a minute or two. If his guess was correct, Betsy had said something about Houston Lamont. Mirrin was oddly defensive on that score. He had not heard her deride the coalmaster for over a month, and all her venom now seemed to be directed at Lamont's wife.

Drew turned on to his back again, screening his eyes, which smarted blearily, against the light. Girls – they were such fools, so petty and self-centred. He could not even understand why they were trotting along to the celebrations at all. Most of the folk in Blacklaw looked down their noses at the Stalkers these days. He could hardly blame them: they were jealous of him, and annoyed at Mirrin for siding with Houston Lamont.

Still, their appearance would supply the gossips with plenty of material. Spitefulness, he supposed, would be repressed for the duration of the evening, but tomorrow, and for a week hence, the Stalkers would be the talk of the middens, and Maggie Fox and her new husband would hardly be mentioned except by their relatives.

As if voicing his thoughts, Mirrin said, 'Come on, Betsy, you're pretty enough. I'm not inclined t'be late t'this beano. If I am, Maggie'll assume I'm puce with envy, and she's not havin' that satisfaction to put on top of all the other pleasures that'll be comin' her way.'

'Fetch Drew, then!'

'Drew: we're near ready.'

He lay motionless on the cot, staring up at the pale jade squares of summer sky which showed through the dirty glass above him.

'Drew: for God's sake!'

A moment later, a broom handle rapped on the underside of the floor boards and caused another slight toppling on his improvised shelf.

234

'All right,' he called.

After all, without him the Stalkers' appearance would be considerably reduced in value.

Rolling from the mattress, he blew out the candle-lamp and dropped down the ladder to complete the family group.

6

Behind each of the twin rows of houses which lined Blacklaw main street, a low brick-built structure served as midden and privy, its functions common to all the residents. In spite of attempts at cleanliness, the odour which wafted from this squat building tended to overripeness and, in summer months, no matter how hot the weather, few families dared throw open their rear room windows. The structure did not extend all the way to the top, for there the houses forked away respectfully from the lozenge of the kirkyard, leaving an area of flat ground dappled with rank grass. This was the setting for most of the outdoor gatherings – the small fairs, the parties, the hellfire conventions of travelling evangelists, and the impromptu performances of Highland tinkers who piped and danced and sang their heart-breaking Gaelic laments for pennies or bread as they passed through Blacklaw from the harvest fields.

The waste was shielded by blackthorns and feathery whinns along the kirk side, and the blunt steeple of that pious building peeped above the greenery to sniff at the proceedings. Though close by, the colliery could not be seen at all, but the shunting and clanging of the back-shift barrows near drowned out the fiddler's tunes at times.

Festivities were under way when the Stalkers arrived. Many of the groom's pals had come directly from the pit, pausing only to sluice off the black grit in the rain barrels at the back of the *Lantern*. It seemed that fastidiousness and a sense of occasion did not extend to all the villagers. Most of the Fox family's friends, of course, had done the decent thing and trigged themselves up a bit to honour the bride and swank their slight superiority over the Williams tribe who were Welsh by origin, Baptists by conviction, and lived in squalor in a fortress of raddled tin shacks in the shadow of the Clayburn coups.

The housewives of Blacklaw had raided their frugal larders to come up with the ingredients of the feast. For the most part, the fare was plain and filling – griddle scones, potato browns, pancakes, bannocks in assorted sizes, raisin buns, custards, dumplings, biscuits, and swollen sultana loaves in square black baking trays. Kitchen tables, scrounged from neighbours, were draped with best cloths and set with borrowed plates and cups. Along the row, the children had already flung manners to the winds and had fallen upon the edibles like little wolves, spilling enough crumbs in the process to satisfy all the stray dogs and mongrel cats who milled about the tables.

Tea flowed in abundance from two mammoth urns, loaned by the Masons' Lodge in exchange for a contribution to their orphans' fund, and there were churns of skimmed milk sent down from Auchenarn where one of Billy Williams's nine brothers was a cowman.

Music exuded from Dick Esslemont's concertina; jigs, reels, strathspeys, and popular songs from the Glasgow music-halls, all struck in the same plaintive key.

Some of the younger adults were whirling away on the bald earth patch by the house backs, but the best time for dancing would come later when dusk cloaked the trees and the eagle-eyed grannies had hobbled back to their hearths and the doors of the *Lantern* had been bolted for the night.

Mostly, the women gathered within striking distance of the urns to drink their fill of strong, stewed tea, nibble scones, criticize the culinary efforts of their friends, and speculate on how long it would be before Maggie Fox would parade a swollen belly round the streets and express her surprise that the bairn was 'so early'.

The miners themselves were little in evidence yet, for it was a proven scientific fact that weddings, like pit-work, incurred a dreadful thirst in a man. Moving discreetly, in groups of three or four, the grooms of yesteryear and the husbands of tomorrow herded each other across the path, through Sunter's Lane and into the jovial fog of the pub's bar parlour, there to toast the bonnie bride and bashful groom in endless jars of ale.

The bonnie bride herself, still wearing the wedding gown which had graced so many Foxes in the past, was soothing her nerves with a measure of neat gin, and wrestling with the yellowing veil and wired headdress which was pinned to her scalp.

With a mug of tea in one hand and a slice of her mother's dumpling warm in the other, Mirrin came up the straggling line of well-wishers, regal as a queen and mischievous as a monkey.

Holding her supper at arms' length, she bent from the waist and pecked at Maggie's cheekbone.

'So y'came,' Maggie hissed. 'Didn't think you'd have the nerve.'

'Nerve enough for anythin',' whispered Mirrin: she drew back, simpering. 'I wouldn't miss your big day for a barrowfu' o' dross, Maggie. Besides, I'd like to meet the lucky lad, of whom I have heard so many favourable comments.'

Maggie blinked: the glass of gin was not her first, but she was still sober enough to recognize the refined insolence in Mirrin's request.

'D'you know where he is?' asked Mirrin.

Setting the measure behind her on the table, Maggie cupped her hand to her mouth and called out, 'Billy.'

It had been a long day for William Williams. The church ceremony had been followed by a seemingly endless afternoon during which his ardour and impatience waxed and waned and was regularly cooled by dips from the carrying kegs and pails which his brothers had on hand. When his anticipation grew too fiery, or when his courage withered into panic, there was always a Williams ready to administer a stoup of the time-honoured remedy, spiked with some lewd advice. During the late afternoon, Billy had napped in the sun on the bed in the rented shack, having blown himself out by lugging Maggie's hamper from her Da's house in Main Street. He had wakened with a dry mouth and panic in his guts, crying for his big brothers to come to his rescue.

But now it was evening, the shadows had lengthened on the grass and the breeze blew cold over the bushes, and Billy's emotions were under control and his senses suitably dulled.

'Billy Williams: I want you.'

Laughter exploded around him.

Brothers Dai and Evan shored his elbows and trotted him obediently forward out of the crowd of supporters and the male kin of the tribe.

It was nice to be wanted, thought Billy, and grinned broadly at his new wife.

Mirrin was prepared for the appearance of a clown or a rough lout, but not for the large, flat-featured youth who stood, beaming and swaying, full of liquor and love. His tight blue suit and short-pegged trousers, the belt twisted under his vest, the tankard dangling in his fist, made him comic, yet the effect of his happy, moon-struck smile was sad and daunted Mirrin by its sincerity.

She glanced curiously at Maggie's narrow, half-wasted, petulant face framed in its yellowing veil.

Oh, tonight there would be no miracles of bliss for either of them: Billy was too drunk, and Maggie too fatigued to be anything but abrasive. But in a week or a month, when the tin shack had been disguised as home and the couple had grown used to each other – what then? Then, perhaps, there would be a sort of love between them in the lulls which living allowed, and Maggie Fox, even spiteful Maggie, would learn the true meaning of the marriage bargain, and have more tenderness granted her than she had wistfully imagined possible.

Mirrin passed her cup to Maggie, put her hand on the groom's shoulder and kissed him.

'Good luck, Billy Williams,' she said. 'You've a good wife there, y'know.'

Billy grinned and nodded.

Startled, Maggie waited for the insult which must surely follow. When it did not, she was embarrassed and put-out, not used to taking Mirrin Stalker's remarks without salt.

'Good luck to you too, Maggie,' Mirrin said, then shifted past the couple and filled her mouth with tea and dumpling to allay her temporary covetousness of the girl she had always disliked.

For a while after that Mirrin stood alone by the thorns, watching the gathering as a stranger might have done. It was true what Kate and her mother had told her about the run of feeling in the village. She had had little experience of it personally, since most of her time was spent now up at the mansion. Soon she would be obliged to stay on the premises. It surprised her that Lamont had not raised the matter before now. If she wanted to serve, then she must serve fully, not keep back the best of the day for herself. In truth, it galled her to be split between the narrow house at Main Street's end and the mansion on the hill. She felt separate from her family, from her former friends, even from herself. It went against the grain of her character to vacillate: nor could she fathom why Lamont had not insisted on full service for full domestic pay. Maybe that bitch of a wife of his was behind it.

When the mug of tea was finished and she had wiped the crumbs from the corners of her lips, Mirrin looked round for Kate, Betsy and Drew.

Betsy was dancing, too dainty for the hulking collier who swung her about on the crook of his arm, but enjoying herself nonetheless and sacrificing some of her airs for the pleasure of the company of her own born kind.

Kate was with Mam, helping out behind the tables, dishing cups of milk for the bairns, and scraping butter thinly on to the surviving bannocks. Most of the food would be gone before the men trailed back from the pub.

At first she could not spot Drew at all, and thought that her brother might have become bored already and returned to the attic and his beloved books. She wasn't much concerned. It was enough that she put eight-tenths of her wage into the stone flour jar and ate a meatless supper six nights in the week for the sake of her brother's education. She was committed by Kate's rash promise to tend his future, not his welfare. She did her share, more than her share, though the job in Lamont's house suited her better than she dared admit. However, she had not forgotten the effort of will it had cost her to go there cap in hand: that had been the worst part of it, the beginning. Now? Well, she would be Lamont's housekeeper as long as Lamont wanted her, and only hoped that she might soon come to terms with the mistress and weld together a truce.

Drew stood apart from the crowd of first-year pit apprentices and second-year hardymen. Not one of the boys had changed out of his moleskins and the hardymen still toted their lamps at their waistclips like badges of maturity. Here was pride in embryo, that new growth her father had often spoken of, the sullen masculine pride which never quite died out in a man no matter how harsh the work or how miserable the take-home pay. It was a coalmaster's toughest chain, yet it had naught to do with the coalmasters of the world, being born and bred into the boys as soon as they could toddle, spooned into them with every bowl of saps, until they thought of the pit as their own and forgot that they were slaves to it and as much in the owners' pockets as the profits of the earth.

Who were they? She peered into the gathering dusk – Henderson, a big brute grown this summer, with coaldust already ingrained into his downy beard and rimming the corners of his eyes. He had been like an overgrown hare in the spring, but a short season's graft at the pit-head had transformed him and made him feral. McLaren was there, too, not so blubbery, though still mump-cheeked. And Danny O'Reilly, and Calder and the two Stewart lads. They had acquired a gallon pail of frothy beer and were dipping their tins into it, all seated on the grass in a ring round the vessel, boasting in quiet voices, and guffawing, and glancing back from time to time to cast eyes at the girls. They were pretending to be men, would, indeed, be men soon, and the better for this period of pretence.

And her brother, lean and stooped-shouldered, stood behind them, staring at them, waiting to be acknowledged: maybe even waiting to be invited to sit himself down and join them – though he wanted only the smug satisfaction of refusing, like as not.

Gloaming darkened the whinn clumps and settled blue and smoky over the roofs of the colliers' rows. A pitch-torch flared, then another, as lads lit the small bonfires which they had collected that afternoon, to give light to the fiddlers' strings.

There were many more dancers now, and the tune was lively. Some young bucks had sauntered back from the pub, pipes in their mouths and a speculative glint in their eyes. One wedding soon led to others, so the sweetiewives said. Across the sward, Maggie danced with her Billy, holding him up, holding him tight, her frail, ivory veil twined round him too.

Mirrin glanced at the apprentices' ring again and noticed that Drew had gone, totally ignored and shunned by the brotherhood of working lads.

A touch on her sleeve brought her attention round.

Loony Lachie Abercorn bowed until forelock almost brushed the grass. He straightened and produced from his tail-coat pocket a plump, green-glass bottle. Tied round the neck with thread a red rosebud nodded on its stem. Loony opened his mouth wide, shook the unusual gift and vigorously indicated that she must take it.

'My, my, Loony!' Mirrin relieved him of the offering. 'Are you not the gallant one tonight? You'll have to be careful or you'll be havin' all the lassies after you.'

Loony fanned his lips wider and pranced up and down. Seizing her hand, he tugged at it and pointed across the wasteground, tapping the bottle, and nodding furiously.

'What is it, Loony?'

'Him, aye, him.'

Rob's bulk was outlined against the bonfire. He seemed larger and more powerful than Mirrin remembered and she realized with a guilty flush that in a month or more she had spared no thought for her father's old friend and her former suitor. Kate had spoken of him a night or so back but she had been too tired to listen properly.

'From Rob Ewing, is it, Lachie?'

Lachie nodded and nodded.

The girl stilled him.

She separated the rose from the thread and, sloping the bottle to the remaining light, read the label – a French wine, from Burgundy.

Sniffing the tranquil perfume of the rose, she glanced up at Rob again. It had been so imaginative of him to put this gift together, but did he suppose her so affected by her sophisticated rank now that only an expensive present would impress her? In fact, she had never lipped wine in her life.

'Is it Lachie I've to thank, or you?' she called.

'Thank him for bein' the messenger.'

Rob came towards her, walking with long purposeful strides, though still not certain of his welcome.

Lachie waited, beaming.

Mirrin reached to her hair and tugged out the ribbon which bound it up. Deftly, she tied a floppy bow about the rose-stem and, with mock gravity, presented the flower to Mr Lauchlan Abercorn.

'There,' she said.

Lachie could not believe it. He performed a mute show of amazement and gratitude, then, on Rob's instruction, trotted off to exhibit his prize to anyone who would give him a little attention.

'How is it with you, Mirrin?' asked Rob.

'Fine, Rob: and with yourself?'

'Fine.' He hesitated. 'Would you be for dancin'?'

'I'm not supple enough in the joints for that.'

'Has housekeeping turned you into an old woman?'

'Not so old that I can't put one foot before the other.'

'Will you take a wee stroll with me, then, since it's such a soft night?'

'I will,' said Mirrin promptly. 'Though I should warn you, you'll set the tongues waggin'.'

'To hell with them,' Rob said. He took her arm and put it through his. 'I'm right glad to see you again, Mirrin.'

They skirted the butt of the kirkyard wall and crossed the corner of a goat pasture, not looking back at the littered trucks of the pit or the high wheel tower which loomed overhead. Sounds of fiddles and concertina, in unintentional harmony, drifted up from the wasteground, diminishing as the couple reached the mouth of the track which had once carried the road from Blacklaw to Northrigg.

Grass and weeds had nibbled it to a dusty footpath. Leaves of birch, thorn and rowan shrouded it, containing the twilight and closing out the music of the wedding party and the raucous din of the mine. Bats flitted across the nave of the pathway, embodiments of dusk and quietness.

Rob put his arm about her waist.

'You ... you don't mind?'

'No,' Mirrin said. 'I like it.'

She handed him the wine bottle and he put it in the pocket of his jacket. They walked on, saying nothing for a time, both resolutely staring ahead into the trees where the path curved and rose a little on to the ridge which overlooked Northrigg a half mile on. The leaves held the heat of the day and the scent of wild flowers and herbs was heavy.

'Mirrin,' Rob said, awkwardly. 'You look bonnier every time I see you.'

'I don't much believe that tale about absence makin' the heart grow fonder,' said Mirrin, suddenly half-afraid of her own emotions.

'It's true, though,' said Rob.

'Rob, Rob,' she murmured. 'You'll just get hurt again.'

'I'm not worried now.' His arm tightened about her waist. She remembered Maggie Fox and Billy, and the loving in the young man's eyes and how Maggie had held her man to her, tightly, tightly. 'It would be better t'be hurt sometimes than this ... this nothingness,' Rob said. 'I want t'see you every day.'

'Then you'd soon hate the sight of me,' Mirrin said.

'It needn't happen to us.'

She stopped, turning in against him, looking up at his face. 'Just what is it you do want, Rob?'

He spoke hoarsely. 'Marriage.'

'Wedding, bedding, and bairns?'

'Aye.'

'And to get me out of Lamont's house?'

'I asked you before.'

'I know you did.'

'Will you, then?'

'Will I what?'

'Consent t'marry me.'

'No, Rob.'

'Christ!'

Once more, he had forced her to refuse and, in so doing, had spoiled the moment which the dusk had brought, the nearness which, had he been less proud, might have brought him closer to fulfilment.

He caught at her, roughly, and pulled her away from the centre of the path. 'Listen,' he said. 'I've loved you for years, about as long as I can remember, an' just seein' you an' talkin' to you there in your father's house was enough. But now it's not. It's all I can do t'hole this hell-hole of a place...'

'Stop, Rob,' she said, breathlessly. 'Please.'

'It isn't *enough* : don't *you* see that, damn you.'

The wind came cool from the direction of Northrigg, rustling and chastening the trees, and bringing, by some strange fluke of contour, the fiddlers' jig, faint and far, far off, from the Black-law patch, the melody hanging in the air then passing away again like elf-music.

Mirrin was afraid.

She could not deny the force of the feelings in her body. Perhaps, she thought later, Rob's violence was simply a response to her passion, transference of her own impulsive longings, so potent that they swept aside his inhibitions and stiff-necked pride. In another, more temperate exchange, she would have credited him with calculation – but it was not so, not then on the path in the gloaming.

His hand caught her hair and pinned her head fast. He brought his mouth against her lips, and kissed her savagely. Fear went out of her, vanished like the tuneful air. Her eyes widened. His skin was not smooth, but pitted and scarred. She could smell the collier's odour from him, sweat and mineral harshness, and feel the breadth of the heaving muscles across his back. Everything beyond her was banished, thrust out of her mind. He clutched her and dragged her deeper into the shrubs, stumbling, and, breaking the contact for an instant, swung her painfully round and pushed her down into the grass.

'Wait : wait,' she said.

Her fingers were steady and adroit, unhooking the tiny pearl buttons of blouse, bodice and chemise, dozens and dozens of useless impediments. She lifted herself on her elbow and slipped down the garments, felt her breasts drag heavily, then come free. She lolled back again, braced on her hands.

Rob was upon her, hands cupping her breasts, his bulk black against the deep lavender afterglow which the sun had left in the sky to the west and which, caught on a gridiron of cloud, glowed like smouldering coals behind the ink-black leaves.

Moths clouded up from the broken stalks, minute and parchment pale: then they were gone as Rob's weight crushed her down deep into the grass, and she saw only roots and fibres struggling from the earth, secret and intimate in their strength. Grass fronds and hair tangled her face, and pleasure ranged ravenously in her loins like some wild creature loosed at last from captivity.

Rob's breathing was loud and ragged. His fists left her breasts. He arched his back. Fresh spasms of pleasure engulfed her. So intense were they that she thrashed her head this way and that and clawed at his shoulders to bring him closer. His fist bunched in her skirts and petticoats, tearing the stitching, swaddling them up so tightly that she could feel the contraction of her belly pressed agonizingly against the cloth. Pain and pleasure confused her, and the only fear in her now was that he would abruptly revert to sanity and haul himself away, leaving her trapped in torrents of need, drowning in her own womanhood.

But the urgency of his hunger was greater than her own – direct, masculine, selfish. Fumbling, he found her and, with no mark of tenderness, lowered his hips. Pain and pleasure separated with a suddenness which made her cry out convulsively and snare him with her arms and legs.

It was quickly over.

He sank all his weight upon her, let out a shuddering sigh, then slid gently to one side and rolled away into the grass.

Still half naked and open, she waited while her reason tilted and floated back like a coin dropping through water.

'Did I hurt you?' he asked.

She did not turn her head.

'No, not enough to complain about.'

'Uh!'

Her arms were leaden as she reached across her breasts and groped for the shoulder-straps of bodice and blouse and, clumsily now, rebuttoned them. That done, she rested, then propping herself up a little, examined herself briefly and untucked the bunched skirts.

Rob was still hidden in the tall grasses. She could see nothing of him but crossed knees and one polished pit boot kicking gently at the air. Was it shame or drowsiness, perhaps even indifference, which kept him apart from her now? Now, when she would have welcomed an embrace and kind words.

'I *was* the first,' he said.

Mirrin frowned, rubbing at a grass stain on her skirt.

'Aye.'

'But . . .?'

'What did you expect, Rob?'

'I dunno.'

'Choirs of cherubs?'

'Was it . . . all right?'

'How would I know?'

He sat up suddenly and, hugging his knees, stared across at her.

'Don't fret,' he said, 'I mean, you've nothin' to worry about.'

'I'm not worried,' Mirrin said.

'I mean, that's it, isn't it,' said Rob. 'You'll have to marry me now.'

'Are you proposin' again?'

'I doubt,' he said, smugly, 'if a proposal's actually needed.'

'Oh, Rob!' she said, lightly; she could not yet believe that he was not joking with her. 'A girl likes all the trimmings.'

'You'll maybe have more than all the trimmings, Mirrin.'

She studied him, peering in the gloom.

'An' just what the hell d'you mean by that?' she asked, at length.

'I mean you might have the beginnings of a bairn . . .'

She was on her knees, leaning.

'Is that why . . .?'

'No, no: now, Mirrin, will you just say when it'll suit you an' I'll do all the arranging.'

'You're serious, aren't you?'

'I've never been more serious.' He spoke in a sepulchral tone.

'It would be better if it was soon, to save folk countin' on their thumbs.'

'Rob...'

'I apologize for what happened,' he said, stiffly. 'It's not the way I would have wanted it.'

'You think that's reason enough for me to change my mind?'

He regarded her solemnly, head on one side.

'It's the least I can do,' he declared. 'Besides, it's not as if I didn't want to marry you.'

'Make an ... make an honest woman out of me, will you!' She leapt to her feet in fury. 'You *bastard*! You smug, arrogant hypocrite! You mealy-mouthed ... Jesus! I thought you were full of ... of *love*: There's nothin' in you but *camphor*. You stink of it.'

'Careful, Mirrin: I'm under no obligation ...'

He reached for her and caught the hem of her skirt. She dragged herself away from him, then kicked out. His palm flew to the place on his brow where her shoe had caught him a glancing blow.

'*You're* under no obligation,' Mirrin raged. '*What about me?* I suppose I'm to crawl over hot coals an' *beg* for you to wed me now. Because I'm just a woman, a nothin', a bit of ... of flesh for you t'stick it in every time the mood's on you!'

'Don't talk like that!'

'I'll talk how I please, an' I'll marry who I please,' she shouted. 'No, don't come one inch nearer, or I'll let you have the other shoe, right in your pious bloody mouth.'

'You may regret behavin' this way, you know.'

'If I'm expecting, you mean? I don't care. But, just for your information, Rob Ewing, I'm no more expecting than you are.'

'How can you...?'

She spoke softly now, sibilantly, with a relish and a venom which cowed him. 'Because I'm a woman, an' know about these things. If you must have the lurid details, it's because I'm due a bleeding tomorrow, an' that'll be rid of any ... any stains you may have left in me.'

As he got to his feet, she drew back from him and stumbled on to the path. But he did not come after her, standing stock-still, hands by his sides, looking then, she thought, more stupid than any one of the Williams tribe, and less of a man even than Lachie Abercorn.

'I'll tell you this, Rob,' she said. 'I did what we did because I wanted to, not because you forced me to it. No, and I liked it, liked it for itself. It might have been better with some other man – it might have been worse. But the fact of it does not grant you the right t'be the last man ever t'give me pleasure. You hear that, *pleasure*.'

'It's true what they say about you,' he bellowed.

'I don't want to hear: I don't want to hear.'

She clapped her hands to her ears, but could not blot out his words.

'You're a whore, Mirrin Stalker. Maybe soon enough you'll have the honesty to be a real one and not just a pretend. You're a foul-mouthed, stuck-up bitch.'

'Tell them then,' she screamed. 'Tell them all what I was like, how good it felt. Tell them when they're propped round the pub swillin' their bloody ale, thinkin' they're gods. It'll do your standin' good, if nothing else. It'll make you *seem* like a man. *Men!*' She twisted her head and, striking like a snake, spat on to the grass at his feet. '*Pigs!*'

Then she turned and fled from the glade which, a half hour ago, had been so tranquil and pretty and romantic. Now it was dirty with night and trammelled by her memories of the rumours which seeped back about the kind of girls who went there and what was done to them.

She held to the path for fifty yards then, imagining that he might follow her and attempt to stop her, she plunged into the thickets, tearing heedlessly on through the brambles and ferns and rank, clinging weeds.

*

Betsy knocked at the corner of the attic: it was hardly a door at all, more like a trap set at a right-angle to the camber of the roof. She had seen the like in the flour-mill and up at the cheese loft in Drennan's farm where she had once been with a friend whose uncle worked there.

'Drew?'

'A moment.'

'Did I wake you?'

'No: come in.'

He opened the trap for her and she scrambled up the last steep, narrow steps into the attic.

The tiny room was warmed by the lingering heat of the day, the warmth given form by the strong beam of the candle-lamp round which big-winged moths batted and whirled foolishly.

Drew wore his nightshirt, and had draped the hunting coat like a cape across his shoulders.

If he had been wearing a pair of cream nap trews instead of the cold cotton shirt, he might have looked quite dashing with the scarlet coat flung across his shoulders and his chest bare. He would have to have his chest bare, of course, and, now she thought about it, Drew just didn't have the sort of chest that would bare well.

'You're back early,' he said, seating himself on the edge of the mattress.

'Almost everyone's gone home,' said Betsy, shrugging. 'It wasn't much of a dance, really.'

'Where are Mam, Mirrin and Kate?'

'Mam and Kate are helping, still.'

'I don't know why they bother,' Drew said. 'After all, it's fairly apparent that as far as this village is concerned the Stalkers are *persona ingrata*.'

'Is that Latin?'

'Aye: it means nobody wants us here.'

'Everybody was quite nice to *me*.'

She shook her curls prettily and tried her profile on him – a waste of effort, of course, because Drew was her twin and never so much as spared a glance in her direction.

'It seems,' said Drew, addressing the oddment of carpet which covered the floorboards, 'it seems, however, that I'm an outcast.'

'Mirrin's gone missin'.'

He looked up. 'Really?'

'Kate's lookin' for her, an' Mam's worried,' Betsy said. 'She went off with Rob Ewing down that path.'

'What path are you talking about?'

Betsy bit her lip. 'Where the . . . the lovers go.'

'Mirrin and Rob Ewing? Never.'

'Don't be so sure.'

'She won't have *him*.'

'Depends on what you mean.' Betsy gathered her skirts and seated herself beside him.

She still felt buoyant with the results of her flirtatious conquests among the younger sons of the village and still had the rhythms of the reels in her head. It was all so crude, and not at all like a real ball would be, but, at least, she had struck dumb a few of her partners and caused them to blush like turkeys; all without saying more than a casual word or two.

Drew peered at his sister.

'No,' he said 'Not Mirrin.'

'She's no different from any other girl.'

Drew licked his bottom lip. 'No different from you!'

Betsy blinked her eyelashes several times, rapid as the wings of a moth. 'What *do* you mean, Drew?'

'Where did you get the coat?'

'Coat?'

'This,' he said, thumbing out the lapel. 'Scarlet hunting coats are not offered for sale at one penny, not in your shop, nor anywhere else.'

'Are you accusing me of lying?'

'Aye.'

'Well, I'm not standing for that.' She flounced up and would have whipped open the door, if he had not caught her from behind. Arms about her waist, he yanked her backwards and fell across the bed with her.

'Let me . . . go.'

His finger insinuated itself into her longest ringlet, specially curled for the occasion, and cocked round it, tugging painfully and rendering her immobile.

'The truth, sister, please,' Drew said.

'I bought it at . . .'

'How much did it really cost?'

'A pen . . .' she began, then cried. 'No, owwhh, don't.'

'How much?'

'I ... don't know.'

'Didn't you buy it?'

'No.'

'Betsy, you didn't *steal* it?'

'No, silly. Let me up.'

He released her hair but placed his elbows across her waist and leaned on it, looking down into her face. 'Did you steal it?'

'I was given it, as a present.'

'By whom?'

'A friend.'

'A gentleman friend, I suppose?'

'Well, why not? He never uses it now. In fact, he hardly ever did use it. It wasn't any use to him, an' he knew I had a brother an' he gave it to me for you. That's all.'

'What's this "gentleman" friend's name?'

'I'm not tellin' you: you'll tell Mam.'

'Is there something t'tell then?'

'No, Drew, honest, there isn't. He's just a gentleman who meets me in Hamilton sometimes.'

'He's not a soldier, is he?'

'No.'

'That's something to be thankful for,' said Drew. 'What do you do together?'

'Not what you think.'

'What do I think?'

She was not afraid of Drew. Being his twin, she understood him well enough, though she was not, alas, endowed with half his intelligence. Whatever she told him would not be relayed downstairs: she could trust him. They were a pair, peas in the same pod.

She said, 'I haven't been ... naughty with him.'

'But he gives you presents?'

'He gave me the huntin' coat, because he had no more use for it. We were talkin' about you, and how you wanted to become a lawyer and how difficult it was, an' he said he had a coat that a lad could wear.'

'What else has he given you?'

'Nothing.'

'Tell me the truth, Betsy.'

'Three ribbons: he gave me the money.'

'An' what did he get in return?'

'My company.'

'He'll want more than that soon.'

'No: he's a gentleman – and he's shy.'

'What age is he?'

'I really ...'

'Older than Rob Ewing, say?'

'A little, probably.'

'Is he married?'

'No.'

'Are you sure of that?'

'He told me he wasn't.'

'Has he made any proposals?'

'Must I tell you again, Drew?'

'Find out what you can about him.'

'But ... Drew, why?'

'So that you may protect yourself, if necessary.'

'How will ...?'

'Listen.'

Kate's voice came clearly from the pavement just below the little attic window. The door opened and the twins heard their mother clumping heavily and wearily into the kitchen.

Kate was saying, 'She'll be fine, Mam: don't fret about her.'

'I can't help it. Mirrin's always been wild.'

'Wild, aye,' Kate answered, 'but she's got Da's commonsense. She'll come to no harm.'

'Where can she be?'

'It's my guess she's had a tiff with Rob an' she's gone t'spend the night with one of her pals.'

'She has no pals.'

'Then she'll have gone back t'mansion. It's after midnight now, Mam: she'll sleep with the maids, in their room, an' be ready t'start early.'

'I wish I could be certain,' said the older woman anxiously.

'Take my word for it,' said Kate. 'Mirrin'll be fine.'

Drew glanced at Betsy.

'You'd better go,' he whispered.

'You won't tell?'

'I have nothin' to tell,' he said. 'But take a wee warning, Betsy : be careful what you do.'

'I like him.'

'Aye – just be cautious, will you?'

Betsy nodded, then opened the door and lowered herself down the steps into the hallway below, calling out, 'Goodnight, Drew.'

The boy did not return to bed immediately. He sat quite motionless on the edge of the mattress, his hands clasped between his knees and his head bowed. He might have been offering up a prayer for his sister's safety but, being the kind of person he was, this was far from the truth. All that filled Drew's thinking, during those silent minutes, was how best he could turn Betsy's budding amour to his own advantage. He had certain qualms that his twin sister's acumen would not be quite as sharp as his own.

As to Mirrin, he spared her no consideration. Long ago he had recognized in her a will and a purpose to match his own, and an almost bland indifference to him as a person and brother. No : dear Mirrin, Drew told himself, was quite capable of looking after herself.

Provided she did nothing to endanger her job at Houston Lamont's house, she could, thought Drew magnanimously, do what the devil she liked.

7

The brass lamps of the Regency pleasure-carriage were silvered by the moon which had lately risen over the stable roofs and now squared the cobbled yard with light. Groom and horse-boy slept soundly in the musty darkness of their gable attic, buried by stout sacks of oats and early corn brought in to lay foundation for the winter stock. Saddles and tack hung from blocks along the whitewashed wall against which the Lamont rigs were ranked. All the conveyances were splendidly brushed and polished, though few were regularly used and remained preserved, like museum pieces, as reminders of Grandfather Lamont's passion for speed.

Here were marshalled phaetons, early landaus, slender-shafted cabriolets, dog carts, high gigs, even a gilded Continental chaise in which the old man, in fits of daring, had raced about his holdings at the risk of a broken neck. Horses not pastured in the four-acre meadow behind the vegetable gardens were stalled in the ell-wing, their sharp aromatic odour mingling with the smell of plush, leather and axle-oil which permeated the long coach-house. The noise of the animals' drowsy champing gave Houston Lamont a sense of companionship which eased the weight of his depression a little. After dusk, he often came here, sometimes with a lamp, ostensibly to inspect the carriages or smooth the horses' coats with curry-comb and dandy brush. More often, he came quietly to brood under the hood of one of the buggies or in the snug shelter of a coach.

The coaching-house was full of happy memories associated with rainy afternoons and make-believe grandeur of childhood games. Dorothy had been Queen here, and he her Consort: he had been Dick Turpin, and Dorothy his ladylove in peril: they had been aristocrats escaping from Paris mobs, lashing imaginary teams across city streets and through wild countryside. None of that magical quality remained in Lamont, only the memory of it.

A more potent memory was of the sickening loneliness of his

first college term, cut off from Blacklaw and his sister's love. Since then he had found warmth scarce, except during the year of his courtship of Edith and the early months of marriage.

It could not be said that he used the stables as a sanctuary to escape Edith, who, on that particular evening, was safe in far-off Edinburgh. Rather, it was a retreat free from the strict, feminine ambience which had moved through the mansion like a fog as the years progressed. In the seclusion of the coach-house, he could be himself, indulge parts of his nature which had no place in the make-up of a coalmaster, that forbidding, decisive, impregnable carapace into which he fitted himself each morning as a knight might don war armour.

The night air was warm. The half-open doors of the long building admitted moonlight. A barn owl hooted and swooped low over the cobbles, casting a brief shadow over the silvered flagstones. Lamont slumped in the carriage bench, facing the shafts. His head rested against the inside of the half-hood and his feet were propped on the painted iron rail which, so his father had once informed him, was designed to prevent ladies and gentlemen 'coming together' in the darkness. The carriage was long, broad and shallow. It smelled not of paint, but of iron and horsehair. He had been sprawled on the bench for an hour or more, moving only to light a cigar, then to stub out the butt against the pitted wheel-rim when he had smoked the tobacco down. He could not define the thoughts which were in his mind. They were clouded and a little confused, drifting between nostalgia and concern for the poverty of the coal markets. Soon he must stir himself, he supposed, and go back indoors to bed. Laziness deterred him from making the effort sooner. In fact, he had just stretched his hand to the riding pillar to hoist himself up when a shadow blotted out the light from the doorway. No owl this, the shadow was large and ragged, stooped like a nun in full habit.

Lamont opened his lips to challenge the person, then as Mirrin Stalker entered the coach-house, he lowered himself back into the dark corner of the carriage.

The girl hesitated in the doorway, bathed in the bright moonlight, then came uncertainly forward. Lamont held his breath.

It was all too clear that the lass was not herself. Her skirts were rumpled and her hair dishevelled. She walked limpingly past the Regency carriage and along the line of the rigs, unaware of his presence. He was not yet inclined to reveal himself, being curious as to what she sought in the coach-house at this late hour. At length, she stopped, leaned against the shafts of a midnight blue phaeton and, hands covering her face, sobbed quietly.

Lamont cleared his throat and drew himself forward on the bench so that she could discern his face. He felt oddly guilty, as if he was the intruder.

Mirrin whipped round. 'Who ... who's there?'

'Lamont.'

'Ah!' Her exclamation was one of relief.

'Are you ... unwell, Mirrin?'

'No, Mr Lamont.'

'May I ask what brings you here at this hour?'

She wiped her eyes with her wrist and swept straggles of hair into a semblance of neatness. Defeat was driven out of her by the need to put on a disciplined face for her employer. 'I ... I wondered if I might be permitted to sleep in the stables, sir, or in one of the carriages. It's not that long 'til morning.'

'Have you no bed at home?'

'Aye, sir: but ...'

'I take it,' said Lamont, gently, 'that the wedding party became rather obstreperous?'

'It did that.'

'You're not ... not hurt, in any way, Mirrin?'

The question was indelicate in one sense; in another the inquiry was logical. Black eyes and bruises were not uncommon in Blacklaw where frustrations were often exorcised in fist fights and the beating of wives and sweethearts.

'I'm just a bit tired,' said Mirrin.

Lamont stepped down from the carriage.

'There's room in the house,' he said.

'No,' the girl said quickly. 'I'd just as soon put my head down here for a bit.'

'A housekeeper's place ...' Lamont began. He paused, then

257

said, 'It's not so long until the winter, Mirrin: you must stay here then, you know.'

'I will, sir,' she promised.

'I will see to it that you have a room of your own.'

'When will that be, Mr Lamont?'

'As soon as you wish.'

'Next week?'

'By all means.'

'Will Mrs Lamont not...?'

'Not at all,' said Lamont, gruffly.

The girl had come closer. He was no longer drowsy. He felt as if a bright lantern had been lighted in his brain. He was almost inclined to comfort the collier's lass, to take her in his arms and soothe her as he might have soothed a child. But she was too independent a spirit, and too attractive. He smothered the impulse quickly, acutely conscious of the quietness of the night and the remoteness of the coach building. It also occurred to him that she might consider him deuced odd to be immured in an old carriage in the dark at this hour of the night.

He said, 'I often come out here, for a stroll.'

'Aye, sir,' said Mirrin.

He said, 'Would you care to tell me what happened?'

'A lad,' Mirrin shrugged. 'He ... he tried ... you know how it is, Mr Lamont, when they've been at the drink.'

'But why come here?'

'I don't rightly know, sir,' Mirrin said. 'It was the first place I thought of.'

'Come, then,' Lamont said. 'If you insist on spending the night in one of my coaches, try this one. It's the most comfortable of the lot.'

He held out his hand to her. She came forward and allowed him to aid her up the step into the carriage. Sighing, she sank back against the leather cushions under the hood.

Lamont said, 'May I sit with you a little while, or are you too tired?'

Did it occur to her, Lamont asked himself, that the servant had no right to refuse the master? How often had he heard that cunning phrase trotted out by one of his less gallant acquaintances to cover the seduction of a parlour maid. It was not in him to approve and, when the talk turned bawdy, he soon found an excuse to leave the company. Some traders and coalmasters called him a prig behind his back, but he cared nothing for their esteem and their slanders did not perturb him. To him, colliers were a class apart, his servants a part of that class. Now, with the Stalker girl, he saw how callous his attitude had been.

Without awaiting her answer, he clambered up on to the flat bench. The curlicues of the painted rail modestly separated them. Throwing himself back against the cushions like some young rake in a music-hall box, he brought out his cigar case and fired up. The black hood framed the girl but a little moonlight crept into the corner under the rim, sufficient to illuminate her eyes, the contour of her breast and her hands folded in the lap of her dress. She was much like a gypsy in her smudged clothing and in manner too, brazen and passive, bold and servile; a bewildering mixture of attitudes – or was that bewilderment within him, a mirror of his own unrest?

'Yes,' he said, breezily, 'I've always liked the coach-house. All these coaches and carriages were my grandfather's. He collected them. It was his one spendthrift weakness, almost a saving grace.'

'The same grandfather, Mr Lamont?'

'Hm?'

'The one who nearly got his block knocked off.'

Lamont laughed. 'His son. He was not without his foibles, you see. Horses and wheeled vehicles. My sister and I...' Curtly he cut himself off. Mirrin Stalker had probably heard rumours about Dorothy. It was not a subject he wished to discuss, so he sternly reminded himself.

'Tell me about your sister, Mr Lamont.'

Ingenuous, not sly: the question was too frank for the girl to be fishing for gossip.

He peered at the burning tip of his cigar.

'I'm sorry,' Mirrin said. 'It's not a thing you'll want to talk about, sir.'

259

'Dorothy lives in England.'

Lamont leaned forward, drew smoke and blew it out. In spite of the railing, he was close enough to the girl now to reach out and touch her. Smoke made a pale cloud against the reflection of light from the doorway. Though she was never far from his thoughts, in four or five years Dorothy's name had hardly crossed his lips. The pressures of restraint had cracked him deep under the surface, like an unshored seam swollen with water vapour. It was not that he chose to unburden himself, rather that he was caught off-guard by the girl's obvious sympathy.

'What *have* you heard of my sister?'

'Only that she was ill, an' doesn't live here because . . .'

'Well?'

'Because you're married.'

'She was sent away to a proper place, where she can receive due care and attention,' he said. 'For her own good, you see.'

There was no trace of disapproval in Mirrin's silence.

Lamont sucked in a shuddering breath. He was like a swimmer about to plunge into a mysterious river, trusting himself to unknown deeps and currents, not knowing where they might carry him or where he would surface.

'Dorothy,' he said, 'is not of sound mind.'

The statement was like a detonator, exploding the wall of reticence which he had built over his feelings. Suddenly he found himself blurting out the truth, not only about Dorothy's illness but about his own sufferings and guilts.

The monologue was frequently incoherent.

Not now recounting familiar events as he had done earlier in the long day, he spoke of Dorothy's childhood, of his separation from her, of his colleges and his training as a coalmaster, of his sister's gradual disassociation from reality, and her ever greater dependence upon him. He spoke of his marriage – only here was he guarded – and of the birth of his son, of the little boy's untimely death and of many other deaths and exits. He spoke of Dorothy's exile, her incarceration in the wilds of Kent in a flowered prison, of recent revivals of symptoms of serious lunacy in her.

For close on two hours he talked, uninterrupted, unprompted. His voice rose and fell querulously in the musty darkness, while pools of silver moonlight shrank and finally dried up in the earth's swing towards morning.

When he had finished, the girl said nothing.

He wondered if his droning confessions of failure and doubt had proved so dull that she had withdrawn into sleep. The cigar butt between his fingers had died. Fumblingly, he groped for the match-box, struck a match and rolled the tobacco in the flame. His mouth was dry, and yet he felt lucid, still, calm and not embarrassed by the intimacies of his revelations.

'Are you awake?'

'Aye.'

'I apologize for talking so much.'

'If you love her,' the girl said, 'how can you stand to be apart from her?'

'I told you the reason: Dorothy needs care and attention.'

'She needs love.'

'May I remind you . . .' He could not follow through with the reprimand. At this time, they were no longer master and servant. He had no right to claim an obligation from her. If any person had told him that he would have spoken thus to a collier's daughter, he would have accused them of making a joke in bad taste. But this girl at least could speak of love without confusing it with lust, or with duty; the two devils which plagued him and which, each in its turn, had brought him down into moroseness and an empty misery.

'Yes,' he admitted. 'She does need love.'

'You should have her here.'

'I cannot.'

'There's those in our street could do with some care an' attention,' Mirrin said. 'They have t'make do with love. It's not a substitute, Mr Lamont: it's the mainstay of us all. Are you afraid of it?'

He did not answer immediately.

Mirrin said, 'What causes the harm – is it the money, or is it the power? Aye, I know what my father would've said t'you, sir. But then he was a simpler man than most folk gave him credit for being; he had no truck with those who evade responsibility.'

'You think I do that – evade responsibility?'

'I saw a girl married today,' Mirrin said. 'Och, she's not much t'look at an' she has a tongue like a viper, but she's discovered that she has the capacity t'love an' to summon love in return. I think you're frightened of *that*, Mr Lamont. D'you imagine it'll weaken you, make you seem less ... less ...'

'My son,' he said. 'You cannot imagine how much I loved him.'

'I loved my father and brothers,' said Mirrin. 'I love them still. I don't blame myself for what happened t'them.'

'No, you blame me instead,' said Lamont.

'I did at the time, but not now.'

'What's changed your mind?'

'That's beside the point,' said Mirrin. 'They're dead an' buried. Your sister's alive. Listen, if she were a collier's daughter, d'you think she would be cast aside? No, Mr Lamont, maybe we couldn't give her "care and attention" in the way you mean, but at least we'd acknowledge her as one of us. That's the difference between your folk and my folk; we have to hold our failures dear and cherish them.'

Lamont rose, making the shallow carriage sway.

Mirrin looked up at him.

She said, 'You're all the lady's got. Why don't you bring her home?'

In the interstices of shadow his face seemed ravaged by anguish. 'Edith, my wife, she doesn't have the temperament to cope ...'

'What's temperament got to do with it? Speak plain, Mr Lamont: you mean your wife won't have her here because your friends might talk. That's not temperament, just a daft kind of fear.'

'No.'

'I listened t'you tonight,' said Mirrin evenly, 'and heard more in the way you spoke than in the words themselves. You're the master in your own home, are you not? Do as you wish to do.'

'Where are your free principles now, Mirrin Stalker? Where are the tenets of your cause? Do they not matter any longer?'

'Oh, they matter,' the girl declared. 'But not where love is concerned. That's first, an' above all. There are no servants and no masters in that house.'

He leaned across the railing, and put his hand against her cheek. Perhaps he would have checked himself. Perhaps he would have drawn her up to him and kissed her, shared the sorrow and anger, the fire which had been between them in the hours since midnight. Slack and pliant, her eyes shining, Mirrin did not resist.

The clatter of the hired chaise boomed up from the stable arch, changing to the chuckle of wheels on pebbles. The driver's hoarse *Hooo-aaah* floated loudly in the still air, and the hoofs of the team of long-distance trotters skated to a halt.

The timing could not have been more flagrantly coincidental.

'It's Edith,' said Lamont, more disappointed than guilty. 'She must have returned to Glasgow last evening and missed the Hamilton connection.'

He leapt down from the carriage, then turned.

'Will you stay here, Mirrin?'

'Yes.'

He smiled ruefully, and shook his head at the irony of fate which, for better or for worse, had broken the bond between them.

*

Mirrin watched him hurry from the stable gate. A grassy lane would take him to the wash-house door and a corridor would lead him directly upstairs. It was comical that the master of the mansion should be required to behave like a sneak-thief. She sank back into the cushioned corner, sheltered by the leather hood. She was physically exhausted, and yet relieved. Something had happened to her, something more important, more momentous than the loss of her maidenhood. Rob's love-making and her flight through the wood seemed far in the past, though sweat was still sticky on her body and her legs hurt. When she had entered the coach-house, riddled with self-pity and despair, she had been on the brink of collapse. Now those alien emotions had passed, and she hardly spared a thought for her squalid adventure in the wake of the wedding party. If anything, she felt more sorry for Rob now than she did for herself.

Though weary, she did not fall asleep. She lay resting in the snug protection of the pleasure-carriage until the first conscientious blackbird tuned his pipes in the trees behind the stables and the lintel of the door became visible against the lightening cobbles outside.

She climbed stiffly from the carriage and made her way into the yard, filled a bucket from the pump and lugged it round to the small lawn behind the coach-house. Stripping off her bodice and petticoats, she washed her body carefully, shivering a little in the fresh dawn air. Around her all the birds were wakening now, and the high crests of the elms were gilded by the sun.

In a moment, before the cook was up and about, she would return to the kitchen and take out the black, prim dress which was kept as a change in the maids' cupboard. She might even tuck her hair up under the daft cap this morning just to keep the waspish Edith happy.

The gloom and depression of yesterday had lifted completely, washed away by the cold pump water. Behind her the tall, blank walls of the mansion lofted into the sunlight, giving her security and the protection she required, so different from the community of pithead troughs and the variable moods of Main Street.

She sluiced the last of the clean water over her breasts and dried herself with her petticoat. Slipping on her dress and carrying her shoes and stockings, she returned the bucket to its nail by the stable gate and walked through the dew-damp grass.

She tried to imagine the woman who had figured so largely in Lamont's confidences, to picture his sister as she had been as a child in this green playground, safe from the hardships and ache of the world. But the image would not congeal, wavering and altering into the face of Houston Lamont as he was now, stern and brooding, yet as solid as the blocks from which the old house had been built. It was almost as if *he* had made love to her, not Rob Ewing: the transference, though strange, did not distress her, and she allowed its warmth to spread within her.

Whistling, she hoisted the bundle higher, and strode into the kitchen to stoke the stove, fill the kettles and set about the business of the day.

8

Maurice McElroy, who regarded himself as an expert in the field, knew that girls as fresh and pretty as Betsy Stalker were rare on the links of Hamilton. Certainly, Maurice's peregrinations about the streets, parks and refreshment arcades gave him authority to endorse his opinion. To borrow an expression then in vogue with certain ladies of the town, however, Maurice McElroy was 'all eye and mouth'. He fell into the category of a spectator whose practical experiences of seduction were limited to a number of strictly commercial encounters and a score of embarrassing misadventures with mill-girls and farmers' daughters, whose morals were not as tarnished as missionary preachers implied.

Betsy Stalker, though, was a filly from a different stable. Not only was she dainty and ravishingly pretty but her ingenuousness was endearingly original and coupled well with the airs she gave herself and her affectations of gentility. Maurice had no doubt that she would eventually succumb to his blandishments. The prospect of that conquest stayed him from rash, impetuous actions which might frighten her off before his fatal charm could bring the campaign to its natural climax.

Failures and humiliations were put behind him. He saw himself as a latter-day Don Juan, a hero whose potted biography had inspired Maurice through the medium of weekly illustrated parts.

In fact, Maurice McElroy was the only child of a widowed lady and dwelled in a cage of adoration. He was firmly tied to his mother's purse-strings by innate laziness and a lack of any remunerative skill. His function in life was to attend to his mother's finances, to look after a small folio of investments from which the family income was drawn. The investments would have managed quite nicely without Maurice's vigilance, for they were amply protected by a shrewd Glasgow broker and an Edinburgh lawyer, and remained secure little money-mills year in and year out no matter the fluctuations of foreign trade or the state of the weather at home.

Even so, Maurice had devised an undemanding daily ritual which gave the impression that he actually performed a service in return for his port and walnuts and the niggardly monthly allowance which his mother doled out. His makeshift chores absorbed no more than an hour per morning and this left the faded young rake – thirty-four on Whitsun past – a prey to boredom, timidity and libidinous fancy. Lacking the stomach to swallow much liquor, the nerve to enjoy gambling, or the wind to become a sportsman, Maurice fell back on the only remaining vice, and squandered many, many hours in pursuit of girls even more dim-witted than he was himself.

The McElroy house, a narrow two-storey lodge on the Hamilton estate, was five miles from town: but Maurice's mother was not short of spies, and discretion was always necessary during his courting tours. For this reason, he did not dare press the delectable Betsy Stalker too hard, or pay her too much attention. He confined their meetings to occasional luncheons in the back room of Reid's Bakery, where his mother's friends would hardly be likely to dine, or to midday picnics in the crowded little park by the river. Friday evening, however, was the high point of his week, and more so now that the days were shortening and dusk came earlier.

The routine permitted few variations. Each Friday, at a quarter to eight, Maurice turned into High Street, purchased a newspaper from the vendor on the corner, and walked at a leisurely pace down the right-hand pavement as far as the grain store. Then he crossed the road and wended his way back on the opposite side to the lane which separated Dalzells' from its humbler neighbours. The fifteen minutes thus spent achieved two things: one, his raffish good looks and aristocratic bearing never failed to draw flattering remarks from the cutters and gutters in the fish market windows: and, two, the Emporium was within his line of vision practically all the way. The newspaper did double duty. Rolled up, it became a substitute cane with which he slapped his thigh. Spread out, it provided protection against dampness on those occasions when he was fortunate enough to persuade Betsy to share a park bench with him in the half hour between supper and the departure of the Blacklaw omnibus.

That evening, lowering cloud indicated that the weekend would probably be washed out by rain and Maurice, cautious as always, had taken the precaution of wearing a light overcoat. He stood by the corner window, apparently scrutinizing a display of winter footwear, in reality watching the rush and scurry of the assistants within after the last customer had been gently eased from the doors and the cashiers had come round with their glossy black Gladstones to clear the tills.

Gas lamps were dimmed and costumes shrouded. The first trickle of senior assistants emerged from the door down the lane. Within minutes the trickle had become a flood and Maurice was obliged to drop his casual disguise and stand on tiptoe to see over the heads of the throng.

Betsy's ringlets bobbed. She was with another girl, a sallow, sad-eyed filly, not in Betsy's class, not even as attractive as Phyllis Rose to whom he had been introduced and upon whom, under other circumstances, he might have directed the full magnetism of his personality.

'Betsy!'

The cry came from his lips before he could prevent it. Three dozen girls stared at him. The flow of counter-hands seemed to freeze for an instant, as if he had bellowed *Fire!* or a bawdy word. He had never been this foolish before, never so anxious to greet her that he had forgotten his station and the need for discretion. Cringing instinctively, he tugged down the brim of his hard felt hat and thumbed up the top-coat collar, covering nose and mouth with the rolled newspaper as a coquette would with her fan.

'Maurie, I do believe you're blushing,' Betsy said.

'Not at all, not at all.'

He collected himself, clicked his heels and inclined a little towards her, offering his arm. Manners, he had learned, were important to this girl; he could afford to be generous with the fruits of his upbringing. He concentrated all his attention on her, blanking out the girls going by, deaf to their cooing and giggling. Best to whisk his victim away. Don Juan would have had a carriage or a barge waiting. Perhaps, next Friday, he would do just that – blow the expense and hire a hackney. Briskly, he drew her away from the windows and across the High Street into the quieter reaches of Riverside.

There were no public houses in the short street, and the evening shadows had already cooled the façades of the houses and small shops. Two drays toiled up from the warehouses at the street's end, and a gang of children chased past the couple in a game of hares and hounds. The din of High Street receded, and Maurice relaxed.

Betsy snuggled a little closer. She smelled of lavender. The turquoise scarf in the collar of her coat matched her eyes to perfection. She had very beautiful eyes, wide and clear, fringed by thick lashes which fluttered in constant bewilderment at the endowments which a steady income bestowed on her beau. He entertained no doubts at all that he was attractive to the girl, but he did not take unfair advantage of her innocence – at least, not yet.

'Has anyone told you how lovely you look?'

'Not today,' she replied.

'And who, if I may ask, told you yesterday?'

'I'm not tellin'.'

'Then I will say it again, just in case nobody told you yesterday – you are a delightful girl, and quite adorable.'

He felt rather than saw her sigh of enchantment.

'Do you like my new scarf?'

'I was in the process of admiring it,' Maurice said.

'It wasn't as expensive as I thought.'

'I see.'

'I bought this with the balance.'

She disengaged her arm and fumbled a vial of *English Maid* scent from her pocket, holding it up to him as they walked. 'I didn't think you'd mind.'

'I wondered why you smelled even more sweet than usual,' he said.

269

'It didn't cost me a lot,' Betsy said. 'But I think it suits me, don't you, Maurice?'

'It might have been pressed and blended for you alone.'

'French costs more. Phyllis Rose says French is a cod, but I think you get what you pay for.'

'I agree with you, Betsy: one does get only what one pays for.'

'Where are we going?'

'To the park.'

'But ... what about somethin' to eat?'

'We'll have time for a bite before the omnibus leaves.'

'I hope so,' said Betsy. 'I'm starved.'

'I wouldn't permit you to go home hungry,' said Maurice, gripping her arm with his elbow.

'Couldn't we have supper first?'

'The shades of night are falling fast,' said Maurice, sagely. 'A brisk turn in the fresh air will do you good. Take it from me, young lady, the keener the appetite the greater its eventual satisfaction.'

For a split-second it seemed to him that she had grasped the secondary meaning of his verbal sport, but her smile reassured him. He slid his arm about her tiny waist to support her over the uneven cobbles where the street dipped and curved to expose the greenery of the park. His wrist rested, as if by accident, against the soft undercurve of her breast. The tip of her tongue, like a kitten's, moistened her upper lip, but she did not change position. This signal of compliance thrilled him so much with its promise that he felt quite weak at the knees.

During the course of their steep descent to the rear gates of the municipal park, Maurice said nothing. The touch of his wrist on her breast was communication enough, and he occupied himself with savouring the prospect of that same full young bosom ungirded and at his mercy. Betsy, as if to cover her collusion in his designs, prattled on about shop matters and materials and money, garrulous enough for both of them.

There had been no rain for over a week now, and the grass was quite dry. Above the beeches and the elms which circled the rear of the parkland, however, the sky was heavy with cloud. That heaviness brought a boon with it, for the walks and bowers were uncommonly deserted and already secret with shadow.

Patience evaporated. At the third little arbour, Maurice released the girl long enough to spread his newspaper on the rustic bench, then pulled her down.

Betsy's response was much less promising. The best that could be said was that she did not take fright. Moistening her lips again, she stared ahead across the grass patch towards the strolling figures on the broad walk in the distance.

Perhaps, thought Maurice in panic, she was calculating the speed with which she could cover that ground. Prudence, like patience, vanished, and his resolve not to intimidate her was forgotten. He reached his arm about her waist and wrestled her to him, showering kisses over her brow and cheekbones, each bobbing caress of her ringlets against his face sending further shocks and charges through him.

Betsy continued to sit quite still, accepting his affection without, apparently, recognizing the raw passion which now lurked behind it.

With a strangulated cry, Maurice suddenly covered one breast with his hand. Imprisoning the girl in his embrace he groped for the buttons of her coat, fumbling them open from the collar to the waist. His fingers reached out to part the garment.

Betsy started.

'Oh, Maurice!'

'No, no,' he groaned. 'No, no. Not now. Adorable.'

Betsy sat bolt upright, her right arm extended, palm uppermost, while Maurice fumbled and nuzzled at the parted garment.

'Rain!'

'Betsy, my creature, my pigeon, my . . .'

'It's *raining*.'

'God, I don't care.'

She stood up.

He grasped at her waist but a neat twist of her hips caused him to miss and he slumped on his elbows on to the bench. The girl stood a pace out from the arbour, her palm still extended.

'Yes, it's pourin',' she announced. 'I mustn't get my hair wet.'

'It's dry,' he croaked, 'in here.'

'No, it's not.'

She walked a few paces along the path, scanning the sky anxiously. 'It's about to come down in buckets. Come on, Maurie, if we hurry . . .'

By a cliff of rhododendron bushes, she paused.

'Do hurry,' she said. 'We can make it dry to that nice chop-house, if you come now.'

She wasn't even teasing him. His declaration of passion had passed unnoticed. He propped himself up. His loins hurt and his hands were trembling. Across the grass swarmed running couples, children, dogs, old wives, like squirrels, pouring out of the park before the storm. Rain bent the leaves like scatterings of lead-shot and the big drops sploshed fatly into the dust.

He got to his feet achingly.

Betsy waited, her arms raised and her hands clasped over her precious hair.

She looked so pretty in the half-light, her skirts shaped by the rising breeze, the leaves bowing and soughing overhead like a silken canopy : so pretty, so desirable, and so utterly indifferent to his plight.

'Maurice, please hurry,' she called.

Next time, he promised himself : oh, yes, next time, in sunshine, rain or a thirty-foot snowdrift, he would do to Miss Stalker what deserved to be done, and to the devil with the consequences either to his reputation or her curls.

'Maurrreee.'

'Coming,' he said. 'Just coming, my love.'

*

Farewells, fond or otherwise, had been made between husband and wife in the latter's bedroom at an ungodly hour of the morning. Houston Lamont seemed uncommonly anxious to be off to the colliery and had hurried through his breakfast with even less formality than usual. He had quit the house on the stroke of eight and Mirrin, attending at the front door, had heard him sigh audibly as he tapped his hat on to his head and ran down the steps to the waiting chaise. Somehow she doubted if that sigh indicated regret at the fact that Edith would shortly be off on one of her social excursions to Edinburgh and that he would be left as a 'taffeta widower' for a week or ten days.

Edith Lamont was a seasoned traveller. She approached each journey, short or long, armed with a reticule full of little paper time-tables and notes of addresses which might prove useful in case of emergency. She did not scamper to board early trains and would not stretch her schedule an inch to make connections at the crowded urban terminals. If the North British Railway Company was not considerate enough to allow for dignity in its female passengers then Edith would not give them the satisfaction of harassing herself just to save a few hours. She travelled with old-style caution, sweeping at a leisurely pace through booking-halls and luggage offices, making use of porters and collectors and even, on occasions, startled firemen and engineers, as if they were all servants placed at her personal disposal by the directors of the railway company.

Though a few society matrons still considered it a trifle *infra dig*, Edith preferred to travel alone. She resented the extra cost of trailing a maid along. Besides, she had no suitable maid and would rather pass herself as independent than be burdened with an uncouth chit who might shame her in the elegant households of the capital.

Aided by the McCormicks, Archie and Sandy had man-handled a mountain of luggage downstairs and out into the driveway. As Edith made her final inspection of the mansion – 'countin' the candlesticks', Mattie called it – the grooms strapped valises, trunks, portmanteaus and band-boxes securely into the bay of the four-wheeler. At Hamilton Station, Sandy and Archie would unload the carriage; hissing impatiently, the through train would wait; porters would stack the collection into the baggage van; the through train would grumble into motion, and carry Edith and her entire wardrobe of clothes off towards Glasgow; Archie and Sandy would grunt with relief, and pity the poor porters and cab-hands who would be pressed into service all along the route and paid a pittance for their labours.

Silk had come increasingly into the panorama of high fashion and Edith, scorning tweed capes and rugs, was dressed like a lady from the quality side of the West Bow. Her flounced bustle was neatly draped at her rear, and the dress shimmered pale blue in the sunlight, the iridescence distracting the onlooker's eyes from the plain features which topped the conglomeration of rich fabrics.

The hall clock indicated that Edith had two hours in hand to trundle the miles to Hamilton. Being, as always, relieved of the stress of unpunctuality, she allowed herself the liberty of a last malicious skirmish with her housekeeper.

Since nine o'clock Mirrin had put up with the mistress's sniping. Only the prospect of being free of the harangues for at least a week enabled her to check her temper and remain polite, obedient and apparently attentive. It occurred to Mirrin that Edith Lamont had rehearsed her speeches and had even made a dead-of-night round of the mansion for the purpose of spotting minute faults in advance. Pencil and tablet in her gloved hand, the woman noted down all marks of slovenliness and handed the list to Mirrin as they stood together by the front door at the end of the tour.

Mirrin had already received a quantity of instructions, all neatly itemized, together with budgeted menus, larder accounts, and a tally of the contents of the wine cellar, down to the last bottle of porter and pipe of ale. There was something so horribly incriminating in Edith's insistence on a detailed inventory, that Mirrin could not help but remark that Mr Lamont would still be on the premises.

Edith's gaze sharpened; she glanced quickly up from her stationery.

'And what do you mean by that?'

'He'll be able to keep check,' Mirrin said.

'Do you imagine that my husband has nothing better to do with his time than ... police the domestics?'

'I ... didn't mean that, madam.'

274

'Explain yourself more eloquently then,' Edith said.

'I meant only that the master will be able t'keep stock of expenditure.'

'That is the housekeeper's task.'

'Aye, madam.' Mirrin sighed.

'Do your chores bore you, Stalker?'

'No, madam.'

Edith pushed the last paper at her, and Mirrin accepted it.

'You, Stalker, are responsible.'

'Yes, madam.'

Outside, the more wayward of the pair of carriage horses snickered and stamped. Gruffly, Sandy Willocks ordered it to 'Bide still a wee, an' haud your wheesht.'

With a snuffle of impatience, the animal settled.

Edith moved out into the sunlight and billowed down the shallow steps to the drive.

Archie had already opened the nearside door and stood at attention by it. His pose emulated the most aristocratic of footmen, though it was totally at odds with his tousled shock of hair, patched jacket and baggy breeks. Suddenly, it came home to Mirrin just how far down the social scale her mistress stood, and how much of a mockery reality made of her aping of the landed gentry. By Blacklaw standards Edith Lamont was wealthy and a fine lady, but among blue-bloods her dresses, carriages and posturings would be immediately recognized and she would be graded like inferior coal and rejected as a mere middle-class trader's wife.

Somehow this grain of understanding comforted Mirrin and strengthened her resolve to see the little tyrant away without giving her the gratification of tears and hot words.

Not one to admit defeat, Edith had saved her cannons for a last, unexpected salvo. She stepped up into the open carriage and signalled to Archie to sneck the door. This the stable lad did, giving the smart brass handle a rub with his cuff to polish away fingermarks. He then trotted round the back and vaulted boisterously up into the seat beside Sandy, demonstrating a lack of decorum which might, at another time, have drawn a rebuke from his mistress.

But Edith had another matter on her mind. Even when Sandy looked round at her and cocked his whip in expectation of the nod which would put the carriage into motion, Edith Lamont continued to study her housekeeper.

If Mirrin was disconcerted by the scrutiny – which she was – she succeeded in hiding it.

The small gloved fist lifted and a crooked finger beckoned. Mirrin stepped closer to the bright black flank of the carriage, looking up at the woman.

'I do not wish to leave in a spirit of ill-feeling,' Edith said, quite loudly enough for the grooms to hear. 'Do you wish me to explain why I have seen fit to document the contents of the house?'

Caught by the verbal snare, Mirrin said nothing.

Edith smiled. 'It is a natural protection against dishonesty.'

'I hope, madam,' said Mirrin, thinly, 'that you don't think the staff here are not t'be trusted?'

'Oh, no! My domestics, including my housekeeper, are honest,' Edith said. 'Of that I am sure.'

'Yes, madam.'

'It is the honesty of their ... *friends* which may leave something to be desired.'

'Friends?'

'Come now, Stalker,' said Edith, with a brittle, icy little laugh. 'I *know* what servants get up to when left unsupervised.'

Puzzled, Mirrin frowned.

'With Mr Lamont off on business most of the day and probably many evenings as well,' Edith explained, 'it would not be unnatural for you to "entertain", shall we say, your admirers.'

'Mrs Lamont ...'

With an airy wave of her hand, Edith continued, 'It happens in the very best of establishments. Lady Catherwood, after last summer's European tour, returned to find that her parlour maid had been *obliged* to marry in her absence; and all the evidence indicated that the ... ah, the deed had been done under Lady Catherwood's roof.'

'I will watch over the servants' behaviour very carefully,' Mirrin promised.

'And who will watch over you?'

'Mrs Lamont, you needn't worry on that score.'

'I cannot believe that a handsome girl like you *has* no admirers.'

'That's as maybe,' said Mirrin. 'But they'll not enter this house, by invitation or otherwise.'

Again Edith blessed her housekeeper with a sweet, understanding smile. 'I'm sure you are sincere, Stalker, but the temptation will be very strong. Indeed, I could hardly blame you . . .'

'You'll have no reason t'blame me. There'll be nobody here but the staff while you're away; nobody t'filch the liquor or the cheese, or the silverware upstairs; nor t'do anything else, either.'

'Good,' said Edith. She looked smilingly at the tip of Sandy's whip, and half-raised her arm to order the carriage to start; then she paused and gave Mirrin one more moment of her attention. 'You do have "admirers", do you not?'

'Not in the way you mean, madam.'

'I heard of a young collier; Ewing, would it be . . .?'

'A friend o' my father's.'

'And of yours, too, I think?' Edith simpered.

Her tone exuded sympathy, a conspiratorial bond in such an *affaire de coeur*, almost as if she were instructing Mirrin to encourage her admirer to use the Lamont mansion as a place of debauch.

'Aye, a friend of mine, too,' Mirrin admitted.

'If he is a young man, perhaps he will not be able to resist the opportunity.'

'I think he will,' said Mirrin, curtly. 'In fact, Mrs Lamont, I don't think y'could drag him through those gates with a double-team of Clydesdale stallions – whether you're here or not.'

'Does he not care for you, then?'

'Aye,' said Mirrin, 'but he's been well schooled. He knows his place, madam – just like the rest of us here.'

Edith snapped her fingers. Sandy flicked the whip accurately across the two glossy rumps. The carriage wheels ground over the gravel as the horses leaned into the shafts.

Mirrin could not hold back.

'Mrs Lamont,' she called. Running a few steps, she caught up with the carriage before it gathered speed. With her hand on the door, Mirrin lifted her face so that her words would not be lost, even though Edith sat rigidly facing the groom's back, eyes fixed. 'Mrs Lamont, if it comforts you at all, I'll give my word that the only man who'll bed down in this house in your absence will be your husband, Mr Lamont himself.'

Edith's upper lip lifted like that of a vixen. Reaching forward, she rapped Sandy on the collar with the crook of her parasol.

'Drive,' she commanded. 'Drive, I say.'

Releasing her hold, Mirrin dropped back and watched the handsome carriage gather speed and roll rapidly off towards the gates. Part of her regretted the impulse which had urged her to have the last word, a last word which implied a power she did not want to possess; yet part of her was triumphant, full of malicious glee that she had defended herself so well and had, in the final swipe of the skirmish, given better than she had got.

Turning, she strode back up to the house, entered the front door and locked it behind her.

Rob Ewing, indeed! She wondered from which direction that rumour had wafted to Edith Lamont's ears. It was absurd, any-how: Rob Ewing didn't dare show his face at the Stalker house in Main Street these days, let alone accost her here in the coalmaster's domain.

That parting shot had had more than a crumb of truth in it: this *was* Houston Lamont's house, not Edith's, not anybody else's. No other man had the right to sleep here.

Startled by the development of the thought, Mirrin gave her-self a little warning shake, then, checking her watch against the clock, took herself down to the kitchen to join the cook in a much-needed cup of tea.

*

The first of the day-shift cages was packed solid with men. The majority were still bleary-eyed and surly in the early hour. Jostling like bullocks to get themselves out of the drizzling rain and down to the levels where money could be earned, they

278

ignored the wheelman-ganger's protests about regulations and the safety act.

Boots drummed on the duckboards; three late-comers hared round the fender from the yard and flung themselves bodily into the crowd. Creaking cables and stays did not perturb the colliers, who took most aspects of their destiny on trust. Besides, the persistent noises were soon soaked up in the clash of the barrier and the high rattling chatter of the pulley-cogs which released power from the winding wheel. Lurching, the floor of the cage dropped and the cargo of caps and mufflers and porridge-pale faces sank below ground.

'Jesus Christ! It's like the tap-room in Hades this mornin'.'

'Shunt up't the back there.'

'Mind what you're doin' wi' that soddin' lamp.'

'Who's takin' up a' the room?'

'Hey, Ormond, you got yon elephant y'call a whippet back there wi' you?'

'Nut me,' Ormond answered. 'Thought maybe you'd brung *your* beast down, Pritchard. It's about time y'gave it a decent burial: poor brute's been dead for weeks b'the look o'it.'

A gust of laughter echoed in the narrow shaft.

The cage was picking up pace now, though its descent was still comparatively leisurely. The wheel operatives would risk nothing with this excessive load on board. Inspection lanterns slid past at intervals, bulbous glass lamps peering from behind shoring timbers like malevolent little eyes. The odours of the deep earth came up in a rush – damp, rust, sweat; mineral, warm, and disturbingly primeval.

'It's no' a whippet Billy Williams wishes he had down with him,' some wag remarked.

'He could make better use of a fox: right, Billy?'

Billy Williams smiled and swayed and said nothing.

'Be a better perker-upper at dinner time than a hunk o'bread an' lard,' Pat Marshall shouted. 'What about puttin' that proposal in writin' t'the Mines Commission? Send the lassies down for the shift break.'

'The only place for women's roastin' on the spits of Hell,' Rob Ewing declared.

His vehemence silenced the colliers for a moment, then George Laverty said, 'Aye, Rob, or flat in the grass by the auld Northrigg track.'

'*Bastard!*'

If there had been room, Rob would have crunched his lamp across his drinking companion's face. As it was, the stir he caused in endeavouring to reach across the throng shook through the ranks and pushed the older men back against the planking.

'Here, lad, easy: easy.'

'Come on, Rob: only a bit o'fun.'

'Aye, you should know all about fun, Rob,' said Pat Marshall. 'Considerin' you've had the best bit o'fun in Blacklaw.'

Only Donald Ormond's prompt action prevented a dangerous brawl in the cage. He pinned Rob's arm behind his back and locked him against the main pillar.

Four blue-glazed lamps announced the level.

With a shuddering jolt the cage grounded. The barrier lifted and miners poured out across the platform into the square.

Rob struggled in Donald's grasp.

'I'll kill Marshall for that,' he raged.

Laughter floated back from one of the seams.

Callum Ewing hefted his short pick and laid the iron bow across his son's heaving chest. 'Contain yourself, son,' he advised. 'The joke's on you, so just accept it.'

Colliers spilled across the square, mingling with night-shift workers on their way to the waiting cage, with the barrowers, bogey-men and pony-handlers who congregated here at the junction of the tunnel mouths. Some seams were low and narrow, but the two main avenues, running east and west, were higher and almost broad enough to accommodate the Northrigg band in column of route.

There were primitive wooden plank-ways down some of the older roads, where, not so long since, the putters and drawers had slaved at their harnesses and sleds to shag coal up from the walls. A few of the stooped old colliers still referred to the vanguard positions where the rubble was dug as 'rooms'. Now, though, with a lattice of iron rails and large bogies to replace the hutches, and a steam-powered winding engine, there was space enough for a parish hall at the shaft bottoms, and storage bays for props and rails and dung-reeking pony-stalls.

Splitting into allocations, the day-shift men headed out along the main road towards the rises, and their sections of the seams.

Rob's voice followed them.

'I'm tellin' you, I'll bloody kill that Marshall.'

'Oh, Mirrrrreeeeeen.'

'Do it again, Mirrrrrreeeeeeen.'

Callum pressed against the pick, but his son was too strong for him, and thrust him aside, wrenching away too from Donald Ormond's grasp.

The apprentices were gawping; even the ponies seemed startled by the outburst as the broad-shouldered young collier ran to the mouth of the road and bellowed along it, 'She's the same as all the rest, Laverty. Call'r what y'like: I don't give a tinker's curse.'

Obscene yelps and smacking sounds filtered back.

'Whores, the lotta them,' Rob cried.

Halted by the throughway of unladen bogies, McNeillage wagged his pinkie in his ear. 'Stop that bullin', Rob Ewin': near blasted m'eardrum wi' your complaints, so y'did.'

'I'll complain all I like,' Rob aimed his spleen directly at the rodent-featured collier, defying him to argue with his condemnation of all womankind.

Recognizing the young man's condition, McNeillage prudently stepped aside, but Donald Ormond, who had come up behind Rob was less inclined to bow before the foibles of youth.

He said, 'You shouldn't talk that way: Alex Stalker was a good friend t'us all.'

'Nobody even mentioned Alex Stalker: it's his bloody daughter, you stupid old goat.'

'Now, now; now, now.'

The train of empty, clanking bogies ground down the track. Rob side-stepped, then glared back at the men behind him.

'If her father'd still been alive, he'd have belted some sense of respect into her,' he said. 'I tell you ...'

'Rob, *look out*!'

'Ewing: your back, for God's sake!'

One drag chain on the bogey had been incorrectly hitched and the side panel leaned out almost at right angles to the iron frame, rivets, like the knuckles of a mailed fist, projecting along its edge.

Warning cries brought Rob spinning round. Ormond lunged to drag him aside. The presence of mind and nimbleness which had protected Rob from harm over the years had been dulled by bitterness. He was not quite speedy enough to avoid the jerking bogey.

The rivet-board struck him square between the eyes.

The contact seemed to brake the whole line of trucks to a halt, set them clanging and chattering down into the gloom. Rob bobbed back like a blown pit-prop, hovered upright in the air for an instant, then toppled sideways against the shoring and slid down the tunnel wall to the ground.

'God Almighty!'

Tossing aside his pick, Callum leaped forward and sank to his knees in front of his son. He held the lamp in one hand and with the other palmed up Rob's sunken chin.

There was no sign of blood. The youngster's lids were closed and his breathing was shallow. The mark of the rivets was visible as a series of indentations on the tight, fair flesh between the bridge of the nose and the hairline. The skin was puckered and fishbelly white against the flush around it.

Gently Callum thumbed up one eyelid.

Rob's pupil stared vacantly back at him.

Turning his head, the elderly collier yelled, 'Hold that damned cage! We've an injury here.'

The message was relayed out of the tunnel. Duly embellished, it reached the workers waiting in the cage as a series of requests involving the immediate attendance of a stretcher party, doctors, managers, and, for some obscure reason, a Roman Catholic priest.

Donald and Callum emerged from the arch, Rob slung between them.

'How is he, Callum? Is he alive?'

Callum nodded, snorted, and moved on towards the waiting cage with all the speed he could muster.

*

Edith Lamont opened her eyes. A watery sun lit the curtains. She altered her position, turning her back on the window and burrowing her head deeper into the pillow. The vacant area of the bed seemed vast; she stretched an arm possessively across it, not seeking her husband so much as the assurance that she was alone.

Though she had been home for almost a fortnight her sojourn in Edinburgh had left lingering traces of discontent. Life in the capital seemed fuller and richer than ever. By contrast, Blacklaw was a sump of boorishness, in which it was impossible to find one single soul not tarred by mendicity.

The source of her restlessness, with regard to Houston, lay in a serious flirtation with a Black Watch captain, who had also been a weekend guest of the Cunninghams. Captain Ramsay had served with Sir Garnet Wolseley's expeditionary force during the Ashantee campaigns, and had entertained the dinner party with tales of the black barbarians and comical King Koffee. Later, in the privacy of the rose arbour, he had expanded his views on the domination of savage regions and, treating Edith as a mature woman of the world, had gone into some detail about his treatment of female slaves in the trade which still survived in parts of North and West Africa. The conversation had taken an unexpectedly personal turn when Captain Ramsay had flattered her figure and compared it to the finest of concubines. Edith had been a little uncertain as to the delicacy of the compliment, but the Captain had left her in no doubt that his youth did not preclude his experiencing a strong attraction towards her. The *risqué* nature of the ensuing *tête-à-tête* had excited Edith inordinately – as no doubt the bold Captain intended. She could recall in detail the witty by-play with which she kept him at bay without frightening him off. It was several years since she had flirted so outrageously. The fact that she was still handsome enough to command the attentions of such a dashing and youthful officer gave her considerable satisfaction. Only with great restraint did she refrain from dropping the final promise which would have brought him to her bedroom that Saturday night. But chance had not been wholly lost. The Cunninghams would invite her again. They thought as little as she did of Houston's manners, and regarded his obsession with coal as rude and unhealthy. Captain Ramsay could wait. He would be garrisoned in Edinburgh throughout the winter; a useful diversion and one which she would not hesitate to employ, if Houston gave her the slightest excuse. The prospect of such a revenge strengthened her and would surely enable her to bring her sullen husband to heel.

She had interrogated Mrs Burns as to anything untoward which may have occurred while she had been away: but servants were loyal to their own, and the cook would admit to nothing. Edith's suspicions were not calmed. Patiently, she had watched and waited for some sign that Houston and the girl, whom he had now installed in the household, had developed a relationship other than that of servant and master.

The door opened. She heard a footfall on the carpet, a heavy tread.

She pretended to be asleep.

'Edith?'

She pinched the sheets to her bosom and raised herself in the bed.

'I've brought your morning tea,' Houston said.

'Have we no servants in this house?'

Houston placed the oval tray on the bedside table.

'I want a word with you, Edith.'

She rubbed her eyes. He was dressed for the city, smart and well groomed in his frock coat and narrow-check trousers. He decanted tea from the silver pot into a bone-china cup, added milk and sugar and stirred it for her. There was an air of determination to him which disturbed Edith and drove the remnants of sleep from her.

'My robe, Houston.'

He brought the quilted silk robe from the chair and waited, teacup in hand, while she struggled up in bed and put on the garment. She settled the sheets and blankets neatly about her, sitting upright, like an invalid.

284

'Thank you,' she said, as he gave her the cup.

She sipped the liquid, then glanced up at him, narrowly.

'Well?'

'I have written to Miss Emerson today,' her husband said. 'I have informed her that I will call for Dorothy in one month's time.'

Edith's head suddenly seemed too heavy for her slender neck and dropped back with a tiny thud against the padded board. Tea spilled into the saucer and a few drops stained the linen sheets.

'Do I understand you, Houston?' she gasped.

'I will bring Dorothy home with me.'

'You will only unsettle her.'

'No,' her husband said. 'She will be happier here.'

'Are you mad?'

'My mind is made up, Edith.'

'*Your* mind is ... What about me, Houston? Am I not to be consulted?'

'I believe I know your opinion, my dear.'

Edith threw the teacup into the tray, swept aside the sheets and pranced out of bed.

'My opinion is that your sister is not fit to be ... to be ...'

'Dorothy needs my care and my love.'

'Who put this notion into your head?'

'It's been on my conscience since my last visit,' Houston said. 'She is virtually a prisoner. At least she will be able to walk in the gardens and grounds here.'

'I forbid you to do it, Houston.'

'It is already done.'

'Cancel it: write again.'

'Dorothy must come home.'

'And what of me?' Edith said. 'Is this *my* home no longer?'

'I do not ask you to attend her,' Houston said.

'I suppose *you* will do that?' Edith sneered. 'Manage the colliery *and* look after a lunatic.'

'The servants ...'

'Ah! It's that girl, isn't it? She put you up to this, to ... to defy me.'

'If you mean Mirrin Stalker, Edith, I assure you she knows nothing of my decision.'

'Where will we put her?'

'In the nursery wing.'

'No, Houston!'

'Mirrin Stalker will take up full duties as a housekeeper. Her room will be close enough to Dorothy's. You need not have your sleep troubled. Indeed, you need not be troubled in any way at all.'

'Have you informed the Stalker girl, yet?'

'Not yet.'

'Perhaps she will not agree to be both housekeeper and night-nurse.'

'In which case,' said Houston. 'I will employ another person to care for Dorothy's needs.'

'It appears that you have given the matter much thought,' said Edith. 'And that you are determined to leave me no choice.'

'None,' said the coalmaster.

Edith realized that threats, tears and temper would serve no purpose now. In all the years of their marriage Houston had seldom defied her. She had always regarded his willingness to concede to her wishes as meekness; suddenly she had an inkling as to the real quality of her husband's past capitulations.

She said, 'Very well, Houston: if that is your decision, I will not stand in your way.'

He bowed formally, but gave no other token of gratitude.

'I will be in Glasgow today,' he said. 'Is there anything you require, Edith?'

She shook her head.

Quietly, the coalmaster left the bedroom.

Edith's control lapsed. She staggered to the edge of the bed and seated herself. Placing a hand across her breast and tucking her elbows into her lap she leaned over like a woman startled by the pangs of childbirth – yet she suffered no pain at all.

Perhaps the recollection of Captain Ramsay consoled her. To her surprise she discovered that her dream of using the young officer as an instrument of revenge had lost all its appeal. The battle would be fought out in this house, and she would fight cleverly to regain that which she had lost – her position, her authority and her husband's devotion. There was no mystery as to the identity of the enemy: not Houston, but that Stalker bitch.

Edith pushed herself from the bed. She would begin at once. She would summon the carriage and be driven to Hamilton where, in Dalzells' fashionable store, she was bound to find some dresses to restore her softness and the winsomeness of her youth.

She rang the bell and waited, impatiently, for one of the servants to answer.

9

Shortly after two o'clock the sun slid from behind the chimney-pots and slanted down the slate roofs of the row opposite the Ewing's cottage.

Rob's eyelids flickered.

Even the faint radiance which managed to penetrate the closed curtains was sufficient to send darts of pain shooting through his skull. He would have closed his eyes again at once if it had not been for the vision of the girl seated close by the bed.

With the window behind her she was little more than a blurred shape; not his mother, though, nor one of his aunts, of that Rob was certain. He goggled, struggling to bring her into clearer focus. His heart gave a peculiar skip in his chest, and pain split his eagerness, forcing him to screw his eyes right shut.

'Mirrin,' he mumbled.

A cool hand stroked his brow.

Smiling, he relaxed.

'Mirrin,' he sighed.

He could remember very little, only that he had been down the pit, and had been involved in some kind of fight with Marshall and Laverty. He wondered which one of them had felled him, and how seriously he was injured.

Cold spread down his nose. He heard gentle splashing sounds like rain dripping from leaves on to grass : nice soothing sounds.

Aye, he must be home in bed : little doubt about that. But what was Mirrin Stalker doing here when she should be up at the big house, Lamont's house, earning her keep as a menial? It did not matter what disaster had brought her here – was he, perhaps, dying and didn't know it? – the mere fact of her presence was comforting.

'Wha' . . .?'

'Wheesht now, Mr Ewing.'

Mr Ewing?

Rob prised open his eyes again.

All he could see was a halo of brick-red earthenware, and a pale object which floated towards him like a puff of foam. He was flat on his back, the blanket squared tightly across him, pinning him, the ears of the bolster sticking up on either side of his cheeks. The object dripped cold water on his lips and he licked them, thankfully.

Some bugger had driven a pick-axe between his lamps and left it there. The pain was iron hard and fixed, and he squinted furiously round what he took to be the shaft.

The foam rose up once more and a delicious coolness eased the wound and melted the iron a little. He actually felt his eyeballs twitch and slacken. The pick-shaft evolved into a plump arm softened by blonde hair. A blouse full of bosom mercifully blotted out the hot light. He saw also a round chin, a full mouth, a straight nose.

The girl laved his brow with the soaking cloth and rested the bowl on his chest.

'Who...?'

'Eileen McMasters.' She leaned closer, her breast only inches from his face. 'From four doors down: y'know.'

'Aye.'

He had vague recollections of a legion of children spawned by wee Mrs McMasters and her hulking husband, Jack, a winding operative in Pit Two. That one of the brood of spindle-limbed bairns could have achieved such mature proportions without his noticing struck him as incredible.

'How long...?'

'They brought you up in a cart this morning.'

'What's the...?'

'About two.'

'God!'

'Doctor's been.'

'Am I...?'

'Nothin' broken, Mr Ewing: just a sore head.'

'My mother?'

'Gone for medicine: your daddy's back at work.'

If the old man had returned to his seam, then death could not be imminent, Rob decided. Though he was not thinking very clearly yet, and he had succumbed to strange, lax emotions, most of which were quite out of keeping with a man who, a moment before, had imagined himself close to the angels.

She was dabbing his forehead now. Her fingers, very tender inside the cloth, made tickling, stroking motions along his brows and up towards his hair.

'I've t'put a bandage on: doctor showed me how.'

Rob said, 'Eileen?'

'Aye, Mr Ewing.'

'I'm thirsty.'

'I've t'give you soup.'

'Fine.'

'Can y'sit up?'

'Dunno.'

'Let me help.'

She put the cloth into the bowl and the bowl on to the floor then dug her arm beneath his shoulders and lifted him, pressing him against her. She puffed and levered at him, then, with an arm about his neck, succeeded in holding him upright long enough to stuff the bolster behind his neck.

Rob took his weight on his elbows, his cheek still against the blouse. Rolling his eyes, in spite of the ache it incurred, he saw her face foreshortened above him, framed by licks of cornblonde hair. She had eyes the colour of the opals in the watchmaker's window in Hamilton High Street. Her skin was warm and she gave off a fragrance that reminded him a bit of washing day, crisp clean sheets snapping in a summer breeze. When she had him in position she went away and he lay like a statue staring vacantly into space.

The stunning effect of the blow between the eyes had almost worn off now, supplanted by another, more enduring kind of stupefaction. He watched her from the corner of his eyes as she worked at the range, a strong, smooth, plumpish girl, and remembered the bad night on the track with Mirrin Stalker. He remembered it in his nerve-ends, unemphatically and without contriteness. That night had created desires in him which demanded satisfaction: he had turned them into rage as best he could, more angry at himself than at Mirrin. Now, still weakened by the clunk on the head, he could not fight them down or alter their exact nature. In this weird situation, he could not pretend to be a prude.

The words came thickly from the back of his throat.

'Eileen?'

'Aye, Mr Ewing?'

'What ... what age are you?'

'Sixteen.'

'Sixteen: then you should call me Rob, don't y'think?'

She smiled but did not answer him at once, bringing the bowl of soup to the bedside. He raised one arm to take the spoon and the muscles dragged at his head, making him groan: at least, that's what he supposed the groan to mean.

'Lie quiet: I'll do it,' Eileen said.

He was naked beneath the blanket, his chest bare and exposed. He wished that his mother would come home – or did he?

The girl placed an arm about his neck again and cautiously steered the spoon into his mouth.

The liquid was thick and scalding hot, but Rob swallowed obediently and immediately opened his lips again, like a gigantic nestling greedy for nourishment. He wished that the bowl was bottomless so that he might lie there for ever with Eileen McMasters's body snuggled close against him.

'You don't remember me at all, Rob, do you?'

'Nuh.'

'Well, it's not surprisin'. I've been at m'auntie's in Wishay this past year. She's been sick and I'd t'help out in her wee shop. I suppose I changed a bit while I was there.'

'Ah,'

'I remember *you* fine, though.'

'Uh.'

'It's back t'the troughs for me come Monday morning: m'auntie's better again, y'know.'

'Hmmmmmm.'

'Soup's good for buildin' up strength: you'll be wantin' more?'

'Aye.'

She dropped the spoon into the empty bowl, but did not withdraw her arm from about him. She contemplated him solemnly.

'My, Rob, y'look fair flushed.'

'I'm fine,' said Rob, feebly. 'Just dandy.'

She smiled, and he noticed, with astonishment, that her eyes were bright with shy adoration.

'You'll remember me next time, won't you?' she asked.

Rob swallowed, nodded and clenched his fists under the blanket. Not trusting himself to speak, he opened his mouth wide, a gesture which sent young Eileen McMasters rushing to the stove to fetch more sustenance for her wounded chieftain.

*

Dominie Guthrie lit a pipe. It was a long-stemmed clay with a shallow bowl, all chipped and blackened, in which a pinch of tarry tobacco burned with a smell like singed rope. Drew had grown accustomed to the reek, to tobacco and ink and chalk and the oily effluvia of the lamp which was lit early these nights with summer dimming into autumn.

The schoolmaster had relaxed with his pupil now that Drew, at sixteen, was no longer under his official jurisdiction. Heels on the desk, book in his lap, head wreathed in pungent smoke, the dominie expounded at random on many subjects which seemed far removed from any academic curriculum.

Since Drew had left school, the work-load had been heavily increased, and his sessions with his tutor had become the only relief to hour upon solitary hour of cramming. The winter months seemed to stretch ahead like some dark unwelcoming tunnel.

But the dominie was a downie bird and understood the trials of scholasticism. He did not devote tutorials to grinding his disciple up small and spent only a portion of the allotted time in testing Drew's knowledge and in setting more exercises. For the rest of the evening, often running late into the night, Mr

Guthrie subtly encouraged the lad to think for himself, to develop agility of mind, confidence in expression and the use of logic in argument. Painlessly the rudiments of philosophy were inculcated into the collier's son, and his understanding of the application of education increased. The method would have been impractical had Drew Stalker not been anxious to please his teacher. He did not hold the dominie in awe now, but respected him and listened with fierce concentration, even when the old man appeared to be indulging in a reminiscence or casual chat.

'A milk churn,' said the dominie. 'You see one on the step: what do you think?'

'That it contains milk.'

'Aye: a natural hypothesis. But what if the churn has a lid on it?'

'I would open the lid.'

'The lid is jammed on tightly.'

'I would test the weight.'

'Against what?'

'My memory of other churns.'

'Could you accurately tell, though, that the weight was not made up by water, or oil, or even sand?'

'No, not with complete accuracy.'

'It is now imperative that you discover the nature of the contents of the churn: how?'

'Prise off the lid with a claw-hammer.'

'Not possible.'

'Well, then, I'd pierce the churn with an awl: can I do that?'

'Why not?' Mr Guthrie jigged his feet, cocked his head and peered at his client through the fog.

Drew's fingers had tightened on his knees, a sure tell-tale that the cogs and pulleys of his reason were taking the strain of the problem.

'I'd do one of two things,' he said. 'I'd obtain a second churn, fill it with milk, weigh it an' compare ... No, the weight of the original churn might vary: that would be imprecise.'

'It would.'

'Then I'd resort to a practical solution,' Drew said. 'I'd use an awl an' mallet to tap into the churn.'

'How?'

'High up on the barrel, so's not to spill the contents,' Drew answered quickly. 'I'd drive a small hole close t'the lid and tilt the churn until some of the liquid flowed out. Sight, taste and smell would indicate its composition.'

'Good, good,' said Mr Guthrie. 'Now, can you form an analogy out of our milk churn?'

'In the light of what we were discussin' before your churn appeared,' said Drew, pacing out his explanation with care, 'I imagine that the vessel represents the human brain.'

'Excellent!'

'A sealed container holding a quantity of material of unknown worth.'

'Call it the memory rather than the brain.'

'Aye. I take the point, Mr Guthrie. But is the memory of limited capacity?'

'Medical science believes that there is no limit to the faculty of memory,' said the dominie. 'But it's knowing how to "tap" it – I like that phrase of yours – that's the real secret.'

'Not what's in there, but how you get it out?'

'Right as rain, Drew.'

The boy considered the problem, seeking, as usual, some practical application of the knowledge he had just acquired.

Puffing on the clay, the dominie waited, offering no prompt to aid the lad's next question. When it came, it caught him unawares.

'My father,' he said.

The pipe-stem hovered an inch from the master's lips, a slender plume of smoke curling from it.

'My father was ruined by memory,' Drew went on. 'He could never put the past out of his mind. It ... it sort of choked him.'

'What sort of memory, Drew?'

'About the hardships.'

'But they were *real* hardships: your father had a hard life.'

'Aye, but was it right of him t'miss out the middle?'

'Miss out the middle? I don't understand.'

'There was what had happened t'him, back in the past, stored away in his memory. An' there was what would happen in the future, to me an' to my sisters an' brothers. But in between – it seems to me, Mr Guthrie, there was just a space, a hollow space: nothin'.'

'The present, you mean?'

'Up when the hooter sounded, an' out t'work.'

'Much as you do – only he went to the seams and you go to your desk.'

'Aye, but . . . but at least it's *my* future I'm slavin' for.'

The boy looked up: his gaze was piercing.

The dominie quailed a little before it. He set the pipe in the clay dish and wiped his mouth with his forefinger: then he took his feet from the desk and rested his elbows on it instead. He had no answer. He could not even concoct an abstraction to satisfy the lad and stave off the myriad of implications which crowded behind the statement. How could he explain in simple terms the intricate system of ethics on which past, present and future, work, accomplishment and reward was founded? *That*, certainly, was not on the curriculum.

'How,' he said, quite aware that the question was a diversion, 'do you separate your memories, Drew?'

'I can hardly remember him, Mr Guthrie,' Drew said. 'Maybe that's how it happens. You put your old memories down under new ones, bury them.'

'Undoubtedly,' murmured the headmaster.

'But I *should* be able t'remember my own Da. I can't remember one word he said t'me. Funny, isn't it?'

The dominie cleared his throat. 'Strange as it may seem, Drew, you *will* remember him again. In ten years, or twenty, the recollections will restore themselves. And when you are my age you will recall your father with more clarity than ever you believed possible. I have no means of proving this: you must just accept my word on it.'

'I . . . I don't miss him, dominie,' Drew said. 'I think it's wrong of me not t'miss him more.'

'You have your sisters, of course.'

'Aye,' Drew said. 'They're all right: but ... but I just don't seem to be able to care.'

A Latin quotation popped into the teacher's mind, but it did not seem an appropriate moment for a classical exhibition.

Drew shrugged his thin shoulders.

'When I think about Da, I realize that I wouldn't be here at all if he'd still been alive.'

'An illogical assumption, Drew.'

'No, it's true enough, Mr Guthrie. He'd never have managed it. I'd have got as far as classes in Hamilton, maybe, an' the chance of a job in a clerk's post under Wyld or over in North-rigg. But that would have been my limit. He'd have kept on dreaming of something better, something different, but he'd never have been able to make it come true.'

'You're being very hard on your father, Drew – and on your-self.'

'My sisters are doing it only because they promised him,' Drew said. 'That was the best he could imagine – t'extract a daft promise with his last breath.'

'I'm ... sorry, Drew,' the dominie said.

'Sorry for what, Mr Guthrie?'

'That I can't help you to understand.'

'It's not important,' Drew said.

'No?'

'How can it be important?' Drew said. 'It's over an' done with: you can't change that.'

With sudden briskness the dominie swept the papers on his desk into a semblance of order. He discovered a cardboard folder and thrust it across the desk towards Drew.

'Additional exercises,' he said, rising. 'Same time on Thurs-day?'

Drew got up too, strapping books and papers together.

'Yes, Mr Guthrie.'

The boy went to the door.

'Drew?'

'Aye, Dominie?'

'The first conjugation in all Latin primers is *amare*, the

Present Indicative Active of the verb "to love". Has it occurred to you to wonder why that is so?'

'Because it is the simplest example.'

'Perhaps there is also another reason,' Mr Guthrie suggested. 'If you think of it, Drew, please let me know.'

'I will,' Drew promised.

But, as the dominie suspected, the young man never did.

*

Conjugations of Latin verbs were not on Rob Ewing's mind that late summer season; if he had paused long enough in his pursuit of Miss McMasters though, he could probably have defined one meaning of *amare* well enough, and would have equated it with passion. He was back at the coal face two days after his accident. The wound on his brow bruised out faster than the green wound which his temporary nurse had made in the region of his heart. His abruptly terminated affair with Mirrin Stalker had taught him a thing or two, convincing him that women were creatures to be used. Each time his hand closed on Eileen's arm or slid round her waist he was gripped by a desire which left him shaken. Beside it, his liking for Mirrin Stalker paled into insignificance. He courted Eileen desperately, seeking her out every night, walking with her, taking her to union meetings in Lanark and Hamilton, to whippet racing at Motherwell and, once, to the variety show in a huge green marquee in the fields near the town of Wishaw.

Callum was not slow to remark the situation.

'Seem's t'me you'd better watch your step, lad, or you'll be findin' yourself in the aisle of the kirk with the McMasters lass. I doubt if you'll bed her any other way than as a husband.'

Rob had no answer to his father's warning.

The substance of it was true. There was an innocence in Eileen which was not assumed. She was a good girl, and good girls in Blacklaw were canny girls. She rebuffed his more ardent demands as gently as she could, never with the suggestion that he had insulted her.

'I want t'be a good wife t'you, Rob. I don't think I can be a good wife until I've growed up a bit more.'

The whirlwind romance lasted into the autumn and reached a climax on the night of the Silver Jubilee celebrations of the building of the Church of Scotland Hall, an event marked by a concert and speeches and the dishing out of tea and scones to all those whose stock stood high enough with the elders to receive a ticket. When the final song had been sung, the Benediction delivered and the harmonium shrouded, a detail of young folk remained behind in the big, damp hall to stack the benches and to gather up rubbish from the floor.

Rob and Eileen were the last couple in the kitchen. It was warm in the stone-floored room, the urns burnished and shiny in the glow from the gas mantles. Eileen, in her best dress, was flushed. Rob could not resist. He grabbed her and might even have proved to her that she already knew all there was to know about being a wife, if the exudations of the building had not stayed him.

He pressed her to him, kissing her hair.

'Oh, Rob: no, not here.'

'You're grown up enough, Eileen.'

'Rob, you'll have t'wait.'

'Sixteen's old enough: m'grannie was a mother at sixteen,' Rob said.

'Times have changed, love.'

'Aye, well, they haven't changed for me. I want an answer. Will you marry me?'

'Yes, Rob, I will marry you.'

'When?'

'Soon.'

'How soon?'

'I don't know. Rob, don't pester me. We've all our lives ahead of us.'

'Eileen . . .'

But she slipped away from him, just as Mirrin had done during his courtship of her. Once more, Rob ground his teeth in frustration, and fell into a mood which could only be described as lunatic.

When he got home that evening, his father was seated in the

wicker chair by the hearth, munching a slice of bread curled round a sausage.

Rob slammed the door.

'Hullo!' said Callum. 'You're back early.'

'Aye.'

'Did y'get a flea in your ear again, son?'

'*None of your bloody business.*'

Rob dashed tea from the pot on the hob and swung the mug in his mouth.

'You'll waken your mother,' said Callum, mildly.

'I don't care.'

Callum bit off a mouthful of bread and sausage and chewed patiently. 'Aye, aye,' he said. 'Y'know, we'll be right glad when you do get married. We could do wi' a bit of peace.'

'She won't have me.'

'Have y'asked her?'

'Aye.'

'What did she say?'

'Wait.'

'At least that's a promise,' said Callum. 'You'll just have t'learn patience, son.'

'I'm sick o'learning patience.'

'Your mother made me wait seven years.'

'I'll be withered up in seven years.'

'Rob,' said Callum, more seriously now. 'Are y'*sure* this is the girl for you?'

'I'm certain.'

'It's none of my business, son, but ... but what ever came between you an' Mirrin Stalker? I never thought there'd be anybody for you but her.'

'Ask *her* that question.'

'I mean, Eileen McMasters's a nice girl, but ...'

'The difference is that Eileen likes me.'

'But Mirrin ...'

'Mirrin Stalker's like all the rest o'them – out for what she can get. You don't think Houston Lamont took her on because she was good at polishin' silver.'

'That's unfair, Rob.'

'Ach, you know the Stalkers got too big for their boots.'

'I know the Stalker girls are havin' a time of it since Alex died. They're strugglin' to put the young 'un . . .'

'I've heard that tale,' Rob interrupted.

'It's an admirable ambition,' Callum said. 'I'm sorry Mirrin never . . .'

'Stop bletherin' about Mirrin Stalker.'

'Son, son : you'll have t'pull yourself together.'

Rob put down the mug and combed his hands across his hair. 'You're right, Da. You're right. It's women. It's Eileen. If only I could be sure . . .'

'Pin her to a date,' said Callum, off-handedly. 'The McMasters are keen t'have her off their hands, an' I hear they approve o'you well enough. Fix a date wi' her, an' that'll pin her down an' help settle your mind.'

Rob slapped his palms on his thighs, and got to his feet.

'You're right, Da.'

The young collier took the kitchen in two strides and yanked open the door.

'Hey, I don't mean *now*,' said Callum.

'Why not now?'

Then Rob was gone.

*

The like of it had never been seen in Blacklaw before. The incident was all the more remarkable because it involved Callum Ewing's lad who, until that summer, had been regarded as a stable young man. Love, however, wreaked havoc with his character. And love cost the neighbours in the centre rows of Main Street a good night's sleep.

It was shortly after midnight when Rob Ewing set up his racket under the McMasters' windows. He had tried the door and found it locked, and, overcome by determination, had refused to wait for an answer. Instead, he stepped to the pavement's edge, pointed his face at the attic window, and let out the most deafening bellow.

'EILEEN.'

If he had been drunk, the whole show would have been

infuriating to the sleepy neighbours. As it was, Blacklaw had never witnessed such a display of honest lust before and found the spectacle both educational and vastly comic. The Mc-Masters, it seemed, were the deepest slumberers in the village. Half the street was up at the windows and doors before Rob's caterwauling roused Eileen, her sisters, brothers, mother and father, and brought them, huddled in nightshirts and shawls, to the door.

By that time, Rob had given up on the door and was concentrating the power of his lungs on the narrow window which jutted out from the slates.

'EILEEN.'

'Who the hell's that?'

'Rob Ewin'.'

'EILEEN.'

'What's he doin'?'

'Shoutin' for the McMasters' lass.'

'Is he drunk?'

'Nup: he seems t'be sober.'

'Poor bastard!'

'EILEEN.'

'Toss a jug o'water on him.'

'Naw, naw: leave him be.'

'First Mirrin Stalker, now this one.'

'EILEEN.'

'Is she ignorin' him?'

'Dunno.'

'EILEEN.'

'Ah, she's at the window now.'

'Thank God for that.'

Back-lit by a single candle and packed into the frame with four sisters, Eileen peered down into the street below.

'Is that you, Rob?'

'AYE, DAMN IT, IT'S ME.'

'Wheesht: you'll wake the whole village.'

'I DON'T GIVE A TUPPENNY DAMN.'

'What is it? What d'you want?'

He could see her corn-blonde hair spilled on either side of her face, and her breasts exposed within the cotton shift, blooming over the sill. Tow-headed, button-nosed sisters were like cherubs around her. Rob was suddenly full of love, suddenly devoid of all anger and impatience, and quite aware of the commotion his declaration of passion was causing.

'I WANT YOU TO MARRY ME.'

'I told you I would.'

'DO YOU LOVE ME?'

'Aye.'

'THEN WHEN WILL YOU MARRY ME?'

'Rob, please, go away. I'll tell you tomorrow.'

'TELL ME TONIGHT, OR I'LL STAND HERE 'TIL DAWN.'

Muffled exclamations came from within the McMasters' house. The street door which had been opened in haste was just as hastily closed. Pressed against it were the three boys of the family and their father, all four convulsed with laughter, choking it back for fear of offending the hefty young suitor. Wringing her hands, Mrs McMasters had been relegated to the narrow stair, from which post she listened to the conversation and wept with shame and excitement. Like Eileen, she was not insensitive to the romantic side of the proposal.

'When I'm seventeen,' Eileen whispered.

'WHAT?'

'When I'm seventeen.'

'WHEN'S THAT?'

'In May: in the month of May, Rob.'

'LOUDER.'

'NEXT MAY.'

'RIGHT! YOU'LL MARRY ME IN MAY?'

'Yes.'

'LOUDER.'

'AYE, ROB, I'LL MARRY YOU IN MAY.'

'PROMISE?'

'I PROMISE.'

Cheers and applause broke from the houses up and down Main Street. Somebody warbled the chorus of the Wedding Hymn in a high falsetto, and the widow next door stepped out to scatter a precious handful of rice over Rob's shoulders.

Though he was now writing with embarrassment at his outburst, Rob manfully played out the scene. He bowed low to the spectators, waved to the windowful of future in-laws, then strode off down the pavement, heading home like a knight from the wars.

Eileen craned from the window, staring after him in awe, wonderment and love.

Fifty yards off, the young collier turned in his tracks, cupped his hands to his mouth and shouted,

'EILEEN, I LOVE YOU.'

Callum waited at the door, thumbs in his belt and the pipe in his mouth.

'By God, son,' he said. 'You've really done it now.'

'Haven't I?' Rob said. 'She'll not wriggle out of that promise.'

'No more will you.'

'Who wants to?' Rob declared and, grinning like a satyr, swaggered ben the house to bed.

Part Three

A Face Towards the Future

I

In September, only six months after the accident which had reached into every home in Blacklaw, Mirrin Stalker left the narrow house at Main Street's end. Though she had been apprehensive about the actual moment of departure, when it arrived she found that she hoisted her basket into the back of the dog-cart and climbed up beside Archie, the stable-lad, without a qualm of sorrow. Perhaps it was the sight of Drew, lured down from his attic by curiosity, which smothered Mirrin's regret and brought an unexpected sense of relief. There had never been much affection between them. Drew was as strong-willed as she was, and both were as stubborn as blind monkeys; but Drew's lack of warmth had grown more apparent since his father's death and could no longer be excused as part of the process of growing up. Not in build, but in manner, he looked every inch a man. The very stance he now adopted, lolling arrogant and silent in the doorway, made Mirrin wish that her severance with this place might be total and permanent.

As it was, Mam and Kate were carrying on as if she was starting a trek to Timbuctoo, not just moving a mile up the hill. Twice per week, or oftener, she would have freedom to return home. Family fetters were not so easily broken; however, her allegiance now was due only to Kate and her mother. Betsy was a selfish, empty-headed flirt, and Drew, as far as Mirrin was concerned, had degenerated into a hopeless case of gallop-ing ambition. So she took her seat in the dog-cart next to Archie and went bowling away from the colliers' row, uphill towards the bronze-leaved oaks, and suffered not a single twinge of conscience.

September had always brought her hope. Ever since she had been a child she had loved this mellow season. Now every month that passed, every blend of weather, carried her further from the spring's tragedies and away from the brash, upstart girl that she had been then. At times, scrutinizing the changes in herself, she was surprised at Lamont's part in bringing them about; not just what he had done for her in practical terms, but the effect that he had on her as a man. In spite of Edith's constant carping, in spite of the awe which she still felt towards Lamont's position in the community, Mirrin could no longer ignore the fact that Houston Lamont was beginning to mean more to her than was quite right and proper. Even more surprising was the fact that she suffered no guilt about it, nor fought to restore her old enmity towards the master. Indeed, the secret acknowledgement made her all the more determined not to let him down and gave her confidence to assume that, within a day or two, she would be thoroughly settled to her new life in the coalmaster's household.

Among her first chores was the readying of the rooms in the dusty east wing's first floor. This part of the house had been used by Lamont's son, the poor mite, and had been deserted since his death. It gave Mirrin peculiar satisfaction to march into these neglected chambers with brooms and mops and dusting feathers and refurbish them, letting in light and air. Her own room was in this part of the house too. It was larger than she had anticipated, comfortably furnished with pieces Lamont had exhumed from attics and cellars, and a far cry from the spartan cell in which the McCormick cousins slept.

Mirrin could not be sure to what extent she had been responsible for Lamont's decision to bring his sister home from the south. She questioned if she had exerted much influence upon him; yet their conversation in the coach-house had been so intimate that she could not reject the possibility that she had helped him find purpose and the courage to defy his wife. It was common knowledge in the servants' quarters that there had been some sort of confrontation between Houston and Edith Lamont. Mirrin's most stern edicts could not quell the gossip which chattered back and forth between cook and maids and even spread out its tentacles to include the groom and casual gardeners. They were all agog at the news that Mr Lamont's sister would shortly return to Blacklaw, and speculation was rife as to her mental condition.

Houston Lamont had given Mirrin the news in person. She had greeted it with enthusiasm. Since that moonlit August night, Lamont had frequently found opportunities to talk with her and, over the weeks, Mirrin was obliged to examine her attitude to the coalmaster in a different light. As a man he stirred her: as employer, and custodian of her family's future, he still intimidated her a little. Instinct suggested that his feelings towards her were equally confused.

At least Edith Lamont's outbursts of petty spite had been stilled by the impending arrival of Houston's sister. Her wardrobe was stocked with colourful new gowns and day-dresses and she took more care over her appearance, struggling to adopt the latest fashions in hair-styling, for example. Her manner too had outwardly softened. She no longer sharply scolded the servants and treated Mirrin with a chill formality, which was a deal better than tartness and temper. Beneath the surface, however, Edith Lamont's mistrust had soured to hatred, and Mirrin was intuitively aware of it and never relaxed her guard.

During the course of the week when Houston Lamont was in Kent, the atmosphere in the house became palpably electric with anticipation and apprehension. Edith removed herself still further from domestic concerns, spent much time in her room, primping and fussing with her appearance, trying on dresses, shoes and gloves, matched against jewellery from her many velvet-lined cases. Charitably, Mirrin assumed that Lamont's wife intended to look her best for Lamont's sister; but, at the back of her mind, she recognized the spirit of competition.

Lamont wisely planned the journey back to Scotland in easy stages, spending *en route* a night in London and another in Edinburgh so that Dorothy could adjust to the change in her routine and, he hoped, find diversion in the cosseting which the grand hotels rendered. He took care to ensure that their suites were connected by an adjoining door and, during the course of the night, looked in on his sister several times. No nightmares troubled her and she slept peacefully, free from anxieties in her brother's keeping.

Dorothy's luggage – a trunk full of clothing and two chests of books – arrived by railway carrier an hour in advance of the branch line train from Edinburgh to Hamilton. Sandy Willocks, the ostler, and Archie, had the coach in the station yard by noon and spent the waiting time giving a last dab of spit and polish to the carriage work and a sheen to the horses' flanks. They were themselves tricked out neat as ninepence in brand-new shirts and hacking jackets, black boots gleaming: the Queen herself could not have arrived to a grander reception.

But Dorothy was tired by her journey and made unsettled, now that its end was near, by the half-remembered sights of Hamilton and the glowering Lanarkshire landscape, brightened though it was by autumnal bunting. The ugly grey coups and skeletal wheel housings, the iron webs of shunting yards, the brick sheds and rusty huts which flanked the road through Northrigg distressed her and she hid her face in Houston's coat over the last miles past Blacklaw and into the avenue of oak-trees.

Though the staff were all assembled, they saw nothing of the master's sister except a glimpse of a tall, angular figure huddled against her brother as she was whisked from the coach and up the steps into the house. Edith, who had sense enough to show compassion at this hour, undertook to attend to the woman personally, and so, for the rest of that afternoon, the servants' curiosity remained unappeased.

*

Mrs Burns sprinkled parsley into the potato pot with one hand and tested the temperature of the basic sauce with the pinkie of the other. She wore a starched apron, matching cap of spotless white linen, and linen cuffs banded over the sleeves of her dress. To judge from the aroma which wafted from the holes in the lid of the great stewpan, she had excelled herself in the selection and dressing of the pair of fowls and had coaxed them to a state of tenderness before which the most invalid appetite must surely quicken. Celery and mushrooms were added to the sauce and Hannah was set to gentle stirring while Mrs Burns, with a frightened glance at the inscrutable wall clock, fiddled with the valves of the ventilated oven within which a rich lemon pudding was just about to erupt deliciously over its rim of puff-pastry.

'If I'd known,' she wailed. 'If I'd only known, I'd have settled them with cutlets an' cold chocolate mould. It's five minutes t'eight an' it'll be all ruint if she's not ready.'

'Poor lady don't know what's wrong wi' her,' said Hannah.

'Eight I was told,' said Mrs Burns, whose sympathy at that juncture was all with her fowls and pudding. 'Eight it should be.'

'It's not eight yet.'

'Where's Mirrin?'

'Checkin' the table, wi' Mattie.'

'I've only got two hands,' said Mrs Burns, apropos of nothing.

'Well, we've done our best,' said Hannah. 'Here, I think this sauce's ready.'

Mrs Burns wailed again.

Normally calm and phlegmatic, she had charted dinner parties for a dozen epicures with less distress than she now displayed over a comparatively simple meal for three. Food, to her way of thinking, was a great panacea whose therapeutic qualities should not be reduced by tardiness.

At that moment, Mirrin pushed through the door. She was straight-backed and unflustered, her black dress making her seem much more mature than nineteen.

'What's happening?' asked Mrs Burns, hoarsely.

'Dinner at eight,' Mirrin said. 'I take it the food is ready?'

'They're all coming?' asked Hannah. 'The sister too?'

'Aye: it seems Miss Dorothy's recovered,' Mirrin replied.

Mrs Burns beamed.

'Trays, please, Hannah,' Mirrin said. 'Then you may fill the soup tureens, both of them. Don't forget t'put the lids on tight to keep them hot.'

'Right,' said Hannah smartly.

Much activity followed, and soon the kitchen was filled with steam and the clash of pans. For the time being Dorothy Lamont was almost forgotten as the four servants made their final preparations and dished the courses into silver servingware.

At one minute past the hour of eight, Edith and her husband descended the staircase from the upper floor with Dorothy between them.

They were greeted by Mirrin's sonorous cliché.

'Dinner is served now, sir.'

'Thank you, Mirrin,' Lamont answered. 'We will take it at once.'

What Mirrin had expected Dorothy Lamont to be like she did not know: she was, however, hardly prepared for the gentleness of the woman who took her seat on her brother's left at the head of the long dining table. The Lamonts were sensible enough not to utilize the full length of the table. Only half of it was covered with the embroidered white linen cloth, so that they all sat within touching distance of each other. As she conducted the progress of the dinner, acting as butler, housekeeper and steward, Mirrin studied the new arrival closely. Dorothy's likeness to Houston was strong, even as to mannerisms; but in her the man's brooding silences were replaced by round-eyed wonder, a naive and slightly apprehensive vacancy of expression. As far as Mirrin could make out, there was little conversation. From time to time though, Lamont reached out and clasped his sister's hand as if to reassure her that there was nothing to fear in the room. Reserve was the key-note in Edith's behaviour; but observing her mistress out of the corner of her eye, Mirrin detected a suppressed hatred glinting through the veil of sisterly courtesy.

At the end of the meal, Mattie cleared away the pudding plates, and Mirrin put out a pyramid of fruits, a bowl of nuts and the port bottle which Lamont had uncorked and decanted himself earlier in the evening. It was only at this juncture that Mirrin became aware of Dorothy's scrutiny. She remarked it only a moment before Lamont did.

'Dorothy, my dear,' he said affably. 'This is Mirrin Stalker who looks after the house. I believe it was she who arranged the sprays of flowers and berries in your room. I told her how fond of them you are.'

Edith's fingers tightened on the stem of her wineglass. Mirrin was not prepared for the radiant smile which lit Dorothy's face, a smile which caused the years to drop away and be replaced by a childlike prettiness.

'I . . . I . . . do like flowers, Mirrin.'

'That's nice, Miss Dorothy,' Mirrin said. 'In summer the gardens are full of them. We still have quite a display, as you'll see tomorrow.'

'I like your hair too.'

Mirrin was a little abashed at such frankness.

Frowning, Dorothy tapped her fingers on the loose coil on top of her head. 'Mine is too soft. I do try to arrange it, but it's too soft. I wish . . .' The wish was too soft too, and could not formulate itself into a proper expression.

Mirrin said gently, 'My sister also has soft hair, Miss Dorothy, but she cheats a wee bit and uses curling irons.'

Abruptly Edith touched the rim of her wineglass with a sugar spoon, making it chime imperiously.

'I do not think,' she said, 'that hair is a suitable subject for the dinner table. You may take away the fruit, Mirrin, and attend to the kitchen, please.'

It was as if a cloud had crossed over Dorothy's brain. Responding less to the words than to the thin, strained sharpness in her sister-in-law's voice, she seemed to cringe and withdraw into herself, visibly shrinking. It was all Mirrin could do to prevent herself from stepping forward to comfort the poor woman. Houston forestalled her, sweeping into the conversation in defiance of his wife's objection.

'If curling irons are the answer, Dorothy,' he said, breezily, 'then why should you not purchase a pair? Mirrin will show you how to use them.'

The cloud whisked away: but Lamont prudently signalled to Mirrin and the girl gathered the fruit on to a tray and quickly carried it from the dining room.

She stood for a moment in the hall, her back against the panelled door. Anger and compassion flickered in her – anger at Edith's tactlessness, compassion for the poor, wandered creature who was so vulnerable that the least word could hurt like the claw of a gin-trap. An infinite capacity for happiness was there too. But, thought Mirrin grimly, there'd be damned little evidence of it left if Edith Lamont had her way.

'So,' Mirrin muttered, 'it'll be up t'me, I suppose, to see that things go right for the lady.'

Toiling up from the kitchen, Mattie caught the sound of Mirrin's words.

'What's that you're sayin', Mirrin?'

'Nothin',' Mirrin answered and handed the girl the laden tray.

'Talkin' t'yourself,' said Mattie. 'Here, you're as bad as her in there.'

'That's enough, Mattie!'

'What do you think of her, then?'

'I think,' said Mirrin, 'that she'll be happy here, and that she'll make a change to the whole household.'

'Aye, but she's a daftie, isn't she?' Mattie said. 'As bad as Loony Lachie, near enough.'

'Never let me hear you say that again,' Mirrin warned.

'Hark at you: you'd think she was *your* sister.'

'Is that not the Christian way to look at it, Mattie?'

'What's religion got t'do with it?'

'The weak, the lame an' the blind: should we not look after them?'

Mattie raised her brows in incomprehension.

Mirrin said, 'Anyway, Miss Dorothy's the sister of the master of this house. Daft or not, she'll get all the attention we can give her. Understand?'

'Is that t'be the way of it, then?'

'Aye, that's t'be the way of it,' said Mirrin. 'An' you might be good enough to let the others know how I feel about it.'

Mattie balanced the tray against her hip, plucked a grape from the bunch on the fruit salver and popped it into her mouth.

'Right,' she said and, chewing noisily, carried the latest scandal below along with the tray.

*

In the autumn of that tragic year the weather seemed to make amends to the folk of Blacklaw for the burdens and sorrows imposed upon them by the spring season. The sun shone warmly and the leaves of the trees changed colour gradually and flurried gently to the grass as if they were reluctant to give way to winter and the dictates of the natural cycle. Even in mid October there were still roses bunched and fat upon their shrubs, and haws and rowan berries glowed glossy red along the hedgerows. Huge sturdy Margarets could still be found blooming in sheltered spots by the briared walls, and Pibroch McCrimmond's fairy-like offerings became embarrassingly plentiful, spilling abundantly out of their baskets. Wasps and butterflies were numerous, and the evening air was full of big-winged moths, like leaves parted from the whinns by an invisible wind. Mild weather and a good harvest gave the colliers an opportunity to recover their health and gird themselves for the cold months ahead.

Dorothy Lamont, too, in her sanctuary behind the mansion's walls, was aided by the encouragement of the Indian summer. She settled rapidly into a happy frame of mind, undisturbed by shadows of the past or the subtle tensions which her presence in the household intensified.

It was not long, though, before her influence was felt among the domestics. From them she drew a cautious kind of protectiveness, and relaxation of inhibition. Archie was a favourite: he too had a simple outlook on life. With great pride, he showed her round the stables, held the horses still as anthracite statues while she stroked their velvety muzzles and fed them crab-apples from McCrimmond's hoard. Mrs Burns exercised a latent talent for producing elaborate puddings in fancy shapes and pyramids, all multi-hued, spangled with angelica, and as ornate as Parisian *chapeaux*. She had in return the reward of all good cooks – compliments honestly delivered by Dorothy in person.

Lamont imposed no restrictions upon his sister's movements and set up no lines of demarcation. She mingled with the servants and joined freely in their chatter. She was permitted to help in the garden: even Pibroch McCrimmond did not flee into hiding when she stumbled into his domain. Instead, he put his collies through their few tricks for her amusement and sang her some ancient Gaelic songs by way of communication. In a remarkably short space of time, gloom seemed to lift from the house on the oaks, and the lilt of forgotten merriment return to it. If only Edith had put aside her pride and jealousy, the golden autumn might have endured unimpaired for ever.

It was, thought Mirrin, a bit like having a child in the house. Miss Dorothy, in her unaffected joys and delights, was so much like a child that her awkwardness and instability of temperament were soon forgotten. But Dorothy was not a child. She was a woman of close to middle-age, Houston Lamont's sister and, according to Edith's warped view, a competitor for the love which she, as wife and mistress of the household, demanded as her exclusive entitlement.

Among the occupants of the coalmaster's house in that prolonged waning of the year 1875, only Mirrin and Lamont were aware that Dorothy had brought more than happiness home with her. Nothing was said : nothing was done : nothing was deliberately omitted from the programme of care. For all that, both housekeeper and husband sensed Edith's growing hatred and were constantly on their guard against anything which might give her cause for a legitimate outburst.

But Edith was intuitively clever, and sensed the real cause of her relegation in status. She did not become openly hostile, but chose rather the opposite approach, feigning a sweetness which, by reason of its insincerity, alienated her husband still further. Gorgeous dresses adorned her stocky body. Creams and lotions, expensive perfumes and rouges appeared on her dressing table and were applied to her face and hands with care. Her exhibitions of affection were gushing and profuse. The effect was too close to vulgarity to appeal to her husband, though Mattie and Hannah were taken in by it and expressed the opinion that the mistress too had blossomed under Miss Dorothy's influence.

In spite of Edith's peculiar reaction, Houston Lamont was almost happy again. In his sister's company he discovered an unstinted warmth and a reason for slackening the bands of pride which Edith had thrown round the household during the past decade.

It was Dorothy's effect on Lamont which gave Mirrin most pleasure, tugging her inexorably closer to her employer and to that day when her confused feelings would crystallize. Though her duties as housekeeper occupied most of her thoughts, that autumn was also punctuated by concern for her mother and elder sister, and her visits to the narrow dwelling at Main Street's end disturbed her.

Flora Stalker, though not ill, had a drawn and ashen look which worried Mirrin considerably. Kate too had lost weight and much of her resilience. Matters were not aided by the malicious villagers who, now that the Stalkers had no man in the pit, treated them as outsiders. Kate accepted the jibes and wicked whispers with typical Stalker toughness, but Flora, who had always depended on the respect of the community, took them much to heart. She was sufficiently influenced by them to lose her certainty as to the wisdom of her late husband's programme for their surviving son. Her attitude towards Mirrin had also been tainted by gossip, and she treated her middle daughter coldly, as if she blamed her for the loss of face.

Mirrin understood the reasons, but felt powerless to ease the situation. She had committed herself to providing a house for the family and to earning enough money to put Drew to Edinburgh. There was no way in which she could do more. But, it seemed, more was required.

Kate accurately put her finger on it one Sunday afternoon when she and Mirrin had an hour alone in the weed-strewn garden behind the row.

'It's Drew,' Kate said. 'Everything's hangin' on him passin' the entrance examination.'

'He'll pass.'

'Aye, or kill himself wi' overwork in the tryin'.'

'Is he sick?'

'Not him,' said Kate. 'But he's drawin' so much out of himself, I'm almost frightened.'

'Have you had a word with Mr Guthrie?'

'I met the dominie, just by chance, last Thursday,' said Kate. 'Well?'

'It's not Drew's studies that worry him,' said Kate. 'It's Drew himself.'

Mirrin asked for no explanation: too well she understood the dominie's concern.

'Drew was set on his career long before Da died, you know,'

Mirrin said. 'How he's turned out is none of our doing.'

'Maybe not,' said Kate. 'But what'll become of him – and us, too – if he fails?'

'Listen, Kate,' said Mirrin, confidentially. 'Drew's too cunning – aye, cunning – t'make a wrong move. He's more aware of what he wants from life than any of us.'

'What'll I do if he does pass?' said Kate.

'So that's it,' Mirrin said. 'That's what's pulling you down: you're worried about the money.'

'What if he gains entrance and I can't afford t'pay the lodgings or the fees, or keep him clothed? It'll not be cheap, y'know, even pared t'the bone.'

'Are we not saving enough?'

'We're saving all we can, but it might *not* be enough, Mirrin. I'm real terrified at the thought that *we* might fail *him*.'

Mirrin shook her head. 'We can do no more.'

'I wonder.'

'What *can* we do? Work nights as well as days?'

'It's not your fault, Mirrin.'

'No more is it yours.'

'I wish I was sure. I wish I *could* be sure.'

'We've a six month in hand.'

'I'm anxious about Betsy, too.'

'What's she been up to?' said Mirrin. 'Come to think of it, where is she?'

'I've no idea.'

'Courtin'?'

'If she is courtin' then it isn't a village lad: I'd have heard some whisper.'

'Have you asked her outright?'

'Aye. She just laughed, an' told me I was daft.'

'Then ask Drew: if his sister's up to anything, you can be certain Drew'll know about it.'

'I wouldn't dare ask him,' Kate confessed. 'All I'd get for my trouble would be that look of his, flat as a gravestone.'

'Betsy's not bringin' in as much money as you thought she would,' said Mirrin. 'Is she?'

'Oh, she's young, an' being in Dalzells' is an awful temptation for her. She can't be expected t'work there dressed like a tinker: but it costs so much . . .'

'I *could* ask for a small increase from Lamont,' Mirrin reluctantly suggested.

'I wasn't droppin' hints, Mirrin,' said Kate.

'I know you weren't,' Mirrin assured her. 'But it's possible Lamont might be persuaded t'pay me a shillin' or two more per week, since I'm helpin' look after his sister. Would it help at all?'

'Every penny would help.'

'I can't promise,' Mirrin said.

'I'd be grateful.'

'Aye,' Mirrin said. 'I just wish it was for your benefit, Kate, and not for his.'

'Drew's not so bad,' said Kate. 'Wait 'til he's a rich an' famous advocate, he'll see us all right for our old age then.'

'Not him,' said Mirrin. 'He'll try t'pretend we don't exist.'

'Oh, no, Mirrin!' said Kate, a little shocked. 'He's loyal, if he's nothin' else.'

'We'll see,' said Mirrin. 'The truth of the matter is that I'd willingly pay him just t'stay out of my life from now on.'

'He's our *brother*, Mirrin.'

'More's the pity.'

*

The ball was of soft India rubber and the racquet, discovered in a garden shed, had several frayed strings, but the game did not seem to suffer through the equipment's imperfections. Unobserved, Mirrin stood by the tree at the corner of the avenue and, smiling to herself, watched Houston Lamont puff after the ball. He picked it up, squeezed it into his large palm, then turned to Dorothy, twenty yards away across the dry grass, and raised both arms.

'Gone,' he said. 'You must have hit it straight out of the county. Shall I send a carriage to look for it?'

'It's there, Houston.'

'Where?'

'In your hand.'

'Oh, no, it's not.'

He advanced, foxily, sidling across the lawn; but Dorothy had already learned those rudimentary deceptions which made the game so much fun, and did not release her grasp upon the racquet or expose the painted tub which stood in lieu of a wicket.

She wagged the racquet, daring him to deceive her.

'Oh, no, it's not, it's not, Houston,' she cried gleefully, in excited confusion. 'It's in your hand.'

Lamont lumbered three or four paces and, with the action of an ironsmith wielding a ninety-pound sledge-hammer, swung his arm in a huge circle and delivered the rubber ball in a floating arc towards the tub.

Dorothy flailed at it, missed, then as the ball trickled along the grass, stopped it with the sole of her shoe, took aim, and drove it across the shoulder of the lawn into the flowerbeds.

Lamont appeared to be flabbergasted: not annoyed, however, for any sign of irritation had a distressing effect on Dorothy. Noisily, he applauded the shot.

'A fine effort, Miss Lamont.'

'Is it lost, Houston?'

'No, it's in the beds.'

'Be careful not to hurt the flowers.'

'I'll be most careful,' promised Lamont, crossing the lawn. 'I wouldn't hurt the flowers for all the coal in Lanarkshire.'

Mirrin emerged from behind the oak tree.

She had been cheered by the sight of Dorothy and Houston Lamont's play, and had sloughed off the cares which her visit home had incurred.

Dorothy's gaunt figure was filling out, and she had lost the nervous habit of picking and smoothing her dress. As for Lamont, he appeared to have no worry in the world, as if a lifetime of sunny Sunday afternoons stretched into the future. Edith probably disapproved of such goings-on on the Sabbath, even though the household had attended morning service in the village kirk and would go again that evening. Two doses of religion in a day surely entitled a person to scratch a wee bit of healthy enjoyment from the afternoon, thought Mirrin. She did not attend church, and stayed behind with Dorothy who, it was felt, might be upset by the many references to death, Hell, brimstone and damnation which larded the minister's sermons.

Lamont did not notice Mirrin. He continued towards the flowerbeds, then suddenly veered off, and laughing, caught Dorothy round the waist and hoisted her from the ground, swinging her this way and that.

'Houston : don't dare. Put me down, Houston!'

On the final turn he caught sight of Mirrin, paused, slightly discomfited, and put Dorothy lightly down again.

'See,' he said, directing his sister's attention. 'Here's Mirrin come to see who's making all the noise.'

'Are you enjoyin' yourself, Miss Dorothy?'

'Yes, Mirrin : we were ... we were playing a game.' She held up the racquet. 'I hit the ball with this.'

'Yes, I saw you,' said Mirrin. 'A grand hit it was, too.'

'Dorothy,' said Lamont, 'see if you can find the ball.'

Mirrin watched the woman cross the lawn, step gingerly into the flowerbed and begin to poke about under the leaves. Her attention was soon distracted from the search by a pair of mauve butterflies and then by the discovery of a cluster of tight yellow rosebuds which promised late blooms. She chattered away to herself as she explored the minutiae of the garden.

Mirrin said, 'What a difference these past weeks have made to your sister, Mr Lamont. You must be fair pleased.'

'I am indeed,' he answered. 'I cannot help wishing, however, that . . .'

Mirrin nodded : she was an expert in wishing. Her mind survived on it, but she had never thought to hear the coalmaster confess to such weakness.

'Miss Dorothy'll be needing some winter dresses soon,' she said. 'I doubt if she has anything heavy enough for our climate in her wardrobe. Besides, it would be good for her to have clothes that were not connected with the ... the place she came from.'

'A splendid idea, Mirrin,' said Lamont. 'We'll make a trip to

Edinburgh. You must come, too, and help her choose. Dorothy would enjoy that. We will have tea in the gardens ... No, perhaps it's too late in the season for that.'

'I'm wonderin' if such a long journey's advisable,' said Mirrin, cautiously. 'I hear from my sister that Dalzells' emporium in Hamilton carries a large stock of the latest fashions.'

'You are right, of course,' Lamont agreed. 'Perhaps we can all bundle into the carriage one afternoon next week ...'

'Perhaps, Mrs Lamont would prefer ...'

'Yes, she may wish to supervise,' Lamont admitted. 'On the other hand she may not wish to be involved.'

Again Mirrin nodded. Edith Lamont would have a dilemma on her hands. She would hardly like to be excluded from a shopping trip : on the other hand, as Lamont said, she would not much care for being seen in fashionable Hamilton in charge of a weak-minded person. Dorothy's behaviour and responses to any new situation were not predictable.

'I'll speak to my wife,' said Lamont.

He glanced across at the flowerbed. Dorothy's head showed above the leaves. She appeared to have discovered something of interest in the earth and was prodding at it with the racquet handle.

'Mr Lamont,' said Mirrin. 'I'm sorry t'have to bring it up at all, but this seems as good an opportunity as any.'

'What is it, Mirrin. Are you unhappy?'

'No, sir, it's certainly not that.' She hesitated, cursing the necessity of putting such a question to him at all. 'I ... I was wonderin' if you could see your way to payin' me a bit extra every week. I think I'm worth it, now, sir.'

Lamont took a handkerchief from his vest pocket and wiped his fingers with it. 'Mirrin,' he said, 'three months ago if I had told you the truth, you would have thought it an excuse. Perhaps now, you will understand. Times are bad, for the master as much as for the man. If it ever leaked out that I paid a housekeeper more than I pay my foremen, then every hot-head in Blacklaw would muster at the street corner bawling his demands.'

322

'It would only be a shillin', sir.'

'You don't need it, do you?'

'No, Mr Lamont: *I* don't need it.'

'But your brother does?'

'Aye.'

'I'll ... consider it, Mirrin.'

'Thank you, Mr Lamont.'

'You do well here, Mirrin,' he said, ruefully. 'But you are not the stuff servants are made of, you know.'

She felt a prickle of resentment, as if he was patronizing her. He had a right to patronize her, of course: she had chosen to be a servant and must accept the sharp division which that occupation demanded.

'What stuff *am* I made of, then?'

He shrugged. 'You don't truly believe that you *serve* my family, Mirrin. You believe that you *help* us.'

'Is there a difference?'

'A vast difference,' said Lamont.

'The difference between the slave and the hireling?'

'Ah, yes,' Lamont said. 'But which is which, Mirrin? We may differ on that point.'

'I'm sorry I asked,' she said, curtly.

'I haven't given my reply.'

'Aye, I think you have, Mr Lamont.'

The debate was interrupted by a sudden scream from Dorothy. Lamont wheeled and began running for the flower-bed, Mirrin close on his heels.

Dorothy was frozen with horror at the far side of the flowerbed. She pointed with the racquet across the narrow strip of lawn into a corner by the old walls. Lamont hugged her tightly, craning to see what real or imagined beast had so frightened her.

'What was it, Dorothy?'

'A ... a ...'

'A rat?' Mirrin prompted. 'Was it a rat with a long tail?'

'Clown,' said Dorothy.

Mirrin went forward: a clown?

'Come away, Dorothy,' said Lamont. But the woman was rooted to the spot, some part of her strong enough to wish to confront her fear.

The animal's appearance startled Mirrin. She had never seen a live badger before. She had heard that they were rife in the woods and fields round Blacklaw and, in the hard snows of February and March, had even been seen by backshift men, foraging in the middens on the end rows. She was not sufficiently informed to recognize the old boar badger who had his sett in the high woods behind McCrimmond's hut, or to realize that the night-beast had been napping in the sun on the stone mound by the wall. Instinctively he had sought an exit route. Finding his path barred by the walls, he scraped and burrowed a shallow trough – all that he could manage in the dry, rock-strewn soil – behind the mounds. The weeds here and the leave-heaps which the gardeners had dumped gave him some protection. Later McCrimmond told her that Grandpa Brock was on the scout for wasps' nests and had plundered a dozen or more that warm autumn.

The white and black mask, long pointed to a button snout and a droll mouth, peered out at her from the inadequate hide.

Mirrin stifled a laugh, and motioned Lamont to bring Dorothy forward.

Holding her tightly, the coalmaster coaxed his sister closer to the strip of wilderness in which her nightmare beast had taken refuge.

'See,' Mirrin said in a low voice. 'See, it's only a Brock, Miss Dorothy.'

'A badger,' Lamont explained.

His grin consoled the frightened woman. She grinned too and would have gone forward to play with the creature if Lamont had not restrained her.

'He's very shy,' whispered Mirrin. 'We're lucky to see him at all, Miss Dorothy. I think he ventured out in the daylight just to admire you.'

'Can I give him apples?'

'We will ask McCrimmond where he lives, and leave some

apples out for him. I think he will like fruit well enough,' Mirrin said.

The badger had tucked his face away now, though they could still hear him rustling and burrowing deeper into the leaves.

'I *should* have him shot, you know,' said Lamont: then instantly regretted the remark.

Dorothy wailed.

Mirrin said, 'He lives here, and he meant no harm.'

'Came to see me.' Dorothy stared into her brother's face. 'He came just to see me. You would not do him harm, Houston?'

'Of course not,' Lamont said quickly. 'I spoke without thinking.'

'Aye,' said Mirrin. 'I suppose old Brockie's as much a part of this place as you are, Mr Lamont: his family might have been here a while longer.'

'Let's leave him, then,' Lamont suggested. 'Give him peace.'

'Will he . . . will he . . . miss us?'

'I doubt it, Miss Dorothy: he's very, very shy. He'll not like too much attention.'

She nodded and smiled, and clasped her brother's arm to draw him away, perhaps still disturbed by the suggestion that he might do the badger injury.

They walked a little way across the lawn again and waited, Dorothy squirming with impatience. After ten long minutes, the low, scuttling shape of the badger showed for an instant at the wall's end as he swarmed over the broken-work and headed off to his home in the high woodland.

'Will he come to see us again?' Dorothy said.

'Perhaps,' said Mirrin.

'After his winter nap?' Dorothy said.

'Aye,' Mirrin answered, though she knew that badgers were abroad all year. 'Aye, when the spring comes.'

With that adventure behind them, Dorothy was suddenly tired, and Mirrin led her off to her bedroom to rest before dinner.

In the excitement, Mirrin had almost forgotten her request

for an increase of a shilling a week. It surprised her when, the following Saturday noon, Edith Lamont accounted her one extra florin in the twist of brown paper which contained her wage.

Mirrin, of course, said nothing to anyone, and gave the money to Kate.

2

Fog choked the valley of the Clyde from estuary to source. It shrouded the peaks of Arran and absorbed Gourock's lights. It swallowed whole the old black rock of Dumbarton castle and drowned Erskine's pastures down to the river's edge. Thickening and darkening, mixing salt with smoke, it crawled east over scattered farms and boatyards and hauled itself stealthily into the city's forest of tenement chimney-pots. Swirling, it filled the pubs and stalls, shops and parlours of every cramped lane and vennel and scalded the lungs of all honest citizens who were daft enough to be out that night.

Glasgow, at the best of times, was too rough for Betsy Stalker's taste. It held none of the glamour of Edinburgh, was throttled by horse-traffic and uncouth folk, far shabbier and meaner than the inhabitants of Hamilton. Her apprehension was intensified that November Saturday both by the sinister pea-souper and by the lateness of the hour. Against her better judgement, she had allowed Maurice to persuade her to accompany him to a Magical Performance in the Candleriggs hall. They had been late enough arriving and had missed the first four acts : since then the fog had worsened.

Supper had been sacrificed as Maurice, a comparative stranger to the city too, had groped and shuffled through the streets in search of the railway station. Betsy clung to her escort, her mouth tucked into her scarf to filter the filthy air. Eventually the station's façade loomed out of the murk; but the girl's relief soon turned to panic when she discovered that few drivers were willing to trust the signals and that it was doubtful if another train would set out for Hamilton that night.

The station was a vast tabernacle of fog, its vaulted roof quite invisible. Gas lamps hung suspended in ghastly yellow cauls which allowed little or no light to reach the ground. Porters, firemen and a few passengers loitered dismally in the concourse awaiting the board's announcement that the station

327

was officially closed. Beyond the rim of the glass dome, the night was a wall of fog, and those engines still at large lowed and hooted mournfully.

'Oh, Maurice,' Betsy said, 'what'll we do?'

'Spend the night in a boarding house, dearest.'

'I can't do that!'

'You may have to, Betsy, my darling.'

'It . . . it wouldn't be right.'

'Under the circumstances . . .'

'M'mother'll be so worried.'

'Doesn't she know where you are?'

'She thinks I'm at a kirk concert in Hamilton with Phyllis Rose.'

'Then she will assume that you have been fog-bound there and are spending the night with your friend.'

'But what if she finds out I didn't?'

There was an expression on Maurice's face which Betsy had detected before and which she had misinterpreted as love. In the fog-shrouded station in the heart of Glasgow, however, the glint of calculation in his eyes was unmistakable, and all the girl's confidence in herself evaporated.

'You need not tell anyone,' said Maurice.

'I want t'go home.'

'I happen to know of a lodging not far from here,' said Maurice. 'The terms are reasonable, and I can guarantee your stay will be . . . pleasant.'

'What do you mean by that, Maurice McElroy?'

'You'll see,' he said. 'We will have supper, and I can just about run to a bottle of wine . . .'

'Are you suggesting . . .?'

'Accept the situation, my love.'

'Maurice . . .' She peered past him into the gloom. '*Look!* They're writin' on that board. Come on.'

Dragging him by the arm, Betsy ran to the blackboard and, with overwhelming relief, read the chalked announcement that a train would leave in five minutes in an attempt to reach Hamilton. Passengers were warned that conditions on the line might strand them, but Betsy hardly gave that a thought. On board the train there would be other people: she would no longer be at Maurice's mercy.

'Betsy, wait.'

'Come on, Maurice: at least we'll be out of here.'

McElroy gave a snarl of frustration which Betsy, who had scampered on ahead, fortunately did not hear. She waited by the barrier until a tired-eyed ticket collector inspected the billets Maurice handed him.

'Will it actually reach Hamilton?' Maurice asked.

'Small chance, sir: if it wasnae for Geordie havin' a bran' new missus in Hamilton, he wouldnae be tryin' the run at all. Like the bloody Earl o'Hell's kilt out there the nicht.'

'Bravo for Geordie,' Betsy cheered. 'I'm sure he'll manage t'get us through.'

The collector gave Maurice a basilisk stare which may have been warmed by a hint of male sympathy: then the couple hurried on up the platform.

It was not as Betsy anticipated. The compartments were empty. Very few people had risked a trip to Glasgow that evening and most of those who had, had decided to lodge in the city overnight. In all the length of the train there were only four other couples – three of them already locked in shameless embraces – and a workman in a cloth cap who obviously did not list sobriety among his virtues.

'In here,' Maurice said, when Betsy had led him almost into the plumes of white steam which jetted from under the engine.

He flung open the carriage door and pushed her inside.

The first class coach was completely deserted.

Betsy took a corner seat. Huddling into the blue plush, she watched anxiously as Maurice slammed and secured the door, rattled down the green linen blind and unhooked the curtains. He crossed the compartment and did the same at the other window.

'Keep the fog out,' he explained gruffly, seating himself beside her and sliding his arm about her waist.

'I like to see where . . .'

'On a night like this?' said Maurice.

'Perhaps we *should* stay . . .'

A whistle sounded. The engine responded with a blast of steam and a forward surge which so seemed to exhaust its power that it paused for a full minute before summoning its links into order, and heaved forward again. The wheels shrieked, the coach swayed and jerked, and the Hamilton-bound train nosed slowly out into the fog.

Betsy straightened the creases in the fingers of her best gloves and, under cover of the handbag on her knee, proceeded to twine and twist fresh wrinkles into them. The pressure of Maurice's arm had increased. It was tight now and rigid, the elbow bent.

Brightly, Betsy looked round the compartment.

'I don't often travel by this mode of conveyance,' she said. 'It's rather comfortable, don't you think, Maurice?'

Maurice smiled, nodded, and laconically remarked, 'Private, too.'

Wheels and rails clattered, making speech impossible for a while, though the engine still pulled and toiled with such slowness that it might have been dragging them up Mont Blanc and not through Glasgow's flat sidings.

The compartment was comfortable, but smelled of coke and fog and damp fabrics. Betsy fixed her gaze on a picture of Rothesay Bay which was framed against the opposite wall. The gas fixture on the ceiling had two loops of chain which swung like pendulums and told her that the rate of speed remained ponderously slow. The tips of the mantles were ribbed by turquoise flame and gave out very little by way of illumination.

The train stopped.

Everything was quiet. Nothing moved beyond the curtained windows. There was no banging of doors or voices, only the sibilant rush of steam and the faint clucking sounds which the mantles made.

Maurice's grip tightened again.

The smile was still on his lips but it had solidified and hardened. She could see his tongue resting on his teeth – and looked away.

Feebly the engine gathered its burden and pulled them on.

Betsy said, 'I did enjoy the magicians. Didn't you?'

'I liked the lady assistant,' Maurice muttered.

'Very ... pretty in her ... spangled dress, but ... somewhat ... vulgar ... did you not feel?'

'I'll wager she could teach us a trick or two.'

'But the man in the scarlet cape with the pigeons,' Betsy babbled. 'I liked him. How did he do that with the chicken? I mean, when he brought the wee chick out of the middle of an orange? I missed havin' a lot of people there, though. It was disappointingly empty an' it would've been better with a whole house full of folk do you go to the shows in Glasgow often Maurice have you ever been to a play I'd like to see a real play sometime but it's hard for me to get away from the emporium early enough 'cept on Sunday an' they don't have real plays on Sundays anywhere though I think they should because kirk is not...'

'How long are you going to keep me waiting, Betsy?'

'What?'

'Unbutton your coat.'

'I'm cold.'

'I will keep you warm.'

'No, Maurice.'

'Unbutton it, my love.'

'I don't want to.'

'I wish to admire your ungirded bosom.'

'*Maurice!*'

'You are so beautiful. I have dreamed of you un ... un ... unclothed, like a water-nymph.'

'*Maurice!*'

'No longer can I ...'

'I hope you're not goin' to misbehave.'

'I worship you, Betsy: every inch of you.'

'Well that's not really very ...'

'I adore you, and ... and ... and I am *rampant* with desire for you.'

'Sit over there.'

'Give me what I crave, Betsy.'

'Stop it.'

But his words had had an unexpected effect.

She was acutely conscious of her body. It did not yield her the same safe, smug kind of pleasure as when she admired it in the mirror after her bath. It no longer seemed quite like her own body. It was as though it had passed out of her possession into the ownership of this man. She felt her breasts constricted by her bodice as if they had grown miraculously larger. She felt indescribable sensations in improper regions between her thighs. She felt breath strangle in her throat.

If he had continued his assault under cover of the stilted compliments which he had borrowed from naughty novelettes, Maurice McElroy might well have received a voluntary offering of the objects he desired. But he had restrained himself too often, could not resist the confined location and found that all his timidity had been left behind on the platform in Glasgow. Even a shady lodging house would not have provided such a rare opportunity for seduction.

The carriages yawed at the stone span of a bridge.

Maurice's lips pored over her neck and face and his nose tangled in her scarf. His hands closed over her breast and kneaded and stroked at it, though she could feel little of the assault under all her layers of winter clothing.

Many things raced through her mind as she felt herself pinned into the corner. All this for a handful of ribbons, some pinchbeck jewellery, a vial of cheap perfume and a red hunting coat for Drew? Did he value her so low? She expected, at worst, a proposal of marriage and would perhaps even have given it serious thought. She had deduced that Maurice was not as rich as many of the toffs who frequented Dalzells', but he had once told her that he expected to inherit substantial property from his mother one day. Betsy did not take into account the food and wine which he had lavished on her, for she considered these things as a just return for the favour of her company.

Now, however, she saw her suitor in his true light, and understood too late the warnings Drew had given her.

She was as vulnerable to McElroy's physical strength as he had been to her feminine wiles.

And she was trapped, trapped with no hope of rescue.

Even at sixteen, Betsy had been schooled in the facts of the sinful life. The dire predictions of teachers and ministers and respectable villagers crowded in on her. She would suffer the leprosy of the defiled; would be an outcast; would die shamefully, riddled with horrible fevers, before she was twenty. She had also wasted her only valuable asset. That loss most of all made her squeal, and slap at Maurice's ears with the fury of a frightened child.

Sprawled on top of her, his shoes awkwardly braced against the cushions of the opposite seat, he grappled with the fastening of his trousers and, with his free hand, sought to find the lacing of her skirt. His lips were wet and slack on her face, supposedly reassuring her with assertions of his devotion.

McElroy's impatience proved his undoing.

His awkwardness gave Betsy a moment to collect her thoughts and, reaching into that pocket of intelligence which she shared with her twin, she suddenly blurted out, 'Touch me again, Maurice McElroy, an' I'll tell your mother.'

It was just the sort of thing she had called out to the bullies of Blacklaw school who had occasionally cornered her and tried to force her to kiss them. Maurice might appear different from Henderson and McLaren and others of that ilk, but he was brother to them under the skin.

Snuffling and panting, he did not appear to hear her at first. She shouted directly into his ear, which happened, at that instant, to be plastered across her mouth.

'I'll tell your mother, if you do.'

So numbing an effect did her words have on him that she might have clubbed him with a pick-axe. He arched up and whipped his hand away from her skirts and then, as she repeated the threat in a clear, steady tone, leapt back and packed himself into the corner seat away from her.

'You wouldn't!' he gasped.

'I would, too.'

'You don't know where . . .'

'Aye, I do : in the big house in the Hamilton policies near Gartcraig.'

'She wouldn't believe you.'

'I'd go straight off this train to her house an' *show* her.'

'I'd say I didn't know you.'

'Phyllis Rose and Jeannie Wilson would vouch for the truth of my story. They've seen us together.'

Betsy had not only regained composure now that she had found a suitable means of keeping the beast at bay, but actually began to enjoy the triumph and sense of power which her wit had won for her. He *was* a miserable specimen after all, in spite of his fine clothes. A collier lad like Rob Ewing or Bob McNair would make mincemeat of him in a trice. He was snivelling: she had never seen a grown man snivel before. She primped herself, set the handbag protectively on her knees, and said, 'I'm not that kind of girl, Maurice McElroy, and would remind you that I only give my company to gentlemen who respect a lady.'

He rose slowly, steadying himself with a palm against the luggage rack, and looked down at her. Once more, she saw that she had been wrong, terribly wrong. The clownish, snivelling wreck had changed, and he appeared more bestial than before, calm too, calmer than she was.

Reaching down, he yoked his hands round her throat.

She branched her arms to break the hold, but his wrists were like iron rods. He swayed into her, not attempting to touch her body now, as if all the lust in him was tapped out by the contact of his fingers with her gullet. When she parted her lips the pressure increased, blocking air from her lungs and stifling her screams into a series of sobbing gurgles.

McElroy's eyes were glaucous.

At that moment, he did not regard her as a girl, as a lover, but as the amalgamation of all the humiliations he had known throughout the years. With his hand fast about her throat, she could neither mock him nor deny him his will. No longer was he looking down into a pretty childish face but into his mother's warty, heavy-jawed countenance. Her accusing eyes, mere slots in sallow bags of fat, seemed to stare back up at him, and the flesh of her neck melted over his fingernails like mutton.

The factor of insanity was not one taken into account in

334

Drew's warnings. Like the tiny portrait printed on a postage stamp, Betsy's dimming mind held the image of her twin brother alone in his attic room. His appearance was tranquil and scholarly, almost godlike in its wisdom and remoteness. Other pictures flickered over it, like the pages of an album riffled very rapidly, each blending into the other – her father's dead face upon the pillow, her brother James in one of his laughing bouts, Douglas smiling at her, his leather cap cocked over one eye; Kate in mourning shawls, and Mam, and Mirrin. It seemed to her that the train wheels, picking up a quicker rhythm, were hammering out little embossed images which fell like coins through the darkness which was softly enveloping her senses – Phyllis Rose, Albert Sutton, Lily, wee Edward, Loony Lachie Abercorn, and the doorman Sergeant in his handsome uniform : then came Maurice McElroy, scarlet-cheeked in scarlet coat.

Brakes howled metallically, the noise changing up into a grating shriek. The plush-lined dungeon ploughed to a standstill so violently that the last portrait in Betsy's gallery fell away. Breath sucked down into her lungs, and confetti danced about her eyes, millions of brightly coloured flecks which, on clearing, left her face to face with reality.

In falling, Maurice had dragged her half out of the corner seat and she lay wilted on her skirts, across the aisle between the cushions.

The carriage door creaked on its hinges, flung wide against the gentle motion of the train. Fog billowed in, a whitish mist, no longer browned by city smoke. The curtains and green linen blind flapped loudly and through the aperture she saw the rails and sleepers of the adjacent line, a rank of fencing and a platform's end. One gas lamp hung like a quarter moon, and by its fleeting light she glimpsed the painted board which told her that Lannerburn had come and gone, taking Maurice McElroy with it.

Running on now into country mists, the train made decent speed. Streams of air dispersed the fog and, before the girl could pick herself up, slammed the carriage door against its lock. Betsy hauled herself to her knees, snatched at the handle and depressed it to make the door secure. Still kneeling, she stared all round the compartment to be sure that her murderous companion had not hidden himself away. But Maurice had gone, vanished into the emptiness which surrounded the wayside station.

Huddled in a corner, shivering with shock and fear, young Betsy Stalker wept copiously until, at long last, driver Geordie limped his train against the ramp at Blacklaw halt and set her free to climb the barrier and scuttle home like a mouse to its hole. The family were all asleep in bed, and she told no one of her experience – not even Drew; not then, not ever.

What sort of passion had driven McElroy to the deed, Betsy did not comprehend; nor did she understand why he had drawn back from killing her, what merciful switch had lit his brain with sanity and shame. Only Maurice McElroy could provide an answer; even he, perhaps, did not know the true reasons for his violent outburst and its abrupt end.

Though she slunk about in fear of meeting him. Maurice had gone out of her life as thoroughly as the dead and, in or out of Hamilton, she never clapped an eye on him again.

*

The steady and alarming fall in the price of coal continued throughout November 1875, bringing despondency to collier and management alike. To some superstitious miners it seemed like a curse inherited from the disaster in the early part of the year. In the eight months since the explosion things had gone from bad to worse. Meetings at the pit and in Blacklaw communal hall kept Houston Lamont engaged until the late hours of the night. Day after day, through all fluctuations of weather, he tightened his grip on the workers under his control, and fought bitter verbal battles with their leaders at formal or impromptu gatherings during the evenings. For all his telling, however, he could not seem to make them understand that he too was at the mercy of the times, caught in a deflationary spiral from which there was no imminent release. He presented the miners with the facts; but they refused to understand and accused him of making excuses. In the trading markets, with ironmasters, shipping magnates, mill owners, and other buyers of coal, Lamont struggled to grab the best prices for his material. For the sake of regular contracts which would enable him to keep a full register of workers in employment, he shaved his own profits.

Throughout the first drab months of winter, he saw little of Dorothy and not much more of Edith. He was up in the cold hours before dawn and back late at night, and, like most men of the village, cared only for a warm fire, hot food, and sleep.

No matter how late the hour, he found Mirrin Stalker still in the kitchen. Long after the cook had retired to her room, she would be sure to have the grate fired in the drawing-room and a meal bubbling in pans on the range. For all that he was a third generation gentleman, Lamont soon came to prefer the cosiness of the kitchen. With no protest from Mirrin, he took his supper informally at the servants' table with his back to the stove and his boots drying on the rack by the vent.

The girl provided the company and treated him, he imagined, as she might have treated her father after a double shift at the coal-face, with a blend of jocular bullying and a practical kind of sympathy.

By the end of the month, the nightly suppers had become a habit. He had shed his standoffishness in the housekeeper's company, and she too had relaxed. She greeted him in informal clothes; not the sombre housekeeper's dress but colourful blouses and old skirts. Sometimes, if he was home before ten, he would find Mrs Burns present, and would gruffly request the cook's permission to eat his meal in the kitchen. Such courtesy, he knew, was necessary, for cooks were most possessive about their kitchens. But it was rare for the cook to tarry long and he was always glad to be alone with Mirrin, upon whom he could unload the cares the day had brought.

'I cannot seem to hammer it into their heads that it's not my fault,' he said.

'But it is your fault, Mr Lamont.'

'I thought you'd changed your mind, Mirrin?'

'I'm still the same girl at heart,' Mirrin replied. 'The difference in me is that now I understand fine what's happening here as well as in Main Street.'

337

'Do they really believe I intend to cause them misery?'

'What will happen, Mr Lamont, if the price slump goes on, if it costs as much to dig the coal out of the ground as the money you receive for the loads?'

'I'll be forced to reduce my labour force: perhaps even close down one of the pits for a period.'

'And that'll mean loss of wages, loss of homes, uprooting, dreadful hardships.'

'Mirrin, I simply cannot sustain such losses out of my own pocket.'

'Can you honestly expect a collier t'consider your problems when they seem so much smaller than his own?'

'Not smaller,' Lamont said; 'more complex.'

'Be that as it may,' said Mirrin; 'the collier sees you driving past in a coach pulled by stallions that are better nourished than his bairns...'

'Even if I sold my stables, my carriages, my house,' interrupted Lamont, 'and ploughed the money into supporting an idle pit, how far would that piece of extra capital stretch? To a few weeks' additional wages, that's all.'

'I'm aware of that, Mr Lamont. But the collier only relates himself to you. You're more than an employer. You own the town. You provide the bread on the table and the milk in the can. When you cease to provide then you are condemned as a selfish exploiter.'

'Do you see me as such?'

'How can I?' said Mirrin. 'Not after what you've done for me and my family.'

'What else do they say about me?'

'You're not invitin' me to spy?'

'Of course not, Mirrin. I am trying to understand the nature of the colliers' mistrust.'

'My brother calls it the result of "feudal legacy".'

'I have heard that phrase used as an insult,' said Lamont. 'But I cannot change things overnight. *Somebody* must hold the reins of power, Mirrin.'

'Miners are not ignorant, Mr Lamont. Most of them can read now. They keep abreast of what's happenin' in the world

338

through newspapers. Fine they know that coal prices are low, that markets are dryin' up. But they hope it won't come t'them. They continue to hope for the miracle that'll bring them back prosperity. In the meanwhile all they can do is cling to what they have, to fight to maintain the ... the ...'

'Status quo?'

'Aye,' said Mirrin. 'That's the Latin for it. The villagers are terrified that you'll slice away the work force prematurely just to save your grand mansion and your horses. They're as selfish as you are, I'll admit, and ascribe to you the same motives.'

'I've always tried to do what's best for the village.'

'How can you expect a miner, born and bred in hunger, disease, disaster and insecurity, to believe that you are on his side? The pit can never be the enemy: you and your kind must stand in place of the devil. I doubt if you'll ever change that, Mr Lamont.'

'But I must try? Is that what you wish to imply, Mirrin?'

The girl was silent. She turned to the range and quietly scooped a ragout from the pot which Mrs Burns had left simmering on the side of the lid. She added potatoes and peas and small yellow turnips to the plate, heaping it up, and put the plate before Lamont. Sensing the coalmaster's mood, Mirrin changed the subject.

She said, 'You'll not have seen Miss Dorothy's new gowns?'

'No,' Lamont said, his mouth full of potato. 'How did she fare in Hamilton?'

'She was as good as gold,' said Mirrin. 'In fact, she charmed the drawers off ... I mean, she was a great favourite with the assistants in Dalzells'. I doubt if they've ever had a customer more appreciative of their wares.'

'What colour did she choose?'

'That's a secret,' said Mirrin, with a wink. 'I wouldn't spoil the surprises by tellin' you.'

'When may I expect to be confronted by my beautified sister?'

'She'll have the day-dress on tomorrow, if you happen to be home. The evening gown ...'

'An evening gown, indeed!'

'The evening gown will be hidden away until the Christmas festivities.'

'Was my wife with you in Hamilton today?'

Mirrin shook her head.

'Just you and Dorothy?'

'Archie drove the gig an' helped with the parcels,' explained Mirrin. 'We drove all the way to Hamilton, in spite of the rain. Archie had a big umbrella with a mare's head carved on the handle. He leapt off the seat an' held the umbrella for Miss Dorothy, an' the chap in uniform at Dalzells' door rushed out an' gave her his arm, opened the doors for her an' snapped his fingers like a pistol-crack to summon a manager to attend to us.'

'You enjoyed it, too?'

'Aye,' said Mirrin with a laugh.

'And what did *you* buy?'

'Nothin',' said Mirrin. 'I had enough fun helping Miss Dorothy. Seamstresses did the alterations on the spot, while we had tea in Wray's; but the evening gown's being done properly.'

'Properly?'

'Measured up, cut and sewn from cloth.'

'As befits a lady,' said Lamont.

'Miss Dorothy stood still as one of those models for an hour while all the tapes and pins and stitchings were put to the material an' tacked.'

Lamont laughed.

'She needed out, Mr Lamont,' said Mirrin, more seriously. 'After bein' shut away for so long, she needs to mix with people.'

'She cannot be allowed out alone.'

Mirrin hesitated. 'No, she can't.'

'Perhaps some day,' said Lamont, wistfully.

'Aye: perhaps.'

The coalmaster mopped gravy from his plate with a pinch of bread, popped the bread into his mouth, then sat back. He sighed contentedly and discreetly slackened the waistband of his trousers.

340

Mirrin placed a cup of tea before him.

He could not quite stifle a yawn and, as if to account for it, the cook's clock whirred and struck eleven wiry notes. Lamont removed a cigar from his case, lit it and blew smoke towards the lamp.

'It's very late, Mirrin.'

'Aye, sir, you must be tired.'

'I am,' said Lamont. 'But I was thinking of you.'

'Och, I'm used to late hours,' the girl said. 'One thing you learn as a collier's lass, that's how to survive on a short night's sleep.'

'You may go to bed now, Mirrin.'

'Not yet, Mr Lamont: I've to stoke the range an' wash up the crocks an' do some other chores.'

'Then I'll finish my tea and cigar and leave you to it, Mirrin,' he said. 'I ... I may be late again tomorrow evening. I have to attend a traders' association meeting in Glasgow.'

'I'll save supper, then.'

'Why do you do this, Mirrin?'

'Do what, Mr Lamont?'

'Always wait up for me: it isn't strictly part of your duties, you know.'

'Maybe not as a housekeeper,' Mirrin said. 'But if I was the woman in any man's home, I'd do just the same for him.'

'Yes,' said Lamont. 'I expect you would.'

A minute later he got to his feet, stretched, and said, 'Has Mrs Lamont been long in her room?'

'Since nine, sir.'

'Good,' he said. 'She'll be fast asleep by now.'

*

Hastily, Edith Lamont laid the squat wax candle on the table close by the door, closed the door with her finger against the lock so that it would make no noise at all, and hurried back to the double bed. She paused only long enough to tug the shoulder and sleeve of her night-gown into casual disarray and expose a portion of her breast, then she hoisted herself on to the mattress, shot her legs between the sheets, stuffed her head into the pillow and, with a swift motion, pulled the blankets

341

and quilt over her face. In spite of the woollen socks she wore, her feet were like lumps of ice. She curled into a foetal position and strove to suppress the shivering which her long vigil by the open bedroom door had brought on. For her patience, she had reaped no reward, and had heard nothing from the kitchen except the muffled clack of a pan and the opening and closing of the basement door. An hour had elapsed between the arrival of her husband's coach and the time he finally elected to come upstairs to his bedroom. What had occurred in that hour, Edith could only surmise.

For a month now, Houston had been taking his ease in the servants' kitchen. He had actually so far renounced his position as to eat supper there like some common jobber sneaked in from the gardens. Naturally, none of the domestics had informed Edith as to what was going on under her nose, but the evidence of her eyes and ears was enough to convince her that her husband was under the thrall of the vulgar girl who had usurped her authority and, perhaps, had even stolen away her marital rights. Edith did not have sufficient confidence in herself to confront Houston with direct accusations now. Instead she had evolved tests and trials for him and set traps with a cunning which no man could master, let alone forsee. She had also written to Captain Ramsay – which was highly indiscreet of her, to say the least – enquiring after his welfare and casually inviting him to spend some portion of the Christmastide in Blacklaw as a house-guest, if he could spare the time from his duties. But the youthful, amorous Captain was a last line of defence. She had lost all curiosity towards him in the past weeks, and had relegated him to the position of a sleeping knight on a far square of the board. Her position was threatened here, in her own home, and it was in her home that she intended to retaliate.

The expensive gowns, the jewels and the perfumes had gone unnoticed by her husband. He had even failed to remark on the size of the bills which came from Dalzells' and Souters', the Glasgow dressmakers. When she asked him for money, he gave it to her without a word – an action generous enough to confirm her belief in his guilt. Feigning sleep, she lay with eyes closed, her breasts almost bared, in a halo of heady perfume, awaiting his arrival from the kitchen.

Since her childhood, she had been trained that a wife was her husband's helpmeet and servant, that she must not be bold in her demands of him – as if any woman would! – but quietly acquiescent when he wished to exercise his conjugal prerogative. Modesty must be mutual, of course, as decorous as possible considering the ugly pinching and positioning which Nature required for the satisfaction of man's ruttish instinct. But, after much observation, Edith had reached the conclusion that men were sheep led easily astray by forward women, by gross flirting and lascivious promises, and found such demonstrations irresistible. Fire was the weapon best used against fire.

The creak of the top step, and of the boards of the corridor told her that he was walking softly so as not to wake her. His heavy tread could not be disguised, nor the strength with which he opened the door and entered the bedroom. The sounds were all familiar; she followed them as she might have followed a playlet. Though her lashes were closed, the changing patterns of light from the candlestick in his hand indicated his direction.

The mattress sagged.

She could feel his scrutiny, did not move.

Now the candle – snuffed out.

The weight of his body in the bed and the crisp whispering of the sheet as he made it tight about him : the bed was broad and he lay a long way from her, on his back, hands clenched on his chest. He seemed to create that momentary tension for the sheer pleasure of releasing it, to feel the slackening of his muscles which soothed him rapidly into a deep sleep.

In the darkness, Edith stirred, manufacturing tiny noises to indicate that she was not quite awake. Lamont did not stir and, as she rolled on her side and brushed against him, inched politely away. She shifted again, allowing the dip of the feather mattress to carry her into the hollow and bring her arms and breast against his ribs.

His breathing was already rhythmic.

She was rigid with tension. Every communication between

her body and her husband's seemed to make her flinch as if she had seared her flesh against hot iron. Her need was now physical – yet she would not surrender to it, or acknowledge it as such. Still, she put it down as a testing. Vaporized by the warmth of her body, the perfume on her forearms and breast released a fragrance which added to her longing – but had no effect at all on the man who lay supine by her side.

'Houston,' she breathed.

His ribs moved and she felt the slight twitch of his left elbow which indicated that he had slackened his grip on the waking world.

'Houston, my dear.'

Even as she tried to plaster herself against him, he wallowed on to his side and turned away from her, adopting that position which at once prepared him for slumber and apparently rebuffed her.

Her arms trailed over him, and he started.

'Houston: hold me.'

'Hm?' he growled, drowsily. 'Yes, goodnight, Edith.'

Tugging a corner of the sheet about his ears, he sank at once into sleep. Within a minute he was snoring gently in a manner that Edith could only regard as smug, boorish and self-satisfied.

Drawing herself away, she turned from him and, biting her knuckles to hold back tears, vowed that she would make him suffer for his indifference. She would make them all suffer – Houston, Dorothy and, most of all, that Stalker bitch.

344

3

Snow fell four days before Christmas, sifting down through the birch boughs and the bare arms of the oaks. It stippled briar and bramble coverts and slid sleekly from the waterproofed leaves of the holly bush around whose base the woman ranged. Fluttering thickly from a dove-grey sky, flakes adhered to Dorothy's sheepskin overcoat and to the fibres of Mirrin's woollen shawl. Gradually, the snowfall obliterated the crenellated edge where the pitheads stood, and the smoky roofs of the colliers' rows, moved on over the brown river to the woods, took into itself the breadth of the valley and marooned the holly-pickers on the evergreen knoll.

Their wicker baskets were not quite full. Mirrin worked the cloth-shears rapidly, snipping pliant twigs and handing the sprigs down to her companion who, with due ceremony, placed them into the basket on her arm.

Though the Lamont estate supported no holly, Dorothy insisted that the season would be incomplete without some sprays to pin above doors and round the mirrors of the hall. Mirrin knew little about Christmas traditions. The colliers regarded Christmas as a holy forerunner to the more secular festivities of Hogmanay. However, she organized a gathering trip, wrapped Dorothy up warm against the damp, and set off towards the river woods where, so Pibroch McCrimmond said, red-berried bushes might be found. He offered to accompany them but Mirrin thought that might spoil the adventure.

She wished that the gardener was with them now.

Snow billowing in brought dusk with it, and made the wintry afternoon seem strangely hostile. Dorothy too was aware of it. She whimpered a little, wrinkling her mouth, as Mirrin packed away the shears and, looking round, chose the path above the river as the shortest route home.

The ground was spongy with leaf-mould, slippery with the sprinkled snow. Mirrin held Dorothy tightly, guiding the woman's awkward steps along the high banking. Below them the river lay stock-still, like gelatine.

Dorothy ceased whimpering, but clung to Mirrin and tried to be brave. The melancholy aspect of the afternoon had blotted out the anticipation of Christmas which had kept her happy for the past three weeks. Mirrin tried to cheer the woman, to fill her mind again with thoughts of carols and candles and the giving and receiving of gifts, of the fine gown she would wear to surprise her brother on Christmas Day. But none of it seemed to matter to Dorothy. Perhaps it was the weather, or the sullen river or, perhaps, Dorothy too was just damp and miserable.

They reached the division in the track where it dipped down towards the water's edge. One fork veered away towards the bridge north of the village; the other threaded on through a coppice to the back gate of the vegetable gardens.

Dorothy suddenly stopped.

Mirrin said, 'This way, Miss Dorothy.'

The woman did not answer.

Her face was warped with horror.

Startled, Mirrin asked, 'What is it? What's wrong?'

Nasal whining noises and a mechanical shaking of her head were all the answers Dorothy Lamont could give. Setting down the basket, Mirrin clasped the woman in her arms. Such treatment, she had discovered, was more effective than a dictionary of reassuring phrases. On this occasion, however, Dorothy could not be consoled. She pushed Mirrin violently away from her and broke into a run. The wicker basket, still clenched in her elbow, bounced against her hip.

'Wait, Miss Dorothy.'

Mirrin ran too, following the woman along the upper path.

The fit passed as abruptly as it had come upon her. Where the first straggling oak tree stalked down from the estate, Dorothy halted, pitched herself against the gnarled trunk and hid her face in her arms. The river was away behind them now, screened by the slope and the drifting snow.

Mirrin leaned against the woman, her hands on the bark, and gently inquired as to what had disturbed her.

Dorothy's features were relaxed again. The terrible glassy stare had melted into tears. She stammered unintelligibly, then became upset by her inability to express the source of her fears. Mirrin patted her and stroked her cheek, saying, 'Never mind, Miss Dorothy, never mind. We'll soon be safe home by the fire.'

And they soon were.

A fire burned brightly in the grate in the woman's room, casting sunny reflections over the tea things which Mattie had set on a card table, with plates of honey scones and dainty cherry cakes.

By five that afternoon, the incident seemed to have been buried in Dorothy Lamont's memory for ever. Even so, Mirrin stayed with her and devised amusements until an hour before dinner when Hannah relieved her.

*

It was no coincidence that Edith Lamont's most outrageous attack on her husband's integrity was made at breakfast the following morning. So erratic had his hours become that she seldom encountered him in private. Even last Sunday's church excursion had been sacrificed in favour of an ungodly Free Speech Meeting in Falkirk which, for reasons best known to himself, her husband had elected to attend. In addition, the post carrier from the village had just delivered a reply to her letter to Captain Ramsay; a reply which contained no hint of the soldier's former ardour and rather coldly informed her that he could not accept her invitation due to a prior engagement at the house of his prospective bride, Miss Arabella Straven, heiress to vast border policies which brewery profits had recently purchased.

Ripped and shredded into particles, the letter had hardly burned away on the coals of the drawing-room fire before Houston Lamont, yawning, entered the room and casually wished his wife good-morning.

Incongruously dressed in a floral tea-gown, Edith stood before the fire in a pose which reminded Lamont of a former governess, a witch of a woman who had terrorized Dorothy and had almost driven him to run away, until his grandfather

347

had wisely dismissed her for thrashing a pantry-boy.

Edith's rigidity was almost vibrant, her fury palpable long before she opened her lips. A nebulous guilt clouded Lamont's mind for a moment. Turning his back on his wife, he strode to the breakfast table, drew out a chair and sat down. Still Edith did not move or utter a word.

Outside, the snow had thawed a little in the night and fretted the edge of the flowerbeds and the lawns quite prettily. It was colder now, however, and the sky was laden with more snow. Even while being drawn inexorably into his wife's mood, Lamont prayed that the fall would not be deep enough to close the troughs and bury the surface trucks. He needed to maintain a high production rate to off-set increased tonnage against reduced load-prices. As yet he had made no wage cuts and had not dispensed with the services of a single hand. But last week's tally had shown a narrow margin of loss, and this week's would show more. Donald Wyld had even suggested that the pits went on to single-shift working by splitting the labour force and offering each man alternate days at a six-tenths' wage.

Arithmetic: calculations.

One night-long blizzard would give him the best excuse in the world. He could shut down production and salve his conscience by calling off the rent tithe for the month – three days before Christmas.

'Did you spare *me* one thought last night?' Edith began.

He glanced up at her, then, to indicate that he had no time to waste on petty recriminations, speared beef on to his plate and immediately forked it into fragments.

Edith's fists were like two hooks against the ruck of the dress.

'One thought for my feelings?'

He ate quickly, neatly.

'When one is in Port Glasgow,' said Lamont, patiently, 'I'm afraid one only spares a thought for getting out again.'

'Do not be glib with me, sir.'

'You are full of seasonal good cheer this morning,' he said, his nonchalance spicing the sarcasm. 'I am glad to see that, Edith.'

'I warned you.'

'Edith, what is the matter now?'

'That ... that ... harlot ...'

'Not again!'

'It seems you cannot have enough of her.'

'What foolishness are you handing me?'

'How dare you sit there, calmly feigning innocence ...'

'I have done nothing.'

'Do you deny that you spend a part of each night with her?'

'Of course I deny it.'

'I have heard you together.'

'You have heard nothing.'

'Skulking in the kitchen ...'

'Ah, so that's it, is it?'

'... after the servants are in bed, and I ...'

'Edith, I eat supper in the kitchen. It is warmer there than in the drawing-room, or the study, or that damned tomb of a dining-room. Besides, I have been much occupied ...'

'Yes. Yes, so you admit it.'

'I have been much occupied with business,' Lamont said, precisely. 'It is unfair to expect the entire staff to wait on me ...'

'Only the Stalker creature.'

'... after ten o'clock of a night. Would you have me dine on cold ham and rice pudding *every* evening?'

'I would have you dine with *me*.'

'I ...'

'And sleep with *me*.'

'Edith, do I understand you correctly? Are you accusing me of having carnal relations with our housekeeper?'

'Dare you deny it to my face?'

'Aye, I *dare* deny it. In fact, I deny it most strenuously.'

'You hypocrite!'

'Edith, I think you are ailing ...'

'Ailing of grief that my husband should conduct himself like a rake-hellion under his own roof.'

Lamont rattled his knife upon the plate's edge, then, lifting knife and fork, helped himself to a third slice of beef, and ate it with apparent relish.

349

Meanwhile Edith had wheeled herself across the floor and stood adjacent to him, her fingers clamped on the chair back.

He no longer even tried to make sense of the avalanche of accusations which tumbled from his wife's lips. She had openly accused him of lusting after Mirrin Stalker and of conducting an affair with the girl; now he was subjected to embellishments on that jealous and demented theme.

Finishing his meal, he paused only to light a cigar, then rose, wished his still ranting wife another good-morning and, without another word, left the room.

It was not until he had crossed the rear yard and found the waiting coach that the import of her words really struck him. He shouted at Sandy to hurry, then, as if pursued by the Hounds of Hell, sprang up into the conveyance and slammed the door.

Sandy Willocks gave the horses the whip and cantered them forward on to the pebbled drive, the wheels casting arcs of small stones behind them. The morning air was keen, and smelled of impending snow.

Looking out at the scene, Lamont felt his momentary anger alter into an inexplicable vigour, tempered by a peculiar sense of having sinned himself free of guilt. Maybe the speed of the coach was responsible; he saw now what pleasure his grandfather must have found in racing round the countryside behind a pair of sporting trotters.

Leaning from the window, Lamont looked back at the house. Mirrin was standing by the pump in the wedge of the kitchen yard. He had only a fleeting glimpse of her, but long enough for him to snatch off his hat and wave, to receive in return a wave from the girl, before the angle brought the first of the oak-trees between them. Laughing, Lamont sank back against the leather, stuck the stump of his cigar in his mouth at a raffish angle.

He could not fathom why he suddenly found Edith's behaviour so richly comic, or why he felt as if a door had opened in his heart. Perhaps it *was* the pace of the coach: or the weather: or Christmas! Perhaps it was a pot-pourri of all three.

Perhaps it had to do with Mirrin Stalker.

Yes, he concluded, as the coach bounced on to the Blacklaw road, undoubtedly it *did* have to do with Mirrin. Edith could rage from now 'til the knell of doom, but he would not give up the pleasure of his late-night kitchen suppers or Mirrin's company for that matter. And if it came to more? Only Mirrin had any say on that score.

The coach lurched and skidded drunkenly. Lamont's heart lurched too, not with fear but with excitement. Craning from the window again, he saw sprays of salt snow flung up from the verge and the coal-black eagerness of the stallions, their polished hooves gouging up mud from the mushy snow pelt.

'Sandy?'

'Aye, sir.'

The groom reached for the checkreins.

'No, they're lusty animals,' Lamont said. 'Let them take it as they will.'

'It's gey slippery this mornin', sir.'

'To hell with that,' Lamont shouted. 'Go on, man, give the lads their heads.'

'Aye, sir,' the coachman answered, eagerly switching his whip across the stallions' cruppers, and entering the bottom of Main Street like a charioteer. He did not rightly know what had got into his master that morning. But if he had to make a guess, that guess would not have gone past the pretty housekeeper, Miss Mirrin Stalker.

*

Even the most deceitful of lovers could not have contrived the circumstances which, that same night, left Houston Lamont and Mirrin Stalker the freedom of the coalmaster's mansion. In a sense it was Edith's doing: by fault and default, she was the prime conspirator in creating climates of love in which she could not share.

At eleven that morning, a couple of hours after her husband had driven to the colliery, she appeared in the drawing-room in all her finery and informed Hannah that she would be lunching in Glasgow prior to calling on her friends, the Misses Crystal, a brace of malicious spinsters who inhabited a house in fashion-

351

able Radnor Terrace. Archie, pressed into service as coachman, jogged the buggy to Blacklaw Station in ample time for his mistress to board the Glasgow train. Before the boy had steered back as far as the kirkyard gates, however, the blizzard's first granular onslaught had swung down with the wind from the north. By four o'clock the whole central plain of Scotland was drowned under a snow blanket which, blowing south, soon cut off the Border passes and the highroads to England.

England's plight was far from Houston Lamont's thoughts as he marshalled managers and gangers and dispatched bellmen into the village streets to wake the night-shift men and drag them from their warm beds. Donald Wyld was ordered to appropriate every shovel in the area, to rank up empty barrows, and shunt the bogies on to the track to the sorting troughs. Four rough sheddings were erected to protect the chutes from the snow's weight, and all standing coal was quickly transferred to the rees by the railhead buffers. Oversmen and clerks, bowlers and starched cuffs notwithstanding, were chased from their offices to try their hands at building earthworks to foil the possibility of drifting. Jock Baird and Willie Inglis boarded the slow cage to inspect the shaft's beams and the mechanics of the winding engine. Pumps too were checked, lest a thaw come hard on the heels of the blizzard. Against the sky, the towers were printed like photographic negatives as twilight seeped across the coal fields from the Lothians to the Clyde and inked out the landscape.

At home, Pibroch McCrimmond directed Sandy's wagon to the best of the autumn logs, then provisioned the kitchens with vegetables and fruits and all the nuts he could basket in time. Before the wind had quite whipped the flakes into cones over the rose thorns, Mattie and Archie were on their way to the village store, each with a one pound Bank of Scotland note wrapped in a detailed list of stores, including many items in which the house was already stocked but which Mirrin, in her caution, thought might run out if the blackade was of long duration. On the whole, a stranger to Scottish climes might have supposed that a foreign horde was sweeping inland from the shores intent on laying siege to every town and hamlet in the land. But it was only the auld enemy – winter – which put the fear of death in many hearts and broke open the meagre jars of saved pence and halfpence as defence against its rigours.

Miss Dorothy, with a blazing coal fire in her room, still experienced some of the urgency and awe which smote the house, and sensed the wonder and drama of heavy snow. Perhaps, thought Mirrin in passing, some echo of the woman's childhood chimed in her too, tinkling like a musical toy in the silences of her mind. Motionless, Miss Dorothy stood by the window, sad-eyed yet calm, watching flakes fall and swirl, driven across the gardens and the bands of trees. Distantly, she heard the shouting of gardener and grooms, the neighing of horses, mostly in new-strawed stalls, and the plaint of saws and hatchets up in the high oak woods. Whatever she remembered of the cold Christmasses of past years, she kept to herself, standing by her window overlooking the wrapped garden.

Since the strange incident by the river, Mirrin had kept a watchful eye on the master's sister. She did not leave her long alone that busy afternoon, but popped in and out, sending Hannah regularly to check the fire. At five o'clock, when the December dark was down, she had the woman brought to the kitchen and arranged a special tea for her before the stoves. In spite of all Mirrin's efforts, there was precious little warmth to be found in the atmosphere upstairs. It was as if the snow had brought ghosts with it to trail their icy robes across the floors and through the vacant chambers of the wings.

Fat loaves of barley bread and black-crusted sultana buns were drawn smoking from the ovens. Sponge tiers, round which the Christmas cake would materialize, were carefully beaten and put to rise, and Dorothy allotted the arduous task of counting minutes on the clock to ensure success to Mrs Burns's best efforts.

Shortly, Archie and Mattie staggered in through the yard door laden with provender, and making way for Sandy Willocks to tip his load of logs into the shelter of the washing room.

When all the groceries were ticked off and shelved, when the last of the logs was forked down from the cart, when the horses

353

had been rubbed down, fed and stalled, and when the sponges had been redeemed from the oven just in the nick of time, then all the servants convened in the kitchen to revive themselves with hot chocolate cups and rum biscuits and amaze themselves with tales and speculations on the general subject of frost and snow.

At length, Mirrin rapped them off to their duties and arranged dinner as usual for the mistress, though doubtful that the solitary place at the dining table would be occupied.

'Na', Mirrin,' Archie confided. 'She'll no' be back this night. I havnae heard the peep o' a train since three. Line's blocked: road's blocked: 'less she's a mind t'flutter hame like a hoodie craw, we'll no' be greetin' the missus this side o' tomorrow's morn.'

'None of your lip, m'lad,' said Mirrin. 'Sandy, will the master get home from the pit, d'you think?'

'Och, aye: he'll haud t'the right path.'

'Can you send a coach for him, or anythin' on wheels?'

'Nut a thing, Mirrin: nae hope o'that.'

'Then will you take a lantern down the hill, just t'make him welcome?'

'Aye, I will: when about?'

'Eight, Sandy: an' hap up well. I'm not wantin' you froze t'the path like a plaster saint.'

Eight came and went, chalked off on the cook's clock and by the chiming of the timepieces in the hall. Outside all was still and silent, all night noises muffled by snow, all neuks and crannies filled with its milky quietness. Snow drifted without halt, dithering down now that the wind had soughed away to harry the colliers of the Border marches. From the mouth of the kitchen yard, Mirrin could make out Sandy's lantern between the trees, like a fairy lamp in the pale, feathery darkness.

At nine, Dorothy could no longer stay awake. Mirrin accompanied her to her room and helped her undress and don the flannel nightgown and slide into the warmed bed. She sat by the woman for a little while; but sleep came quickly to Dorothy Lamont and, after locking up the fire guardian, soon Mirrin returned to the kitchen.

Hannah and Mattie were next to go sleepily to their attic. Mirrin had given them a hot-brick to take the chill off the sheets and a jug of hot tea to sip before sleep. Even Mrs Burns, who had not left her kitchen all day, complained that the cold weather had quite worn her out and, after checking over the pans which contained the master's supper, left Mirrin alone in the basement.

It was ten-thirty before Houston Lamont stumped into the kitchen. He had borrowed Donald Wyld's spare boots and a ragged tweed cap: even so, he was soaked through by his long walk home from the pit-head. Before he took his own supper, however, he went to the cellar, decanted a gill of whisky into a bottle and gave it to the valiant Sandy who had waded through the drifts as far as the colliery gates to accompany his master and light his way home with a storm lantern.

While Lamont changed into dry clothes, Mirrin brought down the heated plates and ladled out his supper. Wrapped in a woollen robe, he sat at the kitchen table and ate without a word. When he had appeased his enormous appetite, tilted his chair and set his heels on the end of the range – exactly like any hard-working collier, Mirrin thought – had lit his cigar and poured out a glass of brandy, only then did he inquire after his wife.

'Where is the mistress, Mirrin?'

'Gone into Glasgow, Mr Lamont: before noon.'

'She'll be stranded.' Lamont shrugged. 'I expect she'll lodge with friends.'

'The Misses Crystal,' Mirrin said.

'Oh, that pair of withered harridans!'

'I hope it doesn't last long, this blizzard.'

'I pray that it doesn't.'

'Have you closed the workings?'

'Not yet,' Lamont said. 'Provided we can keep the stuff moving on the surface, we'll manage. It's the thaw that's always the problem.'

He stretched. Beneath the robe his chest was bare, matted with dark hair. Cord breeches shaped themselves to his muscular thighs and his feet were clad in soft leather slippers.

Casually, he said, 'Did my wife speak with you this morning, Mirrin?'

'No: only with Hannah.'

Lamont nodded.

'Mirrin, my wife believes that we are having a liaison.'

The girl stopped her work at the stove, turned slowly and looked down at him. Last night, he could not have spoken those words outright, nor could he have met her eye.

'A liaison?'

'A casual affair.'

'Do ... do you want me t'leave, Mr Lamont?'

'God, no!'

'But ...'

'You've done nothing, Mirrin: no more have I,' Lamont said. 'But Edith is, perhaps, more perceptive than either of us.'

'In what way?'

'I know it's wrong of me, Mirrin, but I believe myself to be in love with you,' he said, as if the mere suggestion had elements of farce in it. 'Now, you may leave if you wish. I will ... honour my promise about the cottage, and I will find you alternative employment.'

'I don't want to leave,' Mirrin blurted out. 'The mistress has no right t'accuse you ...'

'Mirrin, I'm in love with you. I suppose I've been in that condition since the moment you stepped into this house. It's not an impossible situation, but it is a difficult one. You're an honest girl, and this is not an honest situation.'

'It's up t'me to decide what's honest.'

'The truth is that I can't feel any guilt about it,' Lamont said, with an apologetic laugh. 'Ridiculous, is it not? But you've taken nothing that belonged to Edith, and you have given me ...'

He shrugged, and waved his hand.

'I'm ... sorry,' he said.

'Stop saying you're sorry.'

He looked at her then, abruptly, glanced away.

Mirrin put down the tea kettle decisively, and skirted him, going towards the door.

'Mirrin?'

'I can hear Miss Dorothy.'

'You must have ears like a cat.'

She paused, stepped back from the half-open door and, reaching down, gave him her hand. He clasped it, kissed it, then released her.

For several minutes after the girl had gone, Lamont gazed into the embers which collected in the grate below the stove and let the cigar in his fingers burn away untouched. He experienced no remorse and no uncertainty as to the wisdom of his admission. In bringing the canker of doubt to the surface, he had begun the process of cure. Whatever Edith might say, whatever Mirrin might choose to do, at least he had spoken out and admitted an emotion from his heart.

After a little while, he got to his feet and went quietly upstairs to his sister's bedroom.

Dorothy lay on her side, lips parted, a narrow frown cleaving her brow. Stooped over her, Mirrin held the woman's hand and crooned a Highland lullaby, sweet and lyrical and soft.

'She had a bit of a dream,' Mirrin explained. 'She dreamed of the river and the snow. I don't know why it should distress her. It's so like the song, her favourite, the one about the river always driftin' to the sea and the snows meltin' on the hill.'

'How is she?'

'Oh, it's over now.'

'I'll sit with her, Mirrin.'

Carefully, Mirrin disengaged her hand and shifted back from the bed, allowing Lamont to take her place.

The fire was low in the hearth and, though the drapes were drawn over the windows, the room was full of the sense of the falling snow. It was no longer cold in the upstairs rooms, as if the kitchen's warmth had spread throughout the house. For a half hour, Lamont sat with his sister, not touching her, just watching, until her frown smoothed away and her lips closed and she slept peacefully.

Rising, he changed the night candle which burned constantly in a water-filled bowl, laid a few lumps of new coal on to the ashes and firmly replaced the mesh guardian. He felt contented;

strangely so, for he was stirred by memories of the nursery and the nights when he had returned late from the city and had looked in on Gordon, changing the candle and dressing the fire just as he had done tonight.

At the corridor's end, the tall diamond-paned window held the radiance of the snow, and cast a slat of light across the doors of darkened rooms, sealed off with their cargoes of dusty toys and cabinets of clothes which would never be worn again. There would be children in the village glad of those clothes and toys, Lamont supposed; he was tempted to unlock the nursery there and then, rake out the closets and the contents of the chests and dispose of them. But he could not be that cruel to Edith, could not deprive her of whatever consolation, however morbid, the little relics held. He turned his back on the nursery, paused a moment longer at the door of Dorothy's room, then walked on tip-toe down the corridor towards the dark well of the staircase.

The glow flooded suddenly, just ahead of him, flaring yellow across the brown linoleum. He hesitated, glancing curiously at the open door of Mirrin's bedroom. Perhaps she had left it open by accident.

'Mirrin?'

There was no reply.

The door was wide open, not ajar. The three branches of the wooden candle-stick each held a new tallow, the wicks blossoming with yellow flame, shedding light in profusion across the bed. The colours were like the colours in a rich oil painting, thick and bright and substantial. The composition too, framed by the doorposts, reminded him of an intimate portrait.

She was seated in the bed, the spotless white sheet drawn up neatly to her waist. Within the cotton shift, her breasts hung heavily, and her hair, released, draped her shoulders. She was looking directly at him.

'Mirrin?' he asked again.

She smiled. It was not a grin of calculation, and contained no hint of lewdness. She smiled warmly, and cocking her head, gave him a slight apologetic shrug as if to excuse the piece of

358

drama which she had modestly devised by way of invitation.

Lamont felt again as he had felt that morning, full of strength and assurance.

'May I . . .' he said. 'May I come in?'

'Please do,' Mirrin said.

The coalmaster entered the bedroom with rueful formality and quietly closed the door.

*

The old deal table was now sealed with wax polish, and the ten back-breaking yew-wood chairs, repaired and trimmed piece-meal, were respectable enough to grace any kirk's vestry. The warped boards had been scrubbed and covered with carpeting unearthed from cellars and attics and tacked down, by Mirrin, across all of the floor area except the window bay. The chimney had been swept, the grate scraped and leaded, and a bright fire lit in the iron hearth to relieve the chill atmosphere. It was here that Houston Lamont and Donald Wyld retired after luncheon on a raw afternoon two days before the close of the black year of 1875.

The purpose in adjourning to the boardroom in preference to Lamont's comfortable study was that it contained a table large enough to support all the great ledgers, files and printed data which, like scholars' tomes, the men required to fulfil their task: also, though neither man phrased the feeling, the boardroom seemed a suitable setting ...for confidential plotting and the evolution of strategies which might not benefit the humble colliers of Blacklaw.

Long bills of cramped-hand figures were spread, side by side with relative appendices, and docketed reports of recent Union conferences. The two men moved around the table like billiard players selecting shots. Though no miner would have admitted it, Lamont's concern for maintenance of a *status quo* was based on pride not unmixed with concern for the plight of the district's families. He fought for his pits, of course, not for his men; but the two were so inextricably mixed that he could not contemplate them as separate entities, nor did he try.

Back in 1871, during the Franco-Prussian war, Blacklaw had

benefited from the cry for coal and more coal, and from the high prices which matched high sales. Lamont paid three shillings per darg above the national average and, though that figure had dropped by a shilling and sixpence, had somehow sustained it even when trade was sick and wages tumbling in every colliery in Scotland. Though there were many militant revolutionaries in Lanarkshire, none of Alexander McDonald's henchmen had ever found a real foothold in Blacklaw, and there had been no strike action for two decades. But the surfeit of coal stocks up and down the British Isles and the waning of demand had caused a parallel drop in wages. Lamont and Wyld were only too well aware that, whatever their personal inclinations, Blacklaw colliery could not hope to stand aloof from the effects of national crises.

Unionists were also conscious of the hazards of fostering strife at this unstable juncture. McDonald himself, abetted by Lord Elcho, had climbed down from his agitator's box and seemed anxious to instruct his disciples in the techniques of conciliation and arbitration, a far cry from his previous vulpine attitude towards coalmasters. There was even some ludicrous chat among hard-nosed bosses of 'importing Chinese', heathens who, it seemed, would toil for fifteen hours a day for a mere handful of rice. Fascinating though he found the prospect of Blacklaw pit swarming with tiny yellow men, Lamont saw the proposal as a hollow and childish threat, not fit for the consideration of rational men anywhere.

There was much, however, that he could feasibly do to stiffen turnover and energize his languid profits; much indeed that most masters would have regarded as ordained procedure in a failing market. House rents had been static for twenty years and, by the standards of the mid-seventies, were unrealistically low. He could have founded a 'truck shop' system akin to that used in many other mines, and reaped financial advantage there. But the Lamonts had never favoured that sort of tyranny, and Houston would not consider it now.

Throughout the afternoon, he and Wyld mulled over facts and figures and, about the time the lamps were lit, reached the sorry conclusion that their choice of courses was limited to two most obvious actions. Since neither action was restricted, the decision posed a moral dilemma, hedged round with diplomatic considerations.

Reaching for the tongs, Lamont plucked three large lumps of coal from the brass hod and placed them on the fire. He tamped them safely down, then, still with the tongs in his hand, flung himself on to the nearest of the yew chairs and leaned his elbows on the annual tally sheets.

'How will they react, Donald?'

'Violently, I fear.'

'Do they not see how well off they are?'

'They are blinkered horses, Mr Lamont: they see only Blacklaw and the back shelves of their own larders.'

'Perhaps we should organize a committee of representatives to tour some other collieries: then they might recognize how far above the mean they live here, under my protection.'

'Ah, but they *know* what's happening round about,' said Wyld. 'The best of them are neither blind nor deaf, sir. They just wish to avoid seeing and hearing the truth of it. If you toured them round the vilest towns in the land and rubbed their noses in the poverty of their brethren, they would regard it as a threat of some sort, as blackmail.'

'And so it would be,' murmured Lamont. He held the tongs before him, horn-shaped blades stemming from a large brass rivet, and plied them four or five times, making them click like teeth. 'I would not dare admit it beyond the walls of this room, Donald, but the lost tonnage occasioned by last March's calamity may have been a blessing in disguise.'

For a moment Wyld looked startled.

'No, no,' Lamont explained. 'I do not mean the deaths and injuries and hardships. I mean the loss of so many dargs, a loss which puts us decently behind in the slow-horse race of coaltrading.'

'Too much coal; too few markets?'

'Aye, Donald: but how can you inform a collier that there is *too much* coal when all his life he has been subjected to the order to dig up more and more of the damnable stuff?'

'There are times, Mr Lamont, when I wish that we had a treaty with the workers' movement.'

'A sliding-scale of wages paid against the daily selling price of coal would have been an admirable device.' Lamont clashed the tongs. 'Why would they not accept it? They even rejected out of hand their own hero, McDonald, stripped him of his saintly raiment and branded him a traitor because he supported the proposal.'

'Because it would have taken them out of the hands of the masters,' Wyld suggested, mildly.

'Yet they are never done bawling and brawling to be free of us,' said Lamont. 'I do not understand such a mentality.'

'I think that you do, Mr Lamont. I think that you are depressed at being a natural beast of burden for all the woes of the men and women of Blacklaw.'

To Wyld's surprise, the coalmaster rounded on him angrily. 'I am not one of them, and I am not some martyr, Mr Wyld. I would have you remember that. I try to keep up the traditions installed by my family, but my strength is in the land I own and the capital I have invested. It is *not* in my character.'

'I . . . I'm sorry, sir: I meant no insult.'

'No. Donald, I know you didn't.' Lamont pushed himself to his feet, and dropped the tongs carelessly into the hearth.

Wyld said nothing, standing motionless against the window, just outwith the fall of the lamplight. His estimate of the coalmaster was shrewd, but fundamentally unrevealing. Wyld was neither master nor worker, and made no professional secret of the fact that, in Lamont, he had found an employer who suited him, one who cared for the good opinion of his tenants and who, as much as it was possible for a landed owner to do, navigated his own life to suit the colliers' patterns.

Lamont leaned his fists on the table, his shoulders broad under the tightening material of his coat. His expression was glum as he surveyed the mass of figures and charge-charts which littered that part of the table-top.

'What shall I do for the best?' he asked himself.

Wyld did not venture a reply.

'If I were an ordinary collier,' Lamont went on, musingly, 'what would I settle for?'

At that moment a tentative knock upon the boardroom door disturbed them. The men had been shut off from other society for so long that they were rather startled to realize that the normal routines of the household had gone on outside during the course of their long discussion.

'Come!'

Mirrin entered.

'Yes, Mirrin?'

'I thought you an' Mr Wyld might care for some refreshment, sir?'

Lamont blinked. For four hours now he had not spared one thought for Mirrin Stalker, and yet, in the preceding week there had hardly been a single moment when some portion of his mind had not been concerned with her. She appeared demure and neat and very much like a lady in her dark garments. He felt inordinately proud of her, as if he had somehow rescued her and refashioned her as a model for all colliers' daughters.

Foolish! he told himself: and patronizingly selfish.

'Donald?' he said, turning.

'Tea, I think, sir,' Wyld answered.

'There is whisky, if you wish.'

'No, thank you: we still have much to do, I believe.'

'That is true,' Lamont said: he turned to Mirrin again, trying hard to keep gravity imprinted on his face. 'Tea.'

She gave a little bow and went out.

Lamont glanced curiously at his manager.

Had anything of his relationship with Mirrin showed in his manner? He doubted it; yet he was strangely disappointed by the sudden realization that their love-making must, at all costs, remain a closely-guarded secret and could never be acknowledged by so much as a nod.

Beneath that housekeeper's formal garb was hidden the body of a lithe and sensual young woman – and he had possessed it. Willingly and without a shadow of guilt, she had given herself to him. How could he muster guilt, when he wanted so much

363

to boast about his liaison with the collier's daughter? She was so fine-grained, so mature, and represented a conquest of a different order, a victory over human failings, prejudices, ingrained principles and all the cock-and-bull of radical politics versus capitalism. What he most wished to flaunt, though, was the pleasure he had taken in her arms. In his class of society, braggarts were legion. It was considered a great masculine *coup* to tumble a beautiful, desirable young girl, particularly one who excited admiration in other men, as Mirrin must surely do among the colliers of Blacklaw. Upon her he had put the mark of the *seigneur*, and of that achievement he was ordinately proud.

During the four or five minutes it took Mirrin to return with the tea-trolley, he skirted the subject with outrageous daring.

'Do you recognize my housekeeper, Donald?'

'Alex Stalker's lass, is it not?'

'She suits the role, do you not think?'

'Aye, sir, she looks well in the weeds,' Wyld said. 'I wonder if her father would have approved?'

'He would have howled in dismay, I fancy.'

'Stalker was never one to stand in the way of progress.'

'But would he have billed his daughter's service in a "capitalist's" house as progress, or a retrograde step back into serfdom?' Lamont said. 'He hated me, and all that I ever stood for, Donald.'

'I would question that, Mr Lamont.'

'On what grounds?'

'Stalker was a militant, but, like McDonald, he learned wisdom as he grew older.'

'He blamed me for the deaths of his companions.'

'I wasn't forgetting,' Wyld said. 'But Stalker had ... well, *some* justification for that view.'

'Indeed?'

'You know my opinion on the matter of culpability, sir, and, consequently, I make no excuse for defending colliers like Stalker.'

'Is there nobody else of his calibre?' asked Lamont.

'A few – the Ewings, and the Pritchards.'

'How much weight do they carry?'

'Not a hundredweight to Stalker's ton, unfortunately.'

'You believe he would have supported me, and eased the matter with the men?'

'He would not have supported *you*, Mr Lamont, but he would have accepted the need and the right...'

'And is his daughter made of the same stuff, do you suppose?' Lamont interjected.

The question caught Wyld off-guard. 'His daughter? What does she have to do with it?'

'She ... works here, you know.'

'Aye, but she has no sway with colliers: no woman ever has, at least, not openly.'

'What would she advise?'

'Ach, come now, sir, you're not advocating askin' your housekeeper's advice on this vital...'

'We are not obliged to take her advice – even if she is willing to give it.'

'You would be as well asking the doctor, or the minister...'

'I feel that I know Mirrin Stalker,' Lamont said.

'She may tell you only what you want to hear.'

'Why do you say that, Donald? Do you imagine that I have ... broken her spirit in some cruel way? Oddly, I put trust in that girl, great trust.'

'Mr Lamont ...?'

'Yes, Donald?'

The manager shrugged. 'Ask her, by all means: but, I should warn you, you may be tipping your hand to the rogue element in the pit. You may be giving them warning.'

Lamont smiled. 'If, as you say, Alex Stalker would have mellowed, would have softened, as McDonald has done, then would it not be reasonable to assume that Mirrin may have done the same?'

Wyld opened his mouth, then closed it again. He shook his head ruefully. 'There's no right answer to that. She may not, however, like being ... used.'

'Hm? What do you mean?'

'Only,' Wyld said, quietly, 'that she is still a working-class chiel, no matter her position here in your house.'

Was that the tacit admission he sought? Lamont wondered if he had pressed Wyld into a discreet confession that he had guessed his employer's secret. No.

No?

Lamont might even have inched further down that thorny path, if Mirrin had not again knocked on the boardroom door and, without awaiting an answer, nudged into the room the high-sided trolley laden with tea-things, scones and cut-cake.

From different motives the two men said nothing as the girl poured out tea. Wyld had seated himself at the top end of the table, pushing back the papers; but Lamont remained standing, closer to the hearth. He suspected that Mirrin was aware of their attention, and the faint but tangible tension in the air. There was a slight flush on each cheekbone as she concentrated on decanting the tea from the squat silver-plated pot into the fine china cups. Even when she handed the cups to the men, she did not meet their eyes.

'Shall I leave the trolley, sir?'

'Thank you, Mirrin.'

She turned towards the door.

'Mirrin?'

Hand on the door knob, she paused, then looked back.

'Yes, Mr Lamont?'

'Perhaps you can assist us.'

'In what way?'

She looked at Lamont and then, cautiously, at Wyld.

The manager smiled. 'We've a decision to make, Miss Stalker; we thought the ... benefit of your advice might help us.'

'Is it t'do with the colliery?'

'It has,' said Lamont.

'I'm not well up in business matters.'

'Tell me,' said Wyld, 'if your father was still alive, Miss Stalker, how would he react to a proposal to cut the basic wage?'

Mirrin's eyes widened. 'He'd be ... leapin' mad.'

'Do you know, Mirrin,' Lamont said, 'that there is a national crisis in coal selling?'

'I've heard talk: aye, it's been buildin' up for a couple of years,' Mirrin said. 'Is it that serious?'

'Very serious,' Wyld said. 'Assuming your father was aware of all the facts, would he accept the situation?'

Mirrin frowned, and toyed with the keys at her waist.

'How much of a cut?'

'I'm not sure yet,' said Lamont. 'One shilling and sixpence per darg, probably.'

'Is this t'keep *your* profits intact?'

A little shocked at her interpretation of his motives, Lamont answered quickly. 'It is merely to preserve the pit in full employment.'

'At least that's what you'll tell them,' said Mirrin. 'If y'told my father that, he'd made inquiries into the state of the market; if he found that it was the truth, then he'd grumble, but he'd accept it.'

'What about the rest?' Wyld asked.

'Enough of them would've taken his lead,' said Mirrin. 'But there's little enough point in askin' now, since my father's dead.'

'The alternative,' said Lamont, speaking carefully, 'is to reduce the work force.'

'*Pay off!*'

'Yes,' Lamont said.

'An' give you the edge t'reduce what's left?'

'Oh, really, Mirrin! Do you suppose I'm that sly?'

'Maybe.'

Embarrassed by the girl's outspoken attitude to the coalmaster, Wyld cleared his throat loudly, and got to his feet. 'It's one or the other, Miss Stalker. We thought you might be able to give us some idea what the villagers would feel about it?'

'Why don't you ask *them*, Mr Wyld?'

'I've already consulted with management and senior gaffers: they left the decision to Mr Lamont.'

'Ask the men, then,' Mirrin said promptly.

The familiar fieriness was in her eyes once more, that radical spark, defiant, indefatigable. Her head was tilted back and for a moment Lamont thought the girl would put her hands on her hips in the orator's posture, and bawl them both out like a tap-room militant.

'I mean it, gentlemen,' she said. 'Nobody ever asks a collier anythin': they get *told*, always told.'

'Do you think that if I explained . . .?' Lamont began.

'Democratic principles,' said Mirrin. 'Mr Wyld knows fine what I mean, even if you don't, sir.'

Again Lamont was taken aback. Could this be the same warm and loving girl he had slept with only a few nights past? He put his teacup and saucer on the iron over-mantel, then came forward until he was close enough to touch her. He tried to find in her expression some signal that she did not mean all that she said, some hint that she too had been changed by the events of the last months and by the consolidation of their relationship. All he encountered was the slow-fuse of doubt and anger. She had changed only in appearance. The smart, black dress and adult hair-style only added weight to her words, and assurance to her pose. A hundred women of Mirrin Stalker's calibre, if properly marshalled, could rule the bumbling world of borough politics; and a thousand could take over the governing of the entire country. He had been wrong to imagine that *he* had mellowed her, that *he* had refashioned her out of common clay. Mirrin was still a rock, hard-quarried out of the granite of the Scottish workers' class.

The coalmaster backed down.

'It was unfair to involve you,' he said.

'No, sir,' said Mirrin. 'You were right t'ask. But I won't apologize for the answer I've given – though much use it'll be to you.'

Wyld had approached from the table's end.

'Why do you say that, Miss Stalker?'

'Say what?'

'That your answer will not be heeded?'

'Well, will it?'

'You're making an issue out of a casual question,' Wyld said.

'There's nothin' casual about puttin' families out in the street,' Mirrin said.

'It's not just Blacklaw's problem,' Wyld said. 'Nor is it some trick of the bosses. Something *must* be done.'

'Then it's up to you to do it,' Mirrin declared.

'If we ... if Mr Lamont did put it to the men,' Wyld said, 'what course do you think they would choose?'

'Full employment at reduced wages.'

'Are you sure?'

'All I can say is, Mr Wyld, that it's what my father would've recommended. Give a man a home, an' a place t'work an' you still have him; he's still your man, no matter how bitterly he may descry the fact, an' no matter how hungry he might be. But throw him, or his friends, into the gutter an' you've the biggest sin of all on your conscience.'

'A sin, Mirrin?' said Lamont.

'You've rejected him.'

'Ah!'

'An' if you reject one man, you'll soon find it expedient t'reject others in less stringent circumstances...'

'And we sacrifice *all* sense of unity and loyalty,' added Donald Wyld. 'Yes, I can see the logic in that.'

'Aye, but you're a manager.'

'Do you mean,' asked Lamont, 'that a collier can still feel secure even if he is living on the poverty level?'

'There's some things a bit worse than poverty,' said Mirrin. 'God, but it's a thin line that divides the most of us from poverty at the best of times. If you're miners' spawn, you live with it in the hall cupboard all your life. It's like a wild beast you can hear champin' and ravin' an' daren't let out. But bein' tossed aside is worse, I think. I think that's the biggest fear of all.'

'Rejection?'

'Aye.'

'I won't reject them,' Lamont promised.

'Unless it suits you.'

'Mirrin, am I in the habit of rejecting...?' Lamont bit off the end of the sentence.

Mirrin said, 'I wouldn't know, Mr Lamont: I've hardly had time t'find out.'

369

Silence gathered in the room. The blush on the young woman's cheeks had bloomed to a deep crimson; yet it was not shame that put it there, nor even embarrassment. It was the temper, and the frustration of imagining herself patronized.

'With your permission, Mr Lamont, I'll get back t'my duties,' she said, tightly.

Lamont nodded.

When Mirrin had left the room, the coalmaster poured himself a fresh cup of tea from the pot, heaped sugar into it and drank it slowly, savouring it, and simultaneously giving himself an opportunity to calm down once more.

He lit a cigar, offered the box to Wyld – who refused – then said, 'What do you think, Donald?'

'She has a point,' said Wyld.

'Which particular point?'

'About the fear of bein' flung out.'

'So?'

'I think ... I think we can now *plan* our procedure,' Wyld said. 'Though I believe we should wait a while before embarking on it.'

'Why?'

'In February,' Wyld said, 'the rate of sickness is at its highest.'

'Lord above!' Lamont exclaimed. 'Not even Mirrin thought of that.'

'Perhaps she's too honest.' Wyld busied himself with teapot and milk jug, his back half turned to his employer. 'I'll say this for her, though, she's still as spirited as ever. Frankly, Mr Lamont, I don't know how you put up with her.'

'No,' said Lamont, cagily. 'I am not quite sure myself.'

4

February's frost brought more hardship to Blacklaw folk than the snows of Christmastime and reminded the colliers that their existence depended less on Houston Lamont than on the vagaries of the climate and the hospitality of the land.

The year of 1876 had been ushered in by sheets of rain. Visiting and drinking parties had been sadly curtailed and only a handful of traditionalists had scurried from house to house carrying their lucky gifts and cherished bottles. The *Lantern* had been crowded, though; even those men thick with coughs and ague had managed to hirple to the pub for a bit of Hogmanay cheer.

The Stalker household was among the quietest in the village. There were no men there to kick up noise and give a spark to the start of the year. Drew hardly counted; he treated the day like any other and, if he felt any significance in the occasion, kept his sentiments to himself. For the Stalker women, there had been precious little entertainment. Mirrin had come down in the afternoon, bringing a basket of foodstuffs and a keg of mild ale; gifts from Houston Lamont. She at least had not knuckled under to hard work and winter's bullying. Kate had never seen her sister so healthy. If Mirrin had been handsome before, now she was beautiful, brimming over with vitality, shedding some of her happiness into the quiet house. She had refused to let Mam dwell on the tragedies of the year that was gone, and had encouraged them all to put a face towards the future. She had prattled on to Betsy, who had been very withdrawn of late, and even managed to exchange a few words with Drew. After supper she had left again in an aura of confidence which, in spite of themselves, left the rest of the family cheered.

But that had been two months ago and, since then, the harsh rains which had ceaselessly lashed Scotland throughout January had taken their toll.

Coal sales dropped past the figure which managers and colliers alike had considered rock-bottom. At a meeting in the kirk hall, Donald Wyld had put forward proposals to the miners' representatives. Contrary to Mirrin's prediction, this unique move, instead of boosting the employer's image, had made the majority of colliers highly suspicious. If they were being consulted on policy, things must be very grave indeed. For a week or more rumours were rife that Lamont was on the brink of selling out.

The choice offered the miners was simplicity itself: accept a cut in the basic rate of pay, or have the work force pared to the bone. Militants muttered that Lamont had come out in the open, only to hide a more dastardly intention. They claimed that he planned to reduce wages *and* pay off men. More rational miners, led by Callum Ewing and his son, saw some good in the situation; at long last, they had been treated as individuals capable of thinking. But the Ewings could not stand against the currents of fear, doubt and selfishness which swept through the ranks, or rescue Lamont from hatred.

The mass meeting of the colliers had lasted a half hour. It took place in the yards under the winding towers in the interval between shifts. The morning was bitterly cold, the sky clear as wine and sprinkled with stars, the moon, still silver, glittering high over the village. In company with Wyld and four gaffers, Lamont came from the managers' office. He sprang up on to a platform improvised from a wheel-less bogie and waited patiently until the hubbub finally died.

Without mincing words, he said, 'You've been given the choice of . . .'

'NO. NO. NO.'

'Yes, you have been given the choice. It must be one or the other. I cannot support further losses. The colliery is running at no profit. Maintenance work must be done, and . . .'

His words were lost in a rebellious babel.

'All right,' he shouted. 'At least hear me out.'

The crowd quietened.

Lamont said, 'I am reliably informed that you understand the national situation; that is why I put the choice to you. You have requested a say often enough in the past. Now you have it. Let me explain again – I must reduce wages, or I must reduce the labour force.'

'Mr Lamont: Mr Lamont?'

'Yes.'

'Can y'guarantee this new basic rate, or full employment?'

'No,' Lamont answered. 'I can give no guarantee on either measure.'

'Why?'

'Because I am a seller in a buyer's marketplace.'

'How many hands would go if y'slashed the shifts?'

'One third, in all trades.'

'Christ Almighty!'

'Listen,' Lamont shouted. 'If you think I'm being harsh, I would remind you that I could easily pack my registers with colliers from other regions. The streets of Ayr, Edinburgh, Falkirk and Glasgow are thick with unemployed.'

Voices swelled in incoherent protest.

Calmly Lamont waited until the roar subsided, then went on, 'The very best I can do is to restrict the wage reduction to one fifth of basic in every trade.'

'Including oversmen and managers?'

'Every trade, including staff.'

Strangely, no protests greeted this announcement, though every man present was aware of the plight it would place his family in. Some of the larger families barely managed to struggle on as it was. Had the coalmaster intended to blackmail his men with mention of the hordes of unemployed at large in the country? If so, his cunning worked. It was well known that in most industrial areas there were more men than jobs, and that tramping south to England would not solve the problem, things being just as bad there.

Lamont had them, and they sensed it.

Rob Ewing shouted, 'What do you advise, sir?'

'Do you *want* my advice?' Lamont shouted back. 'Or do you just want somebody to blame?'

'Give us the word, Mr Lamont.'

'Very well, my advice to you is to accept the lower wage rates.'

'Aye, dammit, it would be!'

'Some money is better than no money, is it not?'

'Some bloody money!'

'I will return to Mr Wyld's office now, and leave you to make your decision. Democratically you may wish to vote on it. I want an answer in fifteen minutes and a return to work in twenty.'

Permitting no further opportunity for questions, Lamont vaulted down from the platform and strode off in the direction of the sheds.

There was little argument. A few face-men wanted to hold out for the better wage, but most were afraid that they would be among those paid off, served notice to vacate their homes and thrust upon the open labour market. Worst of all, they might be forced into a parish work-house.

As the first splint of daylight appeared in the sky to the east, a delegation of eight men, including Callum Ewing, Donald Ormond and Jock Baird, carried word to the coalmaster that they preferred to accept a cut rate of pay. Lamont greeted the news with a curt nod, coldly thanked the men for their cooperation and told them to return to work. Somehow his manner suggested that, by duplicity, he had committed them to doing just what he wanted, while foisting off the stigma of greed and brutal self-interest.

As it was, the Arctic weather of February sliced the labour force by a third anyway, and fit miners and their womenfolk, haunted by the phantom of unemployment, worked twice as hard for their money. Even Mirrin Stalker, on whose advice Lamont had given free choice to his men, could not determine if the master had foreseen this pass. Though she shared his love and his confidences, there were many things he still kept secret from her.

*

Frost gripped the land and stretched it taut, split it like chapped skin and healed it superficially with poultices of ice. It padlocked the workings of the pumps and bound up the oily chains of the winding mechanisms. All night long, it groaned and grated in the rafters of the cottages, and creaked out like a

374

bone ailment during the short noon hours. According to the medical correspondent of the *Glasgow Herald*, it was remarkably healthy and invigorating weather: the folk of Blacklaw and its brethren villages would not have agreed. The wet month sowed the seeds of diseases, which the cold month brought to fruition. As much as possible people kept indoors, and the tramp of colliers' boots at change of shifts sounded like an army of armoured Romans clanging up the street. Even the children soon wearied of the winter games, of polished slides and the taste of icicles, and found themselves confined indoors, restricted to scratching patterns on frosted window panes. When, towards the end of the month, the sun sought sanctuary from the snell northern winds and dropped a leaden cloud lid over the Lanarkshire vales, there was hardly a family in the county which did not have at least one member laid up in bed, or worse, buried in the stone-hard earth of the kirkyard.

Blacklaw kirkyard now truly was a place of the dead. Under the oppressive sky nothing moved. The lifeless trees bordering the path were as rigid as the headstones and crosses marking the graves and the few garden flowers in jars embedded in the ground had, long ago, turned black as rotted flesh. No less motionless, Kate Stalker, wrapped in a shawl, stood by the grave that held the remains of her father and brothers. It had been many months since she had last wept for the men of the family, though at the beginning she had shed many tears during her weekly visits here. But grief had not lasted, and she had been spared guilty self-recrimination by the memory of one of her father's favourite adages: 'A man's never dead 'til he's forgotten.' That thought had comforted her because she knew that the Stalkers would not be forgotten in her lifetime. That raw February afternoon, however, she wept less for those below ground than for those above it.

Times had never been so bad; money so scarce. The pits still disgorged their quota of coal, the miners still hewed and the sorters still picked over the troughs, the heavers still shovelled and the barrow-men still trundled their loads to the railhead. But they all worked out of fear now and not out of pride, not even for the money that they earned, for that wage was too scanty now to solve anybody's problems and only created more of its own. Food prices had risen: farmers were hard up too, it seemed. There were no luxuries for anyone that heinous season, and even the brothers Dalzell, so Betsy said, had discharged some of the older assistants, those who tended to cough and splutter over the goods and the customers, or who looked too ill to smile convincingly.

The Stalkers were a little better off than most of their neighbours, at least in terms of income. Though they had no man's wage, Betsy and Mirrin earned more than trough hands. Mirrin was a real champion, bringing home every penny of her wages and often providing bread, ham bones, ox-tripe or a dish of potted head from Lamont's kitchen. Kate did not enquire as to whether the items were come by honestly, for she could not be sure of receiving a direct answer. Of late, Mirrin had become much more defensive about her employer and, even when pressed, would not discuss the affairs of the mansion.

Flora Stalker was still taking orders for knitting and sewing, and managing the household so that a ha'penny did the work of a sixpence. But a lean diet and the cold were taking the stuffing out of her and every day she became more stooped and grey.

Relieved of the burden of the promise, the Stalkers would have survived with something to spare – but the promise hung over them all like a sword, and there was no escaping it. Not that she wanted to escape, Kate reminded herself. Drew deserved it: in spite of his supercilious moods, he had worked harder than any of them. Kate experienced a sudden pride in her brother. Looking down at the grave she found herself nodding just as if her father could see her. Never once had Drew gone to the dominie for his Friday lesson without a florin in his pocket. There had never been a book that the dominie had recommended which they had not been able to buy for him in Hamilton's secondhand market. In a week's time, however, Drew would travel up to Edinburgh to sit the examinations. It had been planned that Mam would accompany him, but there were insufficient funds for that now. Drew would have to undergo the ordeal alone. The fare, the cost of meals, a night's lodging and a few necessary articles of clothing would deplete their savings too much as it was.

Bowed over the grave, Kate tried to smother that part of her which cried out for deliverance and prayed that her brother would *not* pass, would *not* win admission to the Faculty of Law in the May term. Failure in Edinburgh would sap Drew's confidence in himself, but at least it would leave his faith and affection in the family intact. If he did pass – and in her heart Kate was convinced that he would – then she would be confronted with a failure so enormous that she would never be able to hold up her head in Blacklaw again.

The truth was that she did not have the money to secure her brother's lodgings and pay tutorial fees. The cash accumulated from their wages had proved woefully inadequate; without money he just could not go. Tears would not change things. Nobody could help her; no miracles would dump the necessary sum in her lap. By rights, she should tell Drew now, save the valuable shillings it would take to sit the entrance tests – but she could not deprive him of that one day, that glimpse of his goal.

Kate clenched her fists in frustration, and drew the shawl tightly about her head.

'You'll tear it, lass.'

She looked round to see Callum Ewing, hunched in his threadbare jacket, his thin, sharp face dug down into the upturned collar to keep the cutting edge of the wind from his chest.

'Come on now, Kate,' he said, blowing into his cupped hands. 'Stand here long enough in this damned wind and you'll be joinin' them there below.'

'Aye,' she said. 'I suppose it'll be time enough for that soon.'

'By God, Kate Stalker, it's not often I hear that kind o'defeatist talk from you.'

'It's February got into me too, Callum.'

'Neat spirits an' first love are the only things that keep the winter out the heart.' The man grinned. 'No doubt you heard about our Rob?'

'Everybody heard,' said Kate. 'I'd like fine t'have seen him proposin' for myself.'

'If I'd guessed what he was about, I'd have tacked up a tent an' charged admission,' said Callum. He stuck his clay pipe in his mouth, though he had no tobacco to put into the tiny bowl. 'What did our Mirrin say when she heard?'

'Nothin' at all,' said Kate. 'I'm not even sure she did hear – but she must have: Mam would tell her.'

'I had hoped . . . y'know what I mean?'

'We all like Rob,' said Kate.

'All except your Mirrin.'

'She's such a determined one,' said Kate. 'If only he hadn't shown what he felt for her.'

'Hindsight,' said Callum. He offered Kate his arm. 'Still, the McMasters' lass is a nice enough girl, though she's on the young side yet a bit. She's got the handlin' o'Rob, though. Give her a year, an' she'll have our lad right where she wants him. Serve the beggar right, an' all. Him an' his girls.'

'He was never that bad.'

'Ach, no, he's a good lad, in spite of what I say about him.'

The phrase was commonplace, but for some reason triggered memories of her father and brought a sudden flood of tears. Turning, Kate clutched at old Callum Ewing's shoulders and clung to him while the sobs racked her.

'Aye, Kate: aye,' he murmured. 'They were all good lads, right enough.'

'I wish . . . Oh, God, I wish . . .'

'For twenty years,' Callum said, clapping her as he would have done a child, 'it all flows on, sometimes up an' sometimes down. Then, it's over. Things seem the same on the surface, but I wonder if they'll ever be the same again. What'll Rob's sons have to bear, an' your sons, too, Kate, when you marry an' give birth.'

'Callum, Callum!' she wept.

'What is it, lass: what ails you so sore?'

'It's Drew, an' it's . . . it's money.'

'Ach, so that's it.'

'Not . . . not enough.'

'How long d'you have?'

'Ten weeks, at most.'

'Has he passed then?'

'He sits the exam next week.'

'Maybe he'll fail.'

'Oh, no, Drew'll pass.'

'An' you're feared you'll let him down.'

'I promised Da . . .'

'Forget that promise.'

'I can't.'

'Forget about Drew.'

'It's me that'll have t'face him, tell him.'

'He's an educated laddie, now. The dominie might find him a place. He'd be wasted in the pit, right enough.'

'Callum, you don't understand . . .'

'I know pride when I see it.'

'Is that all it is?' Kate asked, pulling away. 'Is it just Stalker pride?'

'Listen, what would it cost, this thing you've t'do for Drew?'

'The dominie estimates twenty pounds a term.'

'*Twenty pounds?* By God, Kate, y'set yourself a high target. How much're you short?'

She would have spoken to no other person in the whole of Blacklaw about this subject: it was private, almost sacred. But Callum Ewing was an old and trusted friend, closer to her, in many ways, than most of her kin.

'We have just seven pounds saved, an' enough t'send him to the examination.'

'Aye, you're gey short, right enough,' said Callum. 'If it had been a pound or even two . . . I can't help, Kate. It's too much.'

'Oh, Callum.' She wept again. 'I would never have asked . . . but . . . but I'm grateful t'you for even thinkin' of it.'

'I suppose there's no way o' accumulatin' . . . Nup, I doubt if there is, not these days.'

'I'll have t'tell him, sooner or later.'

'Best make it later,' Callum advised.

'I don't like lyin' t'him, my own brother.'

'Hold off a wee while, Kate, you never know what might turn up.'

'For the likes of us, Callum, what could turn up?'

Callum could find no answer to the girl's question, and said nothing. He put his arm about her waist and escorted her out of the kirk gate into the head of Main Street.

'Perhaps it's a judgement on us,' Kate said.

'Rubbish!'

'A judgement for committing the sin of tryin' to raise ourselves above our station.'

Callum laughed scornfully and gave her a gentle tap on the rear by way of reprimand.

'Believe that, Kate, an' you'll believe anythin'.'

Kate squared her shoulders.

'Well, at least it'll give the folk round here a snigger.'

Callum took the pipe from his mouth and stabbed the stem at her for emphasis. 'You're knucklin' under, lass: your father would never have done that. He'd have fought right t'the last gasp. Did you not learn that much from him in the weeks before he died?'

Kate nodded.

Her lips pursed and tightened and, Callum was pleased to note, a little of her former determination showed in her expression, even though tears continued to roll down her cheeks.

'Aye,' she said. 'I'll wait: and hope.'

*

The dominie slapped shut the volume *Latin Adjuncts and Primary Phrases*, a collection compiled by the present professor of Legal Studies of Edinburgh University as a monument to posterity. Drew sighed and stretched and leaned closer to the fire which burned in the headmaster's hearth. The boy, Guthrie thought, looked as gaunt as a gargoyle, and about as unhealthy a specimen as you could find in this village of unhealthy specimens. His eyes were red-rimmed and his hair lank and his fingers trembled very slightly like a fever case. Maybe he was a fever case, at that: one without a temperature, though, who could be cured by engagement with the inquisitors in the halls of academe.

Whatever the long dour grind of study had done for Drew's mind, undoubtedly it had matured him physically. Indeed, it might be said that it had robbed him of his boyhood. He no longer looked like a boy, nor even like a youth. In the space of a year, he had acquired the characteristics of a man approaching middle age, and would stand out among the fresh-faced sons of gentlemen who would occupy the desks with him in two days' time. If the invigilators had been instructed to select the most promising legal face, Drew would have been a natural choice. Already he bore a distinct resemblance to one famous advocate whose contact with justice had dried out his humanity and left him vulpine and desiccated. Once Drew lost his accent and acquired the proper icy tone of voice, he would mould readily into a perfect hanging judge.

The dominie kept such idle fancies to himself.

He said, 'Now, whatever you do, you must be bold; bold but calm. Do not attack the papers furiously. Read the questions carefully, choose those most favourable to your range of knowledge, and advance.'

'I will.'

'You appreciate that there are great gaps in your studies. Time's been short, Drew, and some scamping had to be done. If you stumble into such areas in your written presentations or in your oral, do not let it upset you unduly. Finish each question as best you can. Do not guess at answers, unless you have first racked your brain for the information. Impatience is the rock on which many a student has foundered.'

'Yes, Mr Guthrie.'

'Do not be intimidated by the pompousness of your fellow students. Do not indulge in much conversation with them, either before or after the testing. On the other hand, do not be brusque or aloof. Do not endeavour to study tonight, or during the course of your stay in Edinburgh. Eat well in the evenings, take no breakfast except a little tea or coffee, and the lightest of luncheons. Bed early, sleep if you can, but if you cannot, do not lie fretting.'

'Yes, Mr Guthrie.'

'Are you going alone?'

'Yes,' Drew said. 'I prefer it that way.'

'I see.'

The headmaster lifted the lid of a tobacco jar which stood

among the litter on the desk. He fished inside, brought out a silver piece and tossed it across to his pupil.

'What's this?' Drew glanced from the coin to his tutor.

'I doubt if you will be quizzed on coin of the realm,' Guthrie said, 'but that is known in common parlance as a half crown.'

'But...'

'A lucky token: buy good meat with it.'

'Mr Guthrie, I...'

'If I recall correctly, there's a cosy little parlour in Queen's Wynd, not more than a step from the University. When it's all over, Drew – but not before – go there and purchase a decent dinner and a tipple of wine. That's what you must ask for – a tipple of wine. If they inquire about your age, tell them a white lie.'

'Is this corruption, Mr Guthrie?' Drew asked.

The quip surprised the dominie. He laughed, and nodded. 'Aye, lad, pure unbridled depravity. Make the most of it.'

The young man rose, buttoned his ragged jacket and tucked in the scarf ends. He held the half crown towards the lamp and inspected it as if it was a prophet's oracle, then he put it carefully into his breast pocket.

'Thank you, dominie: an' not just for the price of the tipple.'

He held out his hand, jerkily.

The schoolmaster shook hands and clapped him on the shoulder. 'I wish you luck, Drew.'

'I'm grateful for all you've done.'

'It's not over yet, you know: you've a long road ahead of you.'

'I know that,' Drew said. 'But at least I've reached the beginnin'.'

'Remember all I've told you.'

'I will.'

The young man left the study, and the old dominie reached down a pipe from the mantel over the fire. A few grains of tobacco still skulked in the bowl and he touched them with a paper taper lit from the coals. He puffed, spat into the fire, and wandered to the window.

Outside the playing yard was deserted, sugared with frost.

The black ribbons of the children's slides showed on its surface like fissures across an ice floe. Drew emerged from the side door of the building and, hands in pockets and shoulders stooped, walked at his usual philosophical pace across the yard, head bent. Guthrie reckoned that the boy's lips would be mumbling over the vocabularies of the dead languages he had set himself to master.

Suddenly, Drew stopped, staring intently down at his worn boots.

Discreetly, the dominie hid himself behind the window frame and watched curiously.

Drew glanced round furtively, then broke back and cantered towards the doors, angular and cumbersome as a bullock. He started his approach far out of sight and had worked up considerable speed before he reached the lip of the ice slide. Technique had not been forgotten. In perfect balance, he skated down the slope towards the gates, upright and arms akimbo, then dropped into a crouch, fingers gripping knees.

There was an innocent joy in the boy's action which made the old schoolmaster's heart leap for a moment; then Drew Stalker, student of law, whizzed out of the playground and vanished behind the gate-post.

5

Lamont closed the door and pushed the bolt into the latch. The clack of the metal sounded as loud as the discharge of a shotgun fired in warning. He hesitated, staring at the door panel as if expecting some furious retributive fist to thunder upon it and a bullying voice demanding payment for his folly. But there was no sound at all in the deserted corridor. Dorothy was sleeping peacefully; the servants were snug in attic and cellar; and Edith was even further off, 'staying over' with newly-acquired friends in a mansion in bleak Port Glasgow.

Cold weather did not deter Edith from scaling attempts on the ladder of influence. God knows, there were no material benefits to be gained by favouring her hosts, the Edward Foyers, save the satisfaction of adding shipbuilders to her list of acquaintances; a list, Lamont reckoned, which, if printed and bound, would line two long library shelves like a set of the Waverley Novels.

It did not occur to the coalmaster to speculate on the causes of his wife's penchant for spending her nights in the guest-rooms of other folks' houses; nor did he for a single moment imagine that she had slid into an affair. Undoubtedly, Edith had more than her share of that trusting liberty which many wives aspire to and, if she had been cast from a more flexible ore, might have put her husband's laxness to fuller use by taking herself a lover, or a whole stud-book of lovers for that matter, without bothersome negotiation or contrivance. By now Lamont had been left so far behind and knew so few of her friends that he had no means of checking on her doings, even if he had been inclined to do so. But there were no lovers, of course – not for Edith. She craved only the collective attention of society, its constant reassurance that, even without her husband's patronage, she remained a member in good standing of the influential classes.

One act of infidelity might have passed into Lamont's memory as an impulse which, however rash, deserved to be quickly

forgotten. But his love-making with Mirrin did not need justification nor excuse. It stood as a pact, an acknowledgement of
love, and the physical gestures, though gentle and tentative,
had been highly satisfying to both of them. Now, uninvited, he
had come to her room again, this time with an air of formal
authority.

As soon as he turned from the locked door, however, he saw
that she had anticipated him, and that airs and attitudes had no
part in the relationship which would be expressed in the
intimacy of the bedroom.

Two slender wax candles stood on either side of the bed. She
had already turned down the coverlet to expose the clean
white sheet, plump pillows placed together in the centre. He
was not angered by her preparations, nor by the fact that she
had guessed his intention. More truthfully, he had to admit
that her eager acceptance eased the burden of guilt in him and
brought a surge of vigour to his loins.

Mirrin's presence gave the room personality; a skirt and a
black coat hung from a hook on the wall; a brush and comb
and a string of scarlet ribbons stood on the chest of drawers, a
petticoat and workbox on a stool. She had not thought it
necessary this night to present the room as something it was
not, and this signal of acceptance excited him still further.

She was clad in a single cotton shift, her shoulders, arms and
part of her breast quite bare. He tried to think of some
appropriate endearment, but words of that common coin had
lost all their value; instead he obeyed his instinct and touched
her. The movement was bold, demanding, yet not insistent.
Breath caught in her throat. She pushed herself against him,
pressing her breasts against his chest, so that he could feel the
excited thud of her heart.

'How are you?' he asked.

Mirrin smiled at the awkward courtesy of his question.

'Fine.'

'Are you cold?'

'No.'

'May I ... stay?'

'Aye,' she said.

'Mirrin, listen : it's . . .'

She put her palm to his lips, and crushed her body against him once more.

'Hush, now,' she told him. 'There's nobody here but us, Houston. Nobody to hear, or see, or think anythin' about it. Just us. Is that not enough for you?'

'More than enough,' he admitted.

He kissed her.

'Wait,' she murmured.

Sliding out of his arms, she stripped off her shift calmly and unaffectedly and allowed him full view of her body.

Turning, she rolled across the bed and spread herself on the coverlet. Her hair spilled across the pillow. Her arms were relaxed by her sides, hiding nothing. Any trace of false modesty or inhibition would have made the pose seem sacrificial. Any undue movement would have made it lascivious. But Mirrin was neither tense nor lewd.

In years she might be little more than a girl, but she had a woman's shape, breasts high, smooth and heavy, the dark nipples centred in broad aureoles hardly lighter in hue. Her waist would have distressed any fashionable dressmaker; it was not artificially pinched, but curved into her swelling hips and belly with the slight plumpness which marked the best sculpture of the day, and made it both tempting and beautiful. She reminded Lamont of a Viking princess or a Celtic queen, full of courage and passion and pride, yet infinitely more womanly than the staid, powdered marionettes whom contemporary society classed as doyennes of femininity.

She lifted her arms to him.

Tearing at the buttons of his shirt, he threw the garment aside and seated himself on the bed, leaning to kiss her breasts and bury his face in her hair. Her flesh was soft and yielding, and he was harried by his own need to press selfishly into her. But this, he sensed, was not a male prerogative, only the stamp of smoking-room boors who thought of nothing beyond a quick release and the curt pleasure which came at the peak of it.

Lamont caressed the girl's body, flattering her with his touch.

386

She moaned a little. Her eyelids fluttered, closed and opened; smiling at him as he stroked her breasts and belly without apparent urgency, putting his own ardour aside. Mirrin's pleasure gave him pleasure, the heightening of her passion increased his own. There was no conflict of power in it, no selfishness. He had never dared treat Edith this way; she would have been scandalized by the very notion. In all his life he had never before attained such a pitch of sensual harmony with any woman.

Only when he heard Mirrin cry out and felt her raise her body against him, did he consider himself. Pulling off the rest of his clothing, he tugged at the coverlet and slipped under it, drawing Mirrin to him and wrapping her body tightly against his own. He had no need to seek for her. The girl's responsiveness took away and obliterated all clumsiness, and, in an instant, he was swallowed up in her completely.

Rocking, he cradled her in his arms, listening to her rapid, throaty cries. Containing them both within the coverlet, he drove deeply into her again and again until a flood of passion gave him release and left him spent and gasping, still locked in her arms.

When it was over he inclined his head and found her watching him. Her eyes were soft and held none of the mockery he had so often seen in them. He wriggled his hand free and curled a strand of her hair round his finger.

'I should have brought some wine,' he said.

'Next time,' Mirrin said.

'You know, I never dreamed we would ever be here like this again,' Lamont admitted. 'In spite of what happened before, and despite your not having been out of my thoughts since the day you came to work in this house.'

'I'm glad,' the girl said.

She too wriggled her arms and took a tighter hold on him, drawing his face down to hers.

'Ah, Mirrin,' he said. 'I would never have believed that you would ever thaw.'

'Me!' she said. 'I'm not a cold fish, am I?'

'No, but . . .'

'I see,' Mirrin said. 'You planned it all. I am undone.'

For a split second he thought that she was serious, and felt sickening dismay well up in him. He struggled and raised himself on his elbow to study her more closely; then saw that she was grinning.

'Don't be so sober about it all, Houston,' she said.

'I don't profess to understand you.'

'It's because we're so different.'

'I do not feel that we *are* so different.'

'I'm not in the mood for a political argument.'

'Not since we have found such an admirable means of settling our disputes?' Lamont asked, matching her humour.

She lay back on the pillow.

'I don't understand myself, t'tell the truth,' she said. 'I could never have imagined it a year ago.'

'Change is the prerogative of us all.'

'Now there's a daft profundity, if you like,' Mirrin said.

'Do you regret . . .?'

'God, no!' she assured him, quickly. 'How could I regret it? No, I'll never regret what's happened between us.'

'Then that is all there is to say on the matter.'

'But I don't feel any *guilt*.'

'Should you?'

'Aye: everything, an' everybody would tell me I should be sufferin' the pangs of a bad conscience.'

'Perhaps, it's because I love you,' Lamont said. 'That is no smooth lie, Mirrin. I do love you.'

'The magic potion.'

'What?'

'That's what some of the girls call it, the coal-sorters.'

'A magic potion?'

'Aye: they say a lad can get anythin' he wants from a girl if 1e just used "the magic potion" – a few wee drops of love.'

'You mean, if he says he loves the girl, everything is all right?'

Mirrin nodded.

'I'm not lying.'

388

'I know,' she said. 'Anyhow, I think the lassies have it wrong about the recipe for the potion. If you ask me, the love must be in them.'

'Is it in you now, Mirrin?'

'It is.'

'Then say it?'

'Ach, it still sticks a bit t'say a thing like that t'a coalmaster.'

Lamont laughed, and shook his head. He too lay on his back. He held his forearm across his face to keep the direct light of the wax candle from shining into his eyes. He could see the girl beside him clearly, though.

'Surely, Mirrin, you do not think of me as ... as the coalmaster? How can you possibly do that under such circumstances?'

Mirrin shrugged. 'A long schooling.'

'That is ridiculous!'

'Aye, I suppose it is,' the girl said. 'But we're in danger of becoming two people; two times two – four in all.'

'Is that not true of all lovers?'

'Perhaps.'

'Can't you say it?'

'I ... love you.'

'There!'

'Aye, Houston, but it doesn't help me being what I am.'

'But it is what you are that I love.'

'A willing girl; or a collier's lass?'

'Is that what you're afraid of, that I have some ... some warp of character which inclines me to take advantage of my workers?'

'It's hard for me, Houston. It's not givin' up my body that's difficult to accept. It's givin' up my principles.'

'Your hatred of employers and all they stand for?'

'Aye: that's what I meant about there bein' two of you, an' two of me.'

'I am Houston Lamont, coalmaster, and I love Mirrin Stalker, daughter of a miner, and my housekeeper. I'm not distressed by plain facts nor by plain words, Mirrin. Are you?'

'I'm afraid I am. I've lived too long with slogans an' rallying-cries an' all that mumbo-jumbo. I can't be so easy rid of them, Houston.'

'This is hardly a romantic conversation, Mirrin.'

'This can't be a romantic relationship.'

'Why not?'

'Because of what you are; you can see that, can't you?'

Lamont did not answer for a moment, then he said, 'Yes, I can see that, Mirrin.'

'An' on those terms?'

'We must take what we can, and expect no more.'

'Aye,' she said. 'Now put out the candle.'

Reaching, the girl snuffed out the wick of the candle on the left, and Lamont, after a pause, thumbed the flame of that on the right. Darkness enclosed the couple like another coverlet, and Mirrin hugged him.

'Now,' she said. 'Now, like this, Houston, we can be two other people.'

'Yes,' he said. 'Just two . . .'

'Lovers,' Mirrin said, and kissed him gently on the mouth.

*

Drew quickly decided that only a dunderhead could possibly fail to gain entry to classes at Edinburgh University. May term admissions were confined to aspirants to the faculties of Medicine and Law and to a fortunate few whose intellectual potential had captured the interest of the governors and who had been invited to compete for fellowships. The dominie had carelessly neglected to mention that written presentations would be limited to the seven subjects of the *Studium Generale*, and that the standard would not be high. To Drew's relief, he found that he could easily cope with all the manuscript requirements.

The social diversity of the boys who thronged the echoing chambers in South College Street was quite astonishing. Many were obviously gentlemen's sons and graduates of expensive schools. But others seemed as out of place as Drew did, lads of humble origins whose fees had been donated by local patrons or a committee of charitable neighbours. Around the quadrangle and behind the Doric columns lay the seeds of a true

Scottish democracy where learning was recognized as a national asset and merchantable commodity. If Blacklaw's militants could have seen the cross-section of the populace there represented they might have been moved to exchange pit-head platforms for student benches and to preach the primacy of brain-power over brawn.

Drew was a shade put out by the extreme youth of some of his fellows. Several appeared hardly old enough to shed their mothers' apron-strings, wee mites of twelve and thirteen from whose lips Greek and Latin tripped as if they had been weaned on Cicero and Ovid instead of porridge and sour milk.

The oral disputation was rather more of an ordeal. Drew sensed that the invigilation was the nexus of the trial and resolved not to be cowed by the scowling board of examiners. One man intrigued him: he was as common as any collier, with a thick pock-marked complexion and coarse features. Drew could hardly credit that this ruffian was the Chancellor's personal representative, the famous Professor Rayburn, author of many a learned treatise on Metaphysics and Logic. Rayburn put several questions to Drew who, though he could not later recall how he had answered, felt that he had somehow managed to impress the ugly old scholar.

As instructed by Guthrie, Drew had found lodgings in a boarding house in the Warrender Park district where many small establishments catered to the billeting of students. The landlady was a dowdy, kindly widow who fed him a large breakfast for his four shillings and added, at no extra charge, a sermon on the wickedness awaiting young men in the streets of the city. Two resident students lodged with the widow, but Drew saw no sign of them during the nights of his stay.

But it was not his experiences in the University, nor his lodgings which stuck in his memory to be recalled in wistful detail during his rattling trip home in a carriage of the Caledonian Railway Company. Even his brief conversations with the great Professor Rayburn paled into forgetfulness beside his discovery of the unadvertised pleasures which Edinburgh had to offer and which his search for a 'tipple of wine' in Queen's Wynd's *Thistle and Sickle* duly revealed. He debated, later, if it had been part of Guthrie's plan that he should be exposed to the bustle and gaiety of the capital's netherworld, as sugaring for the scholar's pill, perhaps?

Whether the dominie intended it or not, Drew grabbed at the chance to sample a taste of urban living, and his enjoyment was not much spoiled by his shyness or shortage of cash. He had enough for a good dinner of beefsteak and boiled onions, Scotch trifle and clotted cream; all washed down with two – not one – of the tavern's notorious 'tipples' – a tall pewter pot with a glass spy-slot inset into its wall down which, swallow by swallow, the imbiber could watch the rough red wine diminish. He had purchased three stumpy black cheroots, called *Port Morant Rums*, and had smoked them without ill effect. Neither wine nor tobacco seemed to harm his constitution in the least and, indeed, lit up his senses to such a degree that the colour and vivacity of all the sights he had seen were indelibly imprinted on his mind. Never in all his life before had he felt so satisfied and at one with the world as he did that night in the smoky atmosphere of the *Thistle*, sitting back with his feet on a stool, tipple to hand and cheroot clenched in his teeth.

Outside, a sinister grey mist had stolen up from the Forth, enveloping Castle and Cathedral, sifting down over the buttresses and gables and wee windows of the old quarter of the town, seeping into the boards and beams like history itself. Drew was conscious of the precedents; remembered all the famous sons of Scotland who had been drawn to Edinburgh and had – by a slight stretch of the imagination – propped their boot-heels on this very stool, drank from his very tipple-pot and ogled the girls in the parlour with the same recalcitrant hunger.

Everywhere in Edinburgh there were girls: elegant girls in mulberry silks strolling the High Street with their energetic little maids in tow; country girls in plaids and shawls carelessly displaying bare calves along the closes of the Canongate; George Street and North Bridge aristocrats in tight-laced dresses bobbing with sable fur, ladies whose speculative glances – so Drew supposed – belied their aloof manners; counterskippers, neater and sweeter than any ever seen in Lanarkshire

– Betsy excepted – stall-holders' daughters anxious to please, crying eagerly and grinning wickedly and flashing their eyes in promise; tap-room girls with splashed aprons and bulging blouses; girls who kilted up their skirts and jigged to the parlour fiddle and shook their hips and buttocks, and laughed uproariously; small waif-like wenches who waited table and kept their lashes lowered demurely, taut with the fearful hope that some sturdy young blood would take advantage of their lowly station; harlots, sober and drunk, anxious and mocking; and a multitude of sly persuasive whores covering every age from puberty to senility.

Everywhere he walked in the city he saw – *girls*!

Hamilton and Lanark had no displays to equal it, in quantity or quality. Glasgow's flowers were rank weeds compared to the beauties of the capital.

In the *Thistle* he could have taken his pick of a dozen assorted, if he could have summoned the nerve and chinked a bit more silver in his pocket. But, for all his unfamiliarity with city ways, Drew was no fool and did not lose his head and try to buy that which he could not afford. There was no charge for looking, however, and look he did – gazed, stared, wondered, studied and surveyed, until his eyeballs felt like mallet-pegs with so much visual pounding.

The personification of that large part of Edinburgh's appeal lay in the shape of a serving girl in the *Thistle*'s bar parlour. It was not just the girl, of course, but the whole musical, con-vivial, indulgent atmosphere of the place which clung round her that impressed itself upon Drew. She was tall and full-breasted, though not much older than he was himself. She had that flattened, sing-song accent which characterizes the dis-tricts of the River Forth, and her hair was auburn like a rowan leaf in autumn and her eyes were a hazy green. In short, she was the image of one of the heroines of the cheapjack ro-mances which Betsy brought home and which he browsed through to laugh at their maudlin sentimentality and sheer bad grammar. Grammar had no part in it now; not now that he had been confronted by the very embodiment of Romance, in that most Romantic of all cities.

The entire experience was tinted by novel sensations which he was educated enough to recognize as the awakening of masculine maturity. He exulted in the fact that at last his body had caught up with his brain. But the girl – she was lithe and bonnie and seemed to favour him above the other denizens of the tavern. She brushed him with her thigh as she served his meat and touched his cheek with her swelling bosom as she leaned over to clear away his plate; neither gesture had been accidental. He had even exchanged words with her, banteringly, and had held up his end in that disputation as well as he had done in his dialogue with a Professor of Logic and Metaphysics. The girl's answers were pert and subtle; he understood her to mean that she would come home with him later that night if he wanted her to. He did want her to. And he would have done it, done it all, all the things his sisters whispered about and of which Henderson had boasted, and which were essential to the process of becoming mature and sophisticated. He would willingly have taken her back to his room – if he had had a room of his own, that is – to explore all the arcane mysteries of fornication. But he had no room, no private place. Thus, prudently, he had disbanded their union by tipping her tuppence and leaving her with the casual hint that he might stop by again soon.

Side by side with the serving girl stood another figure. Drew did not know what she represented, or why the vision should give him a lingering shock of regret in his belly. She had sidled from a gaslit close at the mouth of the Lawnmarket as he had walked back to Warrender Park. It had not been very late. Most of the hostelries were still ablaze with light, and the streets were not deserted. Yet, it had seemed to Drew as if the city had lost all its people, that there were no other folk in any of the mean wynds or steep-sloping lanes. A crusted lamp dissipated a vaporous glow over the woman who pinned him with a grip like a vice before he could take to his heels in alarm. Behind her the close-arch funnelled down into subterranean depths filled with coils of brownish mist. Light lay scrolled and slimy on the old cobbled walk and vault-like walls, and a red glow, like the dying embers of a coal furnace, showed a dim doorway down in the borders of the mist.

The woman leeched on to his elbow and pulled him closer. She had jet-black hair piled in stiff ringlets which clustered against her skull as ivy clings to church stone. Gilt earrings pierced her lobes, framing the bone-white face in threads of gold as thin as spiders' webs. She was not ugly. Her features were fine, sharp and delicate. Her eyes were dark under carefully painted lashes. Her mouth too was pretty, lips parted to show her tongue and small pearl-white teeth. Two cheap silk capes were draped crosswise round her shoulders, one of shot-scarlet, the other of mottled turquoise.

'How young you are,' she murmured, in an accent as polished as Rhinestones. 'So young, and so handsome a gentleman.'

'What ... d'you want?'

'I want to give myself to you.'

'I ... can't.'

'See.'

Uncoupling the capes, she shook her high shoulders and let the silks slide down her back, exposing her breasts. They were like white bowls, not large, with erect nipples in the centre of each breast, pink as sweetmeats. As she lured his hand towards her nakedness, Drew collected himself and caught at her wrist.

'I have no money,' he said.

She released him at once, peering at him.

'Why, then, did you accost me, you cheat?'

'Because you are beautiful,' Drew said, calmly.

The woman shrugged, not indifferently, but to restore the modesty of the capes. She smiled languorously and cocked her head.

'And you would have me?' she asked.

'If I could,' Drew said.

'No charity, my fine young man?'

'No charity.'

She laughed quietly in her throat.

'If you want me enough ...'

'Aye?'

He did desire this strange female creature, even more than he had wanted the girl. Before she spoke, he knew what she would tell him.

'If you want me enough you will find the price,' she said.

The pronouncement had the quality of an omen, part promise, part threat. The calibre of her delivery caused him to shudder. Abruptly he turned and scampered back the way he had come, veering left into one of the narrow, open lanes which led him, via a hundred worn steps, down into the more populous streets of the new town.

The hour was late when he finally wandered back to his lodgings. The landlady did not chide him that evening, but served him a very stern sermon with his bacon breakfast the following morning. He listened, saying nothing, almost wishing that he did have something to feel guilty about.

The mist had lifted over the Forth. The Castle rock sparkled with light frost, and the walls of the esplanade were stencilled cleanly against a pallid sky. The events of the past forty hours seemed as remote as dreams as he walked to the Caledonian Railway Station and boarded the train which would lead him, eventually, back home to Blacklaw.

As the journey progressed, however, and Edinburgh receded, he began to seriously explore the incidents which had marked the trip, to sort them out and rework them to suit himself. Rayburn, the serving lass, the haunting figure of the whore, were all parcel of a single experience which soon came to seem self-enhancing. From such people he could learn much, much more than any textbook contained. From the Professor he could learn how to make a virtue of a coarse complexion and a rough tongue; from the serving girl he could learn about romance; and from the whore – there was no saying what sort of education she might provide in a private chamber in the vigilant hours of the night.

By the time he reached Bathgate, changed trains, spent his last penny on a mutton pie and smoked the stub of his last cheroot, he had settled some of the sundry problems of mind and matter. The shabby carriage of the Wilsontown, Morningside and Coltness Special was empty and gave him privacy to probe more deeply into the new philosophies which life had cast up for study.

Long before he reached Hamilton, Drew had doubled his arrogance, had gained strength of purpose from his solutions, and added several fresh objectives to his aim. When he finally stepped down to the platform he did so with a swagger which befitted a savant briefly returning home from the capital city. He felt a match for any man, dominie or duke, and, on his own peculiar terms, quite ready to tackle the world.

*

Drew stepped down from the carriage and, clutching his brown paper parcel of belongings to his chest, came on up the platform. His swagger was something to behold, Mirrin thought; not the swing of a proud young man, but so utterly self-possessed as to be almost tyrannical in its arrogance. Looking neither to left nor right, her brother seemed to walk in a vacuum of self-assurance. The faint, fixed smile on his face made him appear even more smug than usual.

Mirrin was at war with herself. She wished that she might see Drew take a fall, smash his overweening pride like Humpty Dumpty's shell; yet it was wicked and callous of her to desire this fate for her remaining brother. Kate and Mam depended on him so much now; he was *their* sole source of pride. That was the way it was with women who were doomed to live vicariously through the achievements of their menfolk; not even obliged to love the puppets which they manipulated from birth to grave, just to accept them as instruments of fulfilment. Now that James and Dougie were dead, all Mam had left was Drew. God knows that's little enough, Mirrin thought, as her brother, still oblivious of her presence, legged it towards the ticket gate.

He would have gone on past her, heading up towards the lane which would take him on to the main Blacklaw road, had she not caught him by the arm and stopped him in his tracks. For an instant there was a quirky flash of alarm in his eyes as she swung him towards her.

'Mirrin!' he exclaimed.

'Who did you expect; the Queen herself?'

'I didn't notice you.'

'You weren't really lookin'.'

'I thought you'd all be at work.'

'I'm in for messages.'

'I see,' Drew said.

'Well?'

'Well what?'

'How did you get on in Edinburgh?'

'All right.'

'Was it difficult?'

'Not particularly.'

'Go on.'

'What?'

'Tell me about it.'

'Not much to tell.'

'Did you manage all the questions?'

'Yes.'

She waited for him to volunteer more news. In truth she wasn't much interested in his academic exploits, except as they would affect their need to find money to buy his student's place. It had never crossed her mind that Drew would actually fail. Recently Houston had informed her that any bright, intelligent lad could be sure of being taken into the college fold, and somehow that piece of impartial information had diminished Drew's ability in her eyes.

'Did you come by the omnibus?' he asked.

'No, I'm drivin' the dog-cart,' Mirrin replied. 'It's over by the cattle pens. I'll drop you off at the house.'

As they walked out of the station and angled across the cobbled forecourt towards the railings of the cattle enclosures which backed on to the grain warehouse and the Caledonian railway haulage sheds, Mirrin said, 'I suppose you were intendin' t'walk home?'

'No sense in wastin' money,' Drew said.

'Did you spend it all?'

'I didn't have much, you know.'

'Enough for tobacco, though.'

'Tobacco?'

'You reek like the dominie's lum.'

'The carriage was musty.'

'Hah!'

'All right, I bought a cheroot. It cost one penny. The dominie gave me somethin' for myself.'

'I suppose you had a drink, too?'

'Yes, a tipple of wine.'

Mirrin shook her head. If it had not been Drew, she would have laughed at his boyish indulgences and teased him about other vices. But the fact that Drew had blewed five or six pence on luxuries galled her. Each of those pennies had been earned by the sweat of Kate's brow, or by Mam's patience with the needle, or by her own labours up at . . . No, that was hardly a proper thread to the argument. The fact remained that Drew had squandered the price of a good family supper on drink and cheroots.

Controlling herself, she said, 'I wouldn't go developin' any addictions, if I were you; if you go up t'Edinburgh, you'll need every farthin' for food.'

'If?'

'I mean . . . if you pass.'

'I will pass: there's no doubt about that.'

'Mister Cocky!'

'I can't possibly fail.'

She would have trotted out one of Mam's adages about Pride and Better Men Than You, but she had no stomach for acting the older sister. She was sorry now that she had gone out of her way to borrow the dog-cart and arrange her shopping expedition so that she could meet him. If Kate had not been so keen for a member of the family to greet the young hero, she would not have made the effort.

Mirrin said, 'That cart: get in.'

Archie had picked the most docile beast in the stable, a small, elderly, brown mare. Its rate of progress was hardly exhilarating, but it was obedient to Mirrin's inexpert handling of the reins and even managed a bit of a trot on downhill stretches with an empty cart behind it.

Drew stepped up and sat on the bench of padded cord, his parcel on his lap. Two hampers of provisions were tucked away under the little gate. Mirrin unfolded a horse rug and threw it to her brother who wrapped it round his legs. She seated herself primly opposite him, cautiously looked all round, then unlaced the reins and shook them optimistically, clicking her tongue.

The little mare cocked its ears.

'Come on, Meg; gee, gee.'

Reluctantly, the animal stirred its hoofs and started off on the wide circle which would steer it out of the area of the pens and into the upper end of the principal throughfare. Mirrin sighed and settled back, letting the leathers ride lightly across her palms, pinched by fingers and thumbs, as Archie had instructed her.

Drew displayed no interest at all in his sister's new-found skill, nor in her navigation. He did not even notice the busy traffic in the streets, as if the scene was so utterly familiar that it bored him. The morning's brightness had dulled, though it was not cold and the threat of rain was slight. For early March the air was very still and smoke from the chimneys on the town's outskirts rose straight into the smoky sky, unwaveringly. Around her shoulders and head Mirrin wore a quilted leather cowl which Archie had loaned her and which made her look, she thought, more like a hangman than a nun. The leather was scuffed and rain-tanned and smelled of the stables, but it was warm to wear and comfortable and she had no reason to appear smart that afternoon. If she encountered anyone she knew, she could always remove it.

For twenty minutes, the couple wheeled along in silence. Hamilton's cottages and outlying villas dropped behind as Mirrin cut away on to a climbing back road which gave firmer ground for the narrow wheels. Trees were winter bare against the bland landscape. Fields lay ready for the plough or some, on the lower plain, were already ploughed, the rich brown earth turned in regular furrows like cord patches on a counterpane.

Suddenly Drew said, 'Did you tell him you were collectin' me?'

Mirrin who had been thinking of other things, said dully, 'Tell who?'

'Him: Lamont?'

'Don't be so daft.'

'It's his cart, isn't it?'

'Aye, but he's too busy t'be bothered with the uses it's put to.'

'So you just ... took it?'

'What's the point of this, Drew?'

'Mere curiosity.'

'If you must know, then, I did ask him if I could take the dog-cart t'Hamilton.'

'An' you mentioned me?'

'No.'

'Oh!'

Mirrin squinted suspiciously at her brother. He had no particular expression imprinted on his face and gave no sign that her answers were of specific interest to him. He continued to stare into the well of the cart, as if it was a boat slowly filling with seepage.

'Drew?' Mirrin said.

'Yes.' The young man looked up. 'There were, in Edinburgh, a large number of boys of my station in life.'

'That doesn't surprise me.'

'All of them aiming, like me, at advancement through learnin'.'

'You'll be at home in their company then.'

'No,' said Drew patiently. 'That's not what I meant.'

'What did you mean?'

'Quite a number have ... patrons.'

'Patrons?'

'Sponsors.'

'Ah, I see,' Mirrin said.

'Local gentlemen.'

'Like Houston Lamont.'

'Precisely,' Drew said.

'But you already have "sponsors".'

'Oh, you mean Kate an' that,' said Drew, airily.

'It doesn't matter where the money comes from, does it?'

'Basically, no,' Drew replied. 'On the other hand, a proper patron would perhaps be more generous . . .'

Mirrin glanced away over the mare's rump, then back at her brother. He was sitting forward now, clasping the parcel to his belly like ballast, head canted as he examined her expression with sly speculative inquiry.

Mirrin said, 'I thought you just wanted t'get there, t'Edinburgh?'

'I do, of course,' Drew said. 'But *when* I get there I don't want to fall short, educationally. I want to be in a position to seize the opportunity for learning to the full.'

'With a full belly, you mean; an' a box of cheroots an' bottles of wine.'

'You're angry?'

'God Almighty, Drew!'

'Ideas above my station?'

'*Aye!*'

'Lamont isn't . . .'

'Lamont isn't what?'

'He's helped us, hasn't he? He's taken an interest in us, since Da died. I mean, he's got you . . .'

'*Will you shut up.*'

'Frankly,' Drew persisted, 'I wouldn't be at all averse t'putting a proposal t'him myself.'

'*You!* You swelled-headed brat, you put a proposal t'the coalmaster? God, that's rich.'

'For twenty or thirty pounds per annum . . .'

'*Shut up, I tell you.*'

Drew sat back, propping his elbow on the side of the rail. Mirrin flicked the reins urging the mare into a sluggish trot. She wanted the journey over with before her rage belched forth in a torrent of abuse, before she so far forgot herself as to tell him exactly what she thought of him.

She had always felt guilty at disliking Drew so much. There was no deep-buried reason why this should be so. He had not been her father's favourite. He was not anybody's favourite.

Indeed, the only close relationship he had within the family was with his twin sister Betsy. Was it the fact that he had been a twin? No, that was ridiculous. He hadn't even been a fractious infant, or a whining child. He had been, now that she thought of it, just about the way he was now – selfish, cold, mean-minded, and sly. Yes – sly! His diplomacy was motivated by cunning, and always had been. Somehow, though he never seemed to make demands, Drew had invariably wound up with the lion's share of what was going.

By rights, by natural law, Betsy should have been the spoiled child, the household's pretty baby. But secretly, enigmatically, Drew had usurped his twin's role. Willy-nilly, given the ghost of a chance, he would gobble them all up. He did not care a jot for any one of them, not even Betsy, nor did he consider the glory he might have brought them in exchange for their sacrifices. He was obsessed only with his desire to springboard out of Blacklaw and shake free for ever from his family. He despised them so much, had been born despising them, it seemed; yet he would make use of them to free himself. That was it, Mirrin decided, that was the wellspring of her hatred for her young brother. He admitted no sense of duty, nor of love; none, none at all.

Suddenly, she saw him threatening her happiness through Houston. The warmth she had enjoyed over the past few weeks might be stolen from her not by Edith Lamont or some accident which led to discovery and scandal but by her own brother's machinations. He would ruthlessly trample on her, on Houston, on anybody who could help him gain his ends. And those ends were shifting and changing and expanding all the time; that was the hell of it. He was insatiable. She could not hope to satisfy him – nobody could.

Snapping the reins, she vented some of her anger by yelling at the mare. Having raised itself to brief effort, the poor animal stubbornly subsided into a shambling walk once more, toiling against the hill.

Northrigg was close in sight, over to the west, and the wheels of Blacklaw and the dense smoke of its engineering forges hove into view, not far distant. Cattle crammed the dyke, snorting and bellowing, full of curiosity like all bullocks. Mirrin shouted at them and they fled, cumbersome and loud, away across the brow of the pasture.

Drew said, 'I didn't mean to offend you.'

Mirrin tugged the leather cowl around her head. She felt close to tears and she would not give him that pleasure.

He said, 'I want nothin' from you, you know.'

'But you'll take it, won't you?'

'If you mean the money . . .'

'What else can we give you?'

'I thought it was arranged: the money side of it.'

'Aye: so what more . . .?'

'You . . . you like Lamont now, don't you?'

'Drew . . .'

'You can tell me.'

'I . . . respect him.'

'What would Da have said to that?'

'Da?'

'However . . .' Drew paused. 'That's idle talk, I suppose, under the circumstances. I take it that you don't actually resent me havin' my opportunity. It's worked out well enough, hasn't it? I mean, Kate's got work, an' you're secure enough up in the big house. Come what might, *that's* not goin' t'change. I mean, if you "respect" him so much, then he'll be aware of it, an' won't toss you out in the gutter, no matter how hard things become at the pit.'

'All that,' said Mirrin, evenly, 'is true.'

'Then you've me t'thank for it – indirectly.'

'So?'

'How much will the market bear?' Drew murmured.

'*What?*'

'Lamont must have friends, influential friends. When I graduate . . .'

'Are you plannin' that far ahead already, then?'

'It would be beneficial t'have contacts in the capital.'

'Make your own. I thought you were hell-bent on chartin' your own course.'

'Five years won't be long in the passin',' Drew remarked. 'If you ... ah ... if you "respect" him enough in the interim ...'

She had never used the crack-whip on the mare, nor on any beast from Lamont's stable; but she used it now, plucking it from its pod and slashing with it at her brother's head. The short, supple thong caught him once across the brow, then laid its trace over the backs of his hands as he protected himself from injury by raising the parcel to cover his face. For a moment Mirrin continued to slash and sabre at the parcel, ripping the brown paper with the thong then, as abruptly as she had mounted the ferocious attack, subsided, throwing the whip down into the well of the cart and lifting the loose rein again, tweaking it to bring the mare to a halt.

Drew peered over the bulge of the parcel.

'What the devil got into you?' he asked, querulously.

'Just get out.'

'Here?'

'Out.'

'I thought you said ...'

'Get out!'

Drew raised his brows, shrugged, then hopped over the side of the low cart, still hugging the torn parcel. Without so much as a glance at him, Mirrin clicked her tongue and slapped the reins. The dog-cart trundled forward and began its descent into the broad valley of the Shennan, into the sprawling wasteland of the colliery villages.

Mirrin did not look back, not until the first of the trucker's sheds lofted scarred walls above her and the hoofs and wheels sucked in blue-black mud; then she swung her head and peered back up the hill. Drew was walking briskly, hugging his parcel, swaggering down the stoop of the road. She had not made much ground on him. Rounding the shed corner she put her brother out of sight. Trotting on, she coaxed the mare into an avenue which led out behind the rumps of the shale bings and would avoid the troughs and houses and bring her home to Houston's mansion by a quiet, green road.

It was not Drew's gall, or his ruthlessness which had infuriated her. It was his ignorance of all human feeling which, at long last, had curdled her dislike into loathing. Whatever transpired in her life or his, she would do not one whit more for him than her duty to Kate demanded. Duty without love, she knew now, could only lead to heartbreak in the end.

6

Spring came early to Blacklaw; the spell of wan sunshine which melted away the frost lingered on and finally encouraged the winter-weary housewives to throw open their doors and drag down the rag-stuffing which lined the windows. Neighbour greeted neighbour again, and after the grumbles about ill-health and shortage of food had been exchanged, got down to the important business of compiling the rotas which would decide on which day each family had the use of the washhouse tub and the sagging drying ropes which stretched across the ground at the rear of the rows. Front stoups were whitened with holystone and chalk-wash. Gutters were cleared of the trash which had frozen into them during the hard winter months. Men dug into the backs of cupboards and unearthed the iron lasts and tins of 'wee tingles' and set about repairing what was left of the family footwear. With no waste of effort, but with little reason to suppose that the coming year would show much improvement on its predecessor, Blacklaw greeted the spring. There was one item of relief, however, which was not discussed yet made its mark on the colliers; an intangible sense of escape from the 'oppressive sorrows of the previous March which, now that a full twelve-month had elapsed, seemed decently remote.

In Lamont's mansion, activity was hectic. Spring-cleaning began with the sunshine on the calendar date of March first. Booming winds provided good drying for the silks, linens and velours which, on Mirrin's instructions, had been stripped from their hangings and steeped in the coppers in the laundry cellar. Dust fled from brooms, and the McCormicks' mops splashed suds into corners which, according to the size of the spiders boarded there, had not sniffed water since Noah grounded his ark on Tinto Hill.

The servants' regular helper was none other than the master's sister. Dorothy enjoyed the domestic upheaval hugely, and seldom left Mirrin's side. In spite of Edith's protests,

Lamont made no attempt to rescue Dorothy from such vulgar company. The servants, and Mirrin in particular, gave her much-needed warmth and affection. He did not even object when Mirrin presented Dorothy with a large frilled apron and a cap to wear during dusting. It was this development which so offended Edith's propriety that she gave up trying to impose herself on other members of the household – her husband included – and withdrew from all contact with any of them.

Edith Lamont had changed much in the months between Christmas and spring. She no longer appeared to care about her duties, and spent many days – cold, raw days at that – wandering from drawing-room to drawing-room round her circle of acquaintances in Glasgow's west end. Edinburgh society, too, summoned her, though less frequently, and she spent several extended weekends as a house-guest of the Cunninghams, the Monteaths and the younger McAlpins.

Neither Mirrin nor Houston Lamont could be certain that their liaison was not being abetted by the mistress of the house; her apparent naivety in leaving them so much alone together disturbed them. Mirrin felt sure that Houston's wife had some sinister ruse in the making, one which would bode ill for them all.

Mirrin was unashamedly in love with her employer. Within a few days of that snowy night in Christmas week, she had given him her heart as well as her body. There was no apologetic formality in their love-making now : it had been replaced by a passion which, in spite of Lamont's assurances to the contrary, Mirrin felt sure showed plainly on their faces. A dozen times all told, Mirrin and Lamont had lain in each others' arms, always in the housekeeper's room, always when Edith was safely away from home and the rest of the household asleep.

There was nothing injudicious in Lamont's attitude to the affair. He was too much in love with Mirrin, and too afraid of losing her, to act like a fool. She was much more than a casual lover : she provided warmth and comfort and the subtle attentions which Edith considered unnecessary to a relationship. He could not quite separate the bounty of her body from the rest of it, however, and found his life permeated with sexual nuances which, instead of making him restless, brought him relaxation and much-needed rest from the rigours of holding the colliery open. In the long run, he supposed, the affair would terminate. He had heard tales of bachelors who had lived out such love-marriages with servants and died in their eighties still clasping the beloved's hand – but they had been single gentlemen, usually squires or clergy. Sooner or later it seemed inevitable that Edith would ferret out the truth, find that her imaginary accusations had taken on substance. In the interim, he determined to enjoy the pleasures of that time in all their forms, and protect himself and Mirrin for as long as he was able.

There was no misery and no real guilt in them; all the folk he truly cared about were happy under his roof. He saw now what his grandfather, and his father, too, had lacked: they had pursued power through possession, and had ruled by the disciplines of tradition. All that had been swept away the moment he had stepped across the threshold of Mirrin's room and into the candle-light which surrounded her bed. It was not as the Bible said: there was no *evil* in adultery, after all. The evil the ministers raved on about was only in the denial of love. He had not known love since Gordon's death, and had known precious little of it even before that time.

Now Mirrin, and his sister, were his household gods, the stars by which he charted the course of his life and steered his conscience through the reefs of Victorian morality. The bright, blustery weather of early spring robbed him of caution, however, and made him vulnerable, not, as it happened, to one of Edith's petty schemes but to the tragedy of the unforeseen.

*

Loony Lachie was one thing, the goodfolk of Blacklaw decided, and Miss Dorothy Lamont was quite another. Their initial sympathy for the coalmaster's sister wore off about the time the weather worsened and, by Lamont's cunning, the miners were put in the cleft-stick of decision-making. It was the latter incident which stuck in the communal craw. Soon after that, the sight of Miss Dorothy, in the charge of Mirrin Stalker, began to have an effect on them, as if the tall, gaunt woman was a totem for her brother's sins. She hadn't enough cheek, of course, ever to show her ugly face in the village itself, but she and that Stalker lass were ay skulkin' about the back of the school and the kirk or down by the Gowrey woods: seen up in Hamilton, too, they were, in and out the posh shops, spendin' the big profits Lamont claimed he wasn't makin'. It wasn't right for the likes of her to be free to wander the streets like a normal buddy.

The whispering campaign was something Mirrin knew about and thoroughly understood. She kept it to herself, shielding her employer, but made sure that Miss Dorothy stayed safely about the house and the gardens. In any case, the weather was too bleak to tempt her out, and it was well into the spring before Dorothy showed much inclination to spread her wings and see a little more of the world beyond the garden walls.

'I want to go out.'

'We'll think about it tomorrow, Miss Dorothy.'

'Today.'

'I'm too busy today: look, come an' help Mattie polish the study. You can wind the Brighouse clock, if you like.'

'I want to go out, Mirrin.'

'I'll tell you what, why don't you go over t'the stables an' see Archie? He'll let you feed the horses.'

'I've fed the horses already.'

'That was yesterday.'

'I . . . I . . . want . . . to go out.'

'No, Miss Dorothy,' Mirrin said, firmly. 'Not just now.'

'Later?'

'Tomorrow.'

'Later.'

Mirrin sighed.

'Wait in the garden, then,' she said. 'I'll try to finish the study cleanin' soon an' then I'll take you up to see Pibroch.'

Dorothy gaped her mouth wide, her head held back and her eyelids lowered. She looked, just then, like a thorough autocrat; but her demand did not materialize. Instead, she opened her eyes again, and said, 'Yes.'

'Wait in the garden, then. I'll be with you as soon as I can.'

Swishing her feather duster like a sabre, Mirrin turned away from the door at the side of the house. She glanced back, saw Miss Dorothy walking and skipping across the cobbles on to the grass, then went on into the house to supervise the annual renovation of the master's sanctuary.

It was an hour before she completed her tasks and returned to the kitchen door in search of Dorothy Lamont.

By that time, it was too late.

*

All through the woodlands beyond the wall the brown leaf mat was shot with crocuses and a second bath of sturdy, virginal snowdrops. A trail of them coaxed Dorothy on. She nodded to the tiny flowers, smiling, bowing and dropping words of praise for their pretty dresses, like some regal lady passing among courtiers. Soon she lost the niggling guilt which her escape through the broken section of the wall had incurred. At first she had acted in defiance of Mirrin : then she had recalled the Brock and wondered if she could find him and persuade him to return and be her garden pet; then the host of spring blossoms had diverted her attention and their dainty, passive patterns had guided her away from the security of the grounds and lured her quickly into forgetfulness.

After a time, her pleasure was marred neither by wilfulness nor doubt and she was entranced by her own independence and made bold by the encouraging sun.

On the western slope of the valley, the trees were struggling to bud and the grass was coming green through the old growths. Fern fronds spread their golden skeletons protectively across the rabbit paths as the contour slipped off into the grazing land to the south and dipped sharply through banks of early daffodils, small and butter pale, down to the flooded river.

The Shennan rose in the Lowther hills, where the snow had lain long in the high air. The melt had begun three days before, with the seep of water loudening in the braes and the level of the burns rising overnight. Elvan Water, the Enterkin, and Shennan, too, had come gradually to flood, the lesser streams cheerfully enough but the Shennan with that dour uncoiling power which said that it fed the industrial Clyde far below the major river's source. It flowed now like a strong brown muscle across the Blacklaw line, rippling and surging between muddy cliffs and coal-blackened outcrops, ignoring the half-drowned willow roots and hawthorns' boughs, and giving out no obvious sounds save the most subtle sucks and gurglings.

Dorothy should have fled from the sight of the river; but she did not. Never would she find it less formidable in its surrounds, not heavy but light and open. For all that, only her new-found courage and her debt to the flowers, kept her on the path to the water's edge. Only then did the nightmare resurrect itself and the river seem a gluttonous thing capable of dreadful destructions. She swung round and stared back up the slope at the trees.

Ferns had covered up her tracks and the little trumpets of the daffodils pointed all hither and thither, directionless and, so Dorothy imagined, crying out for help. She chose a higher path, ran a step or two, then paused, questioning the sources of her fear. Over the winter months, under Mirrin's guidance, she had learned to confront irrationality in herself. She bit her lip, wrenched at her dress, but did not run in panic. Some force, some transient sanity held her above the long rolling currents of brown water. Courage had narrow limits, however; within minutes, she would have baulked and fled. But an unexpected distraction offered itself and took her eye from the Shennan's threat and gave her poor, cluttered mind a single purpose.

Over the brow of the hillside the child came. She was six or seven years old, dressed in a layered cotton smock and protected against the chilly wind by a patched jacket tailored from a discarded cardigan. Her laced boots, several sizes too large for her, flopped comically as she skipped through the grasses. She had a pretty, pert little face, though thin, and eyes that were bright and eager for adventure. Her name was Jinny Sinclair and in each hand she carried a posy of flowers.

*

Hastily Mirrin untied her apron and put it with her puffed cap on to the peg behind the laundry room door. It was not so warm as it appeared and she shivered slightly as she walked

412

along the shadowed avenue and rounded the gable at the front of the house.

'Miss Dorothy.'

The lawns leaned away to the oaks, bland and deserted.

Mirrin frowned, and called again, waiting for an answer. There was no answer, only a very faint echo from the distant trunks in the corner where the walls met. She scrutinized the trees, searching for the dart of colour, mottled turquoise and scarlet, which would show up Miss Dorothy's day-dress in the brown and ochre landscape.

The sun was brittle and dazzling. Mirrin screened her eyes with her forearm and pivoted to look back down the wedge of the shrubbery to the sprawling drying greens behind the kitchens.

'Dorothy.'

Already walking, she called again, passing into sunlight along the frontage of the house, walking faster. The leaves of a beech hedge rustled. She stopped and gazed hopefully towards the rose garden, but the breeze withered away and left the leaves stiff and motionless and unrevealing. She circuited the house once, then headed up through the trees towards McCrimmond's plots, passing the stables and the carriage house on the way. She searched silently, not calling out Dorothy's name now; nor did she consult Archie, though he was there in the stable yard soaping tack. By the time she reached the vegetable gardens, she was wrapped in numb panic. The sensible thing to do was round up the servants and send them out to search for the missing woman : instinct prevented it, some intuitive faculty in her breast. Perhaps she did not want to risk the ridicule of seeming careless with her charge? No, it was deeper than that, and less personal.

At the house-hut in the woods, there was no sign of Pibroch or his dogs. Mirrin searched diligently, searched silently, searched with a calmness which did not mirror her feelings. Certain that Dorothy was not in that quarter of the estate, she returned to the house and, still without a word to anyone, hunted through all its rooms from cellar to servants' attic – and found no trace at all of the missing woman.

By that time Dorothy Lamont had been at large for close on two hours.

*

'Pretty flowers.'

'I picked them.'

'Were you careful?'

'Uh?'

'You didn't hurt them, did you?'

'Flowers canny be hurted.'

'Oh, yes, they can: you have to pick them very ... nicely.'

'What's your name, lady?'

'Dorothy.'

'D'you pick flowers?'

'I have lots of flowers in my garden.'

'My name's Jinny Sinclair: I've got five big brothers in my hoose.'

'I have a brother, too.'

'What's his name, then?'

'Houston.'

'I've had a cough.'

'Are you better now?'

'Aye.'

'Where do you live?'

'In Blacklaw, wi' Mammy an' Daddy an' Jimmy an' Andy an' Joe...'

The bunch was made up of crocuses and daffodils, clutched tightly and shedding velvety petals. In her left hand the child grasped a spray of willow catkins, silken grey buds fat on the twigs. She had augmented the willows with reeds. Jinny Sinclair was like a doll, a little patchwork doll with a fine china face. Dorothy stared at the doll's face, then at the willow catkins. The furry buds were the shade of a gown she had once had, long, long ago. She reached out to touch them. Jinny cut off her flow of chatter, pouted resentfully, and snatched her bouquet of twigs and leaves away.

'Stroke them,' said Dorothy. 'May I?'

'They're mine.'

'Where ... where did you pick them, little girl?'

'Back yonder.'

'Show me.'

'I should be't school today. Mammy put me in the back green.'

'Nice . . . flowers,' said Dorothy.

'Came over the brig from the bakehouse: all b'myself.'

Far across the valley, a train hooted and clanked out of Blacklaw station, the sound loud in the clear morning air. Dorothy and the child both glanced up and watched the puffs of smoke ascending from behind the roofs. From their vantage point, nothing was visible of Blacklaw village except the black slate roofs.

'Will we pick more?' Dorothy suggested.

'Some for you, lady?'

'Yes,' said Dorothy eagerly. 'Where is the tree?'

'Back there.'

'Show it to me.'

'C'mon, then.'

The white willow tree clung to the river bank. A season ago it had been secure on high ground, but subsidence of the clay had brought it down to a leaning angle. Now the Shennan, jealous of the new life which burgeoned on the boughs, arched its back and chaffed and tore at it and, with a fuller flood, would surely have it down.

Behind the willow, alders and bushy whinns clustered thickly. The woman and the child pushed through them and came out on the narrow sward dominated by the knuckled tree roots on an outcrop above the river.

Dorothy stared up at the whippy branches, all speckled with the silver buds. The doll-faced village child was less in awe of the location. Casting aside her spray and posy, she hitched up her skirts and, with a short run and leap, landed cat-like against the trunk and swarmed up into the forks.

The willow tree creaked and swayed.

A bolt of fear passed through Dorothy Lamont.

It was not the rational sort of fear which any adult might have experienced at the child's foolhardiness, but the swamping of a hundred accumulated terrors, some real and many imagined. At the core lay the recollection of the nightmare which had severely troubled her in the early winter. Mated to the scene which now confronted her, the images merged and dream and actuality became one, as if she had caught up with herself at last.

She uttered a guttural cry.

Jinny Sinclair twisted the twigs in her hand and snapped off a pair, dropping them on Dorothy who, reaching helplessly, took the branches on the face and beat and flapped at them as if at snakes. The child laughed and broke off more twigs and showered them down. She was seated cross-legged in the junction of the bole and the branches, perched out over the river.

Tears streamed down Dorothy's face.

She thought of Mirrin, and brought to the forefront of her mind all that Mirrin had told her. Still weeping copiously, but now in some sort of control of herself, she clenched her fists and commanded, 'Come down at once.'

Jinny tossed another handful of catkins on to the lady's head.

She was safe enough up the tree.

She seldom did what anybody told her, and was not awed by this big lady, who cried for no reason.

Dorothy tried to emulate Mirrin.

'*Come down, I say: come down this minute.*'

Grinning impishly, Jinny Sinclair kicked her heels.

Her legs were thin, bare to the knees, skirts lumped about her thighs.

Stepping closer to the cliff edge, Dorothy circled an arm about the willow trunk and, stretching to full height, snared the little girl's ankle.

Jinny wriggled and kicked; the grip was tight enough to hurt.

'Let m'go.'

'Then, will ... you ... come ... *down?*'

'Naw.'

The struggle lasted only a moment; a frail tussle in the frail willow branches, the child tugging and Dorothy tugging, neither with much purchase.

Perhaps it was Jinny's piping complaints, more petulant than afraid, which conjured the man from out of the woods. He came like a dwarf, bounding forth from the whinns, grunting and wheezing with laughter. He was young, broad-backed, bulging-thighed, and his head was huge and misshapen. His lips, slackly grinning, dribbled flecks of saliva. Even as he came to rest on the sward, his hand shot to his face and planted brass teeth into his mouth. His voice changed to a breathy, metallic wail. Blast upon blast chanted out directly at Dorothy Lamont, as he hopped forward again, blowing out his cheeks discordantly, arms swinging.

Dorothy let go her hold on the tree, and on Jinny's ankle.

She tottered, sank, and toppled back over the cliff edge.

The river's roar enveloped her. It was full of gobbling greed now, like some massive animal, a monstrous pet of the creature who had bounded up from the ground. The sticky clay, rough-mixed with shale, caught Dorothy's dress and adhered to it. Involuntarily, her fists closed on the reed tussocks on the verge, and all her muscles contracted, holding her body plastered against the cliff-face. One shoe, draped from her toe, was caught by the water, stripped off and gulpingly devoured. She could still see the beast on the bank above her, though he paid her not the slightest attention.

The happenings were linked into a continuous series of actions. Even as Dorothy fell, Lauchlan Abercorn advanced to the bank, and Jinny Sinclair, scrambling higher, lost her hold, crashed through the pliant boughs and tumbled down on to the current's swift, horse-brown back.

Woman and child were only a few feet from each other. Jinny dangled from the lower branches, snagged by her skirts and patched jacket. Her knees trailed in the water and scored up streamers of foam, releasing from the Shennan's depths an ugly hissing noise which consumed all the other sounds.

Lachie's round head jutted over the cliff-edge. He pushed the mouth-organ forward in his teeth, arched his brows, and nodded.

Soft wet clay cushioned Dorothy.

Lachie's face vanished.

Dorothy inched herself up the banking, digging in her toes, scrambling with her knees. Beside her, the little girl pendulumed, and screamed, and slipped lower, until the river flickered at her heels.

The branch was three or four feet long. Lachie poked it out over the river, and wagged it up and down. The plaintive chanting of the mouth organ was his means of speech, the sound becoming louder and more insistent as he projected the dead branch close to the child, two tinny notes were repeated urgently. He waved and beat with the long branch, impatiently. But Jinny was too terrified to understand. She did nothing to save herself, simply hung by her torn clothing, sinking a little closer to the river with every passing moment.

Lachie now was frantic, furious too at his failure to communicate. He thrashed wildly with the branch, flailing the water and the willow twigs, then striking the child, beating at her head and legs and arms as if to jar sense into her. Dorothy saw the branch break across the little skull, and blood begin to flow. Jinny's head twitched and cocked slackly on her stem-like neck. Still Lachie hacked and smote, dancing up and down, his boots sending shuddering vibrations through the clay.

The willow tree released its burden. Nothing seemed to snap. The smooth, flexible twigs bent slightly and let the bundle slide. Neat and contained, little Jinny Sinclair dropped down into the flood. Brown water flopped open to welcome her body and closed over her hair, leaving nothing but an elongated dimple on the surface, a mark which swirled softly away downstream into the main channel.

Eyes squeezed shut, Dorothy Lamont waited. She exercised no deliberate patience. She waited because she could not bring herself to move, to unite with reality. There was no great weight of terror in her now, nor much awareness of danger. She did not even seek to blot out the vision of the man with the metal mouth. Anyhow, he was no longer in sight.

At length, Dorothy raised her head and opened her eyes. Sluggishly, she propped her elbows over the edge of the grass and, with a weary effort, hauled herself up and on to the flat, solid ground again. There was no sign of the creature, no sign of the little girl child; nothing to remind her of what had occurred. She stared aghast at her pretty dress all smeared and stained with mud. What would Mirrin say? Mirrin would chide her. She ran a few paces left, then looped back to her right, searching, with mounting panic, for some track that she might follow away from this muddy place.

The daffodil heads had massed into a sickly yellow curtain, and the trees on the crest of the slope were matted like a dense thorn hedge. She whimpered a little in frustration, and wiped her hands on her hair. Her stomach and breasts were wet and uncomfortable and cold cloth pasted itself to her legs. She whimpered again, questioningly. She could not imagine what she was doing in this hideous place. She wanted home: she wanted to be in the kitchen, close by the warm stove, to hear Mirrin laughing and watch Mattie pouring tea from the pot with the short blue spout. She wanted to smell the spicy aroma of buns baking, and the warmth of clean clothes. She wanted Mirrin to hold her, and Houston to hold her, and to lie in bed and have Houston hold her hand, and hear his voice talking in the warm quietness of the room with the curtains drawn.

But she could not find the way.

Two posies, one of tiny spring flowers and one composed of willow catkins and slender reeds, lay on the grass. Her panic momentarily arrested, she stooped and lifted them wondering who could have been so careless as to cast such beautiful bunches aside. Holding the spray and the small bouquet close to her breast, she staggered on upstream, whimpering to herself and, after a time, talking to the flowers for company.

7

A dozen men, recruited for the most part from the public bar of the *Lantern*, prepared to march out into the twilit countryside beyond the immediate boundaries west of Blacklaw. Angus Sinclair was the leader among them. He too had been one of the crowd in the public, and had been summoned only latterly by his eldest son, a fresh-faced boy of seventeen. Sinclair had been drinking since the *Lantern* opened its doors. There was nothing unusual in that pastime, for his home was crowded with usurping sons and a wife whose charms had long been defiled by overwork and under-feeding. It was just as well, Sinclair reckoned, that he'd been in the pub. His mates were all on hand, ready and able to swarm out into the gloaming to find his daughter Jinny who, in spite of many a telling, was a daring wee monkey and had probably just got herself lost. Not one to ignore an opportunity for self-dramatization, however, Angus Sinclair marshalled the party with all the strident discipline of a military general. His sons, of whom four were now in the ranks, were dispatched to the colliery store to beg a pot of pitch and, on returning with that article, were further instructed to manufacture torch brands to light the gathering dusk.

While Sinclair established the search pattern and furnished the volunteers with lights, Rita, his wife, was distraughtly combing the backs of the rows and all the many places this side of the colliery fence where her daughter might have hidden.

It was almost full dark before Constable Neave arrived from his house in Northrigg to stamp the proceedings with the portentous weight of the law. Neave was not a heartless man, but he had conducted too many lost-child hunts to be unduly worried by this one. A squint at the father told him that the wee girl was in hiding, like as not, fearful of punishment for a minor mischief.

The organization of proper parties was rendered difficult by the approach of the change of shifts. Some staunch pals of Sinclair's felt obliged to forgo their evening's pay to help out; but the majority forsook the crowd assembled in the *Lantern*'s yard and slunk off to prime their lamps for work.

The confusion lasted a half hour. Only Rita Sinclair's return from a fruitless tour of the wash-house backs restored some sense of urgency to the men. Mr Guthrie was up from the school by then, leading three of his younger teachers. They banded themselves at once and struck off for the area of scrubland along the old Blacklaw–Northrigg track, armed with storm lanterns and an iron hailing funnel. Sinclair and Neave were left to conduct a grave argument as to which of them should lead the remaining volunteers. Waylaid on the trek home from the day-shift, George McNeillage, the Pritchard brothers and Rob Ewing, organizing themselves, headed off across Poulter's Burn in the direction of the quarry holes. Callum, Christy Moran, and an eager contingent of schoolboys undertook to search the colliery sheds and the railway as far down as Blacklaw Halt. Some took it more seriously: others did their duty ruefully, expecting the tot to appear at any moment and have her lug clipped for the trouble she had caused. After all, she had only been missing for six hours.

At last, in the dark, Neave and Sinclair were left with the four Sinclair boys, Davy Henderson, and a sheaf of dripping pitch brands large enough to light their way to the sea and back. Sinclair sank the jug of mulled ale which the landlord had brought him to calm his anxiety, and resolutely shouldered his torch.

'What's left?' Neave asked.

'The river,' Sinclair said, almost lugubriously.

Five minutes later, the little party set off for the bakehouse bridge and the crumbling banks of the Shennan.

*

Houston Lamont tossed his overcoat and hat on to the nearest chair and closed the study door behind him. He had entered the house only a minute before and had had no need to ask Mirrin why she loitered by the door to catch his attention. He could

421

read in her face the fact that some serious crisis had cropped up and, selfishly, assumed that Edith was at the back of it. Glancing towards the stairs, he said, 'What is it?'

'Can we talk in private, Mr Lamont?'

'Mirrin . . .'

'In the study, maybe?'

He had opened the study door and ushered her in. Cramp knotted his stomach and the headache, which had troubled him all day, was suddenly fierce, like a vice pinching his temples. He swept off and discarded his hat and coat. A fire was lit in the grate, and the lamps had already been lighted. Brandy and whisky decanters, newly filled, were on a tray on a wine table by the desk.

'For God's sake, Mirrin, what's wrong?'

'It's Miss Dorothy.'

Lamont sucked in a shuddering breath. 'Ill?'

'I'm not sure.'

'What the devil do you mean . . .?' he blurted out. 'I'm sorry, Mirrin. Have you summoned McKay, the doctor?'

'Not yet.'

'Then what . . .?'

'She went out on her own this afternoon,' Mirrin explained. Her colour was like chalk and her fingers were clenched round the key-chain at her waist as if it were a rosary. 'It was . . . my fault. I left her in the garden. She wanted to go out, into town, I think. I told her I was too busy, an' asked her to wait in the garden until . . .'

'You mean, Dorothy went into Blacklaw alone?'

'No, I don't think she went into the village.'

Lamont poured whisky into a glass and drank. At the back of his mind was an incident which he had noticed on the road home. Glancing from the carriage window, he had seen a group of colliers tramping determinedly down the bottom of Main Street, eight or ten of them. He had thought little of it at the time. Now the picture came clearly into his mind.

'Has she returned?'

'Aye, about a couple of hours ago.'

422

Automatically Lamont swung round and consulted the Brighouse clock in the corner: it showed ten minutes after seven o'clock. He checked its accuracy with his fob-watch.

'What *did* she tell you?'

'Nothing,' Mirrin answered. 'She was covered in mud an' had fallen by the look of her; but ... but, she wasn't distressed. That's what I can't understand. She wouldn't say anything, an' she wasn't weeping or harassed.'

'Where is she now?'

'I put her to bed.'

'She's not alone?'

'Hannah's with her.'

'I must...'

'Houston: I'm afraid.'

'But she is all right: she's home now.'

'I don't know why I'm afraid,' said Mirrin. 'But I am. I'm scared t'death, to tell the truth.'

'It wasn't your fault.' Lamont put down the glass and crossed the room. He would have taken her into his arms, but caution prevented him. The door to the study was not locked, and Edith would be somewhere in the house. 'You mustn't blame yourself, Mirrin. I have never instructed you to make a prisoner of Dorothy. The estate is not a fortress.'

'I searched for an hour or more: then I started out through the far woods. She was wanderin' up through them from the direction of the Shennan, all ... all draggled and filthy. She was hardly even aware of me, at first. She had a spray of flowers in each hand.'

'Perhaps she'd been collecting them: you know how fond ...'

'They were draggled, too.' Mirrin clutched the man's sleeve. 'Houston, Dorothy didn't pick those flowers.'

'How can you tell?'

'They had been *torn* up, ripped from the ground an' the trees. She was *given* them, or ... or *took* them.'

'God! Do you suppose that some ... some man ...?'

'She had no marks on her: none at all, except her hands which are a wee bit scratched.'

'What *do* you suppose happened, Mirrin?'

'I don't know. I tried to question her, but she wouldn't tell me where she'd been, wouldn't say a word.'

'How did she react when you first encountered her?'

'She took my hand an' let me lead her back t'the house peacefully enough. I brought her in through the wall, where it's broken; I suspect that's how she got out. I brought her in, led her up the back stairs . . .'

'Secretly?'

'I suppose so.'

'But why?'

'That's it: I can't say why. Even when I was searchin' for her, I didn't tell anybody she was missin'.'

'Mirrin, you *know* Dorothy isn't violent. She can't have done any harm, not there by the river. I mean, who would be there at that hour? It is more likely that she herself came to harm.' He swallowed the last of the whisky and slammed the glass down on the desk again. 'There appears to be no sense in any of this. I must talk to her.'

Mirrin nodded.

Lamont opened the door, then closed it again.

'Where is Edith?'

'In her room, I think.'

'Does she know about Dorothy?'

'No.'

Lamont opened the door for a second time, and waved Mirrin out into the hallway. The spirits had soothed his stomach but his headache was still severe. He paused in the hall, listening to the house's silence, then, followed by the housekeeper, went quickly upstairs.

Dorothy was propped up on pillows in the bed. Though her lids were leaden and heavy she was not asleep. On a tray before her an egg-cup contained fragments of broken shell. As always, the room seemed snug and secure.

Hannah McCormick rose as her employer entered.

'How is she, Hannah?' Mirrin asked.

'Just . . . just like she is now.'

'Did she eat her tea?'

'Aye: every mouthful. I fed her with a spoon.'

'Has she spoken?'

'No, sir, not a word.'

'You may leave us now, Hannah,' Mirrin said.

Hannah dropped a curtsey and, taking the tea-tray with her, went out soundlessly.

Hands folded in the cradle of her lap, Dorothy Lamont seemed entranced by the pattern of the quilt. There were no nervous signs, no picking of threads, or twitchings. Indeed, she was utterly passive so that her state seemed to border on trance. Even her brother's appearance did not rouse her from her dreamy contemplation of the quilted material.

'Dorothy?'

The coalmaster stood by the foot of the bed.

'Dorothy?'

He shifted on tip-toe to the rush chair and brought it quietly to the bedside. He seated himself, close to the pillows, and leaned over.

'Dorothy?'

He sought her hand, lifted it. It was as limp as a glove, and the gesture did not disturb or distract her.

'How have you been today, my dear?' Lamont asked.

Gently, he crossed his hand before her face and turned her head up and towards him. Her eyes were blind with meek stupor. Lamont peered into them; there was no flicker of recognition and her pupils were colourless and without expression.

Lamont glanced over his shoulder at Mirrin.

'She is in a state of shock, I imagine.'

'Aye: that's what I thought.'

'Send for McKay: send Willocks on the bay stallion.'

'Talk t'her first,' Mirrin suggested.

'Dorothy, how are you?'

The woman's passivity was sinister. Her hand lay across Houston's palm like a fallen leaf. He released her face, but it remained in the position into which he had guided it, head canted and the eyes on him.

Lamont swallowed. 'Where did you go this afternoon, Dorothy?'

The woman did not answer.

'Did you gather pretty flowers?'

She did not answer.

'Mirrin informs me that you brought her two bunches of spring flowers.'

The eyes remained empty.

'Where did you pick such pretty flowers?'

Mirrin's hand touched his shoulder. He leaned back and listened to the girl's suggestion that he question her about the river.

'The effect,' he murmured, 'might be injurious.'

'Do you know for sure that it will?' said Mirrin.

'No.'

'We should ... we *must* find out. How can we heal her if we don't know *what* injured her?'

'Yes,' Lamont said. 'Dorothy?'

He hesitated, gravely studying Dorothy's features. Lifting her hand, he turned it over and inspected the small cuts and abrasions which marred the knuckles and palms. On her right wrist was a long deeper scratch. All traces of mud and grit had been washed away by Mirrin, who had also cleaned her charge's nails with a bristle brush, and combed out her hair. He reached for her left hand too and pulled her into a sitting position, puffing up the pillows behind her. His tone was wheedlingly insistent.

'Dorothy: tell me about the flowers?'

No trace of interest or dismay showed.

'The river?' he said, more loudly. 'What happened at the river? You went to the river. What happened there? Dorothy, tell me about the river.'

For a full, long minute there was no response to his use of the word 'river'. Stupor glazed her pupils, and left her whole body slack.

'*The riv ...*'

It was no gradual awakening.

One instant, the woman was wrapped in trance; the next, she was rigid and upright, hands clawing the air and her lips snapped back in a rictus of pure terror. Great bellowing

426

screams issued from her gaping mouth, flooding out, peal on peal, until Lamont, frightened beyond endurance, clapped his hand across her chin and, using all his strength, pressed her back against the pillows. In his mind was the memory of the file of grim-visaged miners, marching; marching down Main Street towards the bakehouse lane; marching towards the wooden footbridge which crossed the Shennan at its deepest point.

'Mirrin,' he shouted. 'Send Willocks to the village. I want to know what's happened.'

'And the doctor?'

'Yes, of course, bring the doctor.'

Beneath his fingers, Lamont felt Dorothy's tongue writhing wetly, and the stifled pulsation of her screams. He leaned more heavily into her to smother her violent struggles.

Mirrin ran to the bedroom door and flung it open.

The hat had a pigeon's wing set astride the brim and a short cut of ostrich feather to give its wearer height. The winter dress was of quilted silk, with an apron front in shimmering russet. But there was a band of mud about the hem and the black-polished toes of Edith's boots had clay on the welts. She still carried a furled umbrella, and raised it now across the doorway to bar Mirrin's exit.

Edith Lamont surveyed the scene coldly. She seemed to find nothing surprising in the sight of her husband's struggle with his sister. Mirrin was ignored; the mistress of the house addressed herself in clear, calm tones directly to her husband.

'I have been to the walk by the summit of the hill, Houston,' she announced. 'There are men by the bridge; men with lighted torches. They are, I believe, searching for the body of a child.'

'*Christ in Heaven!*'

Edith smiled faintly.

'Perhaps your sister Dorothy will shed light on the poor mite's last resting place,' she said. 'Do you think that may be so, my dear?'

*

They found Loony Lachie on the bridge. It came as no surprise: a plaintive tune had drawn them through the dark, and only one person in all Blacklaw played a mouth organ with such discordant persistence. Lachie was seated on the middle spar of the wooden span. His thighs clutched the rail-post, his legs and feet dangled out over the black sibilant river. His forehead rested on the post. The mouth organ, clenched in his teeth, shifted and slid to the action of his tongue as he incanted his own brand of music. Sinclair would have gone for him on the spot, if Constable Neave had not taken immediate stock of the situation and forestalled murder by his swift intervention.

'What's the daftie's name?' he demanded.

'Lachie Abercorn.'

'Aye, so that's Lachie, is it? Right, who knows him best?'

'We all know 'im.'

The group had come to a halt ten yards from the seated figure who, blissfully unaware of them, continued to make music and contemplate the river. Darts of bloody flame were reflected on the Shennan's rushing surface now, Abercorn held in view by the flare of the massed pitch-brands.

Sinclair growled and thrust forward again, but Neave's bulk blocked the narrow walk.

'Easy, man: easy, now,' the Constable said.

'*The bastard: the daftie'll . . .*'

'Stay here,' said Neave, threateningly. 'I'll talk t'him.'

'*Talk! I'll . . .*'

'You'll do nothin', sir,' Neave warned. 'Now, keep back.'

Tramping slowly forward, the huge young Constable brought himself close to Abercorn who, though fully aware of the uniform's approach, made no move to acknowledge the intruder.

'Hullo, Lachie,' Neave remarked, hearty and casual. 'Bit cold the night, don't y'think?'

Four ascending chords answered him. Neave got down on his haunches, steadying himself against the post. The light was behind him but he ducked his head to allow full illumination on the misshapen face. Abercorn's eyes were round as glass stoppers. Spit glistened all over the board of the tin instrument.

'I'm ... I'm lookin' for a wee lass,' said Neave. 'I'd be obliged if you could help.'

The music ceased abruptly. Lachie bumped his brow lightly against the post as if to drum his brain into working order, to shake the information to the surface.

'Just a wee lass, she is,' said Neave. 'I hear you know all the folk in Blacklaw. I'm from Northrigg, m'self; a bit of a stranger here. D'you like my uniform, Lachie?'

The loony looked at him shyly, grinning crookedly.

'How would you like a button for yourself?'

Lachie nodded, admiring the brass baubles on the man's long jacket front with honest greed. Neave cupped his hand over his midriff and yanked off one button, twisting it until the thread stalk broke. He held it out so that the imbecile could discern the design on its convex surface.

'Like it, Lachie?'

'Ah!'

'Now, I'll give you the button all for yourself, if you just tell me the truth about whether you saw the wee lass or not. Her name's Jinny Sinclair. Her Daddy's name's Angus. Maybe you know him?'

Stumpy fingers made a cockatoo shape, finger and thumb beaked, as Lachie reached for the bauble.

Neave closed his hand over it.

'Jinny Sinclair?' he said. 'Come on, now, Lachie, there's a good lad. Then you'll get your button.'

Abercorn made a strange low barking noise in his throat and spat the mouth organ into his palm. He wiped the wet metal on his hair, then, with considerable care, prodded it down into the high breast pocket of his ragged jacket. Sinclair was shouting and only the commonsense of his young sons restrained him. Torches were spluttering, animate with the restlessness of the knot of men at the bridge end.

'Where is she, Lachie: tell me quick.'

'Dey: dey: dey.'

Abercorn pointed over the bridge. He struggled, extricated

his legs, and, suddenly excited, leapt to his feet, hammering Neave on the chest and gesturing down over the wooden handrail into the water below.

'Dy ... dey ... dey ... dey ... dey.'

'In the water?'

'Dey ... dey . . dey . . dey ...'

'Who put her there? Did she just fall?'

'Dey ... dey ...'

'Lachie: how did she get in the water?'

'Lay ... dey,' Loony said; then with chance clarity, '*Lady*.'

Neave frowned and leaned over the bridge rail.

The patched jacket bulged with trapped air. The skirt had ridden up, floating on the backwash from the prow of debris which had mounded against the timber piles below.

'Lights: bring lights.'

He craned over further.

It was no bundle of rags at all. He saw the filigree strands of hair, and the little legs, as pale and thin as sticklebacks, trailing in the hurrying water, all pulled out lean by the race.

'Oh, God!' he murmured to himself, then set about the sordid business of retrieving for examination the corpse of poor little Jinny Sinclair.

*

It seemed a fitting night for the wind to howl and the rain to lash over Blacklaw, for the elements to add their groat'sworth to the tensions and terrors which the house now held. But the climate was not tuned to man's affairs and the night sky, clearing, exhibited a sickle moon in the space behind the clouds. Mirrin stood in the tiny scullery off the basement kitchen, sipping tea and staring out bleakly into the darkness. Houston Lamont was still upstairs, doing all in his power to calm Dorothy and to reason with Edith. Shortly after her mistress's arrival, Mirrin had left the bedroom.

She swirled the dregs of the tea in the bottom of the cup and consulted them absently. Outside, she could hear the cousins' muted prattle and Mrs Burns's occasional rebukes. She couldn't blame the servants for being so curious: that piercing scream was enough to raise the hackles on anybody's neck. The Mc-

Cormicks knew better than to question her, however, and she had made only a curt explanation to Mrs Burns, telling the cook that Miss Dorothy had taken a 'turn' and was having fever dreams. But the cook was no fool; the sense of impending drama was heavy in the air. Subdued, the cousins engaged in polishing to take their minds off the uneasy feeling which had even descended as far as the kitchen.

Dinner was a cold collation, sliced from the cooked meats kept under cheese-cloth in the chilly slate-floored larder. Mirrin had given instructions that the meal must be kept ready, but not served. Nobody below stairs, Mirrin included, had any notion of what would happen now. She had held back on obeying Houston's last instruction: to summon Doctor McKay at this stage would be imprudent. Besides, though McKay was a good healer, he was more at home with broken bones and burns than with injured psyches and wounded minds. A sedative would be his prescription; the exchange did not seem worth it.

Though there was no connection between the drowned child and Dorothy Lamont as yet, the fact remained that the woman *had* been alone in the region of the river at approximately the time Jinny had drowned. The coincidence was too neat to ignore: Edith Lamont had not been slow to underscore it with her cuttingly cruel remarks.

The wooden door of the scullery burst open suddenly and Hannah, her eyes wide with fright, beckoned Mirrin into the kitchen.

'Mirrin, come quick!'

Mirrin placed the teacup on the window-ledge and walked into the kitchen. She did not know what she expected to see there, but found nothing which might have alarmed Hannah. Mattie, on the other hand, was on tip-toe by the window which peeped, through iron grids, on to the side of the house where the drying greens met the sweep of the front lawn. She was hanging on to the bars like a prisoner striving to catch a glimpse of the gibbet.

'Men,' she declared. 'A whole mob o'them.'

'*Where?*'

'Comin' stormin' up the drive.'

'Will I fetch the master?' Hannah asked.

'No, not yet,' Mirrin said. 'Mrs Burns, will you be good enough to see that all the doors are barred and bolted.'

'What does it mean, then, Mirrin?' asked the cook.

'I think it means that the villagers have taken it into their heads t'blame Miss Dorothy for . . .'

'For what, Mirrin?' Mrs Burns demanded. 'Tell us.'

'A wee girl was drowned,' said Mirrin, already hurrying towards the laundry-room door. 'Some of the villagers seem t'think Miss Dorothy was responsible.'

'But that's daft!' Mattie said. 'Miss Dorothy wouldn't . . .'

'They don't know that,' said Mirrin. 'Where are they?'

'Comin' up t'the front door.' Mattie dropped, panting, to the floor again. 'Can't see them any longer.'

'Right,' said Mirrin. 'I'll find out just what they do want. Mrs Burns: the door, please.'

'But it's Mr Lamont's . . .' Hannah protested.

'Shut your mouth, girl,' Mrs Burns told her. 'Go on, Mirrin: see what they want here.'

Mirrin dropped the bar across the laundry room door, then ran upstairs into the main hall. She could hear them outside. She had heard enough restless crowds in her young life to recognize the mood: uncertain, but on short fuse. Nobody was shouting; the muttering was constrained, save for one protest which rose intermittently above the rest, the voice shrill with outrage and bitterness. Mirrin did not recognize it. She touched her hair, smoothed down her skirts, then flung open the front door and strode out on to the broad top step, drawing the door fast behind her. Breast heaving with exertion and apprehension, she scanned the scene before her.

It was hardly a mob at all: only two adults and four half-grown lads – and Davy Henderson, who had decided to disassociate himself a little from the proceedings and now stood back on the verge of the lawn, looking, Mirrin thought, as if he wanted to cast away his pitch-brand and run like a hare for the safety of the public house. One of the two men wore the uniform of a police Constable. She thought she recognized him as Will Neave from Northrigg, a shared member of the constabulary and not long appointed. He was rigged in a dark serge uniform, but had no imposing hat or helmet on his head. His trousers were caked with clay up to the knees and his tunic was daubed with mud. The other man, quite clearly the victim's father, was Angus Sinclair; the remainder were his sons. She knew Sinclair only slightly, but was aware of his reputation as a drunkard and a trouble-maker.

'What brings you here at this time of the night?' she demanded. 'The coalmaster doesn't much like being disturbed at home.'

'Where the hell is she?' Sinclair demanded, shaking his fist for emphasis. 'Where's that bloody madwoman who done for my wee Jinny?'

'Madwoman?' Mirrin placed her fists on her hips, and stared straight at the Constable. 'What is this, officer? Will you kindly explain?'

'Our business is with Mr Lamont, miss,' Neave said.

'Aye,' shouted Andy Sinclair. 'We've no truck wi' the likes o'you, Mirrin Stalker.'

Mirrin ignored the boy, and his father, and continued to address her questions directly to Neave. 'What business can you have with Mr Lamont that can't wait 'til morning?'

'It's ... it's his sister,' said Neave, apologetically.

'Miss Dorothy?' said Mirrin.

'That bitch o' hell who drowned m'only daughter,' Sinclair yelled. He pressed against the Constable's arm, restraining himself from making a direct assault on the door.

Mirrin saw in him the emptiness of a man who was substituting rage for suffering. She did not doubt that the death of his child had stunned him, but she knew enough of the Sinclair family history to recall that Rita, his wife, had suffered four miscarriages, one at least brought on by her husband's brutal treatment. She could not separate the little victim from the crowds of young children who played up and down Main Street; that failure to put a face to sorrow, salved her sympathy for the moment and gave iron to her denials.

Neave's arm still held Sinclair back. One of the four boys, the youngest, was weeping. The big torch he held in his fists wavered pennants of acrid black smoke across the garden.

'I'm right sorry to hear that your daughter's been drowned,' Mirrin said. 'But what's it got to do with my employer?'

Neave said, 'The sister's not ... not quite right in the head, I'm told.'

'The nature of Miss Dorothy's illness ...'

'Shove her out the road an' we'll go an' shake the truth out the maddy ourselves,' said Sinclair.

'Hold your tongue, man,' Neave said, not sharply. 'It's part of my job t'get at the truth, an' you're not helpin'.'

'Aye, Da, wait a wee,' said one of the boys, seeking to grip his father's hand. Sinclair hauled his arm away.

'Can y'deny that she was there?' he shouted.

'If you mean Miss Dorothy,' said Mirrin, 'you'll have to tell me where, before I can deny anythin'.'

Neave took a pace forward.

'There's ... there's some information come my way to suggest that Mr Lamont's sister was at the scene of the ... well, the incident,' he said, flatly. 'Can you let us have a word wi' her, please.'

'When was the accident?'

'Between three an' five this afternoon.'

'Then Miss Dorothy could not have been connected with it in any way at all,' Mirrin said.

The Constable eyed her curiously.

'She was seen by the river,' he said.

'Impossible!'

'Don't listen t'her, Neave: she's his woman.'

Ignoring the remark, Mirrin said, 'I understand that you've got your duty to do, Constable. If you tell me a bit more, then I'll carry a proper message in to Mr Lamont.'

'The wee girl Sinclair went missin' between one and two o'clock. A search was organized at five, an' I was sent for. A half hour ago we found her body in the Shennan, washed up agin the bridge piles near the bakehouse.'

'An' what makes you think Mr Lamont's sister ...?'

'Tell 'er, Neave: go on, tell 'er.'

434

'Now, I'm not one o'your new detectives,' Neave said. 'But I searched the bank an' found signs o'struggle. There was a stick, a branch, wi' some blood on it, and examination of the body showed injuries t'the head which suggest that maybe the wee lass was ... well, assaulted.'

'What else?'

'Is that no' enough for you, you cow?' Sinclair cried.

Neave sighed: 'I'm sorry, miss: a witness says that Miss Lamont was there.'

'One witness?'

'Aye.'

'Who?'

'Mr Lauchlan Abercorn.'

'*Lachie!*' Mirrin exclaimed. 'Do y'give credence t'an idiot?'

'One idiot t'catch another.'

'Sinclair, that's enough,' Neave warned. To Mirrin, he said, 'The daftie, Abercorn, he wasn't able to tell me much, but he was emphatic that the lady from this house had been there on the spot at the time.'

'I see,' said Mirrin.

'Can we question her?'

'No,' Mirrin said. 'I'll fetch Mr Lamont, an' you can talk with him. But, I'll tell you this, Constable, Lachie's wrong.'

'Are y'sure about that?' asked Neave.

'Miss Lamont's been unwell,' Mirrin said. 'I put her to bed myself – *at half past one.*'

'Don't listen!' Sinclair advised: he looked round for support, meeting only the blank, embarrassed faces of his young sons. Henderson had gone, leaving the pine brand embedded in the grass, still spluttering smoke.

Sinclair caught Neave by the collar. 'Her: *she's* Lamont's whore. Y'can't believe what *she* says.'

Mirrin winced. She had not been aware that talk in the village had been quite so pointed, though she had noticed inquisitive glances cast in her direction.

Neave apologized again.

A hand closed on her arm. Lamont's face was pale and set, his eyes narrowed.

'I have heard what's happened,' he said. 'I understand your grief, Sinclair. But I cannot allow you to invade the privacy of my home and direct such wild and vicious accusations at my sister.'

'Nobody's made any accusations just yet, Mr Lamont,' Neave said, uncomfortably.

'Who are you?'

'Constable Neave.'

'Are you responsible for bringing these men to my house?'

'I . . . accompanied them, sir, to ascertain that there would be no trouble,' said Neave. 'I'm here officially, Mr Lamont, to make preliminary inquiries into the circumstances surroundin' the death of Janet Sinclair.'

'What is the nature of your inquiry?'

'Regardin' your sister . . .'

'I told you once,' Mirrin said, 'an' I'll tell you again – Miss Dorothy never left my sight the whole afternoon.'

Holding her breath, she saw the puzzlement in the boys' faces and the slackening of anger into hurt.

Lamont raised his hand, as if addressing a meeting. 'I will see that the matter is fully investigated. None of you will be penalized, I assure you.'

'It's not for you t'investigate, Mr Lamont,' said Neave, quietly. 'That's a matter for the law.'

Sinclair crumpled suddenly and collapsed against his eldest son's shoulder, weeping.

To Neave, Lamont said, 'Take them out of here. If you have any serious questions, I'll answer them to you or to any other formal authority, not to a . . .'

'It was his daughter, sir,' Neave murmured.

'Yes,' Lamont said. 'Stay home for a couple of days, Sinclair. Your wife will require your comfort. I'll instruct the tally-clerk to credit you with the work hours.'

'Da,' one of the boys said. 'Come on away, now, Da.'

Sobbing brokenly, Sinclair was led away down the drive. All the torches were doused and discarded, bar one which glimmered fitfully at the head of the column as the family moved through the oak trees towards the gates.

Constable Neave loitered on the step.

'Would there be anybody else, Mr Lamont, who saw your sister here this afternoon?' he asked.

Lamont did not hesitate. 'My wife, of course.'

'Ah!' Neave said. 'An' may I have a word with your good lady, sir?'

'Not at the moment, Constable. She is nursing the patient. I would prefer not to disturb her.'

'Thank you, sir,' Neave said. 'An' you, too, Miss.'

Turning, he tramped off down the avenue after the Sinclairs.

Mirrin and Lamont watched until he was out of sight, then moved back into the house. No sounds came from the upper floor, and the hall was deserted. Lamont put his arm about Mirrin's waist and held her to him for a moment.

She stood quiet, tears in her eyes.

'I love you, Mirrin Stalker,' Lamont said softly. 'I'm proud and grateful to . . .'

'Dorothy didn't harm the child,' Mirrin said. 'If I hadn't been sure of that . . . I wouldn't have . . .'

'I know: I know.'

'You'd better go t'her now,' Mirrin said, pushing him away.

*

It was late now, dark outside the house and in. Along the corridors of the nursery wing mice skittered and scraped at the wainscots and nibbled at the mouldering clothes in the wicker hampers in the half-attics. In the hall and in the study the tall clocks ticked away the small hours of the morning.

In Dorothy's bedroom, the night-candle sizzled and guttered at flaws in the tallow. Lamont lay back in the plush armchair, snoring, one foot on the edge of his sister's bed. Dorothy slept too, very deeply, very still under the weight of the bedclothes. Further along the corridor, closer to the dark well of the staircase, the door of Mirrin's room clicked and the hinges shrilled faintly as it opened inward.

Mirrin lay across the bed, still clothed in her black dress. Her hair, untied, spilled across pillow and counterpane. The keys on the chain at her waist hung down and rested their weight on the strip of carpeting by the bedside. The candle in its water-glass holder on the cabinet by the bed had almost burned out and the wick lay floating and flaring on a little clear lake of wax.

The door clicked shut.

Edith wore a full flowered robe, with a quilted collar winged high about her cheeks. She had removed her night-cap and arranged her hair, had even carefully rouged her cheeks and applied powder to her throat, before leaving the empty bedroom. She tucked her thin fingers into the cuffs of the robe now, like a Chinese mandarin, and said, 'I wish to talk with you, Mirrin Stalker.'

Mirrin groaned and turned on to her back, the motion unwittingly sensual and submissive. She opened her eyes and stared at the play of light on the cornices of the ceiling; then sat bolt upright.

'You make an excellent liar, miss,' Edith Lamont said. 'Perhaps my husband was more shrewd than I imagined in bringing a collier's slut into the house. It takes kind to deal with kind, I see.'

'What do you want with me?'

'I heard every word that was said tonight,' Edith told her. 'They believed you, it seems.'

'Why shouldn't they believe me? You know as well as me that Miss Dorothy couldn't do any harm t'anybody.'

'Come now, you cannot believe that the matter will be allowed to rest there.'

'There might be an inquiry,' Mirrin conceded.

'There *will* be an inquiry,' Edith assured her. 'Are you prepared to follow one perjury with another? The young Constable will be back to take statements from the household.'

'The household'll back up what I told him.'

'Perhaps the servants will.'

'Meaning that you won't?'

'I must tell the truth,' said Edith, silkily. 'I will tell it to the Constable and to the Fiscal Magistrate, to anyone who asks me. They will listen to me, you know.'

'What'll you tell them?'

'I will inform them that there has been a conspiracy among members of my staff; that my poor feeble-minded sister-in-law was *not* at home during the course of the afternoon; that she, in fact, was out upon the river bank, and returned home at five o'clock in a remarkably sorry condition.'

Edith floated to a small stool and pushed it under her, enveloping it completely with the skirts of the robe as she sat down. She replaced her hands in her sleeves. 'Our stories will be directly contradictory, of course, but I doubt if the authorities will accept the word of a mere servant against that of a coalmaster's wife.'

'Houston would never...'

'Houston? If you mean *Mr* Lamont , I assure you that he will have little alternative. After all, Stalker, do you suppose that I would display a motive – other than that of conscience – to the law? What could I hope to gain? Hm? I would embroider my account with tears – but I would tell the whole truth in the process. Do you see?'

'I see fine,' Mirrin said. 'But I don't see what you will gain from it.'

'I will *regain* my husband.' She let the words hang in the air for a moment, then continued. 'The choice is entirely yours. You may protect your own position and watch the process by which your precious Miss Dorothy is taken to a place of incarceration, is tried, is found guilty of a hideous crime, is convicted and removed to a criminal madhouse.'

'Or?'

'You leave my house at once.'

'You wouldn't do that t'her; not even you.'

'Would I not? I've waited months now for an opportunity to correct the wrong that's been done me. Houston may have *one* of you : you *or* his sister – but he cannot have both.'

'What if I tell him...?'

'Make *him* choose, you mean? But you're too honest, too respectful for that. Are you so respectful when you bed together? Do you call him *Sir* when he fondles your body? Do you...'

'*Stop it!*'

'It is not within my power to stop it,' Edith said, still blandly, '*You* must do that.'

She rose from the stool, her skirts knocking it over.

Both women paused, listening, but the house remained silent.

'How long do I have t'decide?'

'I would imagine that the Constable will be back here tomorrow in the process of compiling his report. He will ask me to corroborate your story.'

'Tomorrow,' said Mirrin. 'What'll Neave think if he finds I've gone?'

'I will explain that you have returned home for a week or so on family business. He will accept that from me.'

'But what'll folk think?'

'Does that disturb you? No, it's not what they will think that can do harm, it's what they can prove.'

'But if . . .?'

'Do not quibble with me,' Edith said. 'You must decide what is best for my husband. My terms are clear: one or other, Dorothy or you – not both.'

For an hour after Edith Lamont had left, Mirrin sat on the edge of the bed, her hands clasped and her head bowed. The candle spluttered and went out, but she did not move to replace it. The darkness consoled her and contained her thoughts, forcing them in upon herself, forcing her to examine the quality of her love for Houston Lamont, and her position in his household. At length, she groped her way from the bed, lit a fresh candle and put it in the water-glass holder. By its light, she stripped off the tailored black dress and the unpatched petticoats beneath it. She folded the garments and laid them across the bed. She coiled up the key chain and threaded it through the ring and placed the bunch neatly on the pillow. Dressed again in her thin grey skirt and shabby jacket, she packed her few belongings into a bundle and carried them downstairs. She did not pause on the landing to look back into the depths of the nursery wing but, carrying the candle holder, hurried on across the hall into the study.

The two tin miners jerked just as she entered, and laboured

with pick and barrow across the painted clock face, hewing out four units of time and carrying them away for ever. Decanters glowed warmly in the candle-light, but the fire had died and the coldness which accompanied the early spring dawn had already invaded the room. She laid her bundle by the door, went directly to the desk and rummaged upon its top until she found a sheet of plain paper and an envelope. Leaning, not sitting, she cleared space upon the desk's leather top, and took a pen from the row of inkpots on the stands.

There *was* no choice involved. Edith had meant what she said. In the end, Edith had been more cruel than any of them would have imagined possible. She would not now relinquish her chance advantage. How much love could be left between Houston and herself, Mirrin wondered, if Dorothy was subjected to the humiliations of a public trial and then shut away in a madhouse for the rest of her life? Perhaps Houston would even blame her for having persuaded him to bring Dorothy home in the first place. No, she could not believe that of him. But he would be hurt, hurt with wounds which would never heal.

There were many diverse ways in which a man and a woman could prove their love for each other: but none were equal and few were fair, and there was no means of proving in advance which of them nurtured the barbarous seeds of pain.

It must appear to be her decision, her decision alone: in protecting Dorothy, she must also protect Edith.

When she began to write, she was disappointed to discover that few words were needed to mark an end to such an important part of her life.

Without any preface, the letter declared:

'I am going away. The lie I told was for Miss Dorothy's sake. I will stand by it if there is an inquiry. But I am not very proud of what I have become since I came to this house. Do not try to see me, please. I want no more to do with the gentry.
Mirrin Stalker.'

She folded the sheet of paper, slipped it into the envelope and pasted down the flap. In large letters, she addressed it to Mister Houston Lamont and printed the word *Private* above his name. She propped the letter against the ink-stand where he would be sure to find it, then lifted her bundle and went out of the mansion by the kitchen exit.

*

Flora Stalker wakened in the alcove bed, curtained by a cotton patchwork sheet. She could hear the shouts of men in the streets, far off in the distance, and for an instant was filled with panic and the fancy that tragedy had again struck at Blacklaw. But she had no more sons to lose to the pit and that selfish thought comforted her. The shouting died away swiftly and left no aftermath of sound.

Stiffly, she nudged the bolster under her ribs and lay awake, wheezing slightly, in the box-sided bed. The outer door of the house opened and now she heard the familiar bump of the bucket against the post, and the slap of the water as Kate carried the day's supply into the kitchen.

'Kate?'

'No, Mam, it's me.'

'Mirrin?' Flora drew back the curtain.

The fire in the range was already built up and the porridge mixed and put to boil and, even as she watched, Mirrin dipped the filler into the bucket and ladled water into the big iron kettle. Her sleeves were rolled up and she seemed busy and bustling as if she had never been away from this early round of chores.

'What is it? Why are you here?'

'Lie quiet, Mam: it's not time t'wake the others yet.'

'Mirrin, what's wrong?'

'Nothing's wrong: I've left, that's all.'

'Left?'

'I've left that damned house. I'm not workin' there any more.'

'Were you thrown out?'

'No!' Mirrin snapped; then added, 'I left of my own accord.'

'But why, Mirrin, why?'

'Because I'd had enough. Because I wanted to.'

'I'm still your mother, Mirrin: can you not tell me the truth?'

'I'm tellin' you the truth,' the girl said. She set the kettle on the hob and laid the teapot and tea-caddy close by. 'I'm tellin' you the truth. Now don't ever ask me again.'

'But what'll you do now?'

'Work,' Mirrin said, grimly. 'Work at the only job that seems t'fit me.'

'The troughs, you mean?'

'Aye! What else!'

8

The far-flung, crowded corner of the kirkyard provided barely enough space to house the narrow coffin of the youngest Sinclair. Perfunctorily and without fuss, she was interred in the early hours of Thursday afternoon when the colliery was under full employment and not many men were about to spark up a protest out of grief. The three shillings which the coffin-maker extracted from the distraught father had come from funds of the Brothered Miners of Kirkcaldy, a lodge which had flourished in the brave days of '65 when freedom and prosperity seemed within reach of all colliers. Angus Sinclair had paid his dues, even after he had shifted his place of employment to Blacklaw, and continued to render lip-service to the Brotherhood long after it had dissolved. The coffin-price was sent to him by his brother-in-law, once treasurer of the ceremonial band, with the condolences of former drinking companions whose names Sinclair could not remember.

Constable Neave did not attend the funeral. He was occupied in drafting a written report to the Fiscal authority of the County, a task which cost more time and more deliberation than the investigation itself. If he applied himself, he knew that he might prove a case to answer, might even see a man sent to the gallows because of his detective skill. But Neave was no blood-monkey, and tempered his account of the accident at Blacklaw with evasions and distortions of the truth.

In spite of Sinclair's fury, the Constable knew that the wee lass had not been clubbed to death. He knew too that the Stalker girl had lied about Lamont's sister's whereabouts on the afternoon in question; later, he learned that she had been dismissed from service for her loyalty. By that time, it was too late to do anything; Jinny was buried and forgotten and the blame had been shifted elsewhere. Neave regretted the need to account for chance, but the circumstances were too unusual to ignore completely and he wanted no appeal from Sinclair or his drunken gang to blot his own record. So he did what he felt was best, and let it go at that.

It was in this week too that Christy Moran returned from a Delegate Conference in Falkirk and sulkily announced that they had all been tricked by Lamont's assessment of the state of mineral commerce in the land. This duplicity on the coalmaster's part, however, did not encourage Moran to stir up strikes or militant action. He had seen the pitiful state of miners in the Glasgow area where not only had wages been reduced but many of the brethren were working only two full days in the week. He had also witnessed the terrible domestic conditions which prevailed in Maryhill, in Red Toon, in Cunningham's Blairdardie, where men, women and children were crammed into single rooms which streamed with damp and mould, had not a single window or a whole door, and provided no access to sanitary ashpits or clean cooking water. Shilling by shilling the high wages had been pecked away, and starvation and disease were rife across the country. He thought back to the Trade Union promises of Alexander McDonald's heyday, and wondered to himself how he could have been so fortunate as to wind up in Blacklaw where, for all its miseries, life was a paradise compared with most mining areas.

Lamont had deluded them, of course: he had hinted that the price of coal was low. The sorry truth was that the price of coal had never been higher, that greed, not depression, accounted for the falling off in demand. The masters had pressed their pits into gross overproduction. Strikes suited them: strikes cooled the market now. Any district representative who used the old rallying call and the threat of strike action was playing right into the bosses' hands, selling his own kind into reckless slavery. Soon there would be lock-outs, more reductions and a fierce clash of forces. But this time, in this place, he could not bring himself to condone it. For the time being, he laid his militancy aside, cautioned his friends and acquaintances to tread warily and preserve what they had. Moran, like his former godhead, McDonald, had entered a phase of conciliation.

Politics, however personal, had lost their savour for the Ewings. Since Alex Stalker had gone to his grave, their interest in the swings and shifts of unionism had waned, and father and son had drifted closer to the fold of day-to-day workers who never looked much beyond their shovels or the end of their eating forks.

With Callum's health restored and both men working, the Ewings were better off than any other family in the village. Even after Rob's marriage, things would not change much. Eileen McMasters would just flit her goods down a few doors and become one of the family. Rob knew better than to kick for independence at this period. There would be three wages, at least for a spell before Eileen grew fat with another generation of Ewings. His mother, who had not been exhausted by over-work, would care for them all, and everything would just go on as before. The big difference would be that he would not be alone and fevered in his bed and would have something more appetizing than a hot supper to come home to every night. The back room was quiet and his parents were heavy sleepers. To Rob's programme for their future together, Eileen meekly agreed.

Callum tugged his old cap down and shuffled to the door. There was the glint of mischief in his eyes as he nodded good-bye to Eileen, who sat pretty and demure on the chair by the hearth waiting for Rob to finish washing in the cold tub in the back room.

'Goin' out for a wee dawdle, then, Eileen?'

'Ay, Mr Ewing.'

'Not a bad night for it, if you don't mind a cauld hin' end.'

The jest was lost on Eileen.

Phlegmatically, she said, 'I've still got on m'winter petti-coats.'

'Have you now? God, for a minute I thought y'were thick-enin'.'

'Oh, Mr Ewing!'

'B'jings, though, times have fair changed since I did m'courtin',' put in Callum hastily, to make amends for having caused the girl to blush. 'There's you sittin' there pretty as a pictur' while the lad's ben the hoose trivvin' himself up in front o'the mirror.'

'He's just washin' off the dirt.'

'Have y'scrubbed his back yet?' asked Callum wickedly.

'That wouldn't be right.'

'Well, I'm way out, an' his Mam's at the choristers' tea-party in the kirk, so if you've a mind t'practise the art o' back-scrubbin' they'll be nobody here t'stop you.'

'Oh, Mr Ewing!'

'What the hell are you bleatin' about, old man?' growled Rob from the bedroom. 'I'm out and dried an' dressed: so stop that kind o'talk.'

'Away in an' haud the mirror for him, then,' suggested Callum, winking at Eileen.

'Mirror! I'll give y'mirror!' threatened Rob. 'It's well seein' that you never squint in one, or we'd be sweepin' up the broken glass for a week.'

Chuckling, Callum went out and headed across to the public house to refresh himself with a half jug of beer.

Aye, he liked the lass well enough, even if she didn't have Mirrin Stalker's brains and quick wit. She was more passive and that seemed to give her a sensual appeal which Mirrin had but did not exploit. He could well understand why Rob doted on young Miss McMasters. Coughing, he paused to fill his pipe. Still under the shadow of the lean period back in February when he had been too chesty to work for a fortnight and money had been scrape-tight, he extracted a few grains of tobacco from the bowl and returned them to his pouch. Such economies were not strictly necessary right now, but God alone could tell what hardships lay just round the corner. Hands in his pockets, smoke puffing out behind him, he ambled on towards the quiet pub. Things must be bad if the beer trade was feeling the pinch.

Rob's impending marriage was still in his thoughts. He had heard that Mirrin Stalker had given up her job at Lamont's house. He could not honestly say that he was sorry, yet he was disturbed by some of the ugly rumours he'd heard. How much had her contact with the gentry altered and changed Mirrin's convictions? Would she be just as lively and vociferous as before? He had even heard that she would not say a single word against the coalmaster now. But there was so little truth in anything these days, and Mirrin had never been popular with certain elements in Blacklaw. Vaguely, he wondered if Mirrin's coming back to Main Street, back to her old life, would give Rob second thoughts about his marriage to Eileen McMasters. He doubted it. Right now, his big, hulking son was probably admiring something a damned sight more interesting and pretty than his own face in a mirror.

No, Mirrin Stalker's return did not worry him – at least, not much.

*

The communication was couched in flowery language and beautiful copperplate hand-writing and came in a thick cream envelope with an embossed paper seal on the back. Only Drew was unimpressed by the outward trappings: the letter's contents, however, sent him into quiet raptures of delight.

Since his return from Edinburgh, he had thought less of his professional ambitions than of the city itself: he had seen enough to convince him that Edinburgh was the hub of the civilized world, and Blacklaw just a speck of fly-dirt. As the days dragged past, however, he lost confidence, and whiled away the long hours dreaming of Edinburgh as a pilgrim might dream of the Celestial City – without much hope of ever getting there.

One morning in April, the letter arrived. Kate and Betsy had already gone off to work. But Mam and Mirrin were there in the kitchen all agog, and had carefully placed the missive on the table, with a knife beside it – to fall on, maybe, thought Drew wryly. He slit the envelope, extracted the sheet of creamy paper, glanced over the contents, then clenched his fists to the level of his ears.

'I did it!' he said. 'Damn' me: *I did it!*'

Nobody, except Betsy, seemed as pleased as they should have

been. Wisely, Drew tempered his enthusiasm in the bosom of his family and poured out his plans in secret to his twin.

The dominie, however, was elated by his pupil's success; with his tutor Drew was now cool, not haughty but diffident, as if to say that at last they were equals. Through the remainder of the month, the schoolmaster and his young charge continued to meet regularly, at no cost to the Stalkers, to discuss, for the most part, erudite philosophies of law. It did not occur to Guthrie to ask Drew if the family had enough saved to put him to Edinburgh; and it did not occur to Drew to question the fact that his sisters would keep their end of the bargain. After all, they had been working and saving conscientiously all year: his knowledge of domestic economics was woefully immature. At home, nothing was said to daunt his plans or shake his belief that they would fulfil the promise made to his father. Through the weeks of April he lived in anticipation of that May day when he would put Blacklaw behind him and become, at last, a *Civis Universitatis Edinburgensis*, a student of the City of Edinburgh.

It was not for her brother's sake that Mirrin tried so hard to find work. It was not because of Drew that her inability to do so drove her into despondency. She had gone at once to the home pit, only to be told, by Donald Wyld in person, that no more hirings could be made in the near future. She chalked up that refusal to one of Lamont's spiteful orders. The answer at Northrigg colliery was just the same, however; not enough work to go round. That season, it seemed that there were no jobs to be had anywhere, not in the mines, shops, brickworks, trades' offices, or even on farms.

For Mirrin the month was summarized by the slogan:

NO HANDS REQUIRED.

'I wonder what got int' her?'
'Can y'not imagine?'
'Huh! Nobody ever knows what goes on in Mirrin Stalker's mind.'

'Aye, maybe the Lamonts didn't treat her enough like family. She's got a guid conceit o'herself that way, y'know.'

'I wouldn't have thought she'd have had much cause for complaint in *that* direction.'

'Well, I heard from a friend who knows a woman who knows Brenda McCormick's sister, that Lamont was treatin' Mirrin Stalker *real* well. Couldn't have treated her better if she'd been his *wife*.'

'An' what did his wife have t'say about that?'

'I heard . . .'

'Wheesht!'

Though Mirrin's return to her own kind was a nine days' wonder, and most of the gossip was maliciously speculative, it did not escape Flora's ears. Shamed now, and angry, she lost no opportunity of berating Mirrin, though the girl could not determine whether her mother blamed her for taking the housekeeping post or for giving it up.

Nobody was brave enough to interrogate Mirrin outright, for she was more proud and quick-tempered than ever, and hadn't lost her sharp tongue. Maggie Williams, big with her first bairn, had got a right flea in her ear for daring to suggest to Mirrin that if she happened to be in the early stages of motherhood herself, there might be a stray Williams willing to make her an honest woman for a wee cash consideration.

Lifting the basket of soiled clothes she had sorted earlier, Mirrin carried it out to the wash-house at the back of the row. The fire in the little warped grate under the stone boiler was almost out, but it had done its job and the water in the cauldron was almost boiling. Only half aware of what she was doing, she began to feed clothes into it. She was full of anxiety, both for herself and for Kate. Kate worried her. She was so thin, so whittled down by the uncertainty of Drew's future, that Mirrin was afraid she would contract an illness. She pushed the clothing so carelessly into the water that it lumped and knotted. She had no right to feel sorry for herself: only for Kate. What had she ever done to be proud of? The bone-white boiler stick jabbed at the tangle, and lathered up suds from the sticky almonds of soap. No, there was no scope for pride in anything that had happened in the Lamont house. She could not now even think of Houston without guilt and, what was worse, without a growing animosity.

The old habit of blaming the coalmaster for everything was reasserting itself – and that too was unfair. Houston had not taken advantage of her: on the contrary. It might have been to her credit that she had saved Dorothy Lamont, had she not done so at the cost of honesty, and the almost certain sacrifice of Loony Lachie.

The rumour was strong that the Parish Board had taken an interest in Lachie Abercorn, that he would soon be sacrificed to the legal machine and, at best, committed to an asylum. She thought of the dafties of the world as its free men, of Lachie in particular as the spirit of liberty of Blacklaw – a stupid analogy, of course. He fed in the bakehouse, or the back of the village store, was given farthings by the drunks in the *Lantern* yard, slept warm in the railway sheds or in somebody's washhouse, talked to the stray dogs and cats, and played his music. He was free, all right, and she saw in his grinning silences now a contempt for the slave system which he refused to join.

And she, Mirrin Stalker, had perhaps put an end to that too.

Everything she had touched had turned rotten.

Pounding the suds into agitated froth, she sent up clouds of steam, which filled the low outhouse like a fog. Mirrin did not notice her sister's arrival, and, lifting the stick higher, speared madly at the clothes in the cauldron and shouted out like a soldier bayoneting down a hated enemy.

'Does that help?' Kate asked.

With the stick held high, Mirrin whipped round.

'If it does, maybe I could have a shot,' Kate said.

'Aye, it helps,' Mirrin said.

'I've decided t'tell Drew.'

'When?'

'Tonight.'

'He'll go mad.'

'Aye.'

'How bad is the position?'

'He can't go,' said Kate. 'Besides, we could lose the house at any time, now that you're ...'

'It wasn't my fault,' Mirrin snapped.

'No, no, love: I didn't mean it t'sound ...'

'I know: I'm sorry. If only I could get decent work.'

'Work! God knows, there's enough of that in the world: it's payment that's so scarce.'

Mirrin leaned against the warm boiler, and shouldered the stick. Sweat glistened on her face and arms, and the front of her blouse clung to her body. 'If Lamont puts us out, I'll kill him.'

'I don't think you meant that.'

'Don't I?'

'What happened?' Kate asked.

Mirrin turned round abruptly. 'Nothin'.'

'Was it him, or her?'

'Her, if you must know.'

'Did she resent you?'

'Aye: she hated me. Och, I wasn't the only one she hated. She's a born bloody hatred-monger. Kate, I was happy there. Does that sound funny comin' from me, from a Stalker? I was happy up in that mansion-house.'

'And with him?'

Listlessly now, Mirrin stirred the sinking froth with the edge of the spurtle. 'Aye, with him especially.'

Kate said nothing.

'You must never tell anybody, Kate: never,' Mirrin said quietly. 'I love Houston Lamont. Imagine! Me, a collier's daughter admitting that. But I did love him – in every sense of the word. Mam suspects, an' thinks the worst of me for it. But it wasn't like that at all. Believe me, Kate, I don't regret what I did, not one moment of it. I may pretend t'myself that I do, but all I regret is the way that it ended. None of the rest of it was deceitful. There was so much ...'

Suddenly Kate's arms wound round her, drawing her about, and the sisters were weeping. Their weakness and their need of comfort was safely shrouded in steam, and nobody saw them, nobody in all Blacklaw guessed that the Stalkers' secrets caused them so much suffering.

'Perhaps you'll see him again : go back,' Kate said.

'No : it's past now,' Mirrin sobbed. 'It's all past, Kate.'

But she was wrong.

*

Kate did not tell Drew the dismal news that night. Mirrin was tempted to do the deed herself. She could corner him up there in his attic and unburden herself of a few harsh facts about Kate's sacrifices just to steel him for the blow, but she also hesitated. She did not want to usurp her elder sister's authority – or, perhaps, she too was just a little afraid of the effect of the disappointment on her brother's stability. He had grown up so much, and had changed so often in the past year, that he seemed like a total stranger to her. Not for Drew the silly airs and graces which Betsy had first affected when she got the job in Dalzells' : his was an adult, deep-grained quality, based on the assurance that he would soon be better than them, and quit of Blacklaw. What lay behind his arrogance, neither of his sisters could be quite certain. Both delayed the inevitable confrontation. They even discussed plans for his comfort and welfare with the enthusiastic Betsy. Flora, too, was kept in the dark about the true state of affairs. As a precaution, Kate removed the flour jar which contained the meagre savings and hid it under the floorboards in her bedroom cupboard.

For another five days, there was no change in the situation. Mirrin roved further and further afield in her seach for employment. The talk about putting a face towards the future seemed as grimly ironic as Free Miners' gala days and the tattered, unwashed bunting of the Union's parade flags. There was no sure future for any of them. As if to rub home that fact, Mirrin was privileged to witness, at first hand, the last act of her involvement with the coalmaster's household.

She had tramped home after a hard morning's walk round Hamilton's warehouses, none of which were interested in taking on hands. With her boots off and her feet on the cool ledge of the hob, she was resting, sipping tea and contemplating just where in the county a girl might find a job. Her reverie was abruptly interrupted when Flora Stalker slammed into the kitchen, and declared, 'Terrible, so it is: a proper disgrace.'

'What is it now?'

'See for yourself, if you're curious.'

Upset and indignant, Flora pushed on into the back room and slammed that door too. Mirrin frowned and wondered what could possibly have roused her mother to such a passion of contempt. Still in her stocking-feet, she went out on to the pavement.

It was a still morning, dull and hazy, and might turn to either rain or sunshine in the latter part of the afternoon. Up near where the street narrowed at the mouth of the Kirk Lane a dozen or so women were jeering at the antics of a couple of men in biscuit-brown uniforms, the like of which Mirrin had never seen before. Almost against her will, she wandered up the hill towards the group. The broken pavement pricked her feet, but she hardly noticed. There was a horse-drawn van, like a small cattle float, drawn up near the lane's end, a tight brown tarpaulin, bearing no legend, battened across its spars. The horse was a docile, aged beast, which waited patiently between the shafts. The uniformed men, though not so motionless, were patient too – or, perhaps, experienced would be a better word, Mirrin thought. They flanked the Kirk Lane, for all the world like whippet racers at a trap, waiting to watch their dogs spring out.

It was no dog they were after, however.

Lachie had been cornered twice already, and the chase had gone on by fits and starts for an hour or more, shifting down from the coups behind the colliery, through the shacks on the wasteland, into the back courts of the village itself. Lachie's escape route was haphazard, and had less sense to it than that of a hunted animal. He had his dens and his earths, too, his snug, secret dreys, scattered about through Blacklaw. But they were no longer safe refuge, and had not been built by the daftie to hide him from his fellow men.

The brown uniforms had helpers. The villagers were ambivalent in their attitude to Lachie. They resented the authority of the asylum patrol, but could not side with a creature who had taken the place of a bogeyman for many of them and whose irrationality was a source of fear. Since word had got about that Lachie was involved in Jinny Sinclair's drowning, he had been cast off by most of his former friends, rejected out of hand. Now, the village women chose to jeer at the uniforms, but not to impede them in their task. Instead, reports were shouted out as to Lachie's whereabouts, and advice on methods of capture was freely given.

Mirrin felt suddenly sick.

The tea she had drunk gagged her, and she gave a spluttering little cry. She was still twenty yards short of the group of spectators and could bring herself to go no further. But she could see all that they could see – Loony Lachie sitting astride the wall, one leg on the kirkyard side, the other hanging into the lane. The mouth organ was in his hand, and he was grinning and conducting some inaudible chorus with massive sweeps of his arms.

'Bring your rope then.'

'Aye, string'm like a steer.'

'All he is, anyhow: a wild animal.'

'Clout him wi' something.'

'Have y'not got batons?'

'Aye, missus,' one of the uniforms retorted. 'We've got batons, but we're no' keen t'use them.'

'Scared you'll break them?'

'Would an' all, on his big head.'

'What d'you think, Rab?' one uniform asked his companion.

'Hell, aye! I've had about enough o'this chasin'.'

'Righto! I'll get the stuff.'

The man strode purposefully to the van, unlocked a padlocked gate in the rear and, a moment later, reappeared carrying two long polished batons on leather straps and a net woven from hempen rope.

'Aye, they'll get y'now, Loony.'

Lachie stopped conducting his imaginary choir, pressed the

mouth organ between his palms and crooned into it, regarding the officials with interest.

One uniformed man shook out the net, spread it in the dirt, then folded it carefully and draped it over his forearm like a cloak. He stuck his baton into his belt and approached Lachie directly. His partner crept down the street a little way and slunk through the kirkyard gate. In an instant, Lachie was down off the wall. He stumbled, regained balance, and galloped round the corner and across the backs of the rows.

'Bloody hell!' the uniform muttered.

Spectators shifted to find new vantage points and the two uniformed men united again at the lane's end.

Mirrin heard the senior say, 'Nothin' for it, then, Rab. We'll have t'net him and put him out.'

Their patience and efficiency horrified Mirrin, that workmanlike approach to battery. Even if it took them all day, she had no doubt that Lachie, broken and bleeding, would become their prisoner.

She walked forward.

'If I bring him to you, will y'not hit him?' she said.

The officials of the parish looked at her curiously.

'Friend of yours?'

'Aye.'

They glanced at each other.

'Can y'get him for us?'

'I think so.'

'Righto.'

Mirrin went into the lane and down into the area of the backs. There was no sign of Lachie, but two women, leaning from windows, shouted to her and pointed. He had taken refuge behind a broken cart under thorn bushes, where the children had made a little den. Mirrin stopped twenty yards short of the hiding place.

'Lachie?' she called. 'Mr Lauchlan Abercorn, will you give me a dance?'

His whistling was casual and unconcerned.

'It's me, Lachie : it's Mirrin Stalker.'

His head appeared over the edge of the cart, popping up and down again like a puppet in its box.

'Lachie?'

The head popped up.

'I see you, Lachie.'

The head vanished.

Mirrin went forward a little way, talking quietly, persuasively. After several minutes, the jig started up, in tune for once; a moment later Lachie crawled out from his retreat, leapt to his feet and performed a clumsy, high-kicking dance to his own theme. Not smiling, Mirrin clapped her hands in time to the rhythm, watching the bushes tremble.

'That's it, Lachie: that's the way.'

Encouraged and trusting, the daftie spurred himself to greater efforts, cavorting, prancing up and down, the mouth organ wailing. He squared to Mirrin, his face beaming and his eyes full of merriment.

She clapped louder.

The thorns parted. A uniform appeared, then, off to her right, another brown figure. Stealthily, they flanked Lachie, coming at him from the rear in pincers formation.

'Dance, Lachie,' Mirrin shouted. 'Go on, dance.'

Tied round with string, the loony's boots flopped crazily in the dirt. He bit into the instrument, sucking and blowing, raised his arms and pirouetted; once round, and then again – then stopped. Arms still lifted, he stared at Mirrin in rebuke.

The uniforms sprinted the last few yards. The net fanned out. It seemed to hover over the little, broad-shouldered man for an eternity, then swamped him. He fell to his knees, tearing at the mesh, tangling himself, then bunched up and rolled on the ground.

'*Nooooo.*'

Mirrin screamed as the official batons cracked down upon Lachie's skull. The cheering of the women in the closes cut off.

They hit him four times; then he was still. They did not even look at her as they stooped and wrapped the net tightly round

457

Lachie's body. His weight was considerable. It cost the uniforms much effort to lug their burden across the backs, down Kirk Lane and heave it into the back of the van.

The mouth organ lay in the dirt. Mirrin picked it up. The women had gone now, all of them, slinking back to their domestic tasks. There was nothing to see, nothing to amuse them.

Running hard, Mirrin came out into the street.

The aged nag started and swung its head to stare past its blinkers. Within the body of the van Lachie had been unwrapped from the mesh. One of the uniforms folded the net and stowed it away in its compartment, but did not relinquish the baton which he tucked into his belt. His companion was already waiting on the driver's bench and neither of them so much as spared Mirrin a glance.

Aimlessly, she loitered on the pavement, clutching the mouth organ in her fist. She could see Lachie within the van, conscious but groggy. Blood flowed copiously from a split on his brow. He did not seem to notice the wound and blood trickled and dripped over his thighs on to the planking. The official clanged the cage door, padlocked it, stepped round the side of the conveyance, paused, nodded curtly at Mirrin, said, 'Much obliged,' then went on round to his seat at the front.

Reins cracked, and the driver's guttural order coaxed the horse into action. The iron-rimmed wheels rumbled on the cobbles.

Mirrin could still see Loony, bemused and numb, swaying against the shrouds.

'Lachie,' she shouted. 'Here, Lachie.'

Sprinting, she caught the bars, hauled herself up against them and pushed the mouth organ through the grid. It landed on the boards close to him, but he hardly seemed aware of it. His big, ugly head had a majestic dignity as it lay pillowed on the stiff tarpaulin. Vacantly, he surveyed the girl for an instant, then closed his eyes and let two globular tears trickle down his cheeks.

The horse picked up its hoofs into a trot. The van gathered

speed. Mirrin dropped and fell sprawling into the gutter. She did not raise herself at once, but crouched on all fours staring into the gloomy cavern behind the bars. Forty yards up the slope, the van swung round the corner by the colliery fence. Mirrin got to her feet.

Even as she turned to run home, the noise arrested her. It filtered discordantly from behind the cart, wistful, faint and sad. The van trundled out of sight on to the Lanark road. The chant of the mouth organ lingered a little longer, then it too dwindled and was gone.

That was the last of Lachie's tunes ever heard in Blacklaw, and he was never seen again at large and free in his old stamping grounds and innocuous haunts.

*

Coming from the bedroom, Flora Stalker found her daughter crouched on the floor, face buried in the cushion of the chair that had once been her father's. Sobs racked her, a sore weeping which reached deep into her body and shook her visibly.

Flora dropped to her knees and lifted the girl's tear-streaked face gently. She did not know what to say to comfort her; with sudden insight, she realized that she had never had the right words to give to Mirrin. Mirrin was so different, so much like her father. A wave of tenderness swept over her. She cradled the girl's head against her breast and crooned to her until the sobbing diminished and with a final rending sob, Mirrin was still.

'What is it, love? Nothin' can be that bad now.'

'Aye, Mam, it can.'

'Was it what they did to the daftie?'

'That – an' other things,' Mirrin said. 'Och, it was the way they trapped him, an' laughed at him, then took him away from the places he was happiest in.'

'It's like that for a lot of us,' Flora said. 'We think we're travellin' in a nice wee circle, an' instead we're bein' swept away.'

'Are we bein' swept away?'

Flora shook her head. She fished a cloth from her apron

459

pocket and applied it to her daughter's nose. Mirrin blew obediently, then settled on her elbow and regarded her mother curiously.

'D'you miss m'father very much, Mam?' she asked.

'Aye.'

'But ... but how? I mean, what does that kind of hurt feel like?'

'I wish I could tell you, lass, but I can't. There's no right words for it. It's just ... an emptiness, that's all.'

'Does it not get better?'

'It changes,' Flora said. 'I suppose that's for the better.'

Mirrin stared up into her mother's face. It was the face now of an old woman, yet Flora Stalker had not lived much more than half her promised span. What was left for Flora Stalker – twenty-five or thirty years of emptiness? What memories could she have accrued to help her through the nights – a fluted sea-shell in a drawer, a cherry-cloth hat on top of the wardrobe? Not much for a lifetime of hard labour and suffering. Suddenly, Mirrin understood a little of her brother's greedy ambition.

There were hills beyond the Lothians, rivers which did not flow into the Clyde, villages and towns where men did not have black dust ingrained into their pores and the barking cough of bronchial diseases. There were cities where the women were still young at forty, and lively at fifty. There were far harbours, even in this time and in this land, where happiness was constant and not just the lull between periods of tears. Honesty and industry might be extolled as the greatest of virtues, but what good did they do; what did it mean, if the virtue itself was pared down out of need and continual sacrifice?

'Mirrin, don't keek at me like that.'

'What?'

'As if ... well, as if you hated me.'

'I don't hate you, Mother,' Mirrin said. She could not explain that she pitied her: pity was worse than hatred in many ways. She hugged the big woman to her and then, comforted and with her determination partially restored, got to her feet.

'You'll be all right, Mam,' she said.

Flora nodded: she had heard that tone before, that casual, hearty voice which covered the fact that Mirrin had made up her mind and would not be stopped.

Nothing Flora Stalker, Kate or Betsy could say would change Mirrin's decision to leave Blacklaw and seek work, and happiness, elsewhere. Not even Houston Lamont could do that. In fact, his intervention only made it easier for Mirrin to strike out on her own.

9

Jock Baird brought the letter that same night. He arrived only minutes after the shift hooter had sounded, and well in advance of Kate. He handed it directly to Mirrin and, when asked if he knew the nature of its contents, shook his head.

'Eviction notice, I suppose,' Mirrin said, grimly.

'May be,' Jock said. 'What'll you do then?'

'Tent out,' Mirrin said.

'Aye, there's a wheen o'camps in the north part o'the county already, I'm told,' Jock said. 'Eviction strikers, an' families too impoverished t'meet the rent.'

'Thank God, it's near summer.'

'Well, good luck t'you, anyway, lass.'

'Thanks, Jock.'

She closed the door soundlessly. Her mother was out at the privy in the backs and Drew had gone up to the school to talk with the dominie.

She turned the letter over in her hand. Somehow, she did not feel dread, or dismay. The writing was firm and upright – Lamont's own hand. It was addressed to her, in her name alone. Still standing in the tiny hall, she slit the flap with her thumb-nail, took out the sheet of colliery notepaper and read the message. It was no eviction, after all. Houston wanted to see her. It was his first attempt at contact in the month since she had walked out. So much came through to her even from the touch of her fingers on the paper. She could imagine him reaching for the mottled box which contained the official stationery, dipping the pen into the pot, and leaning forward in his chair. The picture was vivid, almost unbearably so. She crumpled the sheet and its envelope in her fist and crushed them up small. In the kitchen, she tucked them down into the back of the fire in the range and watched them burn away.

There was no point in telling her mother, or Kate. She knew what they would say – Mam, at least. They would condemn him for daring to make contact with her again. She went into

462

the bedroom, closed the door and lit the candle by the fragment of mirror. She looked so tired, not pretty even. Her hair was untidy, though that could be repaired, and her eyes were lustreless. From the cupboard she took out her clean blouse and skirt and the only pair of boots she had that still had enough leather on the uppers to be worth polishing.

The back door opened, and Flora entered the kitchen.

'Mirrin?'

'I'm in here.'

'No sign o'Kate yet?'

'Not yet : she'll be soon.'

'Did y'put on the potatoes?'

'Aye.'

'Are y'all right?'

'I'm fine.'

'What are y'doin'?'

'Sortin' my hair.'

'Oh!'

'Yes,' said Mirrin, more to herself than to her mother. 'Yes, I think I'll go out later on.'

* * *

As a suitably private meeting place, Houston Lamont had chosen the coppice on the high ground to the north of Blacklaw. There was a fine, high view from the hill. The Shennan was hidden behind the coups of older workings which had stood untouched for a half century and had even given root to grass and shrubs on their lower shelves. West and south the coppice bounded farmland and a track led from it to the pasture behind the Lamont estate.

The dull day's cloud had lifted in the evening. Only a half hour before, the sun had set in solemn golden glory and there was still enough twilight to show Mirrin the path which wended up from the back spur of the village. A breeze rode over the shoulder of the hillock, blowing towards Northrigg and Blacklaw. It bore no taint of damp and dust but a hint of the new season's growth and even, perhaps, of the distant sea.

Once, Mirrin paused to catch her breath.

Below she could trace the patterns of the little grey dwellings uniformly arranged in the shadow of the coal rees and the winding wheels. She could even pick out the last narrow house in the row, the house in which she'd been born. How many years it seemed since she had been a child romping tomboyishly in the fields behind the Poulter's burn and on the wasteground where the railway yards now spun their iron webs. But she daren't count in years: there didn't seem to be enough of them to debit with four deaths, a withering of hope and the realization that nothing ever turned out right.

She turned again to the climb, her strong, young body making light of the steepness of the upper path. She felt comfortable in the shabby clothes, with the leather belt buckled round her waist and her sleeves rolled up. Dressed like any collier's lass, she was better prepared to meet Houston Lamont than she would have been in finery.

Though she was early, Lamont had already reached the rendezvous. The chaise was back among the trees where the track swung off to connect one farm with its neighbour. The stallion was cropping the verge contentedly to the limit of the hobble rope which the coalmaster had attached to its rein. Houston Lamont waited by the only conifer in the coppice which reached above the beeches. Even in the fading light, Mirrin could see that his face was leaner, harder, and that his smile, when it came, did not soften by one iota the rigid lines of his mouth.

'I was not sure if you would come.'

'You should've known me better than that,' Mirrin said. 'Don't I always do what I'm told?'

'Not always.'

'The truth is, I felt I owed it to you.'

'Why?'

'Because of the letter.'

Reaching into the inner pocket of his jacket, he withdrew her letter, in much the same state as she'd left it, only a little more tightly folded. He shook it out. 'Tell me, what manner of fool did you take me for? Did you really think I would believe this?'

'It's the truth,' she said.

'No, Mirrin. I want the truth, from your own lips.'

'If that's all you got me here for, Mr Lamont,' she said, angrily, 'then it wasn't worth the climb.'

'Don't torment me, Mirrin,' he said. 'I *know* why you wrote this letter, and why you left as suddenly as you did.'

'That's ... fine, then.'

'Darling,' Lamont said: the endearment no longer came easily. 'Mirrin, did you think you could deceive me? I love you too deeply, not to know you well.'

The change in his tone was unexpected. Mirrin felt herself trembling. She did not want his arms about her, did not need them, was afraid to allow him to draw too close.

He said, 'It wasn't difficult to guess your reason. Now, I know what happened.'

'Do you?'

'About my wife.'

'Houston, leave me alone.'

'Is that what you wish?'

'It's as it must be.'

'Dorothy asks for you, from time to time.'

'How is Miss Dorothy?'

'Ill, depressed,' he answered. 'She has slipped back, I'm afraid. Perhaps I was wrong to bring her here, to encourage her love. It can be a terrible prop, taking too much weight, can it not: love, I mean?'

'Aye,' Mirrin said. 'But until it breaks ...'

'Dorothy's more of a prisoner than ever now,' Lamont went on, quickly. 'I dare not allow her out of the house unsupervised. In fact, she shows no inclination to leave her room. She has gone back to the picture books. They are her diversion: facsimiles of gardens and flowers and trees. The substance and the reality frighten her.'

'And ... and your wife?'

'She is well,' said Lamont, drily.

'And happy, I suppose?'

'Edith will never be happy: I'm not sure if she would have found some ... something, if our son had lived. Perhaps.'

'But she has you back, at least.'

'I'm there,' said Lamont. 'I am one of her prisoners, like Dorothy. Like you too, I suppose, Mirrin. We talked of this once, do you remember?'

'I remember.'

'Nobody is free,' the coalmaster declared, with a violence which suggested that he had been forced into the admission. 'Nobody. There is nothing we can do to break down the walls, is there?'

Mirrin sighed. 'Not together, Houston; only apart.'

With sudden briskness, he removed two long envelopes from his inner pocket and held them out to her. 'In one you will find a title deed to your house. Your family may stay in it as long as they wish. Nobody will be able to break the legality of the deed, I assure you. Only in the event of there being nobody of Stalker blood left, will the property revert to me or my kin.'

'No,' said Mirrin. 'No, no!'

'In the other, is a letter of instruction to Mr Gow Havershaw, a lawyer of George Street in Edinburgh. Havershaw will administrate a grant of twenty pounds per annum, drawn in your brother's name.'

'No, no, Houston!'

'Havershaw will also find lodgings suitable for your brother, and will undertake to apprentice him on completion of his studies. Take them.'

'I can't.'

'Because you are too proud?'

'I don't want your money, or your gifts.'

'I wish you to have them, Mirrin.'

'How did you calculate it, coalmaster: so much for sharing your bed, so much for perjury, so much . . .?'

She swung her hand to strike him. He caught her wrist and drew her against him, holding her.

'If I gave you the house and its grounds, my horses, the pit and all the land you can see from this hill, Mirrin, I would still be short of the price of a bribe. What I give you is nothing; a token, that's all. Do you not believe in me enough to see that?'

She did not weep, for part of his strength was hers too now. Instead, she reached up and touched his face with her hand, impressing it upon her fingertips as if she was blind and had no other way of recording it upon her memory.

'As long as I live, Mirrin,' he said.

'Yes,' she said. 'Yes.'

He swung away from her, and strode through the trees towards the carriage. She heard the horse snort and, a moment later, the sound of the wheels, and the brushing of the leaves on the hood of the chaise. Stooping, she lifted the envelopes from the ground where she had dropped them.

Hope was so easy to record: the stroke of a pen on paper, the action of shaping a signature to a command. Like a miracle, the answer to her family's problems was contained in two long envelopes hardly weighing a goldsmith's gramme. But there was no easy solution to *her* problem, no means of signing a deed to seal up love in perpetuity, all neat and lawyer's legal.

How could she ever learn to live with the accident of love, the error of giving her heart to a man who should have been her enemy and have remained immured in his own stockade? At least in death there was an end to change, and a kind of permanence. She could think of her father and her brothers as they had been, not carry them with her to be tainted by the future.

What had happened between Houston Lamont and herself had been both simple and unbearably complex. The mark of it would rest on her heart for many years to come.

Suddenly, she was running, stumbling and sliding down the hill towards the lights, towards the streets of the village in which she had been born and, many, many months ago, had, for a brief moment of time, been young.

*

Drew Stalker's fury was as seemingly cold and calculated as that of a theatrical performer who mimes madness without being in any way affected by it. Kate could hardly have chosen a less opportune moment to inform him that his plans would be scotched by lack of money and that his enrolment in Edinburgh University must be cancelled.

The young man had returned from the dominie's study in an unusually good mood. He had seated himself at the table and

467

had even complimented his mother on the watery stew with which she had flavoured the potatoes. He had not seemed inclined to hide himself behind a book that evening, and, when Betsy arrived from Hamilton, immediately began to regale her with Guthrie's latest scraps of information on the bounties of the capital city. Flora too appeared to be entranced by Drew's enthusiasm and listened raptly, without understanding much of what he said.

It was all too much for Kate who, with the stew pot in one hand and the kettle in the other, turned round suddenly and blurted out, 'You're not goin', Drew.'

'Of course I am.'

'I say you're not.'

'You can't prevent me : I passed the tests. I've been accepted.'

'You can't go because we've no money t'pay for it.'

'Money !'

'Aye, money : we've none, at least, not enough.'

Drew pushed away his plate, and smiled uncertainly.

'I must say, Kate, this is in rather poor taste.'

'*Drew, we can't afford it.*'

'Now, Drew : now,' said Betsy, beginning to lift herself from her place. 'She doesn't mean it '

'*She does!*' Kate shouted, clanging down the pot and kettle. 'We've scrimped and saved as best we could . . .'

'I gave you so *much*,' Betsy cried. 'What've you *done* with it?'

'It's all there, in the bedroom cupboard; every last brass farthin' that we haven't been obliged t'spend just t'keep body an' soul together,' Kate said. 'If you don't believe me, Drew, go an' look for yourself. You'll find the weekly tallies in the jar, too.'

Drew glanced from Betsy to his mother, as if expecting them to contradict Kate and produce a box or a jar of their own, spilling sovereigns from it to refute his older sister's lie.

'Best do as she says,' Betsy advised.

Flora shook her head sadly.

Drew rose and walked stiffly through into his sisters' room.

leaving the door wide to the wall. He flung open the cupboard door and peered inside.

'Under the boards,' Kate told him.

Crouching, he yanked up the loose plank, dug out the big stone jar and carried it through to the kitchen. Knocking off the lid, he tilted it until the contents tipped out on to the table among the plates. He fished inside, scraping the sides with his fingers, and brought out the tally sheets which Kate had kept assiduously week by week since the previous March. He stared at them, flicked over the pages, then checked the final total against the sight of the coins which were spread about the table.

'Is that all? Is that *it*? Is that *everything*?'

'Aye, Drew, I'm afraid it is.'

'She never told me,' Flora Stalker said.

'*You cheats!*' Betsy shrieked.

'That's enough, Betsy,' Kate warned.

Gently, Drew put the flour jar down. His eyes were unseeing, filmed by disbelief.

'Why didn't you tell us before?' Betsy stormed.

She had edged round the table and stood squarely before Kate, screaming up into her face. It was as if she spoke not only for her twin but even in his voice, using the childish accusations which he might have used.

For fully a minute, Drew said and did nothing. Kate pushed Betsy suddenly, sending the little girl sprawling into a corner. She reached across the table and grasped Drew by his hair and shook him.

'Say somethin'; say anythin',' she demanded.

'I worked this,' he began, coolly. 'I worked this ... house out of me. Yes, that's what it was. I did it to get out.' His voice rose in pitch, leaping up an octave until it seemed to harmonize with Betsy's wailing, to be an extension of it. 'Do you think I did it because of a promise? What about that promise, Kate? Why did you fail?'

Kate released him. 'God knows, Drew, I tried.'

She slumped against the table. Flora heaved herself to her

feet and, stretching out her arm, offered the young man her left hand.

'There's m'ring, son,' she said. 'We can sell that. It's not worth much, but . . .'

He slapped the hand aside.

'It's worth nothing,' he told her. 'Look at it, worn away. It was probably worth nothin' when he bought it from some tinker's stall.'

Flora Stalker stood stunned, and even Betsy fell silent. But Drew was in full flood, enough words in him, dammed up over the years, to make his loquacity endless. Before Kate could reach him, he had stepped back, then forward again, round the table's end, his palm outstretched like a claw.

'I want what's mine,' he said. 'Where is it?'

'It's . . . not . . . anywhere.'

'Damn' you!' he said. 'Are you just another thick-headed colliery bitch? Is that what you are? What'll you do now, strike me? If *he'd* been alive, he'd have made sure you kept your promise. Ah, yes, I know; you loved them, Da and James and Dougie; do anythin' for *them*. All they had t'do was snap their thick fingers an' the rest of you would jump. But what about me? Is it because I'm different, because I'm not smeared with coalpit dirt an' reek of sweat, an' earn coppers for you all like . . . like a damned slave?'

Even Kate could not bring herself to silence him. She felt that much of what he said might be true, that his terrible accusations reflected so much on her that to stop him now would be but another act of selfish pride. She sank back on to a wooden chair, head hanging, and in that position of servility and contriteness, received all his slanders on herself.

For ten minutes or more there was no let or halt to the young man's invective. He berated them all, one by one. He cursed his father and his brothers, and his misfortune to be the last begotten son, and only a twin at that – of such weaklings. He used words that none of them had ever heard before, some erudite, some foreign, but all plaited into a rope of obscene abuse with which he flayed them remorselessly.

At length, he ceased, turned and walked out.

Not one of the weeping women stirred.

The sound of their son and brother was still in the house. The noises of his movements in the hall and then the attic were much louder and angrier than the timbre of his voice had been. They heard him stamping, the crash of books swept from the shelves and the violent battering of the bed as he upended it, the shattering glass of the student's lamp and the crackle of its trampled shade. The sounds and vibrations of his anger shook the house to its foundations. None of the women spoke, or moved to prevent the costly damage. They could hardly grudge Drew a scouring out of the prison he had built for himself over the past year. It was as if they had released a demon of destruction, a physical manifestation of all the rage and anguish they had suppressed in themselves.

Finally, the noises trailed off into uncanny silence.

It was at this point that Mirrin let herself in through the kitchen door. At a glance, she took in the essence of what had occurred since she had left an hour before. The envelopes in her hand might atone for despair and adjust the balance of their future. But Lamont's gifts had come too late: the damage to the Stalkers' family pride was quite irreparable.

*

The name of Fair Mile Field was older than the farm hamlet on which Blacklaw was founded, older even than the sweetwater well at Northrigg which was mentioned in domestic annals going back five centuries. The Field was a stretch of flat grass on the moor which roofed the subterranean vaults of rich black coal, two miles from Blacklaw and three from Northrigg. For as long as records had been kept there were accounts of a May Fair there, a fragment of tradition which imparted to the colliers a sense of continuity with the golden age of the past. The year of the Blacklaw disaster was the first in living memory in which May Saturday had not seen a trek of packmen, tinkers and miners out to Fair Mile: that year the folk of Blacklaw had walked unseeing past the flat of the moor, tainted as it was by drifted soot thrown out by the March explosions.

But the seasons of grief were over. From the crack of dawn

the men of the two communities met on the field to shore up stalls and booths, and mark out tracks for races, tug o'war tournaments and the fiercely competitive pit-prop event, the nearest thing the Highlanders among them could get to tossing the caber. In the lee of the moor's only trees, boards were laid for dancing. Paper chains, bunting and little tin lanterns were hung round, and benches put out for the members of Northrigg colliery band who would provide music during the course of the afternoon.

Though poverty had hit the area hard, the colliers struggled to put aside their depression and enter into the spirit of the occasion. Local shops' stocks of ribbon and cheap fretted edging were soon exhausted. Farmers' sons and daughters came down out of the hills with eggs, cheese and junkets to sell, and the tinker kind assembled to make a week of it by hawking the beats from Hamilton to Lannerburn. There were bagpipers, too, Argyll men mostly, who would squeeze out a rant for a copper: and a fellow from Ayr, accoutred like the Bard, who would recite any work by Rabbie Burns most stirringly for a capful of small change.

Within the Stalkers' house there was little excitement, though they had more reason than most to celebrate. The following morning, Drew would embark on his journey to Edinburgh, and his new valise stood packed and ready by his bed. Mirrin too was leaving the village on the Sunday train, bound for Glasgow in a bid to find work.

Surprisingly, neither Flora nor Kate had put up a protest when she had announced her intention. Since she had presented them with Lamont's generous gifts, both women had regarded her with suspicion. They would never understand what sacrifice Mirrin had made to gain the deed and the grant. Drew's torrent of abuse had confused them. Even Kate, kind-hearted and generous, had been strained by her brother's accusations. The family was split, and nothing could mend it. It would be as well if Mirrin left, then Kate and Flora could begin to find in the community that forgiveness and acceptance which meant so much to them. Betsy would prosper in Dalzells': the roof over their heads was secure: Drew's future was assured. None of it was accountable to luck or to charity, and the mystery of the price Mirrin had paid soured and tormented her kin. That brave promise made a year ago, and its ultimate fulfilment, had taken too much from them all.

Before noon, Flora Stalker went off alone to the Fair Mile Field, carrying a basket of sultana scones as her contribution to the children's feast. In the latter part of the afternoon, Betsy and Drew set off together for the dancing. They were both smart and well-dressed young adults, set apart from their contemporaries and former school friends. Arms linked, the Stalker twins walked sedately up the length of Main Street and veered left along Kirk Lane. Neither spared so much as a passing glance for the tombstones in that corner of the yard where their father and brothers lay. They were too engrossed in conversation to be even remotely conscious of the past.

'Perhaps,' Drew admitted, 'I was a trifle harsh on them.'

'Not at all,' said Betsy loyally. 'I thought most of your remarks were perfectly justified.'

'If only Mirrin hadn't been quite so tardy in wheedlin' that grant from Lamont.'

'How do you suppose she did it?'

'Come now!' said Drew. 'Can't you guess?'

'Oh, I can guess,' said Betsy. 'But guessin' isn't knowin', is it?'

'The evidence is plain.'

'You sound like a lawyer already.'

'Well, I shall be,' Drew said. 'I'm set on that.'

'Drew, you remember your promise?'

'What promise?'

Betsy's eyes filled with alarm. 'You said I could come t'Edinburgh an' stay with you when you were settled.'

'Oh, that!' he said. 'No, I haven't changed my mind. But it'll take a while, you know. In the meantime, I want you to promise that you'll stick at Dalzells', save every penny you can, an' not do anythin' foolish. Do you take my meaning?'

'I take your meanin'.'

'No more "gentlemen" like McElroy.'

'How do you know about him?'

Drew grinned, smugly. 'I happened t'meet Phyllis Rose Mc-Bean one Saturday evening: she's very talkative.'

'Aye, well, you don't have t'worry; there'll be no more like McElroy, I can assure you of that.'

'That's a good girl,' Drew said.

'I don't care how hard I've t'work,' Betsy said. 'So long as I've got your promise that you'll take me out of this pit-town as soon as you possibly can. What chance have I got of makin' a decent marriage in this miserable place?'

'I'm glad you recognize that fact,' Drew said.

'You will send for me?'

'I told you, yes.'

'Promise.'

Drew paused and inspected her critically. She had grown even prettier lately, had shed some of her adolescent fat. But it suited her, made her appear more dainty and sweet. There were plenty of pretty girls in Edinburgh, he'd noticed, but few were as attractive as his sister. With decent clothes and careful grooming, she would be quite an asset. He secured her arm again and went on towards the crowds and the bunting.

'Promise, Drew,' she insisted, anxiously.

'Oh, yes,' he said. 'I promise.'

*

Dusk spread intricate shadows over the rough framework of stalls and tables and the debris of the afternoon's festivities. In the fading light the bunting no longer seemed shabby but took on the texture of silk and rippled in the little wind which had sprung up from the west and brought with it the threat of rain. Prizes had been given out, the blankets and cooking pots and food hampers donated by local gentry and the pit managers and masters. Games and races had been the highlight of the day's events: poverty showed in other competitions. The baking displays had been poor and hardly worth the effort of judging. But that now was history, of little concern to the couples who drifted up through the early gloaming to join in the dance.

Children and old folk had wandered home, though a number of boys and girls still dodged about the empty stalls, taunting the tinkers, jeering at members of the brass band who were packing their instruments to make way for the fiddlers and accordionists who would play for the dance. Barrels of beer had been carted up from the public houses and the trestles on which they stood were focal points for the miners who, now washed and spruced up, had just come off the day shift. Even in the lull before the evening's programme got underway, there was laughter and noise and, true to the mining tradition, voluble arguments on every subject under the sun. From the edge of the boards, by the tinkers' booths, Mirrin watched the dance begin.

She saw Drew dancing with Betsy, and saw the faint stir the young couple caused among the crowd, leaving a trail of whispered comments in their wake. It was typical of Blacklaw folk: they would never deign to acknowledge Drew's achievement among themselves, but, by God, they were quick enough to brag of it to the brethren from Northrigg, just as if they had contributed to the lad's success. Perhaps they had, though: perhaps it was colliers' courage which had inspired Drew, without his being aware of it. But she would never boast of her young brother, not to anyone. Too vividly could she recall the pain in her mother's eyes that night a week ago when she had returned from her meeting with Houston Lamont. She would never forgive Drew for his arrant cruelty: never. In fact, she hoped that they might never see each other again. He was too much like her, in some ways, to make her comfortable in his company, or leave her proud of his progress.

Kate was dancing with Colin Pritchard, kicking up her heels. Younger miners no longer saw her as a suitable partner: already, poor Kate was too much like an elder sister. Her only hope of marriage was to one of the older bachelors, the kind who sought a housekeeper rather than a bedmate. That kind of marriage contract might not be so bad, after all. Love, Mirrin thought, was too colourful an illusion to survive in the hodden-grey rains of Blacklaw.

As night came, and with it a little smirr of rain, the hissing lanterns seemed to shed their light over a painted frieze of all the days of Mirrin's life, good and bad. She noticed Maggie

Williams, big-bellied and complaining, trying to drag Billy away from the beer table; saw Donald Wyld in heated debate with Callum, and pompous wee Dunlop, still in his half-crown flat hat, arguing the toss with George McNeillage. She watched Davy Henderson, his upper lip sprouting a wispy moustache, dancing with Edna Brown and thumping McLaren on the back every time they passed each other on the boards. Christy Moran had found a girl from Northrigg who would talk politics 'til dawn, and Dominie Guthrie and Doctor McKay were examining the medicinal benefits of whisky nipped neat from a leather flask.

But the faces missing from the throng meant more to Mirrin than any there — James, Dougie, Lily, and her father; Loony Lachie, too. Nor was there anyone from the mansion. She would have liked to see them incorporated into the swirling motions of the dance — Nelly Burns, Archie, Pibroch, Miss Dorothy, and Houston; Houston in particular, his strong, taciturn face breaking into a reluctant smile at the skirl of the accordion and the squeak of the fiddle strings. It would be a fine thing, she thought, if he would come now in his carriage and step down and take her in his arms, dance round and round under the misty lamps, dance with her in the middle of all her folk — and not be ashamed. But that was a dream, and could never happen, not in this life.

'Mirrin.'

She snapped out of her reverie.

Rob Ewing stood before her, healthy, handsome and as stolid as ever. Involuntarily she slid her shoulder round the post of the booth, drawing herself away from the eyes of the crowd.

'Rob,' she said. 'I haven't had a chance t'congratulate you.'

'Thanks.'

'When's the event?'

'The end o'the month.'

'I hear she's a bonny lass.'

'Aye.'

'Where is she, then?'

'Dancin' with m'father.'

'Better keep an eye on him,' Mirrin said.

476

'Is it true you're leavin'?' asked Rob, soberly.

'First thing in the mornin'.'

'Surely not for good?'

'That depends.'

'On whether you find work?'

'On whether the world's better outside Blacklaw, than in,' Mirrin answered.

'I wish you'd stay.'

'Do you – still?'

'Aye, I'm ...'

'Marry your lass, an' forget all about me, Rob.'

'I'm ... scared for you, Mirrin,' he blurted out. 'I'm scared what'll happen if you leave here.'

'I'm more scared what'll happen if I stay.' She gave him a gentle shove with the palm of her hand. 'Go on, Rob Ewing: goodbyes are not right for the likes of us.'

He studied her critically for a moment, and she saw surprise in his eyes, surprise at discovering that his feeling for her had waned – not all of it, but enough. He could manage fine without her now, and could even endure the memories. He nodded, and swung away.

While they had been talking the music had ceased. Rain drifted heavily now across the deserted boards. The colliers and their womenfolk, laughing and merry, sought shelter under the big black tarpaulin which protected the trestles. They were still hopeful that the cloud would soon scud past, reveal the stars again and allow the dancing to continue far into the night.

Mirrin knotted her scarf over her hair and slipped down the side aisle between the stalls. A wrinkled crone peered up at her from under a turtle basket, held out her hand, and said, 'Fortune, missy? Good fortunes told?'

'Not me, old one.' Mirrin paused, fished a halfpence from her pocket and dropped it into the tinker's lap. 'I think I prefer to keep my future to myself.'

Far across the moor Fair Mile Field receded, its sounds and lanterns sinking softly into the falling rain. Mirrin walked on and did not look back, going on past the colliery fence, the railway sheds, the kirkyard lying silent under the looming shadow of the winding wheel. She felt no sadness now at leaving Blacklaw. Beyond its rows and dun coups, beyond its surrounding hills were other villages and towns, other cities, other men. If luck was with her she might one day find another man like Houston Lamont, not bound to a pit and the coalmaster's trade.

The fiddler's last strathspey still lingered in her mind. Whistling, she took up its step and walked briskly down the long steep hill to the narrow house at Main Street's end.

Daphne du Maurier
Rebecca 80p

'Last night I dreamt I went to Manderley again . . .

One of the most appealing heroines in all of fiction, with a special magic that enthrals every reader . . .

Rebecca is know to millions through its outstandingly successful stage and screen versions ; and the characters in this timeless romance are hauntingly real.

Brilliantly conceived, masterfully executed, Daphne du Maurier's unforgettable tale of love, mystery and suspense is a story-telling triumph that will be read and re-read.

The Progress of Julius 70p

Julius Levy sacrificed everything to a ruthless ambition. From quick-witted urchin caught up in the Franco-Prussian war he plunged headlong into the adventure and vice of Algiers. Then to England, where his dreams came true with a swiftness that would have frightened a man less sure of his destiny.

The Loving Spirit 75p

A powerful exuberant romance of Cornwall, through three generations of passion and drama, of sailing ships and the glory of wind and sea.

Janet Coombe was born with the loving spirit, and passed it on to her son Joseph. When it reappears in her great-granddaughter Jennifer, the barrier of the years breaks down as they are carried beyond all prudence in their need to love and be loved.

'Miss du Maurier creates on the grand scale . . . a rich vein of humour and satire, observation, sympathy, courage, a sense of the romantic are here' OBSERVER

Hilary Ford
Castle Malindine 70p

Convinced he is the true Marquess of Kheilleagh, Bella Harley's father takes her to Ireland to establish his rightful inheritance. At Kheilleagh they find the present Marquess ruling his oppressed tenants with arrogance, cruelty and contempt . . . Then the peasants rise up against their oppressor, and Bella faces an ordeal of terror in the grim recesses of Castle Malindine.

Sarnia 60p

Her mother's past threatened Sarnia Lorimer's life and sanity . . . A visit to Guernsey in the summer of 1832 brought Sarnia face-to-face with the father she had thought dead. Soon she realized that beneath the lavish entertainments provided by her new-found cousins lurked dark and menacing forces . . .

You can buy these and other Pan books from booksellers and newsagents; or direct from the following address:
Pan Books, Sales Office, Cavaye Place, London SW10 9PG
Send purchase price plus 15p for the first book and 10p for each additional book, to allow for postage and packing
Prices quoted are applicable in UK

While every effort is made to keep prices low, it is sometimes necessary to increase prices at short notice. Pan Books reserve the right to show on covers new retail prices which may differ from those advertised in the text or elsewhere